FAMILIES AND EDUCATORS AS PARTNERS

SECOND EDITION

Robert E. Rockwell
Southern Illinois University, Edwardsville

Lynda C. Andre
Edwardsville Community Schools

Mary K. Hawley
Alton Community Schools

WADSWORTH
CENGAGE Learning

Australia • Brazil • Japan • Korea • Mexico • Singapore • Spain • United Kingdom • United States

WADSWORTH
CENGAGE Learning

Families and Educators as Partners, Second Edition
Robert E. Rockwell, Lynda C. Andre, Mary K. Hawley

Executive Editor: Marcus Boggs

Acquisitions Editor: Christopher Shortt

Assistant Editor: Caitlin Cox

Technology Project Manager: Ashley Cronin

Marketing Manager: Kara Parsons

Marketing Communications Manager: Martha Pfeiffer

Project Manager, Editorial Production: Samen Iqbal

Creative Director: Rob Hugel

Art Director: Maria Epes

Print Buyer: Paula Vang

Permissions Editor: Roberta Broyer

Production Service: Rebecca Logan, Newgen–Austin

Photo Researcher: Deanna Ettinger

Copy Editor: Jonelle Seitz

Cover Designer: Bartay Studio

Cover Image: © Anthony Redpath/CORBIS

Compositor: Newgen

For product information and technology assistance, contact us at **Cengage Learning Customer & Sales Support, 1-800-354-9706**.

For permission to use material from this text or product, submit all requests online at **www.cengage.com/permissions**. Further permissions questions can be e-mailed to **permissionrequest@cengage.com**.

Library of Congress Control Number: 2008937274

ISBN-13: 978-1-4283-1828-1

ISBN-10: 1-4283-1828-3

Wadsworth
10 Davis Drive
Belmont, CA 94002-3098
USA

Cengage Learning is a leading provider of customized learning solutions with office locations around the globe, including Singapore, the United Kingdom, Australia, Mexico, Brazil, and Japan. Locate your local office at **www.cengage.com/international**.

Cengage Learning products are represented in Canada by Nelson Education, Ltd.

To learn more about Wadsworth, visit **www.cengage.com/wadsworth**.

Purchase any of our products at your local college store or at our preferred online store **www.ichapters.com**.

Printed in the United States of America
1 2 3 4 5 6 7 12 11 10 09 08

To Donna, who has been a friend, wife, parent, grandmother, and great-grandmother extraordinaire. To Susan and Janet, my daughters, who are living the joys of grandparenthood. To my grandchildren, Teri, Robert, Amanda, Kathryn, and Michael, and my great-grandchildren, Tyler, Megan, Ethan, and Mya, who continue to give me endless happiness.
And to my late mother, Erma Lee, for bringing me into this world. I love you all.
—*Robert E. Rockwell*

To Michael and Lauren, Chris and Jen, Lindsay, and Betsy for the inspiration they provide. To my husband for his support and encouragement. To my mother and father, who taught me the importance of it all!
—*Lynda C. Andre*

With love and gratitude to all who have taught me family involvement: my mother and father; my children, Erin and Joel, who have been my first and best teachers; and to the special families who have shared their children and their lives with me over the years.
—*Mary K. Hawley*

Contents

Preface

Families and Educators as Partners is written for everyone in education, both public and private, concerned with building partnerships with parents. Such involvement bridges prenatal, neonatal, infant stimulation, preschool, kindergarten, primary, and elementary levels. Its impact extends to students of family involvement in community colleges and universities; professionals involved in the development, administration, and evaluation of programs; and educations of all kinds in home, classroom, or child-care settings.

As a child's first caregiver and teacher, a parent has both the right and the responsibility to be involved in the child's formal education. Early childhood programs need to begin to involve parents, guardians, and families in this education. It has never been possible to help children grow and develop without mutual respect and cooperation between home and school. Today, this cooperation is more important than ever to children's achievement.

Research has clearly shown that parental involvement is a critical variable in a child's education. Studies conducted in a variety of educational and care settings over the past 30 years suggest that parents/guardians who established a strong learning environment in the home, who stimulated interest in learning, and who supported their children's natural curiosity fostered attitudes that were important to success. Parents and families who were involved with programs and schools also developed more positive attitudes toward the school and its goals.

Early childhood programs and elementary schools must not only welcome parents and families, but actively encourage and seek their participation in the education of their children. Teachers and administrators must have the skill and desire to involve all families in meaningful roles within the school community. Parents of cultural, ethnic, and familial differences must perceive the educational program as "their" own.

There are many approaches to family involvement, and a teacher or an administrator can easily become overwhelmed and confused. The main strength of this book is that it organizes and presents strategies and techniques in an easily accessible way that enables the reader to understand them and to know when to implement each one.

Families and Educators as Partners is divided into three parts:

- Part One focuses on some of the specific issues and challenges in implementing parent and family involvement: why involvement is necessary (Chapter 1), how parents, families, and teachers can learn to become partners in children's education (Chapter 2), special information on working with families from diverse backgrounds (Chapter 3), and families with children who have special needs (Chapter 4).

- Part Two describes several categories of strategies for communicating successfully with parents and families: written correspondence (Chapter 5), verbal communications (Chapter 6), home visits and how to make them effective (Chapter 7), strategies for successful parent and family group meetings (Chapter 8), and parent–teacher conferences (Chapter 9).

- Part Three discusses support systems for parent and family involvement: volunteers (Chapter 10), parent empowerment as decision makers (Chapter 11), and community networks (Chapter 12).

Some important features of this book include individual chapter student learning outcomes; boldface key terms; practical, experienced-based examples; questions for discussion, expansion, and application; case studies; and website resources. Throughout this book, we have utilized several key vocabulary words that deal with parental and family involvement interchangeably. Please keep this in mind as you read, and assign the context that best fits your individual frame of reference.

Some important definitions are:

Early childhood: Period of a child's life from birth through age 8.

Parent: Biological parent(s), family member, or designated primary caregiver of the child, including a stepparent, grandparent, or foster parent.

Early childhood professional: Any adult who interacts with children and families and who is identified with an early childhood program. This could be an early interventionist, therapist, social worker, child-care provider, classroom assistant, or other staff member. Used interchangeably with teacher/educator.

Program: Any attendance center for children in a private, public, not-for-profit preschool, child-care, community, or agency program. Used interchangeably with elementary school.

Administrator: Individual involved in a leadership role for management, direction, and supervision of personnel or programs. Includes principals, directors, and coordinators.

Acknowledgments

We are grateful to our reviewers.

At Cengage Wadsworth Learning, we thank Philip Mandel and Chris Shortt and their team.

Thanks also to our families and friends for their unfailing patience, encouragement, and support.

Mary K.'s special acknowledgements: Loving thanks to my mother, Mildred M. Pervinsek for her ongoing support, careful review, and valuable feedback on the draft revision. Sincere appreciation is also extended to Chet Brandt and Pat Traylor from the Illinois Early Childhood Intervention Clearinghouse, who supported my research and allowed generous extensions on library loans.

Lastly, Lynda and Mary K. offer a special thanks to Bob Rockwell, our teacher, mentor, and friend.

About the Authors

Dr. Robert E. Rockwell received his PhD from St. Louis University and is now professor emeritus and former Program Director of Early Childhood Education in the Department of Curriculum and Instruction at Southern Illinois University, Edwardsville. He is the author of numerous books and articles addressing early childhood topics including parent involvement, language and literacy, fitness and nutrition, and science education that are available throughout the world. He has had many years of personal experience as a teacher, administrator, and consultant developing parent–teacher partnerships that work. He has lectured and conducted workshops throughout the United States, Europe, and Australia. Bob is the father of two daughters and has five grandchildren and four great-grandchildren.

Lynda C. Andre received her EdD in instructional process and MS in early childhood education from Southern Illinois University, Edwardsville, and her BS in child development from Western Illinois University. Lynda has worked extensively with children and parents for the past 30 years. An early childhood teacher with experience in preschool through third grade, she taught kindergarten in the Edwardsville Community Schools, was the coordinator of a Model Early Childhood Parental Training program, taught parent involvement classes at Southern Illinois University, and is currently the Assistant Superintendent for Curriculum and Instruction for the Edwardsville Community Schools. Lynda is the mother of four children.

Mary K. Hawley received her MS in early childhood special education from Southern Illinois University, Edwardsville, and her BS in elementary education from Illinois State University. She has over 30 years experience teaching children in early childhood special education, preschool, primary school, and middle school in both rural and urban settings. She also taught education courses at Blackburn College and a variety of parenting classes throughout the area.

Mary K. has worked for the University of Illinois Extension and, for eight years, was the director of STARnet Region IV, a project of the Illinois State

Board of Education offering resources, support training, and consultation to professionals and families of children with special needs in the southern 38 counties of Illinois. Mary K. has been a presenter, consultant, grant writer, and curriculum developer who has utilized a wide variety of strategies for parent involvement in her own classrooms. She is currently teaching in an inclusive preschool program with Alton Public Schools. Mary K. is, most importantly, the mother of two adult children, Erin and Joel.

PART ONE

OPPORTUNITIES AND CHALLENGES

CHAPTER 1
Why Family Involvement?

STUDENT LEARNING OUTCOMES

After reading this chapter, you should be able to

- Define parent and family involvement in education programs.

- Outline Epstein's model of parent involvement.

- Discuss and support a rationale for family involvement.

- Explain how involvement benefits children, parents, families, and programs.

- Identify challenges to family involvement.

- Describe federal, state, and local initiatives that support involvement.

Educators have long recognized the need for communication and collaboration with the **parents** and **families** of the children they teach. The home–program and home–school connections and attitudes developed during the preschool and elementary years are valuable in enhancing a positive impact on a child's development. Family members can gain an understanding of their important role during these formative years and can assist programs by sharing their experiences and resources. Yet, despite the best of intentions, family involvement can be elusive, thereby causing confusion and frustration for staff members. Why should we try to involve parents and families? This chapter will examine the definition, rationale, benefits, and challenges of involving parents and families in the child's **educational program**.

CHANGING TIMES, CHANGING EXPECTATIONS

Parenthood is historically accepted as a natural part of human life, one that carries with it the responsibility and challenge of nurturing children's growth and development. Yet in today's complex society, we recognize that parenting abilities, skills, and insights don't necessarily come with the birth of a baby, nor are they necessarily embedded within a parent's experience. Raising physically and emotionally healthy children equipped with the necessary skills to meet the challenges of the world they will inherit has become a formidable challenge for today's parents.

Home–school connections developed during the early years are valuable. *Courtesy of ECE Photo Library.*

An explosion of research and knowledge surrounding children's development and educational success has flooded the media over the past 50 years. The public has been showered with books, magazines, television and electronic media, websites, and blogs that reveal "new" aspects of child development or parenting. "Experts" have shared their knowledge and opinions on how parents should raise their children and what impacts particular family, educational, or societal situations have upon the young. Although families have accepted this public approach to parent education and counseling that was once directed exclusively to families in therapy or crisis situations, the profusion of information on child rearing and learning is often perplexing and mind-boggling.

In the process of deciphering this often-conflicting information on child development and education, parents may become overanxious about doing what is right for their children. With so many education options available, it has become increasingly difficult for families to identify what is best for their children. The desire to have children maximize their early learning potential sometimes results in expectations for children to demonstrate academic abilities and skills at younger ages. This has created a consumer market for education programs in all aspects of learning, including technology, languages, music, art, and movement. Families often seek information and guidance from educators and other professionals as well as other parents.

On the other hand, many families are unaware of the value that early exposure to a stimulating learning environment has upon their child's later development and academic success. These parents may be uninformed of the early education options available or may encounter difficulties in accessing educational services, while others may have their kindergartener enrolled in a full schedule of enrichment activities such as violin lessons, dance, beginner sports, or foreign language classes. The existence of this disparity is cause for concern among professionals in education, social science, and government. It has been the incentive cited for the development and funding of many **parent involvement** programs.

Families Face Change

Over the past 50 years, there have been dramatic changes in individual lifestyles and in society at large. As a result, the family, one of the oldest human institutions, has been challenged and changed. The 1950 family stereotype, consisting of a working father, a mother who stays home, and two or more children, has become increasingly rare in today's economic climate. In an age where one in two marriages ends in divorce, children commonly spend part of their childhood living with a single parent, while the relationship with the noncustodial parent may fade in time or become restricted by distance, visiting rights, or new family configurations. It is common for children to be born to a single parent who may or may not have a consistent partner during the child's preschool or elementary years. Whatever the situation, over time, adults frequently find their parenting roles extending to nonbiological children as well. The dynamics of blended families— those that include stepchildren and stepsiblings—impact the family system dramatically. Consequently, today's child may see the family portrait change several times during his or her childhood.

Teen pregnancies create a generation of children parenting children. The stresses of being a young parent, the dilemmas of balancing personal growth, continuing education, work, and parental responsibilities within a different social framework, along with the harsh economic realities of basic needs, place many young families at risk.

Grandparents and extended family members, once nearby for parenting assistance and advice, may be physically distant in an age of employment mobility. Consequently, family members may visit infrequently, and the family system may lack a traditional source of support, increasing the family's sense of isolation. As the fabric of support in the community unravels, family stress escalates and optimism for parenting success is compromised.

When parents are unable to fulfill their responsibilities to their children, grandparents, extended family members, or other individuals in the community often assume a dominant parenting role. Young mothers and fathers and their children may move back into a parental home until adult education is completed or stable employment allows the family to proceed and succeed on its own.

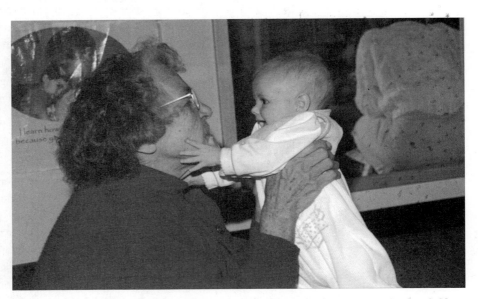

Grandparents or extended family members may become primary caregivers for children and provide support to families. *Courtesy of ECE Photo Library.*

Economic and financial realities have dramatically changed the dynamics of family life. Today, most women are employed outside the home, either full or part time. Many mothers are also continuing their education while parenting young children. Consequently, young children are commonly cared for by family members or are in child-care settings, playgroups, or one of a variety of public and private early education programs for all or part of their day. School-aged children also may experience multiple transitions between home, school, and before- and after-school care. Families across all income levels experience greater stress from the dual responsibilities of work and family life. Child poverty and homelessness have risen to record levels, and inadequate nutrition, health care, and housing undermine the early development of a growing number of children. As the result of these and other factors, a family overwhelmed by the demands of daily living may perceive a young child's development to have a lower priority amidst other family concerns.

Parent Involvement Redefined

These variations in families have broadened the definition of *parent* and have increased the complexity of involving family members in early childhood programs and elementary schools. Today, *parent* may refer to a single adult, to a couple of either gender, to other family members (such as grandparents, aunts, or older siblings), or to **foster parents** who serve in a parenting role. Teachers then need to be prepared to build partnerships with several parents and family members who are active in a child's life in different configurations and are concerned about the child's development, education, and future. Programming for parents must extend to meet the concerns of a broader family group. Effective family involvement can provide and secure valuable additional support for families facing new situations, whether it is the birth of a baby, the diagnosis of a disability, or the guardianship of a grandchild. Understanding the family context or family system to which a child belongs enables the educator to better design strategies for family involvement.

What actually is parent or family involvement? Many programs have defined parent involvement through a model that uses a specified format for parent–educator interactions, such as home visitation, conferences, or parent education classes. Yet, parent–family involvement exists in a broad continuum of activities and strategies. Parent or family involvement, therefore, is the practice of any activity that empowers parents and families to participate in the educational processes of children either at home or in a program or school setting. Because educating children has become a responsibility shared between families and professionals, the authors of this text support a philosophy of partnership between home and the school or center. Throughout these chapters, the terms *parent involvement* and *family involvement* are used interchangeably out of respect for the diversity of supportive relationships in the lives of children today. Keep in mind that, for some families, participation is restricted to biological parents or other individuals who have legal responsibilities for a child.

PARTNERSHIPS WITH FAMILIES; DEVELOPMENTAL COLLABORATIONS

This partnership philosophy is the critical foundation of family involvement activities. In it, parents are recognized as children's first and most important teachers, and the home is considered the first school a child attends. Families are typically co-supporters of children in their development and education. Teachers are viewed as sensitive, caring, and supportive partners in the education process. In this partnership, the relationship between all parties is guided by a common concern for the well-being, development, and education of the children. The empowerment process for these mutual relationships requires sensitivity, trust, flexibility, responsive listening, and a supportive, nurturing attitude (Swick, 2003).

This collaboration goes beyond parent education. It builds, often slowly, upon mutual respect and trust. Through active communication and support, adults are empowered to recognize and fulfill their roles as parents. Teachers share with families their knowledge of child development, as well as practical information and strategies to assist young learners in developing their potential, all the while recognizing the special needs of the child, family, and educational program. Families educate teachers about their child's strengths and needs as well as family interests and concerns. They also can share how they might become resources for the educational program.

This bridge from home to school allows families to have a valued and meaningful presence in the program. Parental time, skills, and experience are shared at the center or school, at home, and through connections with other families and community resources. Parents are partners in joint decision making that affects their child's program and in the selection and design of parent support activities. They often are active as program advisors, evaluators, developers, and, sometimes, team administrators. This home–center bridge also allows staff to bring pertinent, individualized information into children's homes through special communication strategies and activities.

It becomes evident that the concept of parent involvement encompasses a wide variety of options. Commitment is the key to them all. Without the dedication and perseverance of administrators, educators, and the families they serve, education would lose one of the most valuable factors in effective programming: parent involvement.

Administrators, teachers, and parents are all part of the parent involvement team. *Courtesy of ECE Photo Library.*

Program Activities Define Family Involvement

The activities of the program or school define the organization's broad or narrow interpretation of family involvement. Some share information through a prescriptive program of parenting education on a wide variety of topics, which may be explored using a parent textbook, a speaker, or a multimedia presentation during a group meeting. On the other hand, some define parent involvement by more informal strategies for communicating with families. Administrators and teachers may communicate with parents through websites, newsletters, notes, telephone calls, e-mails, or short conversations in person. Families may become involved in the activities of the curriculum at home via interactive homework assignments, an activity calendar, or lending library kits, or they may volunteer to prepare items for the classroom. Many programs and classrooms have an "open-door policy" that allows parents to visit, read to children, or join their child at lunch. Programs and schools are continually experimenting with strategies for involving families that meet both program goals and the needs of the families they serve.

Epstein's Six Types of Parent Involvement

Joyce Epstein, a leading researcher in school–family–community partnerships, has led the way in studying teachers' practices regarding parent involvement and the effects of family–school connections on students, parents, and teachers. She has identified six types of parent involvement that contribute to successful model programs. Detailed examples of how to implement these strategies can be found in later chapters.

The six aspects of Epstein's model of parent involvement are Parenting, Communicating, Volunteering, Learning at Home, Decision Making, and Collaborating with the Community (Epstein, 2002).

1. Parenting

Goal: To Help All Families Establish Home Environments to Support Learning and Positive Parenting. Schools have the obligation to recognize that the family exerts the greatest influence over the child in terms of determining the success or failure the child experiences in school. Attitudes toward literacy and education, the ability to provide a healthy and safe environment, and the development of language all begin at home. Programs and schools that acknowledge the family's importance can utilize opportunities to understand family background, culture, concerns, and goals. Educators respect family strengths and knowledge of the child, are supportive of diverse home environments at each developmental stage or grade level, and recognize individuals' efforts regarding parenting and child-rearing skill building. As a result, programs and schools learn to be sensitive to working cooperatively with parents by developing a better understanding of them. National organizations, such as the **National Association for the Education of Young Children (NAEYC),** provide supports for families, educators, caregivers, and programs to provide guidance on developmentally appropriate practices for children from birth through age eight. Sharing and support may be offered through parent education programs, support groups, rooms and spaces, questionnaires and surveys, and resource libraries as well as in social service directories and on websites.

2. Communicating

Goal: To Design Effective Forms of Communication to Reach Parents.

Communication between parents and schools is often about school activities and student progress. A strong parent involvement program includes effective two-way channels that fit the needs of the individual family and school community. The attitudes parents develop about the program and its teachers will often stem from their contacts with program staff members. A parent involvement program in the early childhood and primary levels carries the increased responsibility to initiate a positive rapport with parents, since these experiences may shape attitudes toward schools that last throughout the child's educational career. Families with older children have questions and face different challenges as their children mature. Positive interactions with teachers can enhance effective parental responses to a child's progress or difficulties as well as increase positive attitudes and support toward schools.

Because parents have widely differing expectations, attitudes, and prejudices toward schools and teachers based upon their own experiences, a variety of approaches are needed to reach and involve each family. The following methods of communication have been used successfully:

- Notes and letters
- Activity calendars
- Parent conferences or meetings
- E-mails
- Home visits
- Notebooks or passport journals
- Surveys or questionnaires
- Web pages
- Classroom or school newsletters
- Telephone calls
- Parent handbooks

- Learning compacts
- Orientation meetings or open houses
- Portfolio or progress reporting

See Chapters 5 and 6 for descriptions of and implementation suggestions for verbal and written communications.

3. Volunteering

Goal: To Recruit, Train, and Organize Parent Help and Support. This type of parent involvement refers to parents as volunteers, both in and out of the center or school. Parent volunteers better understand a teacher's job and tend to be more comfortable in schools. They also experience positive attitudes toward parents and feel their participation is valued both in the classroom and the school. Traditionally, volunteering has included everything from assisting during field trips, in the classroom, or in the library to helping with fundraising projects or clerical chores in the office. While these opportunities still exist, volunteering has expanded in an effort to involve working parents and those busy at home with small children. Alternative activities for at-home volunteers allow family members to participate when it is convenient for them and maintain a feeling of connectedness to their child's classroom. Some alternative activities include:

- Using a classroom phone tree to coordinate volunteers for projects
- Recording stories for children
- Fundraising
- Constructing instructional games or materials
- Maintaining and constructing playground or classroom equipment
- Sharing talents, skills, hobbies, and resources

See Chapter 10 for additional information and implementation suggestions for developing a volunteer program.

4. Learning at Home

Goal: To Provide Ideas and Materials to Help Parents Help Their Child at Home. The fourth component in this model concerns parent involvement in learning activities in the home. One important aspect of promoting the parents-as-teacher philosophy involves giving parents the proper tools with which to teach their child. Often parents feel inadequate and ill prepared to support their children academically. The assumption that educators have the sole knowledge of appropriate methods for instruction is erroneous. Each family needs to be guided to realize that they have important advantages critical to their child's learning: they know their child on multiple levels (emotionally, socially, behaviorally, and physically); they have a history with their child; they are aware of the child's likes, dislikes, interests, strengths, and weaknesses; and they have the opportunity to build a supportive, ongoing relationship with the child. They also know how to support, encourage, and help students at home during the year within the context of the family setting. Teachers can contribute to parental success by sharing learning strategies and educational expectations with them. The following are some activities that can support this:

- Homework or help lines
- Updates on what is being studied in class
- Web pages
- Parent meetings or conferences
- Workshops or seminars
- Books on loan
- Articles on various parent concerns
- Activity bags to support and extend curriculum at home

5. Decision Making

Goal: To Recruit and Train Parent Leaders. The formation of a parent advisory council or **Parent Teacher Association or Organization (PTA/PTO)** represents advocacy, leadership, and governance on the part of parents, indicating a bond between schools and families. Parents in decision-making roles have a powerful effect on the curriculum and policies that a program chooses to adopt, and, by getting involved, they show concern, commitment, and responsibility toward the program or school. This level of participation is referred to as "empowerment." It is at this point that families and teachers reach a level of trust and respect, working together as members of an educational community. At this level, a family member may participate as an advisory board member or a member of a curriculum committee, promote or advocate for the student program, or utilize family or professional resources to connect to the community.

Decision making as a parent involvement strategy will be expanded upon in Chapter 11.

6. Collaborating with the Community

Goal: To Coordinate Community Resources and Services. Coordinating community services and resources for individual families may have once been the exclusive role of a school social worker or counselor. Today, sharing information with families and students about child-focused services, community resources, and events is part of a community-building relationship that has the school as a contributing member. Participating in a community network of schools, libraries, hospitals, service agencies, government resources, community colleges, businesses, and organizations increases the level of services available to children and families through collaboration and networking. Activities that can be the product of these collaborations include directories of local or regional services, calendars of meetings and school events, GED or adult education programs, school-based vaccination or physical clinics, family library initiatives, and financial support for school programs. Chapter 12 provides additional examples regarding the collaborative links between education and community networks.

THE VALUE OF PARENT AND FAMILY INVOLVEMENT: SUPPORT FROM RESEARCH AND THE LAW

One of the goals of education is to support and encourage children to develop their potential for learning. As partners with families, another goal for schools and programs is to support parents and families in this joint responsibility. Parent involvement is a multifaceted component of education, and the rationale supporting it is multidimensional as well. Why value parent involvement? What benefits does it provide in early childhood programs and elementary schools?

Education is the business of transmitting information to and developing abilities in the learner. Successful strategies for parenting education have been identified and accepted over time. These truisms or beliefs are linked to logical and practical concepts concerning parent interaction. From these selected ideas, recommended practices have evolved. The following statements are samples of experience-based successes.

- Programming for parent involvement can help families by providing sound information on parenting, child development, and the importance of appropriate educational experiences.
- Parents learn to better focus their parenting energies on activities that are developmentally suitable and accomplishable within the daily routine. This increases support for the child's learning and actively engages parents in the process, which enhances their enjoyment and appreciation of the unique individual their child is becoming, while supporting concept development and educational skill building.
- With a greater number of families in stressful situations, parent involvement programming can encourage the development of positive parenting and coping skills, which promote desirable adult–child interactions as well as realistic expectations for learning and social/emotional behaviors.
- Professionals involved with families can assist them in locating needed human services within the community and foster a supportive, caring network for children.

- Families are unique systems that face intricate challenges to survival. Families struggle to understand complex life situations, deal with frustrations, and develop coping strategies that protect vulnerable members—typically, the children.

Parenting is one role in life that few adults are fully prepared to undertake. Historically, there has been national support for family education to enhance parenting skills. In the 1970s, Keniston and the Carnegie Council on Children (1977) recognized that all families, not just the "needy" families who then were the beneficiaries of many federal initiatives, would benefit from support in raising their children. In 1994, the Carnegie Corporation Task Force issued *Starting Points: Meeting the Needs of Our Youngest Children.* This study documented the effectiveness of positive parenting practices, parental social supports, and early childhood development stimulation in enabling children to achieve a good start in life. The report also warned that inadequate social policies and a devaluing of children and the family are compromising the country's future workforce and citizenry. It upheld that all young people should be prepared for parenthood and receive information about child development, child-rearing models, parenting skills, and the significance of environment upon children.

The United States Department of Education and other governmental agencies, as well as organizations like the National Coalition for Parent Involvement in Education and the National Parent Teachers Association (PTA), have promoted the benefits of home–school partnerships for children, families, teachers, schools, and communities. Studies have documented that parent involvement in a child's education is a major factor in determining success in school, regardless of the economic, ethnic, or cultural background of the family. The National PTA Standards for Parent/Family Involvement were reflected in numerous pieces of legislation in the 2000s (Parent Teacher Association). These standards are:

1. **Communicating:** Communication between home and school is regular, two-way, and meaningful.

2. **Parenting:** Parenting skills are promoted and supported.

3. **Student learning:** Parents play an integral role in assisting student learning.

4. **Volunteering:** Parents are welcome in the school, and their support and assistance are sought.

5. **School decision making and advocacy:** Parents are full partners in the decisions that affect children and families.

6. **Collaborating with community:** Community resources are used to strengthen schools, families, and student learning.

The National Association of State School Boards of Education, in its research-based publication, *Creating Good Schools for Young Children, Right From the Start*

(Cummings, 1995), stated that parental involvement is essential. Strategies the organization recommended that remain relevant today include the following:

- Promote an environment in which parents are valued as primary influences in their children's lives and are essential partners in the education of their children.
- Recognize that the self-esteem of parents is integral to the development of the child and should be enhanced by the parents' positive interactions with the school.
- Promote an exchange of ideas and information between teachers and parents that will benefit the children.
- Ensure opportunities and access for parents to observe and volunteer in classrooms.
- Include parents in decision making about their children and in the program overall.

Impact of Parent Involvement on Children and Families

Research findings have repeatedly substantiated the benefits of family involvement for students, parents, and teachers (Wherry, 2007a; Wherry 2007b). The sections that follow provide a historical framework and detail the various benefits.

The Impact on Children: The Early Childhood Years.

During the early years of childhood, the best strategies for family involvement offer avenues of information and access to a network of supports that can adapt to particular family needs and interests. These opportunities encourage parents to see themselves as the child's most important teachers and empower them to support their young child's efforts to learn and expand opportunities to do so. Having recognized the many benefits of family involvement for the child, family, and program, early childhood programs have a long history of nurturing children's development in partnerships with parents. Many federal education programs developed during the 1960s studied the effects of parent involvement that opened doors for parents to become active participants in their children's education. The effects of programs that aim to enhance parental competence in child-rearing practice showed that the quality of care that parents give their children does make a difference in their future education and lives.

Parent involvement in a child's program and educational activities is critical to sustaining program accomplishments after a young child's participation in an early education program. The Perry Preschool Project, which included a parenting education component, studied the lives of 123 children born in poverty and at high risk of failing in school. The comparison of individuals who received a high-quality preschool program and those who did not determined that at age 40, those who received the preschool program had higher earnings, were more likely to hold a job, had committed fewer crimes, and were more likely to have graduated from high school than the adults who did not have preschool (Schweinhart, Montie, Xiang, Barnett, Belfield, & Nores, 2005).

Research has validated the importance of parent involvement and early childhood education. *Courtesy of ECE Photo Library.*

When parents are interested in and involved with their child's program, they support the child's need for attention and provide motivation for future learning. This was substantiated during the historic early years of the Head Start and Follow Through programs. After researching parental involvement in the Follow Through program, Ira Gordon concluded in 1977 that all forms of parent involvement help a child, but the more roles parents can play in the program and the longer the involvement lasts, the more positive the effects will be. In addition, younger siblings, who are exposed to positive parental attitudes and educational activities, also benefit.

The Impact on Children: The Elementary Years. Research with older children builds evidence that parent involvement is critical to student and school improvement as well (Henderson & Berla, 1994; Wherry, 2007b). Parent involvement provides students with benefits including the following:

- Higher quality homework and completion of weekend homework
- Higher grades, test scores, and graduation rates

- Increased self-esteem and motivation
- Reduced behavior problems and lower rates of suspension
- Better school attendance
- Decreased use of drugs and alcohol
- Greater enrollment in post-secondary education
- Improved attitudes toward school and better homework habits
- Improved math and reading skills

Parents do not have to be well educated to help their children; parental involvement benefits all children, but especially those from low-income and minority families (Henderson & Berla, 1994). Children whose parents are involved in their educational program recognize that their parents are an integral part of learning and see them in different roles at home. Children begin to value education more when they experience the connection between home and school. Most importantly, children who share learning experiences with parents feel special and cared about (Eldridge, 2001).

Benefits of parent involvement in the elementary grades include higher-quality homework, better grades, and positive attitudes toward school. *Courtesy of ECE Photo Library.*

The critical message is that parent involvement and support in a child's education is the best predictor of school success across all income levels (Epstein, 1996). Unfortunately, some types of family involvement do tend to decline as children move through the upper elementary grades, although involvement continues to have a positive effect on student achievement through high school (Weiss, Kreider, Lopez, & Chatman, 2005).

Family Benefits. Parents, regardless of background, who are involved in their children's schools tend to have children who do well in school. Research indicates that a planned program of parent involvement has a positive impact on parents as well. When parents are involved, they:

- Believe they should help
- Demonstrate greater confidence in themselves as parents and their ability to help their child learn
- Understand more about the educational program
- Experience increased awareness of their own and other's challenges in parenting
- Change their behavior at home to be more supportive of their child
- Appreciate teacher efforts more
- Demonstrate increased confidence in the school and experience feelings of support
- Improve communication and relationships with children and teachers
- Express higher educational expectations for their child
- Exhibit stronger decision-making skills
- Project an improved attitude toward school and educational personnel
- Are known in their child's program and treated with greater respect by teachers and administrators
- Communicate their concerns to teachers and administrators and have increased opportunity to have their concerns recognized

Involved parents also are better able to define appropriate levels of expectations for their child's development and begin to perceive their child's developing abilities and skills. Parents have greater access to teachers and other parents and develop an appreciation for their own parenting abilities. The noted social scientist Urie Bronfenbrenner commented on the far-reaching effects of family involvement. He stated:

> Not only do parents become more effective as parents, but also they become more effective as people. It's a matter of higher self-esteem. Once they saw they could do something about their child's education, they saw they could do something about housing, their community,

and their jobs. . . . [T]he family is the most effective and economical system for fostering and sustaining the development of the child. The evidence indicates further that the involvement of the child's family as an active participant is critical to the success of any intervention program. (Bronfenbrenner, 1974)

Impact of Parent Involvement on Teachers and Programs

Concern about the effectiveness of our nation's schools has spread across the United States. The public is frequently confronted with media reports of inadequacies in the educational preparation of our youth. Although many components enter into the success of school programs, parental involvement consistently ranks high among the characteristics of effective programs and schools, according to researchers, practitioners, and policy makers. Yet not all programs actively encourage parent involvement, and not all families realize how to become involved.

The benefits of actively involving parents in the classrooms and family awareness of the diversity of involvement opportunities begin with the classroom teacher. Aside from the practical assistance that parents offer, teachers who involve parents gain new insights about the children they teach and can enrich their curriculum with fresh, new resources in the parents themselves. Teachers also experience the following benefits:

- Improved morale
- Increased support from families
- Increased teaching effectiveness
- Greater job satisfaction
- Higher opinions of parents
- Improved communication and relationships with students, families, and communities
- Increased support from the families and communities (Henderson & Berla, 1994; Wherry, 2007b)

The value of parental involvement has not gone unnoticed by leadership organizations in education. A variety of professional educational organizations, including the following, offer support for family involvement:

Association for Childhood Education International

American School Counselor Association

Council of Chief State School Officers

Education Commission of the States

National Alliance of Black School Educators

National Association of Elementary School Principals

National Association for the Education of Young Children

National Association of State Boards of Education

National Association of School Psychologists

National Education Association

National Association of School Boards of Education

Parent Teacher Association

In addition, the North Central Regional Educational Laboratory, the Parent Institute, and the National Council for Parent Involvement in Education are among many others that promote parent involvement.

The variable political climate, the nature of politics, and the difficult fiscal and moral issues faced by all levels of government make the realization of goals within the economic and educational agendas of the United States a challenge for lawmakers and citizens alike. Within the local program and school district, however, the value of parent involvement can be recognized and implemented. With school referendums and fundraising support for valued programs and student opportunities facing communities on a regular basis, parent involvement is an investment in the schools and programs as well. In times of fiscal uncertainty, community support has proven critical for the continuing survival of school programs. Parent involvement at the local level increases community support for schools. Likewise, family support and involvement by schools and programs demonstrates commitment to families and communities.

Since there is such widespread support from leadership organizations affecting education and evidence that it benefits children, families, programs, schools, and communities, why is parent involvement still elusive?

CHALLENGES TO PARENT INVOLVEMENT

Involving families is no easy task, and making it a priority as an educator takes commitment, caring, and creativity. There are, however, identifiable barriers to family involvement that may contribute to the challenges toward involving all families. The multidimensional process of parental participation can be made more challenging by a variety of factors that limit communication and cooperation. Many factors impede parent involvement from family, professional, and programmatic perspectives. Educators who become aware of these potential deterrents can enhance the potential for the success of their personal family involvement efforts.

Family Factors

Many parents are enthusiastic supporters of their child's education and respond to each note, invitation, and conference appointment sent home. Educators must realize, however, that it is not easy for all families to become involved in program activities. When families do not respond as expected, there are often justifiable reasons. Each family system operates with individuals at different ages and stages in their own personal development, which impact their ability to be involved. For many families, a major barrier to involvement is a lack of time. Working parents are often unable to attend program events during the day because of inflexible work schedules—some may face a penalty if they take off work. Evening events may be jeopardized by the competing demands of home, family, and work commitments. Parents may choose to spend this time catching up on home responsibilities rather than attending meetings. Occasionally, families must choose participation for one child over others. For example, during a parent–teacher conference night, parents may need to attend conferences for many children in different school buildings within the few hours set aside for these meetings. Conferences for children who are having difficulties may take precedence over meetings for children who are doing well. Sickness or other medical problems sometimes prevent participation. Parents may be afflicted with stress-related problems, constant fatigue, or depression. Evening meetings may cause concerns for personal safety in some areas. Families also may have difficulty securing adequate child care, especially if the family includes a child with special needs. For some families, there may be an overwhelming number of personal problems involving basic needs, like available or dependable transportation, or difficulties with family relationships, which affect involvement with the program. In light of personal problems and family situations, parents may be unable to make involvement at school a priority.

Parents may choose to be uninvolved because of intrapersonal or interpersonal difficulties. Some parents may have difficulty seeing themselves as the "first teacher" and feel intimidated by the teacher's demeanor or overwhelmed by an educator's expectations, whether real or imagined. Parents may not realize why they need to be partners with programs and schools in the education of their children. They may feel that parenting is their job, and teaching children is the educator's job. To them, school and home should be separate and may view the parent involvement overtures as intrusion rather than assistance. Some parents may lack self-confidence and do not value themselves as participants in the parent program. They may feel they lack the skills to adequately participate or do not know how to become involved.

These feelings may be compounded by different linguistic, cultural, or socioeconomic backgrounds. As programs and schools become more diverse, non-English-speaking families may be especially challenged by language and cultural expectations. Communication skills and understanding of language (whether English or professional or educator jargon) can be a challenge for families. Parents whose own school experiences were not positive may feel uncomfortable interacting with teachers again. Just returning to a school building may be intimidating and bring back unpleasant memories of educational difficulties or social discrimination. Consequently, parents may feel mistrust when dealing with educators and staff members. Some families may take offense at an educator offering any suggestions about their children, or parents may react negatively when a child repeatedly comes home and declares, "My teacher says . . . ," thereby confronting parents on a particular action or statement.

Many parents view teachers as authority figures and are quite respectful of educators. Some families may feel they are being helpful by keeping a respectful distance or consider it disrespectful to ask questions of the teacher. Some children, especially if they perceive difficulties, may discourage parents from becoming involved, as they don't want to be "spied on" or anticipate negative comments from parents or peers.

Professional Factors

Educators can also have difficulties with parent involvement. They may object to expanding their responsibilities to include parents. Frequently, a lack of time is cited by busy teachers, who may feel that planning lessons for the children is enough of a responsibility. Many educators are working parents who share the same constraints of fatigue, stress, and home–work conflicts, especially when it comes to evening events that follow a demanding day on the job. Sometimes, educators take on parent involvement activities without compensation, and some educators may not desire to make the commitment to involve parents because they feel intimidated by parents who may ask questions or want explanations for what is happening in the classroom. Some are concerned that parents may challenge the school personnel's professional judgment and want to assume control of the school. Major roadblocks to parent involvement include feeling insufficiently trained to work with families and overwhelmed by the problems families may face, difficulties in relating to or communicating with culturally different families, and discouragement because of past problems with parent involvement. Some teachers do feel there should be a professional separation from families and insist on formality in communicating with families. Young teachers may also feel threatened by parents who are older than they or who question their expertise. Some teachers may feel anxious about interacting with parents who are prominent members in the community or who are significantly wealthier than they. Teachers also may be hesitant to have parents in their classroom because they are afraid of scrutiny or are just protective of their classroom "turf."

Teachers can become frustrated by their inability to reach the parents who might benefit from involvement the most. Some parents, by rejecting active participation in their child's program, may appear to want the teacher to take over some parental responsibilities. Other parents may want educators to "fix" what they perceive as the problem, insisting that the solution be simple, fail-proof, and immediate. Frustration over these demands may prompt teachers to abandon efforts toward parent involvement.

Programmatic Barriers

Not all programs actively encourage and support parent involvement. Programmatic barriers to parent involvement may occur at either the philosophical or practical level (see Table 1.1). Insufficient parent involvement may be due to a lack of administrative support. There may be an absence of policy guidelines regarding parent involvement or a lack of coordinated planning to execute activities in an organized manner. Inadequate staff time or money for family programs can be a barrier to parent activities. Occasionally, parent involvement programming is concentrated at particular levels (early childhood or elementary) and is not available system-wide. This may occur when schools receive special grant or program funding. Previous difficulties in reaching or sustaining participation from a significant number of parents or of a particular target segment of the parent population may discourage administrators from attempting to reestablish parent programming. This is most likely to be evident when there are a large number of working or single parents in the target program.

Despite the obstacles, families want to know more. They are aware of the differences in education for their children compared to their own school experiences. Parents are typically receptive to new information about how to help their children or learn more about the challenges facing them. Since the majority of adults raise their children in a way similar to the way their parents raised them, they may find their knowledge inadequate to the challenges their children present. Parents are eager to learn skills that will lessen parenting frustrations and help their children succeed in school. They realize they don't have all the answers and are willing to listen and try new techniques. Despite sometimes overwhelming conditions, they never give up hope. This optimism is a definite motivation for professionals. By working with families, individuals who entered teaching to make a positive difference can find the affirmation and reassurance they need to continue.

Table 1.1 Positive Responses to Parent Involvement Challenges

Challenge	Ideas
Difficulties establishing rapport	▪ Recognize parents as persons with unique skills, interests, and talents. ▪ Be sensitive to parental feelings and situations. Use reflective listening. ▪ Ask families what they prefer. What parent involvement activities are most valued and productive? Use discussions, surveys, or short questionnaires to allow parents to evaluate the partnership. ▪ Extend a genuine and warm welcome. ▪ Individualize your communication strategies with parents. ▪ Give parents positive feedback to emphasize what they *are* doing for their child and the skills their child has developed. ▪ Listen to parents with undivided attention. ▪ Be open and honest. Treat parents like equal partners. ▪ Make repeated special efforts. ▪ Reflect on and analyze your attitudes and behaviors with families. Do you reveal any bias? ▪ Monitor your nonverbal communication—visual contact and gestures, physical space or classroom environment, and appearance. ▪ Help family members understand why they are important to their child's success. ▪ Ask parents what they feel is important for their child's success this year and use their comments to individualize your involvement plan for them. ▪ Avoid jargon. Keep the conversation nontechnical and concrete. Provide interpreters if needed for conferences and meetings.
Lack of understanding	▪ Ask parents what they want to know more about or what resources they can share at school. ▪ Give parents specific information on how to help their child at home. ▪ Give them tools to help track their child's progress.
You are uncomfortable with parents	▪ Determine what feelings may be influencing your attitude/behavior. ▪ Talk to teachers who appear to have good family partnerships. Ask what is working for them. ▪ Ask your administrator for staff development in parent involvement. ▪ Search out resource information online and in print to create your own in-service.
Little response to involvement efforts	▪ Ask parents what they would like and how best to communicate—phone, notes, e-mail, or in person. Use various strategies. ▪ Be available to parents. ▪ Invite parents *and* extended family to participate. Encourage parents to bring a guest. ▪ Enlist children's help to design and write personalized invitations. ▪ *Don't give up!*
Lack of parental time	▪ Offer flexible options for parent communication such as a chat during a home visit or a telephone conference instead of one in person. Offer a variety of meeting times and places if possible. Utilize a home-to-school notebook, e-mail, or electronic messages.

Challenge	Ideas
Transportation difficulties	■ Encourage parents to invite someone to the event who might be able to provide transportation as well as support. ■ Help parents link up for ride sharing. ■ Check for availability of funds for public transportation.
Child care	■ Provide on-site, supervised care using volunteers. (Some high school students may need community service time.) ■ Combine the parent event with child activities.

FEDERAL, STATE, AND LOCAL INCENTIVES FOR PARENT INVOLVEMENT

In the past 50 years, the issues and benefits of involving parents have captured the interest of federal, state, and local policy makers. Fueled by a history of successful efforts that have brought widely documented positive outcomes in intellectual development for participating children and increased awareness of child development as a result of family involvement, commitment to the parent–school partnership continues to grow.

Federal Initiatives

At the federal level, several major initiatives have mandated parent involvement components in programs serving economically disadvantaged or educationally at-risk preschoolers. Head Start has been this country's most extensive investment in preschool education. Since its inception in 1965, Head Start has piloted innovative strategies for involving low-income families with young children aged 3 through 5. The Early Head Start and Parent and Child Centers, which are supported by the national Head Start program, are comprehensive child development and family support programs that serve expectant mothers and children younger than 3. These programs ask parents to make a commitment, aim to prevent deficits in the child's development, and strengthen parenting skills and confidence. Chapter I of the Title I federal program includes the family-focused Even Start initiative. Even Start integrates early childhood education and adult GED education by cooperating with federal programs that offer adult education, literacy skill promotion, employment training, and preschool education. Guidelines include parent involvement in the planning, design, and implementation of programs, as well as parent training in centers and homes.

Numerous laws, including the Elementary and Secondary Education Act (ESEA) and the Individuals with Disabilities Education Act (IDEA), require meaningful parent involvement. In January of 2002, the ESEA was signed into law as the No Child Left Behind Act. This legislation required schools to issue an annual school report card that shows parents how students at large perform on required standardized tests and how teacher qualifications meet the requirements for professionals. It also made provisions for parents to transfer their children to better-performing public schools within their district if particular conditions were met. Parents were required to be involved in the planning, evaluation, and improvement of the various programs and receive understandable descriptions of curricular and student assessments. Although the specifics of the legislation may change with the times, the Elementary and Secondary Education Act will continue to impact the roles of families in schools as it is revisited and reauthorized to reflect current issues in our country. Additional information can be obtained at www.ed.gov, the U.S. Department of Education website.

Federal legislation also has provided the impetus for parents to become involved in the educational planning and evaluation of children with disabilities through IDEA. Since 1975, federal laws have authorized public education to serve children with disabilities. Parent advocacy, through the judicial and legislative branches of government, has contributed to the rights of parents in providing services for their children with special needs. Parental participation in developing the individual education plan, as a multidisciplinary team member, has been protected and increasingly expanded with each reauthorization of IDEA. Since 1986, services for infants and toddlers with disabilities are to be directed to the family, as well as the child, under an individualized family service plan. This plan could include referrals to community resource providers, parental training, counseling, and home visits. Succeeding reauthorizations of IDEA have strengthened the provisions and regulations for family-centered programming at the state and local coordination levels to require family involvement with all aspects of planning for the education of children with special needs. Additional information on parent involvement regarding families who have children with special needs is available in Chapter 4.

The Child Care and Development Block Grants, funded by Congress in 1990, continue to support a national system of safe and affordable child care targeting low income, working families and promote quality child care for all. Parents and child-care providers can help set child-care standards and policies at national, state, and local levels. Resource and referral programs are funded to educate parents about child-care choices, licensing requirements, and complaint procedures.

State and Local Initiatives

Public school early childhood programs, spearheaded by state governments nationwide, often target children who are at risk due to physical, environmental, or developmental concerns. These programs typically include a focus on parent involvement. While some of these initiatives are federally supported, a growing number of states have begun their own initiatives to provide family support and education. All children from birth to kindergarten age and their parents are eligible for Minnesota's Early Childhood and Family Education Program, which was begun in 1975. One of the oldest state efforts, it operates through local school districts to provide parent discussion groups, classes, home visits, newsletters, access to toys and books, and developmental strategies to support parental efforts in raising children.

Family involvement is also a component of states' school improvement plans. Federal and state program initiatives frequently foster collaborations at the local level that contribute to the development of local parenting programs. These programs meet needs by merging government and community support. Since 1985, Missouri has operated the Parents As Teachers program that operates through school districts to offer information and parent education via home visits, group meetings, and parent resource centers in the schools.

Many programs have discovered the importance of building a stronger educational and political base. Family Support America, originally founded as the Family Resource Coalition, is a national organization begun in 1981 as a consortium of diverse community-based programs involving parents. The coalition has communicated the importance of parent involvement and has promoted the development of research and programs nationwide. Locally, many community groups, businesses, and organizations offer parenting resources, parent training, and group meetings on parent involvement. The National PTA has produced strong leadership in promoting collaborative interactions between parents and schools. Utilizing the organization's support and resources, local PTA programs can go far beyond fundraising and token parent involvement. Communication, cooperation, and collaboration provide the grassroots advocacy to bring about acceptance and appreciation for the value of parent involvement.

SUMMARY

Parent involvement can be defined in many ways and is supported by varied rationales that target the partnerships between individual parents and teachers and the relationships between educational programs and parent communities. There is no one-size-fits-all family involvement program. While difficulties can challenge the success of communication and collaboration, parent involvement provides enormous benefits for children, families, programs and schools, and communities.

Educators can be the catalysts who make parent involvement work for the benefit of all. To reap the rewards of positive parent collaborations, educators must demonstrate interpersonal skills, develop effective strategies, and maintain a commitment to the process. Family involvement has been the focus of research to identify effective qualities and strategies. Joyce Epstein and others support a rationale for involvement that benefits children, families, and programs. Federal, state, and local initiatives have required and supported family involvement despite the challenges it may present. Involving families requires an ongoing dedication to personal growth as a professional, supported by comprehensive preservice and in-service programs. Teachers may need to collaborate with others to muster philosophical and financial support for parenting initiatives. Working together, educators and policy makers can successfully meet the challenges of parent involvement and make meaningful partnerships a reality to benefit children, families, and communities.

ACTIVITIES FOR DISCUSSION, EXPANSION, AND APPLICATION

1. Select three educational settings in your community. Contact members of the program staff and interview them to determine the following:
   - How does their program define parent involvement? Do they have a policy statement or mission statement? What does their choice of parent involvement activities reveal about their philosophy of parent involvement?
   - Describe activities and strategies used to involve parents. How do staff members support these efforts?
   - What benefits do staff members perceive for children, families, and the program?
   - What challenges to participation do parents face that may prevent them from becoming actively involved? What has been (or can be) done to overcome these challenges?

2. In a small group, discuss the reasons to support parent involvement for families, programs, and communities. By group consensus, list the three most significant reasons your community should promote family involvement.

3. In multiple studies, researchers have discovered differences in parent involvement strategies used by programs and schools. Conduct your own

community research, individually or within a team. Interview the parents of children in preschool, kindergarten or primary grades, and middle or upper grades. Ask them:

- What opportunities are available for parents to be involved in your child's program/school?
- How does the teacher invite your support?
- What activities have you been involved in?
- What factors encouraged your participation?
- What may have discouraged you from participating?

Analyze the similarities and differences among the parents you interviewed according to the program or school, ages of the children, and your perception of the parental characteristics.

4. Imagine yourself to be a parent, an educator, and an administrator. What rewards and frustrations (or barriers) regarding parent involvement would you expect to encounter? Support your answers.

5. Identify federal, state, and community initiatives utilized in your area to promote family involvement. How long have the programs been in existence? Are they selective or restrictive in determining who can participate? What strategies or activities do they use that encourage parent involvement? How does the community perceive the value and effectiveness of the parent components? What criticisms have you heard?

6. What do Epstein's Model Parent Involvement Components, the National PTS Standards for Parent Involvement, and the National Association of State School Boards of Education's statement on parent involvement have in common?

CASE STUDY

Germayia Cole is a first year preschool teacher in an ethnically and socioeconomically diverse program. At the beginning of the year, teachers hold a parent orientation meeting to introduce themselves and the curriculum to families of children in their classes. Germayia is excited about the opportunity to get families involved and win their support. She had a positive student-teaching experience in another program that had a strong family involvement policy. Her cooperating teacher there was a veteran teacher who utilized classroom volunteers, sent home "weekend bags" for child–family homework, and utilized weekly notes to keep families aware of classroom events. Her new program appears to support family involvement, but Germayia isn't sure where to start. Using the Epstein model of parent involvement, information concerning barriers and benefits presented in this chapter, and your own intuition, what advice can you give her?

1. What activities should she give priority to this year?

2. The children come from a variety of family backgrounds. Identify any potential barriers to family involvement Germayia should be aware of. How can she anticipate and overcome them?

3. What should she include in her orientation "sales pitch" as a rationale for having families become involved in their child's program this year?

USEFUL WEBSITES

www.csos.jhu.edu/P2000/center.htm

Center on School, Family, and Community Partnerships. Directed by Joyce Epstein, the center conducts research and publishes about best practices, policies, student learning, and school improvement for parents and professionals. The TIPS (Teachers Involving Parents in Schoolwork) resources (guides, CDs, and videos) are designed to help parents become more involved.

www.ed.gov/about/offices/list/oii/index.html

U.S. Department of Education Parent Information and Resource Centers. This site provides information on educational services provided through the No Child Left Behind legislation and current issues in education. A variety of teaching resources are also available.

www.familysupportamerica.org

Family Support America. This organization provides resources and information regarding family support practices and assists local efforts through networking and training (formerly the Family Resource Coalition).

www.nhsa.org

National Head Start Association. This is the official website for Head Start Program information.

www.patnc.org

Parents as Teachers National Center, Inc. This organization is a leading international birth-to-kindergarten parent education and family support program that offers training and resources.

REFERENCES

Bronfenbrenner, U. (1974). Developmental research, public policy, and the ecology of childhood. *Child Development, 45,* 1–5.

Carnegie Corporation Task Force. (1994). *Starting points: Meeting the needs of our youngest children.* New York: Carnegie Corporation.

Cummings, C. (1995). *Creating good schools for young children: Right from the start.* Alexandria, VA: National Association of State Boards of Education.

Eldridge, D. (2001). Parent involvement: It's worth the effort. *Young Children, 55*(4), 65–69.

Epstein, J. (1996). Perspectives and premises on research and policy for school, family, and community partnerships. In A. Booth & J. Dunn (Eds.), *Family–school links: How do they affect educational outcomes?* (pp. 209–246). Madwah, NJ: Lawrence Erlbaum Associates.

Epstein, J. (2002). *School and family partnerships: Preparing educators and improving schools.* Boulder, CO: Westview.

Gordon, I. (1977). The application of infant research: Policy-making at the local level. In M. Scott & S. Grimmett (Eds.), *Current issues in child development* (118–124). Washington, DC: National Association for the Education of Young Children.

Henderson, A. T., & Berla, N. (1994). *A new generation of evidence: The family is critical to student achievement.* St. Louis: Danforth Foundation; Flint, MI: Mott (C.S.) Foundation.

Keniston, K., & The Carnegie Council on Children. (1977). *All our children: The American family under pressure.* New York: Harcourt, Brace, Jovanovich.

Parent Teacher Association. *PTA, parent involvement, and the law.* Retrieved July 7, 2008, from http://www.pta.org/archive_article_details-1118251961500.html.

Schweinhart, L., Montie, J., Xiang, Z., Barnett, W., Belfield, C., & Nores, M. (2005). Lifetime effects: The High/Scope Perry Preschool study through age 40. *Monographs of the High/Scope Educational Research Foundation, 14.* Ypsilanti, MI: High/Scope Press.

Swick, K. (2003). Communication concepts for strengthening family–school–community partnerships. *Early Childhood Education Journal, 30*(4), 275–280.

Weiss, H., Kreider, H., Lopez, M., & Chatman, C. (2005) *Preparing educators to involve families from theory to practice.* Thousand Oaks, CA: Sage Publications.

Wherry, J. (2007a). *Barriers to parental involvement—and what can be done: A research analysis.* Retrieved July 7, 2008, from http://www.parent-institute.com/educator/resources/articles/obstacles.php.

Wherry, J. (2007b). *Selected parent involvement research.* Retrieved July 7, 2008, from http://www.parent-institute.com/educator/resources/research/research.php.

KEY TERMS

Educator—Any adult associated with a program or school who interacts with children and families. For purposes of this text, this could be an early interventionist, therapist, social worker, child-care provider, teacher, classroom assistant, or other staff member serving children from birth through the elementary years.

Parent/Family—Typically the biological father and/or mother of a child, but may include others assuming a parenting role in a child's life, such as grandparents, extended family, primary caregiver, and so on.

Educational Program—A private, public, not-for-profit, preschool, child-care, community, government, or agency program that serves children from birth through the elementary years.

Parent/Family Involvement—A continuum of activities or strategies that empower parents and families to participate in a child's educational process either at home or within a program or school setting.

Foster Parent—A certified "stand-in" parent who temporarily cares for minor-aged children who have been removed from their biological family or other custodial adults by state authority.

NAEYC—The National Association for the Education of Young Children, a not-for-profit international organization representing early childhood teachers in programs, schools, and family- and center-based child care.

PTA/PTO—Parent Teacher Associations/Parent Teacher Organizations are organizations that promote family involvement in programs and schools.

CHAPTER 2

Special Considerations in Partnering with Families

STUDENT LEARNING OUTCOMES

After reading this chapter, you should be able to

- Recognize that all families have strengths.

- Analyze a family-centered philosophy in family–teacher partnerships.

- Explain parental and professional prerequisites to engaging parents as partners.

- Identify demographic and societal factors influencing the family unit.

- Outline strategies for enhancing family partnerships for difficult-to-reach families.

- Explain supportive interactions for families in stressful situations.

- Discuss involvement of fathers and ways educators can facilitate their participation.

As explored in Chapter 1, the American family portrait has undergone significant change since 1950. Statistics on the changing demographics of American society provide dramatic evidence that families are facing continued and extraordinary lifestyle stresses. These complex changes in modern life affect children of all socioeconomic levels, in all areas of the country. Consequently, few children or families are immune to periods of social, emotional, or physical trauma. Because programs and schools increasingly reflect our society, educators can expect to work with greater numbers of children and families challenged by life's circumstances or in crisis as the result of them. There is no magic formula or prescription for perfecting family involvement. It will be vital for educators to develop personal and professional skills to reach and involve diverse families along with the skills needed to educate children in the years ahead.

ALL FAMILIES HAVE STRENGTHS

Each family possesses strengths that can help it respond to its needs. **Family strengths** are considered to be the family's abilities to meet the various needs of its members and maintain equilibrium within the family itself. These abilities or strengths may lie in the values, attitudes, and beliefs that characterize the family's lifestyle. Families may be committed to sticking together in difficult times, be willing to make personal sacrifices in order to help each other, take pride in members' accomplishments, or have a clear set of family rules and beliefs that define acceptable and desired behaviors. Strengths also may be reflected in the knowledge, skills, and capabilities of individual family members. For instance, some family members may be able to look on the bright side of troubling circumstances or know how to locate informal supports to help during a crisis. Families also develop mutually supportive behaviors in their interpersonal relationships, which promote positive family interactions. They may make time to be together, listen to an individual's point of view, discuss different ways to deal with problems, share feelings and concerns, and demonstrate a willingness to help each other. The following family values are characteristic family strengths:

- **Love:** Strong emotional bonds between various immediate and extended family members—adults and children.
- **Communication:** Responsive listening and support for family concerns and life activities.
- **Togetherness:** Sharing and support in carrying out roles and responsibilities to meet the family's needs.
- **Consideration:** Sensitivity to the needs, feelings, and problems of various family members.
- **Commitment:** A willingness to support the family and work through problems.
- **Respect:** Valuing the individuality of each member of the family.

Interactive family involvement strategies can reinforce parents' positive efforts in building family relationships and parenting. Whatever the form or degree, all families have strengths.

All families, regardless of members' ages or circumstances, have strengths. *Courtesy of ECE Photo Library.*

No family, however, is completely self-sufficient. Because of this, many professionals in the helping professions who work with families may focus on observed weaknesses, not strengths. This results in a biased view that sees only what is not working well for the family and encourages a tendency to "do for them" rather than promoting the family members' abilities to do for themselves. If teachers hope to develop a true partnership with parents and families that will foster the holistic development of children, they must learn to recognize the strengths inherent in every family system.

Family Systems

A **family system** provides the loving and secure environment in which children learn and develop. Olsen and DeFrain (2000) state: "In family systems theory, everything that happens to any family member is seen as having an impact on everyone else in the family. This is because family members are interrelated and operate as a group or system." Family members' unique characteristics, emotional interconnectedness, and interactive styles are considered part of their family system as well. Each family system utilizes various methods of meeting needs and sustaining the family in dynamic, ever-changing ways. Since the days of cave dwellers, the reality of raising children and meeting the needs of the family unit has required a group effort. The group and the method of sharing support may be unique for each family. Today's supportive contacts may require connections with family members hundreds of miles away, a babysitting cooperative organized by neighborhood moms, a class on parenting skills offered by the school or program, or financial assistance from the government to meet basic needs.

Parenting classes can provide knowledge and guidance about child growth and development, homework strategies, and discipline. *Courtesy of ECE Photo Library.*

Naturally, the parents are the family's greatest assets. That is not to imply that all parents possess every skill to respond appropriately to all the dilemmas that arise in raising children or survive unaffected through difficult times. Parenting isn't an instinctive skill and, unfortunately, babies don't come with instructions. Moving from the stage of single person or couple to that of parent is a major physical, psychological, and social adjustment. The dynamics of each individual's growth and development—the ages and stages of life as a human being—add overlapping complexities to each family system. Consequently, the development of any family system is not consistent or entirely predictable. Families strive to achieve a sense of functional balance. The balance of daily life is affected by such factors as the roles and influences of various family members, life stressors, and situations that challenge family beliefs. Most parents at one time or another require resource information—whether from extended family, a parenting magazine, or an educator or other professional. When considering a child's personality, motivation, behaviors, and skills, educators must consider each child as a part of his or her own unique family system.

Parents as First Teachers

Parents are resources—to themselves, to other families, and to the educators working with the children. Families typically have some formal or informal **family networks** in place to help meet their needs. These supportive resources can be family, friends, church groups, or community organizations. They may be embedded within the value system of the family and may appear within a religious, social, or cultural context. Families under stress may not immediately recognize supports that are already in place, such as the extended family or local service organizations. A caring educator can assist them in recognizing, accessing, and maximizing resources available to them. Different families find different solutions to similar problems and needs, and the experience developed by one family may be shared and thereby benefit another. Given options for self-help, peer support, and other network linkages, parents can make the decisions most appropriate for them.

FAMILY-CENTERED PHILOSOPHY AND PRACTICE

Chapter 1 documented the positive connection between the home and school as symbiotic learning environments key to a child's progress and achievement. To work most effectively with children, the sensitive teacher recognizes the importance of family systems and understands the circumstances at home. The teacher also must personally project a commitment to family involvement through a strong personal outreach and nonjudgmental attitude. This is the groundwork for a family-centered approach to parent involvement. Recognizing that parent involvement is an indicator of best practices in education doesn't make partnerships automatically happen. There is a critical gap between theory and practice. Establishing and maintaining parental contacts may sometimes be challenging or even quite difficult for educators because of the complexity of family issues. A first step is to believe that family involvement and the positive interactions it fosters are vital to an educator's practice in the classroom and worth the effort.

Dangers of Distancing

In the gap between theory and practice, the biggest obstacle can be the distancing that appears between parent and educator. The concept of accepting parents as "experts" can be confusing and even threatening to the teacher. Yet within the context of a family partnership, parents hold the most knowledge about their family and especially about their children. Educators are resources, not authorities who know what is absolutely best for families and children. The educator can assist parents in developing a nurturing learning environment at home and even help parents identify options and develop strategies to address problems. Best practice in family involvement reflects the collaborative process of parent and educator working together in the best interest of the child. It is not prescriptive or controlling. Educators who undertake any type of family involvement program must first, in their minds and hearts, understand their own motivation and role in developing dynamic relationships with parents.

Foundations of Respect

The educator's philosophy concerning parents can underscore or undermine the framework of trust and respect in the family–teacher relationship. As the diversity of families increases, the understanding and appreciation of cultural and ethnic backgrounds and the acceptance of dissimilar value systems and lifestyles will become increasingly important for the educator who values parent involvement. (**Cultural diversity** is explored in depth in Chapter 3.) Families are sensitive to the economic, linguistic, structural, cultural, or ethnic differences between themselves and other parents or the teacher. Consistent efforts should be made to communicate family strengths, to give consideration to unique problems or concerns, and to respond to them in a sensitive manner. Through responsive listening and actively tuning in to parents' verbal and nonverbal messages, teachers can project openness to parental ideas about their children's development and learning. Controlling the impulse to talk too much, "talk down," correct or advise in a pushy manner, or move too fast in parent–teacher communications is also critical in developing rapport with families. Being accessible to families is important. Sharing contact information, as illustrated in Table 2.1, indicates personal confidence and openness. Young teachers often worry about how parents will accept them due to their age or lack of personal parenting experience. When a teacher demonstrates credibility as a professional (through confident, child-centered

Table 2.1 Invite Families to Communicate

In order to promote a two-way, equal partnership with families, it is important to give them some appropriate ways to contact you. Print out a card with your information on it. Some teachers don't mind if parents call them at home and find that most parents never do this unless absolutely necessary. Modify this example to meet your needs.

Hello!
My name is Mrs. Andrea Goodteacher, your child's first-grade teacher at Stony Creek School.
If you would like to contact me, please feel free to use any of the methods below:
Send me a note with your child.
Call the school at 123-4567. The secretary will take a message and leave it in my mailbox. I will return your call later in the day. Let the secretary know what telephone number I can use to reach you and the time(s) you can be reached at that number.
E-mail me at agoodteacher@stonycreekschool.org.
If needed, call me at home between 6 and 8 p.m. at 765-4321.

behaviors, knowledge of teaching, good classroom management skills, etc.), parents gain assurance that the teacher is reliable. These qualities encourage a comfortable climate for building a partnership.

One initial strategy toward family partnership is to learn about the families of the children. It is important to become familiar with the family's composition, interests, situations, and values without being intrusive. Inviting parents to share information about the child and family through a simple questionnaire at the beginning of the school year is one way to broaden and strengthen this partnership. (See Table 2.2 for potential questionnaire items.) This process provides preliminary background to better understand the child and to individualize future parent contacts. In some programs, information is gathered through a social-health history form or a personal interview when the child enters the school or program. This can also be done individually on a home visit or as part of an orientation meeting at the center or school. Carefully prepared written or verbal surveys can communicate to parents that staff members are flexible and are sincerely interested in encouraging a "needs-fit" involvement match for each family. Information gathered using surveys can be used to make a simple chart like the one in Table 2.3. The chart organizes key information about the children and adults in each family and can help identify special family needs, strengths, and possible solutions for challenges to parent involvement.

Table 2.2 Beginning-of-School Questionnaire

Parents can fill out a simple questionnaire when their child begins school to help a teacher become acquainted with their child and family. It also introduces parents to potential opportunities for becoming involved in the classroom. Select the items that are most applicable.

Help Me Get to Know Your Child

Hi,

I'm looking forward to getting to know your child here at school, but you are the expert! Please share the following information about your child so I can be prepared to support him or her physically, socially, and emotionally as well as educationally this year. This information will be kept confidential. Thank you for your support. I look forward to working with you as a partner for your child's success!

Sincerely,

My child is _____. His/her nickname is _____.

Family
Brothers' names and ages/grades
Sisters' names and ages/grades
Do any of them attend this school?
Any other family members at home who will be working with your child? (grandparents, aunts, uncles, etc.)
Any pets? What kind(s)? Name(s)?

Free time activities
What are your child's favorite free time activities?
Favorite toys, television shows, movies, or video games?

Table 2.2 Continued

Does he/she take any special lessons (music, dance, gymnastics, swim, foreign language, etc.) outside of school? Which ones?
Does he/she play any sports? Which ones?
Does he/she belong to any organizations? (scouts, 4-H, YMCA, Boys and Girls Club, etc.)

Health
Are there any health concerns/conditions I need to be aware of at school?
Recent surgeries/procedures?
Asthma or seizures?
Allergies or food sensitivities?
Regular medications? What kind(s) and when taken?

It might help me to know about . . .
Regular child care—before and/or after school?
If yes, where?
Any fears or anxiety? About?
Any painful or traumatic events that still affect him or her?
Any regular separations from family members?
Languages other than English your child hears or uses in the family?
Any special religious or cultural traditions/practices?
How do you describe your child's personality?

Do you have any questions or concerns about your child's:
Learning, speech or communication, movement, or skills in . . . ?
Health, eating habits, or sleep routines?
Behaviors?
Other?

Is there anything else I should be aware of as your child's teacher?
I like to let you know about the good things that happen at school. How can I best share information with you?
It is better for you to (please check one):
☐ Receive a note sent home with your child
☐ Receive a telephone call at # _____
         (Best time: _____)
☐ Receive an e-mail at _____

Is there anyone else I need to send classroom news to or invite to parent conferences?
Name   Relationship   Address

Do you need duplicate classroom notes/newsletters for others? Yes_____ No_____

Families are very important, and I invite you to participate in classroom activities this year. Can you:

Home Activities
  1. Help occasionally with preparing games or materials? (I can supply materials and patterns.)

  2. Use a computer to put digital photos into a slide show?

  3. Other?

School Activities

1. Volunteer occasionally in the classroom to work with the children?

2. Be a "Guest Reader" to read a story aloud to a group of children?

3. Bring a "show and tell" item or skill to share with the children? (Tell me more.)

4. Know someone who can visit to share his/her occupation/hobby (such as a firefighter, law enforcement officer, dog trainer, pet owner, etc.)?

5. Other?

Table 2.3 Identifying Family Needs, Strengths, and Solutions

Child	Adults in Family System	Potential Barriers & Strengths	Ideas to Overcome Challenges
Lindsey	Mom, Aunt Kerry	Single mom, works days, needs child care for 4 sibs, aunt single and may help, Dad visits occasionally. Wants to "help Lindsey."	Provide activities for daily routine at home, meet during lunch? Send notes to Dad too.
Misha	Pat and Jim—foster parents	Misha may return to biological mom during the semester. Has visitation every other week. Two other foster children in home.	Meet with foster mom, caseworker?
Luke	Sarah	Luke born when Sarah was 16. Both live with Sarah's parents, have financial & emotional support. Sarah finished GED, works at restaurant, likes aerobics.	Maybe will do a movement class with K–1.
Noah	Joel and Amy	Both parents work, uncle is firefighter. Joel wants to bring train set to school.	Send calendar for babysitter.

ENGAGING PARENTS AND FAMILIES: PREREQUISITES TO PARTNERSHIPS

Professionals may get discouraged when families fail to respond to their best efforts to encourage a partnership. Sometimes obvious barriers, such as a lack of transportation or child care, stand in the way of involvement, but sometimes there does not appear to be an obvious reason. At these times, the teacher must have an honest, heart-searching look at his or her attitudes and behaviors. A courageous teacher can approach a colleague or parent with whom there is good rapport to ask for assistance in analyzing the situation.

There are some hard and simple truths to the business of family partnerships. In order to actively participate in a parent–teacher partnership, parents must have some degree of readiness, or the capability to respond to the requirements of the partnership. These abilities center on four themes: parent self-image, parent self-control (optimism and sense of control over one's relationships and actions), parent development or maturation, and interpersonal skills. By consistently reinforcing the importance of parents as first—and best—teachers and recognizing positive parenting behaviors, teachers can communicate respect for the inherent value of each parent. Teachers can empower parents to view themselves as capable people by honestly helping them recognize individual and family strengths, potential options, and choices.

Parent Self-Image

How parents view themselves (with a positive or negative self-image) is reflected in all their actions, especially in their acceptance of the parenting role and in how they interact with authority figures such as teachers. Some parents may think they have nothing to contribute to their child's education because they have a limited view of the role of "teacher" or because they feel they have not been successful enough in the societal view of education or life success.

Parent Self-Control

People tend to see themselves as a victor or a victim—or a combination of both—depending on the situation. This is sometimes referred to as the **locus of control.** When circumstances are difficult (and always have been), parents may feel that they have no control over what happens to them. Eventually, it becomes difficult for them to believe that they have the power of self-determination. Parents who are simply overwhelmed with meeting basic needs may feel they cannot undertake a less crucial or unfamiliar obligation—for example, meeting with a teacher.

Parent Development and Maturation

Educators sometimes tend to forget that development continues throughout a lifetime. As people mature (as individuals as well as parents) they learn to cope with changes in relationships, and they develop a perspective about life experiences. Just because two people are physically mature enough to conceive a child, it does not mean that they have the emotional maturity to parent effectively. Parents may not yet have the willingness to put the needs of the child before their own. This can create difficult dilemmas for the teacher and the child.

Parenting skills often develop with experience. The first-born child, initiating a mother or father into the ranks of parenthood, may be considered a "first teacher." Parents often recognize that they become more relaxed and parent quite differently with the last child in comparison with their first-born. Older children in the family will frequently notice this within the context of privileges or opportunities. The youngest may have more privileges at a younger age than did the oldest children.

Interpersonal Skills

Interpersonal skill building is related to self-confidence, self-esteem, and the belief that "I am valuable as a person and can support others." A parent's life experience may not have empowered him or her to develop these types of skills, and this "disability" is brought into the parent–teacher encounter. Parents' rates of development in these three areas are varied and diverse. Nurturing experiences between parents and teachers in the early years of educating their children offer opportunities for individual growth and success in interpersonal skill building that can reap benefits for both children and their parents.

Challenges for Educators

In addition to the internal limitations that may hinder parent involvement, most families face increased stresses from the rapidly changing political, economic, and societal forces around them. Inflation, unemployment, and job insecurity may jeopardize dreams of a better life. A tidal wave of poverty, substance abuse, increased violence, abuse, neglect, and disease has engulfed an increasing number of families. Inadequacies in employment, child care, housing, and health care threaten parents' hopes for their children's future. Most educators will eventually work with children and families facing many types of crises, and they need to be aware of how these situations may affect families.

It isn't surprising that a great many families have special needs or that they look to the classroom teacher for assistance. These needs may involve maintaining adequate food or housing or juggling two demanding parental careers, or they may be severe enough to require intervention during a crisis of family violence. Some families may seek guidance in helping their children cope during the adjustment to a new baby, a move, a divorce, or the death of a grandparent. Many families may need assistance in understanding the normal challenges of having a rapidly growing child in the household and a reminder of the many joys that accompany having children. It is critical to remember that, just as each family has a composite of needs, it also possesses unique abilities to respond to those needs.

Insights and Strategies for Reaching Unresponsive Parents

Some families have strong skills and come to the program or school ready to become involved. However, as described earlier, more families than ever before are influenced by societal and economic factors that affect their capacity to become full partners with their child's teacher. Teachers must understand where parents are developmentally and respond with sensitivity to their life circumstances. By labeling parents as "difficult" or "problem" parents, educators often subconsciously alienate them.

Regardless of first impressions, most parents are indeed reachable and have a strong desire to be involved. Schools, however, may not truly attempt to involve them, may not be knowledgeable of effective parent involvement strategies, or may not be sensitive enough to overcome cultural and socioeconomic barriers (Warner, 1994). Parents revealed the following obstacles to school involvement:

- The perception that non-middle-class children were viewed and treated differently.
- Communication from schools to parents was mostly negative.
- The perception that families were deficient in some way and that fault lay with the parents. The focus was on their problems.
- Among poverty-level families, parents revealed a low assessment of their ability to be involved in their children's schooling.

Research varies greatly in drawing specific conclusions about the groups of parents whom teachers may categorize as "difficult to reach." Outcomes for their children may be reported to be positive or negative depending on the study, the researcher, and the decade in which the research was done. Parents are very much aware of their circumstances and also may be aware of society's views of families like theirs. Sensitivity to these assumptions will color parent interactions with the program or school.

Unfortunately, teachers can be influenced by societal and personal biases as well. The presence of certain characteristics (teen, unemployed, or low-income parents, for example) does not imply that a family will demonstrate particular attitudes or behaviors (such as low self-esteem or poor parenting skills). Each family is a unique group of individuals with a unique history, support structure, and set of resources. Consequently, the best source of information about a family is the family itself. Teachers may work with families and children who belong to a different socioeconomic group—either lower or higher—than they. Each experience can be intimidating in its own ways, and the educator must learn to develop a comfort level in pursuing a relationship with all families.

Facilitating a trusting partnership with families is the foundation of family–school collaboration. In order to share critical and relevant information, the family must trust the teacher. Some families may not wish to share what they consider private matters with anyone outside of their extended family or circle of friends. That is to be respected; confidentiality is a critical element in building trust. The National Association for the Education of Young Children has developed a Code of Ethical Conduct to assist teachers in working thoughtfully with families. This information is found on pages 155–158 of the *Home, School, and Community Relations Professional Enhancement* text (Gestwicki, 2007). Building trust requires individualizing the relationship and communication strategies employed with parents. Some parents may need more encouragement to begin a relationship; others may need only a request in the classroom newsletter.

Individualizing family involvement strategies requires that the teacher try various methods to share information. Communication may be in writing, by telephone, via e-mail, or in person. Ask families what they prefer. People are most responsive when conversations begin and end with a positive comment about the family and the child. Sharing some personalized information or anecdote about the child regarding his or her interests, mannerisms, or habits demonstrates to the family that the teacher knows the child as an individual, thus gaining teacher credibility in the eyes of the family. Chapters 5 and 6 will discuss communication in detail; however, these are some important reminders. Above all, listen to parents. By giving them attention and respect, teachers communicate that parents are important. Accept their feelings and differences of opinion by using active listening techniques and a calm, professional demeanor.

Teachers who listen with sensitivity and are responsive to parental views show respect and build rapport. *Courtesy of ECE Photo Library.*

Respect privacy and guard confidentiality about the child, the family, and their situation. Mistrust can easily destroy any positive relationship-building efforts if information is shared about their child (or any other child) with anyone other than the parents. Be available to families by promptly responding to notes, phone calls, and e-mails and by sharing information or resources that could be helpful.

Supporting Families in Crisis

No family is immune to crisis. Some crises (a grandparent's death or a separation) may be anticipated, while others (a home fire, accident, or act of domestic violence) may happen without warning. Whatever crisis occurs, it brings additional stress to a family's existing situation. Sometimes teachers can provide supportive interactions with parents, especially those with whom a trusting relationship has already been built.

Parents and educators often encounter limits to parental involvement during crisis situations. When a family enters a crisis, individual members may need the intensive resources of family preservation and support services. Since the children's educational setting may be one of the few familiar routines, the teacher is often in a pivotal position to help the family. Educators should know who provides sources of assistance in the area. Schools and programs commonly keep community resource information available for staff and families. There are many ways the teacher can work within the program to help the family:

- Provide a structured and predictable classroom environment. Children affected by constant stress and upheavals at home can find security and relief in a supportive, familiar routine.

- Maintain continuity with the home. Supporting families as well as children is a goal of an active parent involvement program.

- Assist parents and children in interpreting and adjusting to life transitions. Conversation, sharing books that deal with a similar situation, and modeling can be supportive. Libraries and the Internet can be valuable resources for children's literature that addresses stressful scenarios in proactive ways. Carol Gestwicki's *Home, School, and Community Relations Professional Enhancement* text (2007) includes a chapter on books for children that may be of help in locating appropriate titles.

- Encourage positive coping techniques and make referrals to other helping professionals when appropriate.

FAMILY STATUS AND STRESS: IMPLICATIONS FOR EDUCATORS

Family configurations and the context of parenting have become increasingly diverse. Piece by piece, statistics reveal a complex picture puzzle for families with children. This picture is composed of, for example, dual-income families, single parents, blended families, and families subjected to multiple risk factors created by life events or poverty. Not all parents, of course, will find themselves influenced by these lifestyle forces, but teachers in early childhood programs and elementary classrooms will inevitably have children who are affected by some of them. Unfortunately, when a situation affects family status and well-being, it may not be an isolated experience. One situation may result in other resulting stresses. For example, parents may divorce, and the mother may become a single parent struggling with the economic realities of minimum wage employment or of returning to school to further her education. This could necessitate dependence upon her parents for child care or even housing until her life direction improves. Families of children in early childhood programs and in elementary schools throughout the country become statistics that are collected and analyzed by sociologists and economists. It is the teacher working with the children and their families who sees the faces behind the numbers reported on the evening news.

Many facets of changing family lifestyles have become commonplace (e.g., dual-income families or divorced parents); consequently, the stress that accompanies them may be underestimated. Adults establish their unique family structures while simultaneously developing career and other life goals. As many women postpone childbearing or have children in second marriages, older parents are becoming more common. This, too, presents challenges, as parents at different life stages interact with teachers and schools. Children may spend less time with their own family due to the number of waking hours spent in child care, with a nanny, or with a home care provider. These are common family dynamics that place many families and children under stress.

The sections that follow are not intended to make generalizations or predict outcomes for particular groups of families. There are too many individual variables within families and overlapping characteristics among groups to do that. Research, however, does offer some consistent guidance for educators and others in the helping professions for working with families in special circumstances. The suggestions or implications for teachers detailed in one section are not necessarily exclusive; the information may well apply to and benefit other children or families.

Working Parents

In 2004, according to the Children's Defense Fund, 64 percent of mothers with children younger than 6 and 78 percent of mothers with children under the age of 18 were in the civilian workforce. The lack of quality child care and the inability of lower-earning mothers to take advantage of it due to the underfunding of support programs have created a child care nightmare for many families (Children's Defense Fund, 2005). The increase in the number of mothers in the workplace reflects both the current economic instability and an increase in the number of families headed by single mothers. Both parents working outside the home have, in fact, become a model of family life in the United States. Mothers may continue their careers after maternity leave, work part time, or seek employment with family-friendly employers who permit flexible work arrangements. When a mother has a job, she must deal with many issues that can complicate home life. Conflict often arises between her role as provider and nurturer, which she must manage along with the complex life routines and emotional responses that result from leaving her children in another's care.

Child Care Challenges Affect Families. When a child is sick or injured, the immediate need for emergency care can create a crisis that can negatively affect a mother's sense of "capable coping." A woman's satisfaction with her dual roles often hinges on many factors, including the degree to which her husband or partner shares in the household chores and child care, her job satisfaction, how comfortable she is with child care arrangements, and the perception of how her employment affects her children. The level of the mother's education has a significant effect on her morale and attitudes regarding the attention her children require. Mothers with higher educational levels who are employed outside the home appear to compensate by spending more time with their children during non-work hours and weekends. They also are more likely to verbally stimulate their children and be more interactive with them. Naturally, a mother's job outside the home magnifies the problem of time—there never seems to be enough of it. Fathers, too, are affected when the mother is employed. They often must step into roles involving housework and child care that they have little preparation for or that are considered "women's work" within their own social circle. When mothers are working full time, a more highly involved father takes on child care duties alongside his wife (Garanzini, 1995).

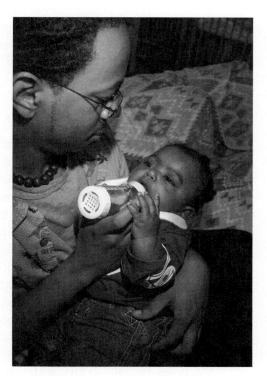

Dads are often more involved with their children's care today. *Courtesy of ECE Photo Library.*

Child Care Challenges for Children. Nationally, child care has become a major public policy issue. Concerns about child safety; physical, emotional, and social development; staffing within child care centers; and the issue of the availability of quality care appear regularly in the media. Studies of working mothers from a variety of family structures indicate that a critical variable in determining long-term effects on children is the way stress is handled in the family. Garanzini (1995) targets this concept: "It is the stress and strain of daily living, that is, the management of complex schedules, the juggling of resources and limited budgets, dealing with intrusion and unforeseen emergencies, that complicate family life."

Research has indicated that children may have negative reactions to maternal absence, potentially affecting school performance, when mothers work more than forty hours per week outside the home. Likewise, children who spend much of their day in child care and in before- or after-school care are sometimes more aggressive and peer oriented. This may be due to the amount of stress a child feels due to the multiple transitions and adjustments required in the course of a day —often four or more between home, child care, school, child care, and home again. Some children miss the lack of an unscheduled, less demanding break in the daily routine. Children may show stress from being over-scheduled or even "burned out." Classroom teachers sometimes are challenged in having children that need training to be more teacher- or adult-oriented and less demanding. Likewise, children may lack the impulse control needed for positive classroom adjustment (Garanzini, 1995).

Some dual-income families are further challenged by the emotional and physical realities of long workdays and commutes, extensive job-related travel away from home, or working more than one job. In all of these scenarios, the key factor regarding children's adjustment and school performance is the organization and management of the home environment. Open communication, clear rules, and parental control of situations allow children to cope and concentrate on school, friendships, and other matters of childhood. By being honest with children and with each other and having practical home routines and care, parents can best help children be both flexible to inevitable daily changes and secure in knowing they are respected, listened to, and loved.

Today there is an increase in dual-career homes, where women maintain their careers and professional life while raising their children. These differ from homes with two working parents where the focus of the family is on raising the children and the second income, although extremely helpful, is supplemental. In a dual-career family, both adults consider their careers and raising children equal priorities and responsibilities. Dual-career families are often less flexible with time and variations in routine. Parents may become especially stretched when the child is sick, has academic difficulties, or seeks time or attention from parents beyond what is available. Promotions, career shifts, or opportunities for career advancement, and the accompanying emotional implications, may further strain the family. Assistance for the family may frequently be purchased services—nannies, housekeepers, tutors, and so on. School personnel have reported that parents may place more responsibility for child care and support upon the school. Teachers may need to be especially sensitive to physical and emotional indicators of stress for children in these circumstances (Garazini, 1995).

Working parents may spend much of the day away from their child and may be sensitive to their child's stress responses. *Courtesy of ECE Photo Library.*

Implications for Educators. A family's satisfaction with the organization and harmony within a single- or dual-income family will play an important role in the parent–teacher relationship. Potential concerns may include time management, child-care arrangements (before and after school, transportation, quality, and cost), attitudinal conflicts, overwork, financial concerns, emotional, physical or relationship stress, and health-related issues. Many educators personally experience this first hand, as many spend all or part of their careers as working parents.

Schools can help families by becoming sensitive to the way homework is assigned. Working parents may be more likely to be involved with home support if assignments have extended or flexible deadlines or are designated as "weekend work." Because of parental work schedules and home commitments, opportunities for communication may be limited. A special folder, notebook, or zip-top plastic bag used only for home–school communication may simplify message transfer and help children be more responsible for carrying home special "mail." Telephone calls, notes, library loan materials, and flexible meeting times may also foster ongoing communication. E-mail messages or information on school or classroom websites may effectively keep working parents in touch with school events and classroom activities. Announcements of meetings and events should be given far enough in advance so that parents will have ample time to make arrangements. Likewise, care should be taken to maintain emergency numbers and child-care preferences in case there is an unexpected adjustment to the school day. Maintenance of current, functional phone numbers should be emphasized as part of every child's emergency information.

Flexibility in scheduling family events is typically appreciated by working parents. Parents could be given options to schedule conferences in the early morning, during lunch, in the evening, or on weekends. Meetings with parents can be held in person or over the phone. Evening events may be preferred, especially if child care is included on site. If possible, meetings before school or in the early evening could include simple refreshments to encourage attendance.

To feel involved, working parents may need alternatives to traditional classroom volunteering. Teachers can offer opportunities that benefit the program and are feasible for working mothers and fathers. (See Chapter 10 for additional ideas on program volunteers.) Learning activities that are tied to family home routines, such as reading or math practice that is part of meal preparation or charting a television-viewing schedule, make skill review meaningful. By looking at family involvement from the perspective of the working parent, it may be easier to share empathetic options for home support.

Divorce, Remarriage, and Blended Families

Divorce represents not only the end of a marriage, but the end of a family system as well. As divorce becomes more commonplace, researchers continue to study the effects of separation and divorce on the family unit and on children at different ages. About 50 percent of all divorces occur in the first seven years of marriage. Consequently, children affected by this major life transition are often young. Since the majority of men and women remarry following a divorce, stepfamilies or blended families now make up 20 percent of all two-parent families with children under age 18 (Gestwicki, 2007). Consequently, an increasing number of children throughout their school years will bring their developmental concerns to school following a divorce and remarriage. The events that lead to divorce and the arrangements made when one is agreed upon are unique to each family. The divorce affects each family member differently, both at the time of the parents' separation and later. Family members, especially children, may experience fears of abandonment, grief, guilt, depression, and rejection. The family may need to adjust to the effects of a smaller income, a change in residence, or a different standard of living, even though child support is part of the divorce agreement. A mother may need to increase hours of work, thereby impacting the hours she can spend with the children.

Implications of Divorce for Families and Children. How well adults handle their personal issues and assist their children in making the necessary transitions often determines how long the period of disharmony lasts and how great a psychological impact the divorce will have. All members of the family are affected by the adjustments to new family configurations and possibly new homes, new routines, and other new life patterns, but for children the adjustments can continue for much of their childhood and into their adult life.

Divorce impacts children in various ways. Many parents and children deal successfully with the new circumstances and cope well, despite the changes in the family configuration. Cooperative joint custody arrangements can help create positive structures for the transition to a new lifestyle. Even so, children may need to adjust to two homes and often two distinct sets of rules and parenting styles. Returning to a sense of normalcy both at school and with peers can be one of the most challenging adjustments children of divorced parents must make.

Children are also adversely affected when parents, stressed by interpersonal upheaval, temporarily put parenting on a back burner—they may be simply unable to parent until they can sufficiently rebuild their own lives. During this time, children may be affected by inconsistent parenting as the custodial parent juggles the responsibilities of being a single parent and, sometimes, the sole family provider. The consistency of routine and security of family life as children knew them are disrupted. For young children, whose lives are solely focused within the family, divorce seems to bring their world to an end (Heatherington & Kelly, 2002).

Research continues on the long-term effects of divorce on children as they mature. Regardless, families in complex situations like divorce have a great number of factors that affect individuals, both positively and negatively. Divorce does cause stress for adults and children that may last to some degree for a number of years. However, children who have the most difficulties often are those who had problems before the divorce occurred. Children can be resilient and learn healing and coping strategies that can carry them through the turmoil of divorce (Emery, 1999).

In time, most divorced people remarry, frequently to other parents with children. Children in these **blended families** have a great many adjustments to make in accepting new parents and siblings, settling issues of rivalry and territory, and becoming acquainted with new sets of extended families including grandparents, aunts, uncles, cousins, and so on. Stepparents may find it difficult to establish a satisfactory relationship with their stepchildren, despite their eagerness to be accepted. Fathers may feel guilty about not living with their own children, while stepmothers may have a difficult time shaking the "wicked stepmother" image and establishing expectations for the household. Stepparents may be concerned about developing a strong marital bond while at the same time developing bonds with an "instant family." Children may feel torn between parents and have loyalty issues between their old and new families. Parents have been known to overindulge children to increase acceptance of the new situation. Developing a workable parenting arrangement is an ongoing task, especially as children mature. Noncustodial parents also may harbor anger and resentment about the divorce, which can influence their relationship with the children and their participation in the children's education.

Implications for Educators.
Teachers should be aware that children and parents react differently to separation and divorce. Divorce is a major change, and the family may need extra support, patience, and reassurance from a relatively stable school environment. During a family upheaval, parents and teachers may be challenged by a child's increased aggression and noncompliance. Some children may exhibit symptoms of sadness, fear, developmental regression, and loneliness. Older children may show moodiness or withdrawal, inability to attend, frequent physical complaints, or challenging behaviors. Children react differently to the reduced contact with the noncustodial parent and commonly deal with feelings of loss, anger, and guilt. Helping the parents understand what is happening from the child's perspective and offering practical options is a supportive partnership response. Parents may reflect feelings of anger, guilt, and worry to the teacher. Teachers can suggest professional and parent resources on divorce, including contact information from local support services that specialize in family counseling or sponsor support groups.

Teachers should be kept informed of the legal and informal agreements regarding child care and whether there are any restrictions to family visits at school or with child transportation arrangements. There also may be changes of address and telephone numbers or additions to the child's emergency contact list. Parents who are on an emotional roller coaster may need to vent their anger and frustrations. Teachers should be careful to remain professional and refrain from taking sides, while acting as a reflective listener to sensitive conversations that occur at school. Teachers can help parents keep adult conversations private and away from the child as much as possible.

As mentioned before, in times of upheaval, as is the case for many family stressors, the stable routine of a child's program or classroom can help maintain a sense of security for children and lessen the effects of stress at home. Regular program or school activities and established limits for behavioral expectations can be gently and firmly communicated to the child. Teachers can be open and understanding to a child's emotional state. Listening with a sensitive ear to the child's feelings can help them feel less afraid and alone. Children may want to draw or write in a journal to express their feelings. Some may talk freely about what is happening to their family. Teachers can provide a safe sounding board to support the child while refraining from taking sides. Children may be so focused on life changes at home that they may neglect schoolwork and social activities. Teachers may need to be prepared to address this in the classroom. Some schools have support groups led by social workers or counselors for children going through divorce and related home situations.

All parents should be included and made welcome in the program or school's parent involvement activities. If interested, noncustodial parents should receive their own invitations to meetings, conferences, field trips, and other events. These can be mailed to noncustodial parents, or phone calls can be made to keep them involved. Separate conferences can also be offered for discussing a child's progress and report card. Teachers should be sensitive to parental desires to be involved and aware of differences in last names. When making gifts or cards, children should be encouraged to make as many as they need for their families. Teachers should also be sensitive to visitation patterns for weekdays, weekends, holidays, and vacations in order to understand children's behaviors upon returning to school. Teachers may especially be aware of changes in attendance, attitude, or behavior on Monday or after holidays when children may have been visiting with the noncustodial parent.

A teacher who shares information about stressors and typical situations affecting children during divorce, remarriage, and in developing stepparent relationships can help a family adjust. Building upon an open and caring relationship with the family, the teacher can be an ally in helping parents and children adjust to change. The teacher can be a reassuring link for families and can assist them in recognizing their new strengths. Many excellent books can help children and parents talk about the concerns of a new lifestyle. Although books are no replacement for counseling if it is needed, teachers can help families by suggesting family-sensitive children's literature available from the classroom or school library or offer a bibliography of titles available from public library systems. Care should be taken in selecting books for use with children. Children's classic stories often portray negative images that are confusing to young children. Stepparents, especially stepmothers, have suffered from a stereotypically negative image. Family-sensitive literature and curriculum materials now available for early childhood classes may become the classics of children's literature in years to come.

Since the majority of parents whose marriage ends in divorce do remarry, programs and schools are increasingly seeing children in blended families or stepfamilies, in which children from one marriage are being reared by a biological parent and a stepparent or in a family with children from each parent's previous relationships. These families may also include children from the new marriage. Families with "yours, mine, and ours" children are yet another family system seen in society and in programs and schools today.

Single-Parent Families

In single-parent families, one adult usually undertakes all the parental roles typically shared by two persons. These include economic support, child care, housekeeping, recreation and leisure time management, emotional support, and companionship for the children. Consequently, the single parent is at risk for strain and task overload—both physical and emotional. Often the psychological stress and distress of the parenting situation are related to the age, educational level, parenting style, individual capability, and values of the parent. Typically the single parent is female; however, fathers may assume the full-time caregiver role as well. Single-parent fathers are subject to similar role strain, although fathers may not acknowledge serious child-rearing difficulties as readily.

Single parenthood can occur for many reasons. Although separation or divorce is a common cause, an increasing percentage of single parents are mothers who have never married, including those who are in a long-term relationship with the child's father but are technically single. When parents separate or when one parent dies, the family may confront emotional and economic loss, possible relocation and the accompanying loss of friends and family support networks, and health insurance and security concerns. The children's reaction and adjustment to these issues may add to the difficulty of the situation. Many families are headed by a parent in a married relationship, but due to the prolonged absence of one partner the other is in a position of being virtually single. One parent may be in military service, incarcerated, or away from the family due to job assignments. This type of family situation requires the same considerations as a single parent family.

Effective Single Parenting. Single-parent households, even low-income single-parent households, do not necessarily mean low-quality parenting. The following key factors contribute to a healthy, functional, single-parent home:

1. Family characteristics such as the presence of clear authority and open communication, as well as the parent's personal abilities
2. Family coping, accommodation, and acceptance of environmental stressors, such as unexpected illness
3. Family supports from relatives, friends, and community agencies such as safe housing, education, and health care

Garanzini (1995) reported that mothers who adapted to typical family challenges and had good coping strategies had less depression and a more active social network. They also had higher self-esteem and a sense of control in their lives. They usually had help with children, but authority regarding decision making and discipline was clearly the parent's. Mothers in effective single-parent homes gave more feedback to their children's positive and negative behavior and disciplined by giving warnings and consequences. This firm authority remained the mother's prerogative even when there were grandparents in the home. The opposite was true for unhealthy home situations.

Successful discipline in single-parent homes involves giving feedback about behavioral expectations as well as warnings and consequences. *Courtesy of ECE Photo Library.*

If there isn't a father in the home, many mothers are concerned about the lack of a male role model, and noncompliance in young boys often creates particular problems for their mothers. Separation from a truly significant other may affect children in much the same way as a divorce. Women must also deal with their own emotional and relationship needs while balancing the potential effect different partners may have on the children.

Implications for Educators. Single parents may depend upon their children's school or program to provide a needed stable environment and respite for the parent. Educators may provide valuable guidance, reassurance, and support during the adjustment process and beyond. Practical and emotional problems (limited parental education, child management difficulties, homework assistance, etc.) may be overwhelming, so sensitivity to issues and family needs is important. Requests for classroom donations or volunteers should be made with sensitivity to parents' feelings and their capacity to respond. Some mothers and fathers may feel self-conscious about being a single parent. Some single parents may feel a social bias, actual or perceived, about being single or never having been married. The strain of single decision making, dealing with discipline, and one's personal needs often creates challenges that ebb and flow for individuals parenting solo. Some may shield their discomfort with a smoke screen of indifference.

Concerns common to other working parents may be heightened for single parents. Because work and school schedules may not coincide, there may be a concern about who is watching the child when a parent isn't available. Often, older children are given the responsibility of supervising younger ones. A positive action on the part of a teacher would be to be aware of before- and after-school care (often available as part of the school's extended day outreach) and make that information available to the parent. Schools and churches in many communities provide this type of care. Single working parents may want more contact and consultation with teachers. They might also be responsive to a parent-to-parent group. Teachers should make sure that all school event publicity is bias-free and open to parents who do not fit a typical family structure. Families may feel left out if many events are restricted to one parent or type of family member and not open to others (for example, Mother's Breakfast and Dad's Night are more restrictive than Buddy Breakfast and Guy's Night).

In developing a caring and open partnership with single parents, teachers need to know the current family support persons for when an emergency arises, as well as the surnames of adults and children in the household. It is important for the teacher to be aware of changes in living arrangements and any potential need for family assistance with basic needs, such as food, housing, and so on. Teachers are often the first professionals to become aware of a family's changing needs, and they often assume the role of "first responder" in referring families to school support persons, such as social workers or counselors, or sharing this information themselves.

Families in Poverty

As the number of positions in manufacturing and management decline and those in service industries increase, many wage earners find themselves at risk of unemployment, reduction of hours, or becoming underemployed in an era of downsizing. The median income of both men and women working full time fell in 2005, and the poverty rate rose to 12.6 percent, according to a 2006 report by the Center on Budget and Policy Priorities. In addition, Americans living in poverty grew increasingly poor, with 43 percent falling below half of the poverty line. Basically, the poor are getting poorer. Contrary to popular myth, the majority of poor children are not on welfare. Three out of four poor children live in families where someone works, and one in three poor children lives with a full-time, year-round worker. In addition, 22 million adults and 13 million children live in households suffering from hunger or "food insecurity without hunger." In fact, two incomes at above minimum wage are needed to maintain a standard of living similar to that of preceding generations. The realities of daily existence continue to undermine many families' hopes for a better life. According to a 2005 report by the Children's Defense Fund, the earnings of a single parent of two working full time would meet only 40 percent of the estimated cost of raising two children. As the costs of housing, food, utilities, and transportation increase, low-income families struggle with the widening gap between what they earn and what they need to cover their basic needs.

Poverty Risk Factors and Children.

Poor families face more risk factors than do members of other groups mentioned in this chapter, although parents from any of those groups may also be economically deprived. Multiple risk factors subject children and families to developmental and dysfunctional problems. Lifestyle risks include inadequacies in housing, environmental safety, and sanitation. Poor neighborhoods are prone to older housing, environmental exposure to lead or toxins in structural materials or the soil, and higher incidences of violence, substance abuse, and crime. Poor working parents may be exposed to monotonous or hazardous working conditions. Although the government is attempting to increase health care benefits for children and families in poverty, health care is often inadequate or even nonexistent. These factors create stressors on parents who want a better life for their families. Parents may feel they lack any control over their situation, which fosters a pervasive feeling of hopelessness. Despite their best efforts, mothers may be piecing together multiple part-time jobs (all without benefits) and still have difficulty making ends meet. Hunger, poor nutrition, and child abuse are major related problems. Family beliefs about child development, adult interaction, and discipline vary greatly, as they do within the population at large. In children, the emotional stress may manifest itself in behaviors similar to posttraumatic stress disorder: short attention span, weak impulse control, speech delays, sleep disturbances, depression, or aggression. Parents may have difficulty responding with sensitivity to these behaviors and may be dealing with behavior management and guidance problems at home. Economically deprived families often focus on basic survival needs, and parental involvement may become a low priority.

Implications for Educators. Families living in poverty face many challenges in daily existence, but they do love and care about their children. Teachers need to be aware of modifying requests made of these parents. Literacy skill levels may be lower in families in poverty, so care should be taken to be sure notes and newsletters are written at an effective reading level. Consequently, communicating information solely in writing may be less effective. Parents may respond best to individual invitations and personal contacts. If a family is receptive, frequent informal contacts and visits may be important links for home–school connections. Poverty, illiteracy, and poor health tend to reduce the parents' ability to respond to stress in their lives and to program or school expectations for family involvement. Parent ownership and leadership of the partnership process is crucial. Opportunities should be provided for parents to invest themselves by making or locating usable materials for teaching tools, giving assistance when their schedule permits, and so on. Additional help from community, governmental, and social service agencies may be needed. Libraries, common spaces, and bulletin boards could include resource information on family welfare issues such as nutrition, shelter, clothing, health, child care, and employment and appropriate application forms. Some families may be struggling for the first time with low-income issues and be embarrassed about their new situation. Family programs and activities can focus on empowering strategies and provide suggestions for healthy meal planning, advice about easy home repairs, job application and interview tips, or even a school-wide clothing swap supplemented by clothing from community donations. The school or program may provide the location for these types of meetings in collaboration with other area agencies. Since extra clothing may not be readily supplied by the home, the teacher may need to keep some items at school in case of a clothing emergency. A one-size-fits-most sweatshirt for cool weather recess, for example, may help a child feel more comfortable and less conspicuous.

Parents may appreciate regular, short, and positive notes about their child. Take and share photos of their children (especially of children and parents together), as these may be the only pictures some families will have. Some families in poverty may have had inconsistent parenting models, and they may have a difficult time parenting and encouraging their own children. Parents need specific information about their children and general information about typical development and behaviors during childhood. Suggestions for encouraging a positive learning environment at home should be shared in an individualized, sensitive manner.

Families may also find it helpful to talk with other families at the center or school. Establishing a special place for families is one way to foster trust and communication. Parenting information in short, easy-to-read pamphlets or flyers should be available. Holiday activities and cultural events provide teachers with additional opportunities for positive parent contact. Teachers should understand also that it might be a real hardship for parents to leave work for school events, as employers may tolerate little absenteeism from work regardless of the reason. Providing options, such as telephone conferences, may greatly reduce stress on parents who want to be involved, but have honest difficulties in following traditional practices.

Teen Parenthood

Teen parenthood has its own special problems. Not yet finished with the complex issues of adolescence, a young woman assumes the role of parent as well. Only about half of teen moms finish high school. This fact alone puts both mother and child at risk, as maternal education levels correlate with children's future academic success. Support systems may include parents, extended family, or friends. In addition, teen parents often need help from programs that assist with literacy, GED preparation, employment, family planning, and life skills. Programs targeting this group of parents have made inroads in assisting with special parenting skill-building programs in high schools and with flexible GED initiatives. Relationships between adolescents and their parents can be strained, and the increased dependency on parents that results from pregnancy and childrearing can increase conflict in the home. The biological father may not be in a position or have the capacity to help the young woman through pregnancy and the early years of parenting. Girls in teen parent programs, consequently, often develop their own individual support systems among peers. Grandparents or extended family members often assume the role of parent and become primary contacts for educators.

Children of Teen Parents Face Additional Risks. Adolescent pregnancy is a major contributor to the increase in single-mother families. Since teen parents are less likely to complete high school or go on to college and are more likely to require public assistance, children of teen parents face additional risks as they are more likely to perform poorly in school and are at a greater risk of abuse or neglect. Sons of teen mothers are more likely to become incarcerated, and daughters of teens are more likely to become teen moms themselves (Children's Defense Fund, 2005).

Implications for Educators. The number of teen mothers has had an impact on the role of teachers. The mother's age at the birth of the oldest child can affect her ability to assume the responsibilities of parenting during a child's early years, middle childhood, and adolescence. Consequently, the issues of teen parenthood affect not only educators working with children in early childhood programs. As their children enter and progress through school, mothers may be especially uncomfortable in educational settings and may lack the confidence or initiative to ask questions. Programs and schools at any level may not be comfortable environments because they remind them of difficult times in their own lives as students. Resuming contact with "school" as a parent may be especially intimidating. There may be a greater need for transportation and on-site child care in order for parents to participate in program events. A special group organized for younger parents may be attractive. Young parents are usually interested in learning about their children and may learn best by practicing skills in a role-play setting or by making materials to help their child learn at home. Incentives for attendance and participation may encourage involvement, and personal contact by someone from a parent-to-parent network may also help. These programs can be provided by an agency but hosted by a program or school.

Homeless Families

Homelessness is a reality for many families in communities large and small, urban and rural. The new definition of the **homeless** under the McKinney Homeless Assistance Act of 1987 includes those who do not have a regular place to sleep at night, those who may temporarily sleep in a shelter or residence, or those who stay in the home of another while seeking more permanent housing because of economic hardship, domestic violence, or abuse. The definition also includes those who may spend the night in a house but in a place not ordinarily used as sleeping quarters. Statistics provided by the Children's Defense Fund (2005) are alarming. Under this definition, families with children compose 40 percent of the homeless population in America. There is great concern about the lack of progress in assuring that all families have decent and stable housing, which is recognized as vital to children's development. Without a stable home in which to grow, homeless children typically develop more severe health, developmental, psychological, behavioral, and nutritional difficulties than other poor children do. They are more vulnerable to the effects of lead poisoning, educational dysfunction, emotional stress, and family separation. Many families are also highly transient and move frequently. This type of situation may create additional problems, as children may experience a series of temporary housing arrangements but do not live in a regular place to call "home."

Effects of Homelessness on Children. The trauma of homelessness also includes the loss of stability, security, social and family networks, privacy, and the emotional grounding that comes from "going home." Homelessness isn't reserved for the poor. In an emergency situation, such as spouse abuse, a woman and her children may seek refuge in a community shelter. Such a situation can produce anxiety about the uncertainty of each day and fear of the violence that may arrive at any moment. Shelters cannot offer children the safety, comfort, or security they need, nor can they provide the age-appropriate opportunities for exploration and stimulation children require for healthy development.

Because the world of homeless children is chaotic, the program or school may be the only place where they can participate in the normal activities of childhood. These children may participate in additional public or private programs or receive services in a special shelter program. Typically, shelter programs have limitations on how long families can stay and on the types of services and programs offered. The conditions that produce the homeless situation are often the same ones that contribute to short enrollment in a program or school.

Implications for Educators. Parents who live in emergency housing are struggling with overwhelming demands. Although contact with families may be short, teachers working with these families can best assist parents in the following ways:

1. Help parents appreciate and understand their children. Provide information about their children's abilities, interests, play, communication, and behaviors. Short, regular reports, especially about the positive things their child does, can be reassuring to parents. Share photos of their child enjoying school activities. Help them to feel they are still decision makers in their child's life.

2. Respect and support the unique needs of the parents. Many parents of homeless children are vulnerable individuals in need of nurturing themselves. Parents may need assistance with transportation in order to attend conferences and meetings. The teacher can supply bus tokens in order to attend events or assist with other arrangements. They may also need child care or permission to bring siblings to events. Teachers could supply activities for children during the meeting and anticipate interruptions. The family space could have refreshments, or parents could join their children for breakfast, snack, or lunch. Extra clothing, toys, books, or food can also be available for emergency use. Around holiday times, teachers should be especially sensitive to the family's need to provide positive memories for their child. Activities such as simple gift-making centers can be part of the program, as can events with other families, such as "fun day" programs, class picnics, sports days, and so on.

3. Provide information and/or support services to families. Teachers can help families fill out applications for assistance for breakfast and lunch or waivers for activities. They can also become a liaison between parents and other needed service providers. Encourage a trusting, nonjudgmental atmosphere where individuals can share stresses or problems. Teachers should also communicate with shelter staff whenever possible.

4. Keep expectations for the child reasonable. Critical survival issues are a priority. Temporary housing may not provide an appropriate place for children to play or for families to even be alone, so allowances can be made for assignments with older children. Families can be encouraged to help their child by practicing basic skills that do not need materials, like recognizing colors, shapes, and letters and practicing spelling words or math facts. Children may have difficulty paying attention or participating since their sleep may be disturbed by unfamiliar circumstances in their shelter or temporary home. Often, they move with few personal possessions and are in need of clothing, a replacement book bag, and other supplies in order to help reduce the stigma of homelessness. There also may be anxiety about keeping what they have safe. Since meals and food may be available on a different schedule than they have been used to, children may eat more or attempt to hoard food for later.

5. Maintain predictable and supportive routines. Assign children a special, personal space, so they have a spot to call their own. Help them make transitions in their day as needed, giving clear, advance notice of changes. Teachers can also supply children with a variety of drawing materials and a supply of paper or a notebook and invite them to express themselves. If a move to another program or school is anticipated, teachers can help the child deal effectively with the practical and emotional aspects of the change (Swick, 2004).

Children and families may be in a situation in which abuse (to children or adults) is suspected. Needless to say, extreme sensitivity is required. Educators are mandated reporters and each school or program should have a protocol for reporting abuse. It is critical that teachers become aware of the guidelines if follow-through actions are required. A resource section on violence and abuse is available on pages 160–168 of the *Home, School, and Community Relations Professional Enhancement* text by Carol Gestwicki (2007).

Family Violence and Neglect

Many kinds of violence affect the lives of young children and families each day. Children exposed to violence can be in the classroom at any time. The statistics are sobering. Between 1998 and 2002, family violence accounted for 11 percent of all reported and unreported violence. Females accounted for 73 percent of all victims of family violence. Of this number, 84 percent were victims of spousal abuse. A significant number of females were also abused by a boyfriend or girlfriend. Family violence crosses all cultures, races, and economic groups, but most family violence victims were white, and the majority were between the ages of 25 and 54—typical ages for parents with children in the home. Forty percent of the family violence victims were injured during the incident, and domestic violence was the most common cause of family homelessness (Durose, Harlow, Lanagan, Motivans, Rantala, & Smith, 2005).

Effects of Violence on Children.
Children exposed to violence, even if they are not the targets of violence, have reactions similar to those exposed to serious maltreatment. Survivors of violence exposure often have long-term effects of the trauma throughout their lives. Reported cases of abused and/or neglected children increase each year. As a result, the numbers of children in foster homes, group homes, or institutional settings in the child welfare system are growing; sadly, infants make up the largest percentage of children entering this type of care. Although many states have family preservation programs in place, for many children, they are not sufficiently effective to operate in a timely enough manner.

Exposure to other violence—both in the media and in the neighborhood— also has a major impact on children. Children's exposure to media violence concerns social scientists, public health experts, and many parents. Studies show that, in children, exposure to violence on television and in video games is associated with increased aggression, desensitization to violence, depression, and fear. According to Eric Jensen (2006), young children's brains absorb all the violent information (voices, actions, persons, situations, etc.) but cannot "delete" it. Consequently, young children may exhibit behaviors that result from their exposure to violence, whether real or on television, video games, or other media. This exposure may shape their social and cognitive understandings throughout childhood.

Today, nearly all children have increased access to violent television programming, and gun violence is prevalent. Children growing up in violent neighborhoods may feel helpless and fearful. They often have difficulty sleeping, sometimes as the result of increased nightmares or night terrors; they may demonstrate increased hypervigilance, anxiety, or depression; and they may withdraw or have difficulty paying attention. If symptoms are severe and occur for extended lengths of time, posttraumatic stress disorder may need to be considered as a medical diagnosis. Families, too, are affected. They often lose confidence in their parenting abilities and are so traumatized that they find it difficult to be emotionally responsive to their children (Saxe, Chawla, & Stoddard, 2003).

Implications for Educators. Teachers play a pivotal role in teaching expectations for learning and behavior. Programs that promote prosocial values, character education, and positive behavioral responses should become an important part of the classroom culture. Beverly Johns (2000) provides these suggestions for teachers:

- Teach children to recognize choices for peaceful or aggressive behaviors. Teach them that they are in control of their behavior choices, and guide them in making good choices with appropriate words or actions.
- Become sensitive to acts of minor aggression in the classroom. Although small, touches, expressions, words, and so on can escalate to more serious forms of interpersonal violence. Adopt a "no tolerance" approach.
- Prohibit any videos from classroom use that depict violence or other actions, such as inappropriate language or actions, that violate school expectations for students.
- Be alert for use of violent video games, reading material, and so on for free-time use at school.
- Make sure Halloween decorations, themes, and activities reflect a happy, amusing, peace-filled holiday, rather than a bloody, gory, terror-filled one.

When children and families have been victims of violence, a teacher's expression of personal feelings and condolences can help the survivors in their efforts to reconstruct their lives. Teachers should be aware of children's emotional responses, which can manifest in anxiety, hyperactivity, fears, sleep disturbances, and bedwetting. The family should also be coached to recognize these behaviors as symptoms of their child's experience. Survivors may benefit from the local and national support groups formed expressly to assist those experiencing similar crises. Victims of abuse should be directed to local shelters for women and children, where counseling and other support services are available. Local police or social service departments, as well as county, state, and national organizations, can provide other assistance. Crises often require special counseling skills, and teachers should be prepared to direct families to appropriate local services.

Foster and Adoptive Families

All families share a special bond that creates their family system. Foster and adoptive families are unique in that the family connections are created by legal agreement.

Foster Families. Parents choose to become foster parents for a variety of reasons. They may have different motivations in taking in children, different commitments to their foster children, and a different view of their role as caregiver–nurturer. Some foster parents are motivated by the extra income provided them; however, the majority view themselves as substitute parents and attempt to create a stable, albeit temporary, home for children in their care. It is unfortunate that 15 to 20 percent of foster parents exhibit significant problems relating to their parenting style, such as deficiencies in behavior management and effective discipline strategies, their understanding of children's development and emotional needs, and their expectations of children in their care (Gorman, 2004). Teachers' interest in and support of foster families may contribute to foster parents' choice to continue to care for a child rather than asking for him or her to be placed elsewhere. Because foster parents may not have intimate knowledge of child development and parenting children at particular ages and stages, teachers can share information so foster families have realistic expectations for their foster children, especially those with special needs. The training to become foster parents may not have addressed working with teachers or even the special needs that are related to the child's need for foster placement (such as physical, cognitive, behavioral differences or exposure to drugs or other substances). Children in foster care frequently demonstrate challenges, which may include a poor self-concept, fears, depression, anger and aggression, and problems with attention and social skills.

Adoptive Families. Adoptive parents are a diverse group as well. Some were foster parents who desired to make the relationship with the children permanent. Some cannot conceive children of their own or want to enlarge their family by nurturing children in need of a "forever home." Some children in a blended family are adopted by the stepparent. An increasing number of adoptive families are formed by single-parent, multiracial, or international adoptions. Depending on the circumstances that prompt the relinquishing of biological parental rights, adopted children may have experienced such difficulties as abuse, neglect, abandonment, death of parents, or removal from the country or neighborhood of their birth. There is an increased potential for problems that impact academic and social-emotional areas with adopted children. Some issues relate to effects of poor prenatal health care or exposure to environmental toxins or substance abuse. This type of problem can be significant in adoptions from countries where a lack of health care and alcohol or other substance abuse is common.

Implications for Educators. Children who were adopted as infants or very young children may only remember their adoptive family, but they may still have physical or emotional challenges that stem from their social and health history. Children who have been adopted later in childhood or who have been in foster care for many years are more likely to exhibit disorders of attachment.

This can affect not only bonding at home but also relationships with teachers and peers.

Many children question who they are and want to know their birth family's story. They may make up their own version or accept what their adoptive parents share, but they tend to seek answers as they grow older. Most children ask, "Where did I come from?" at some point in their early life. For adopted children, the answer is quite different from the answer given a biological child, and questions may crop up anytime. Birthdays and holidays may inspire additional periods of questioning or emotions about the past. It is important for teachers to be aware of what information families have been sharing with the child about their adoption.

When topics of home, parents, and families are part of the curriculum, teachers should use the opportunity to include the wide variety of family configurations in today's world, not just within the particular group of children. Care should be taken in requesting children to supply baby photos or make a family tree, as adopted and foster children may not have the required information or memorabilia. Instead, children can be asked to share the names and photos of people who are important to them in their family. This strategy reflects the wide variety of family configurations and provides for the inclusion of information of a native culture or country (Gestwicki, 2007).

Grandparents and Extended Family in the Parenting Role

Approximately one in twelve children is living in a household headed by grandparents or other extended family. The 2000 U.S. Census showed that more than 2.4 million grandparents are responsible for meeting the basic needs of their grandchildren. New terms have evolved to describe this different kind of family. In **kinship care families** and **grandfamilies,** grandparents or other relatives raise children when the biological parents are unable to do so. In times past and in many cultures today, it has been common for households to have several generations living under one roof. In this case, however, children are cared for by extended family because the parents cannot meet the needs of the children. Depending upon the circumstances, grandparents or another family member may or may not have legal custody of the children, or they may even adopt them. Sometimes the child is removed from the parent's care by the state and placed with a grandfamily as part of the formal foster care system. The child may also be placed informally in a relative's home.

It is not unusual for a single mother to move her family in with grandparents or another family member. Grandparents may assume responsibility for the care and parenting of grandchildren in case of chronic illness or military service, but domestic violence, child abuse and neglect, incarceration, alcohol and drug abuse, and HIV/AIDS may also be factors.

Emotional Implications for Grandfamilies.
Grandparents have a great deal to offer their grandchildren. Oftentimes, grandfathers who had little time to spend with their own children during their growing years find not only pleasure in playing and spending time with grandchildren but also that those relationships develop into genuine friendships as the children mature. Grandparents also benefit from an enhanced role with their grandchildren. The connection grandchildren have to the future creates an emotional and spiritual link for grandparents. They gain an increased sense of purpose and self-esteem as their role in a child's life increases. This can enhance the quality of life and contribute to the older generation's mental health as well (Gestwicki, 2007).

Grandparents are a vital family link and have a great deal to offer their grandchildren. *Courtesy of ECE Photo Library.*

Grandparents may not necessarily be retired or in compromised health. Grandparents themselves may be single, working full time, or still have younger children of their own in the house. They may believe that this will be a temporary arrangement and that the birth parents will assume responsibility as soon as they are able. In actuality, the dependent relationship may last years, and the extended family may make a permanent commitment to the children. Often, the family who opens their home to a child is avoiding the otherwise inevitable placement of the child within the foster care system at large. Grandparents or extended family may feel a gamut of emotions. Some genuinely welcome the return to an active parenting role with their grandchildren in the household. They may view it as the best of circumstances for all of them. Some grandparents may not have ever planned on having grandchildren live with them, although they love their grandchildren dearly. At times, they may be angry or resentful toward the parents for putting them in this situation. Having the children in the household may create a drain on finances and the human resources of time and energy, especially if there are disabilities, medical problems, or behavioral issues to deal with. Grandparents or family members who find themselves in the parenting role again may feel they do not fit into their familiar social group of friends but that they don't feel comfortable with younger parents, either.

Implications for Educators.
Since this generational support system is more common, schools, state agencies on aging, the AARP, university extension services, churches, and grassroots grandparent groups are often able to provide information and group support. The Children's Defense Fund has a variety of online resources for those interested in grandfamilies and kinship care at www .childrensdefense.org. The AARP (www.aarp.org/grandparents) also has supportive materials available to families. Teachers can help share both local and national resources to help grandparents and extended family members realize they are not alone.

Grandparents or extended family members may feel overwhelmed with the differences in the child-care and educational systems today. Technology, curricular jargon, testing, early childhood program expectations, and even the subject matter taught today can be confusing and foreign to them. Today's schools may be quite different from the schools their own children attended. Teachers can help them better understand curricula and encourage any questions they may have. Grandparents may feel unqualified to help their grandchildren even with the basic skills focused on in early childhood or with homework for older children, so teachers can share tips on what may work for them at home. Some grandparents, however, may want to have increased contact with the program or school and are a valuable source of assistance. They have lifetime skills and experiences that can be helpful for younger children to see and hear about. Their backgrounds may provide assistance with tutoring students with English as a second language, grant writing, or even helping children maintain a school garden or learn to play chess. They may also be dependable, for example, as pet sitters for the class pet during holidays. This may help them feel more connected and involved with the program and with their grandchildren.

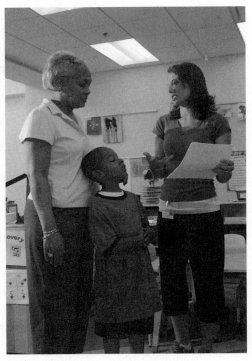

Teachers can help grandparents understand the changes in education and suggest ways they can help their grandchildren at home. *Courtesy of ECE Photo Library.*

Children in these custodial or supportive situations may be more challenging children. Abuse, neglect, substance exposure, and health concerns may all have associated emotional and behavioral concerns. It may be more difficult for grandparents to get children to obey them and comply with homework responsibilities and related activities. A teacher's sensitivity to the feelings and challenges in the home, combined with positive and practical strategies to use at home, is usually welcomed. Teachers should be respectful of family dynamics but ensure that the family members who should be contacted with information about the child are clearly identified. Notes can be sent home with the understanding that anyone in the family is welcome to participate in a school event. It is important to also know who has legal custody of the children in regards to permissions and notification of meetings. Copies of the school newsletter and classroom notes can be sent to those who are prominent in the child's life. Providing support and practical encouragement to grandparents and family members can help develop a strong and much-appreciated partnership with the home.

Utilizing Community Resources

In addition to program- or school-based resources, educators may be working with community-based family support initiatives and personnel who promote healthy child development, improve family literacy, prepare children for school, reduce child abuse and neglect, and support teen parents. These support services may include home visits or drop-in centers that provide child care for families participating in classes, group meetings, and social activities. Often these services have a variety of trained personnel who collaborate with schools and other agencies within the community. These programs provide excellent resources and can refer teachers to additional sources of assistance for families. Many community agency coalitions have directories of family resource services available. Teachers may want to get a copy of such a directory or learn who may have a copy within the school. Social workers, counselors, and others who work with families within the program or district are great resources for family assistance. The teacher may be in contact with a family caseworker or with other educators working with younger siblings in an Early Head Start or early intervention program. There are many other professionals available to help the classroom educator in working with families. Table 2.4 identifies supports commonly available to assist educators and families. Additional resources and information are available on the Internet, through the library system, or from the websites and publications suggested throughout this text.

Table 2.4 Family Support Professionals

Type of Professional	Services Provided	Professional Organization
Marriage and family therapists	Counseling for family members having difficulty coping with life	American Association for Marriage and Family Therapy www.aamft.org
Pastoral counselors	Counseling for families within a religious context	American Association of Pastoral Counselors www.aapc.org
Registered nurses	Help with medical concerns	American Nurses Association www.nursingworld.org
Social workers	Information about community resources that assist children and families; some may do some counseling	National Association of Social Workers www.socialworkers.org
Mental health counselors	Individual and family counseling	American Mental Health Counselors Association www.amhca.org

INVOLVING FATHERS

Fathers have long been neglected in parent involvement programs and strategies. To many educators, minimal participation by fathers is not surprising in schools and programs. Fathers report that some teachers are often shocked by their interest in participating actively in their child's educational life. Yet, fathers are now involved in their children's lives as never before. They are routinely present in the birthing room during the baby's delivery and actively assist with caring for children in the home. An increasing number of fathers of preschool and school-aged children are highly involved in their children's activities. As family-centered practices become more common in education, sensitive professionals have increased opportunities to empower fathers, stepfathers, partners, and grandfathers as active participants in children's lives.

Most people recognize that men and women parent differently. Gender differences may be attributed to opportunity (time and proximity), encouragement, and cultural conditioning, rather than a biological distinction. Fathers may be competent primary caregivers for their infants and children. These children are active, vigorous, and interested in the external environment. A Child Trends Brief reports that higher levels of father involvement in children's routines and activities are associated with fewer behavior problems, higher levels of sociability, and a high level of performance on standardized developmental tests among children and adolescents (Brown, Michelsen, Halle, & Moore, 2001).

Roles of Fathers in Children's Development

Fathers (and those in fathering roles) need to recognize ways to make positive contributions in all facets of their children's lives. For some, the rules of fathering have changed dramatically. There may be few role models in their lives that demonstrate an involved method of fatherhood, and they may feel they have missed some critical information and education on how to do it. Fathers have, however, a unique role to play in their children's lives. According to May (1992), men's strengths lie in areas such as playfulness, leadership, adventure, independence, and responsibility. Fathers can be encouraged to play with and teach their children one-on-one in a style that is comfortable for them. Men communicate, play, and discipline children differently than women do. Children benefit from that unique interest and support as they grow and develop.

Men have unique and important roles to play in children's lives. *Courtesy of ECE Photo Library.*

Many programs target fathers, including those for dads of Head Start preschoolers, for fathers of children with disabilities, and for teen and minority fathers. The most successful programs have provided a chance for men to participate in parenting or other educational programming, to discuss their feelings with other fathers in groups led by men, and to interact with their children in a play setting. These programs are designed around the interests of the fathers and have resulted in improved communication and a closer, richer relationship with their children (Levine, 1993).

Fathers, whether they live with their biological children or not, can be effective parents and serious partners in rearing their children. They can fulfill the caregiver role well, even though the media often portrays them as incompetent and comical. After a divorce, some fathers who previously were not involved in their children's lives become more involved. However, this is not necessarily the case, as many fathers become less involved. Financial issues such as the expenses of lawyer fees, court costs, costs related to dividing assets, and child support can affect access to children. A denial of visitation privileges, as well as rejection or lack of interest by the children may also affect father involvement. Some fathers experience a severe disconnectedness from their children's lives and a sense of loss that is emotionally traumatizing. To compensate, they may reduce contact or withdraw completely from their children.

Implications for Educators

Often, program activities for men limit father participation to traditionally "male" jobs, such as construction projects. Many men may prefer to develop computer-generated movies or slide shows to highlight photos of children doing classroom activities, create a list of books boys like to read (and dads like to read to them), or advocate for the needs of children in the community or at the state or national level.

Fathers, life partners, grandfathers, uncles, stepfathers, and stepgrand-fathers all have a role to play, as a new model of fathering is emerging. Men are often ignored as potential classroom volunteers or PTA members, yet they have a very important role to play in the cognitive, physical, and social development of their children. Because most educators are female, teachers must learn how to work positively with men and make an effort to overcome any fears or preconceptions about male stereotypes. Welcoming and encouraging fathers (and other male family members) may take a conscious effort, but it will pay off. Here are some ideas to promote becoming more "guy friendly."

● Project the expectation that it is normal for men to be involved and be supported in the fathering role. It is very important for children to develop a close, supportive relationship with their father or male role model. Teachers need to assume the attitude that men are welcome and be willing to help them feel comfortable through meaningful involvement.

- Get to know the fathers as well as the mothers and siblings of children.

- Make phone calls home (especially those positive "warm calls") at a time when both parents are home and available to talk. Many fathers may not be able to meet during the traditional work day, so this is an important way to introduce father involvement.

- Write information in classroom or program records so that it is respectful to both parents.

- Don't neglect fathers not living in the home or other father figures in the children's lives. Copies of permission agreements, newsletters, program information, and other materials should be sent to the father as well as to the home where the child lives.

- Be flexible. Schedule appointments and program activities to accommodate the father's work schedule when possible. For example, if parent–teacher conferences are held during an afternoon and evening, reserve some appointments in the evening to allow fathers to participate.

- Be respectful of a separated or divorced father's feelings about meeting with the teacher if his former spouse will be there. Actively keeping the focus of the meeting on the child can help reduce friction, as can making a separate conference arrangement.

- Support special events of interest to men in family event planning. "Guys Night Out," Buddy Breakfast, or "Our Special Saturday" can include any male figure in a child's life. Programs and parent organizations often collaborate in sponsoring these events.

- Engage a group of fathers to work together on a project to benefit the children.

- Alert families to area support programs for men in parenting roles. Try to locate those led by men for men. There are a number of parenting sites for men on the Internet. Share these with families.

- Recommend the inclusion of materials and books for men in the family space and keep informed about other options for involving men in local programs. Include books that have men as key characters in your library.

States and organizations are continuing outreach initiatives to encourage father involvement. From the statewide Minnesota Fathers & Families Network to the regional Men & Kids Project of Urbana, Illinois, programs are being developed to support the role of fathers in our changing society. Various media resources are available to help those interested in organizing fathers' groups. The Minnesota Fathering Alliance (1992), for example, publishes a guide for working with fathers. In 1994, the National Fatherhood Initiative was organized to promote responsible fatherhood; support dads in all social groups, ages, and stages; and maintain a national focus on fatherhood through a bi-partisan taskforce in the U.S. Congress. The organization's website, www.fatherhood.org, features articles and research, training supports, "fatherly advice," and a weekly e-mail service. Its various initiatives include help for military families and deployed fathers, support for expectant fathers, and a program for incarcerated fathers. Some fathers' groups provide special interest support. The Fathers Network, www.fathersnetwork.org, advocates for and provides resources and support to men who have children with special needs. There are a number of books that focus specifically on father involvement and provide detailed guides for a variety of programs and ways to facilitate involvement. In their comprehensive guide to involving fathers, Fagan and Palm (2004) encourage teachers and administrators to "not reinvent the wheel" when it comes to specific programming for father involvement. Instead, they can utilize programs, events, and services that are already working for families and build upon that success by actively including fathers.

SUMMARY

This chapter has investigated some of the many issues facing families today and has explored some of the implications for building family–teacher partnerships. It is critical to keep in mind that all families (as well as all children) have strengths. Working with children and families facing personal challenges requires great dedication and concern—critical prerequisites for teachers in today's world. Teachers often choose education as a career because it provides an opportunity to "make a difference." In some programs and schools, there are adequate support personnel such as social workers, family involvement specialists, and counselors to refer families and children to supports. In others, the teacher needs to be more proactive and aware of community services and programs in order to be prepared to support families and children.

A family-centered philosophy is vital to developing a positive family–teacher partnership. Both families and professionals need to have prerequisite abilities and skills before they can be effective partners. As families respond to the wide variety of demographic and societal factors that influence them, they may appear difficult to reach. Developing sensitivities and strategies to support families in stressful situations is key to being an effective professional partner. Teachers should become knowledgeable about the range of special services available to parents and be a resource and referral for families if necessary. Children in trying circumstances may be undergoing life-changing events, and the teacher is in a pivotal role to make a significant difference.

Working with families in crisis may trigger strong emotions: pity, anger, rescue fantasies, and so on. Situations with families may also elicit personal experiences or emotions from the educator's own life. Determining the source of these feelings may help a teacher keep them from negatively affecting current family partnerships. Teachers also must anticipate being the target of strong feelings expressed by parents and must maintain an objective viewpoint. They should pay particular attention to the needs and feelings of the parents and be prepared to keep them separate from those of the children.

The more stressed parents are, the more emotional or dependent they may appear to be. This tendency can be recognized and accepted, although parents should be encouraged to develop the skills and confidence to solve their own problems. Educators need to realize that parents under stress will have difficulty making commitments and organizing their lives. Parent involvement expectations may need to be modified under a number of circumstances. This should be communicated to families in a sensitive and supportive manner. Children and families have resilient qualities that can help them survive any crisis. Teachers are often in a most important position to support them.

Fathers are sometimes overlooked or misunderstood as program partners. In relationships with the family and child, the mother often plays a predominant role. Educators can develop and use strategies to enhance the comfort level and participation of the men in a child's life. This can foster an increased understanding of children's abilities and the important role men play in their development.

ACTIVITIES FOR DISCUSSION, EXPANSION, AND APPLICATION

1. Interview teachers, program directors or principals, and social workers or counselors from programs in your community. Using their input and your personal observations, discuss the demographic and societal factors affecting families in your area. How do these impact the early childhood and elementary programs and services available for families?

2. Consider a family with which you are familiar. Determine its strengths and possible areas of stress or concern. As an educator, how would you approach family members, respond to their concerns, adapt your family involvement strategies, and encourage their involvement?

3. Develop a checklist or chart that could be used in either the development or evaluation of a family involvement initiative. It should include (a) statements to evaluate the quality of activities, and (b) indicators to determine the degree to which family-centered philosophies of parent involvement are integrated into them.

4. Select one group of parents or families whose involvement could present a challenge. Outline the characteristics and potential barriers to involvement. What could a teacher do to adapt strategies to the group's unique needs?

5. What type of family would be most challenging for you to engage in involvement activities? Why? Based on this analysis, how would you have to adjust your attitudes, responses, and so on to make the partnership successful?

CASE STUDY

Blake, a student in your kindergarten class, is typically a serious student, quiet and attentive. On Monday, he comes into the classroom sullen and less social than usual. During seatwork time, you notice he has stopped his work several times to look out the windows. Once he appears to be wiping his eyes. At recess he gets into a pushing argument with two of his best buddies and has a time out on the playground. You suspect something has happened, but your gentle questions in the privacy of the empty classroom before lunch yield no clues. You decide to wait and see how Blake behaves tomorrow. He is absent for the rest of the week but has not been called in sick. His older sister, Molly, hasn't been at school either, but her teacher isn't aware of any problem. You suspect that there has been an unexpected illness or death in the family. On Friday afternoon while your class is in music, you call his mother, Kim, at home. She has always been involved, responsive to classroom requests, and a regular volunteer in the room, listening to children read aloud. Mike, her husband, developed a movie of classroom photos to show at open house and was on the planning committee for the school "Guys Night" program. You feel you have a good rapport with the family.

Kim apologizes for not calling before and shares that she, Blake, and Molly have had a difficult week. She and her husband of nine years have separated and are going to divorce. The children have been staying with her parents until things are "less ugly" at home, but they will be back to school on Monday. She isn't sure how things are going to work out. Previously a stay-at-home mom, Kim mentions probably needing to look for a job. You can hear her voice quiver as she says her parents are not supporting her in this decision and she is worried about Blake's reactions. How do you react?

1. What would be the best supportive first response to this information?

2. What could you do in the classroom to help Blake adjust to the changes at home and in his life?

3. What changes in Blake's school performance and behaviors could you anticipate?

4. How will you respond to any potential differences in Blake?

5. What would you offer to Kim in order to recognize and support her? What would you offer to Mike?

USEFUL WEBSITES

www.aarp.org/grandparents

AARP Grandparent Information Center. This site helps grandparents who are raising grandchildren cope with their primary caregiver roles. It serves as a clearinghouse where grandparents and service providers can obtain information and referral to available national and local resources for child care, legal services, and family services.

www.childrensdefense.org

Children's Defense Fund. This organization collects and publishes data, develops programs, and advocates on issues affecting all children and families, especially those who are poor, are minorities, or have disabilities.

www.familiesandwork.org

Family and Work Institute. This institute conducts policy research on multiple issues related to the changing demographics of the workforce and the changing workplace and its affects on work and family life.

www.fatherhood.org

National Fatherhood Initiative. This organization supports family- and father-friendly policies and offers father-friendly resources online. The website includes a checklist to determine if a school or program is "father-friendly."

www.naeyc.org

National Association for the Education of Young Children. The NAEYC is a leader in resource development and advocacy for quality education and child care for children and families from birth through age 8. The organization's publication, *Young Children,* and a wide variety of books, guides, and pamphlets provide resources for families, teachers, and administrators.

REFERENCES

Brown, B., Michelsen, E., Halle, T., & Moore, K. (2001). Fathers' activities with their kids. *Child Trends Research Brief.* Retrieved July 1, 2007, from http://www.childtrends.org/Files/June_2001.pdf.

Center on Budget and Policy Priorities. (2006). Poverty remains higher, and median income for non-elderly is lower, than when recession hit bottom. Retrieved July 1, 2007, from http://www.cbpp.org/8-29-06pov.htm.

Children's Defense Fund. (2005). *The state of America's children 2005.* Washington, DC: Children's Defense Fund.

Durose, M., Harlow, C., Lanagan, P., Motivans, M., Rantala, R., & Smith, E. (2005). *Family Violence Statistics*. Washington, DC: U.S. Department of Justice.

Emery, R. E. (1999). *Marriage, divorce, and children's adjustment*. Thousand Oaks, CA: Sage Publications.

Fagan, J., & Palm, G. (2004). *Fathers and early childhood programs*. Clifton Park, NY: Delmar Learning.

Garanzini, M. (1995). *Child centered, family sensitive schools: An educator's guide to family dynamics*. Washington, DC: National Catholic Education Association.

Gestwicki, C. (2007). *Home, school, and community relations*. Clifton Park, NY: Thomson Delmar Learning.

Gestwicki, C. (2007). *Home, school, and community relations, Professional enhancement series resource*. Clifton Park, NY: Thomson Delmar Learning.

Gorman, J. (2004). *Working with challenging parents of students with special needs*. Thousand Oaks, CA: Corwin Press.

Heatherington, M., & Kelly, J. (2002). *For better or for worse: Divorce reconsidered*. New York: W. W. Norton.

Jensen, E. (2006). *Enriching the brain: How to maximize everyone's learning potential*. Hoboken, NJ: Jossey-Bass.

Johns, B. (2000). Give peace a chance with research based advice for teachers. *The Education Digest, 65*(9), 14–20.

Levine, J. (1993). Involving fathers in Head Start: A framework for public policy and program development. *Families in Society, 74*(1), 4–19.

May, J. (1992). *Circles of care and understanding: Support programs for fathers of children with special needs*. Bethesda, MD: Association for the Care of Children's Health.

Minnesota Fathering Alliance. (1992). *Working with fathers*. Stillwater, MN: Nu Ink Unlimited.

Olsen, D., & DeFrain, J. (2000). *Marriage and the family: Diversity and strengths*. Mountain View, CA: Mayfield Publishing.

Saxe, G., Chawla, N., & Stoddard, F. (2003). Child stress disorders checklist: a measure of ASD and PTSD in children. *Journal of the American Academy of Child and Adolescent Psychiatry, 42*(5), 561–570.

Swick, K. (2004). Communicating effectively with parents and families who are homeless. *Early Childhood Education Journal, 32*(3), 211–215.

Warner, C. (1994). *Promoting your school*. Thousand Oaks, CA: Corwin Press.

KEY TERMS

Family Strengths—Ability of the family to respond to the various needs of its members and maintain balance within the group determined by family values, attitudes, and beliefs.

Family System—The dynamic relationship among members within a family group that meets and sustains the needs of the family. These include unique communication styles, values, beliefs, interpersonal interactions, emotional connections, behaviors, environment, and history of past experiences.

Family Network—The formal or informal supports that help meet a family's needs, such as family members, friends, and faith or community organizations.

Cultural Diversity—Economic, cultural, linguistic, compositional, or ethnic differences among different families.

Locus of Control—An individual's belief in self-determination and his or her capability to meet life challenges.

Blended Family—Also called a stepfamily. When one parent with children marries or enters into a relationship with another person who assumes the role of co-caregiver, the family unit may be considered a blended family. The nonbiological parent is a stepparent. Sometimes both are custodial parents who have children that contribute to this new family system.

Homeless—Individuals who do not have a regular place to sleep at night and who may temporarily sleep in a shelter or residence, or those who stay in the home of another while seeking more permanent housing because of economic hardship, domestic violence, or abuse. The definition also includes those who may spend the night in a house, but in a place not ordinarily used as sleeping quarters.

Adoptive Parents—Individuals who have legally assumed custody for a child and are raising him or her as their own child.

Kinship Care Family—A family composition in which extended family members, such as aunts, uncles, cousins, siblings, and so on, are temporarily or permanently caring for and raising children related to them.

Grandfamily—A family composition in which grandparents are temporarily or permanently the primary caregivers for grandchildren in their home.

CHAPTER 3

Working with Families from Diverse Cultures

STUDENT LEARNING OUTCOMES

After reading this chapter, you should be able to

- Define diversity in the school or child-care setting.

- Identify ways in which families differ from one another.

- Discuss the role of the teacher's attitude in parent involvement.

- Analyze educational practices that present barriers to parent involvement.

- Explain common barriers to parent involvement from the parents' perspective.

- Evaluate strategies and techniques that help remove barriers between families and schools.

In educational settings, diversity means more than racial differences. Educators encounter families from diverse backgrounds, cultures, and family structures. Because today's family is changing, educators and administrators find it increasingly important to redefine strategies that establish and maintain lines of communication between home and school. Teachers must examine their attitudes and eliminate any biases so they can fully accept each child and his or her family network.

In the context of this text, **diversity** refers to the inclusion of children and families of any cultural background or religious origin who are a part of family configurations that include those headed by a single parent of either sex, blended families, families with teen parents, families headed by gay or lesbian parents, and families in which children are in the custody of adults other than biological parents. Diversity, then, is the blending of many separate and unique families. Toward the goal of building partnerships with schools, each family possesses individual strengths that deserve to be recognized and tapped.

This chapter will focus on four main topics. First, the ways in which families differ from one another will be described. Issues such as family structure and patterns, value systems and socialization, perceptions of authority, degree of isolation, and degree of permanence in the community all impact a family's attitudes and beliefs toward schools. Second, practices related to teacher attitudes and the effects they have on how well families are accepted by teachers and staff will be discussed. Third, barriers to parent involvement—from the parent perspective—will be explored. Research has shown that parents often perceive invisible walls to parent involvement that may exist despite written policy to the contrary (Hosley, Gensheimer, & Yang, 2003). Concluding this chapter is a discussion of methods to overcome barriers, from both the parents' and the teachers' perspectives, and a discussion of areas of focus for the administrator.

VIEWPOINT ON DIVERSITY

Numerous articles and books that explore issues related to diversity focus solely on the multicultural aspects of education. A great deal of attention is paid to these issues, especially as they relate to the curriculum and their effects on young children's attitudes. Often a chart or graph is created that categorizes information about group values, family structures, and attitudes toward education. Such a "recipe approach" promotes stereotypical attitudes. While cultural issues are often the most noticeable and, in some cases, problematic because of language barriers, there are similarities in the concerns and needs of all children whose background or family structure differs from the mainstream community in which they live. Many families share feelings of isolation, a lack of awareness of expectations, and concern about whether or not their children's needs to ensure school success will be met.

As educators, we must broaden our definition of diversity and utilize the same strategies to reach all parents. Without such efforts, many families "fall through the cracks," and opportunities for involvement are wasted. For this reason, the authors have chosen not to simplify the attitudes, beliefs, and values of diverse groups of people into a few words or phrases. Instead, we will discuss the universal strategies and techniques that apply to *all* parents, and we will explore methods of increasing parent involvement based on individual family needs (Berger, 2008).

WAYS IN WHICH FAMILIES DIFFER

Basic differences exist among all families, across all socioeconomic and racial lines. Differences may have more to do with family heritage and life experiences than ethnicity. In addition to the more visible differences at the socioeconomic level, there are other criteria that distinguish families from one another, including the degree of permanence in the community, family configuration, values socialization, and perceptions of authority.

Degree of Permanence

Central to establishing parent involvement is an understanding of the degree of permanence each family has within the community. Employment status, reasons for living in the area, and length of time in this country all impact the commitment parents feel to a school, neighborhood, and community. Families may be educated, employed, and permanent citizens of the United States. They may be recent immigrants, employed, and working toward citizenship by adopting the new traditions and values of the current culture, yet continuing to embrace some cultural traditions from their country of origin. Families may be refugees who fled their homeland under duress and are continuing to live under enormous amounts of stress and poor economic conditions. Parents who are migrant workers may be part-time members of a community that serves as a place of temporary employment for weeks or months.

Families rely on teachers to help children adjust to new schools or centers. *Courtesy of ECE Photo Library.*

Teachers should resist forming preconceived ideas about any parent based on name or race; doing so creates invisible walls to participation. Rather, parent needs for involvement should be determined *after* meeting families and discussing mutually desired goals for their children.

Family Configurations

Families of the 2000s are more complex than at any other time in history. The 1950s version of the nuclear family (a two-parent family in which the father is employed full time, the mother does not work outside the home, and all of the children are born after the parents' marriage) is now but one of the many combinations of children and adults labeled as a family. Consider these other facts about the American family that were published from data collected in the 2000 Census:

- Single parents account for 27 percent of family households with children under 18.
- One in two children will live in a single-parent family at some point in childhood.
- More than 2 million fathers are primary caregivers of children under 18, a 62 percent increase since 1990.
- One child out of 25 lives with neither parent.
- 2.4 million grandparents are the primary caregivers for the children in their families.
- 2.8 million children under age 18 and nearly 7 million Americans of all ages identify as more than one race.
- More than 4.5 million married and unmarried couples in the United States are of mixed races or ethnicities.
- Estimates show that approximately 2 million American children under the age of 18 are being raised by their lesbian and gay parents.
- The number of unmarried partner households has increased by 72 percent in the last decade, from 3 million in 1990 to more than 5 million in 2000. These figures include both same-sex and different-sex couples.
- One-third of lesbian households and one-fifth of gay male households have children.

In addition, racial and ethnic diversity continues to increase over time and families in schools and child care centers reflect this changing demographic in America. Consider that the number of multiracial babies born since the 1970s has increased more than 260 percent, compared with a 15 percent increase of single race babies. The implication for educators is that the number of biracial or multi-racial children enrolled in their programs may exceed the number of children from a single ethnic background. For this reason, educators who welcome families as individuals first, and heritage second, are likely to build stronger relationships with parents. Then, parents can let educators know of their individual needs, which are likely more similar to than different from those of other families (Wardle, 2001).

How do these trends affect parent involvement in schools? Teachers must continually expand their list of strategies that will reach *all* parents, including nonliterate parents, adults with limited English proficiency, families with multiple ethnic heritages, **noncustodial parents** who wish to remain involved in their children's education, extended families with two or three generations of a family under one roof sharing responsibility for the children, blended families, single parents of both sexes, and teenage parents.

Educators also must be open to developing relationships with adults who may be significant in a child's life but are not biological parents, such as foster parents and grandparents. These conditions occur across all socioeconomic and racial lines. To make assumptions based on stereotypical information is not serving parents fairly. Rather, educators need to take responsibility for making face-to-face contact with families before interpreting their needs for communication, involvement, and assistance (Harry, 1997).

Socialization and Values

Socialization refers to the qualities and attributes, those that are required for adult roles in a particular society or ethnic orientation, which families encourage in their children. Socialization relates to such issues as level of independence, cooperativeness versus competitiveness, individuality versus group goals, tactility (comfort levels of touch from another person), and aggression. Families are not the only agents assisting children in adapting to their environment—schools assume a large degree of the responsibility as well. Historically, one of the school's primary roles has been to perpetuate society's knowledge, skills, customs, and beliefs (Kliebard, 1987; Stott & Halpern, 2003). The difficulty lies in the conflict between these two sets of knowledge. Children who come from a family outside of the mainstream, dominant culture may experience dissonance when integrating what is taught at home and at school. This applies to children in ethnically different as well as in nontraditional families. Children often are caught in a struggle to meet the expectations of family and school. Some of the more general ways in which families differ include the following:

1. **Work ethic:** Standards for industriousness, level of ambition expected of children, value placed on competition both in school and in personal relationships, and degree of emphasis on cooperation within peer groups all vary within and between cultures and may impact student or parent response to school expectations.

2. **Communication style:** Appropriate communication styles vary according to cultural standards. This includes how children may address adults verbally, maintenance of eye contact, silence, distance, emotional expressiveness, and body movements.

3. **Basis for ascribed status:** Cultures differ in their methods of assigning status to individuals. Level of education, occupation, class of birth, and family heritage are common criteria for assigning high, middle, or low status within a culture.

4. **Value of achievement versus heritage:** Some cultures may place more value on the heritage, or family line, than on individual accomplishments. Children from these cultures may be expected to achieve for their families and not for themselves.

5. **Role definition in family and community:** Some cultures place equal value on the child's responsibilities at home and school; others value school performance as a reflection of the family honor. Gender roles in the home may be specifically prescribed and may conflict with philosophies of gender equality in the schools.

Within a culture, there may exist tremendous variations between subgroups. For example, while there is a population in the United States identified as Native American, it is made up of more than 250 federally recognized tribes, each with unique beliefs, customs, and languages. While it is difficult to make generalizations about all groups, there may be certain core beliefs that are shared by many. Gaining familiarity with these core attitudes, values, and behaviors can aid teachers in discovering basic sociocultural orientations.

Another factor to consider is that some minority families may be in a state of transition. Transition may refer to a physical transition due to a recent relocation to this country or the neighborhood. It may also refer to the family's attempt to merge a new culture with a former culture; this type of transition may take longer for individual members of the family. It is not uncommon for a mother who is home with children to be less comfortable with the language, customs, and culture of a new setting compared to her children who attend school each day.

Cultures change through the years, so the degree of cultural orientation that children bring with them into the classroom will vary contingent on the strength of their ethnic identification and how acculturated their parents are. Many families fall between the two extremes of traditional orientation and full assimilation. By addressing each family individually, without preconceived notions, educators make it possible for each set of parents and children to have their needs met realistically and fairly.

Perceptions of Authority and the Role of the School

Educators may gain insight into parent attitudes toward involvement by discovering how strongly they feel about their culture's traditional views of education. Cultures differ on the appropriate role parents are to assume in their child's education. In some groups, formal schooling is reserved for the elite. Parents who have never been part of the educational system have difficulty understanding the roles and responsibilities of parent involvement in this society. In other groups, the school and its teachers are highly respected but not viewed as having a collaborative relationship with parents. In such a culture, school assumes a role of authority similar to the position of the church.

There are also families who, because of chronic poverty, unemployment, and poor school experiences, have negative attitudes toward education and teachers. These are parents who have little to do with their children's schooling, and they offer minimal support for the teacher's efforts to communicate. Included in this group may be parents who have had difficulties obtaining special education services or meeting immunization requirements so their children can enter school.

Degree of Isolation

Another factor that affects parents' willingness to become involved is their degree of isolation within the school community. In some cases, isolation occurs because the parents are not residents of the community (for example, when special needs students are bused into neighboring communities to receive services). Parents are limited in their opportunities to socialize with other parents and are likely to receive less communication from the school.

There is also the isolation that exists for parents who are not connected to other parents in their situation. For example, teenage mothers are often socially isolated from their peers and from other teen parents. They may also feel excluded from the mainstream group of parents once their child enters school. New immigrants may experience a great sense of isolation when they are separated from extended families and are unable to locate families of similar background with which to bond.

Families also experience isolation if the community is not accepting of their lifestyle or culture. Conditions of cultural difference, prejudice, and the unequal distribution of economic and political power extend to all institutions in the community, including the educational institutions. It is apparent, then, that to encourage parent and family involvement, schools must be accepting of the diversity within their family population.

TEACHER ATTITUDES AND SCHOOL PRACTICES INFLUENCING PARENT INVOLVEMENT

Teacher Attitudes

In creating opportunities for parent involvement, educators must look at their own practices and attitudes to examine how, if at all, existing biases, beliefs, and prejudices affect their ability to nurture involvement. We are all greatly influenced by the culture in which we were raised; attitudes, beliefs, and values stem from this environment. In order to provide a welcoming atmosphere for families from cultures or family structures different from one's own, there are two steps to take:

1. Develop an awareness of your own cultural and family values and beliefs and a recognition of how they influence your attitudes and behaviors.

2. Develop an understanding of the cultural values and lifestyle choices of your students' parents and how those values and choices influence their attitudes and beliefs. To do this, consider the questions in Table 3.1 as a springboard to acknowledging individual cultural heritages. Answers may help professionals clarify their attitudes and serve as a starting point when considering other family situations.

Table 3.1 Acknowledging Your Cultural Heritage

1. What ethnic group, socioeconomic class, religion, age group, and community do you belong to?
2. What experiences have you had with people from other ethnic groups, socioeconomic classes, religions, age groups, or communities?
3. What were those experiences? How did you feel about them?
4. When you were growing up, what did your parents and other significant adults in your life say about people who were different from your family?
5. What do you find embarrassing about your ethnic group, socioeconomic class, religion, age, or community? What would you like to change? Why?
6. What sociocultural factors in your background might contribute to your being rejected by members of other cultures?
7. What personal qualities do you have that will help you establish interpersonal relationships with persons from other cultures? What personal qualities may be detrimental?

Randall-David, 1989.

Many of the difficulties that are experienced stem from the outmoded idea of the United States as a melting pot. In reality, it is a rich, diverse mix of people resembling a "quilt, rich in colors, textures, and patterns that make up the fabric of our society" (Randall-David, 1989). In order to address such diversity, it is critical to examine some of the unintentional ways in which educators discourage parents from participating in their children's education.

1. Teachers may believe they're not prejudiced. Even when a teacher believes he or she is not biased against people of other races or lifestyles, it is possible for biased beliefs to sneak into everyday language. Phrases like "running around like wild Indians" or "throwing like a girl" may be a part of our everyday language, but little thought is given to how the words will affect impressionable children. Whether intentional or not, prejudice hurts, and it builds walls that impede communication.

2. Some teachers are proud of being "color blind." Many teachers, in an effort to display openness to all children, espouse the belief that "all children are the same to me." Sociologists have found that "all the same" generally refers to the Euro-American culture and that this is the standard of acceptable sameness. Refusal to acknowledge the evident differences between children's cultures and traditions does not allow the opportunity to explore ways of coping with diversity in the real world.

3. Teachers may employ the "tourist approach" to introducing multicultural activities into the classroom. The tourist approach, while once thought to be an ideal way to expose children to various holidays, foods, and customs, usually perpetuates stereotypes. Children focus on the exotic differences between people and tend not to see the similarities of life experiences, family, and day-to-day problems common to everyone. This approach also lends itself to a one-time exposure to a culture and, therefore, variety is not integrated into daily curriculum in a meaningful way (Koeppel & Mulrooney, 1992).

4. Teachers believe that Caucasian children are unaffected by diversity. All children, whether exposed to diversity through their classroom populations or not, need to be aware of our society's cultural richness and diversity in order to adequately prepare them to cope with the real world. Curricula and books that perpetuate stereotypes do children a disservice by reinforcing myths and biases.

5. Teachers of Euro-American descent often believe that children from minorities are "culturally deprived." Children who are not of the dominant culture and who are assumed to be deprived may not be allowed to experience the respect and value their individual heritage deserves. It is necessary to a child's self-esteem that his or her family's traditions, customs, and holidays are regarded with equal importance to others celebrated. Maintaining pride in one's heritage is an important key to helping children bridge the gap between home and school.

6. **"At risk" does not mean "deficient."** Each child brings experiences and thoughts to school about which he or she can talk, write, and read (Walker-Dalhouse & Dalhouse, 2001). Pellegrini (1991) summarized that children labeled as at-risk who experience school failure do so because of "unfamiliarity with the rules governing the learning context of the school." Success can be achieved, in part, by the use of curriculum materials that reflect a child's heritage and offer opportunities to express language.

Educational Practices

Several educational practices promote the concept that minority children are less capable learners. This perception creates a self-fulfilling prophecy: Diversity creates lowered expectations, which result in lower levels of academic achievement. Teachers need to become advocates for their students' parents to ensure that students are not being unfairly placed in remedial classes or special education rooms, or labeled as slow learners, based solely on diversity issues. Seeking ways to draw out parents who might otherwise feel unwelcome in a school system is a beginning. What should follow is the commitment on the part of the staff to developing and maintaining a working relationship with families for the benefit of their children.

The following is a partial list of educational practices that tend to limit children from diverse backgrounds and have a lasting impact on low-income and minority students. Some of these practices persist when "different" is seen as "deficient."

1. **Kindergarten retention, academic tracking, and ability grouping convey a message of limited worth to children who belong to a minority group or who are economically disadvantaged (Walker-Dalhouse, 1993).** Children who do not match the social expectations of schools tend to become labeled as low achievers and do not receive the same encouragement to succeed as other children. In fact, labels often follow children into subsequent grades. Parents of children so labeled tend to be less involved and feel their presence and opinions are less desired in the schools. When this occurs, negative feelings and damaging stereotypes persevere and are likely to return, full circle, in the next generation.

Awareness and acceptance of cultural diversity is critical. *Courtesy of ECE Photo Library.*

2. Programs designed for English as a Second Language (ESL) students or English Language Learners (ELL) often operate on a "deficit philosophy." When such programs are viewed as compensatory in nature, a child's ability to maintain a native language suffers at the expense of acquiring English. It is generally believed that language learning and cultural enhancement occur when the emphasis is on preserving the bilingual capabilities of young children rather than substituting one language for another (Tabors, 1998).

3. Schools that fail to acknowledge the changing composition of families and family life restrict many parents from full participation in their children's education. Educational practices of each school need to be continually revised and updated to meet the unique needs of the population being served. When schools adhere to outmoded practices such as daytime classroom volunteering, daytime conferences, limited phone access to both teachers and administrators, and daytime registrations, orientations, and screenings, it is logical that many parents will be unable to participate. Acknowledgment of changing lifestyles and parenting needs presents to educators the challenge of creating new, more accessible channels of communication and opportunities for teacher contact.

4. There is a lack of emphasis placed on teacher training about family stresses and family structures. Teachers need accurate, practical information about the kinds of stresses that many kinds of families endure (Coleman, 1991). Cultural differences may require background knowledge and training so that trusting relationships can be created. An increasing number of diverse families, along with the many stresses all families face, make it necessary for teachers to have additional training in order to create family-friendly schools.

PARENT PERCEPTIONS OF BARRIERS TO INVOLVEMENT

An examination of practices within individual schools often can uncover the barriers to parent involvement. Parents may perceive difficulties in developing a relationship with or an interest in their schools for the following reasons:

1. There are poor language and communication efforts between the school and the home. Without meaningful, understandable communication, families with a language or reading barrier are less likely to feel a part of their children's education. Parents who sense that the school is uninterested or biased against their family structure also may find it difficult to maintain an interest in the school (Coleman, 1991). Written, spoken, taped, individual, and group communication should be developed. Face-to-face contact, group meetings with other parents, and printed information covering relevant areas of curriculum, conferencing skills, school policies, evaluation methods, and discipline are necessary for transmitting available information to the greatest number of parents.

2. Parents often feel that schools do not value their input on important matters. Many parents, especially those who represent minority cultures or who are themselves undereducated, feel that their opinions about the school are not valued by teachers or administrators. Common complaints include the attitude that teachers want parents to only do menial tasks and that decision making is better off in the hands of educators. Clerical work, fundraising, and being a room parent are the typical roles that parents in general are assigned.

3. Parents from minority cultures or migrant populations, or those who are illiterate or do not have jobs, may have feelings of inadequacy that can inhibit the growth of positive relationships between home and school. Parents who have low self-esteem may find it overwhelming to take an active role in their child's education. Because many cultures assign the responsibility of formal education to teachers alone, parent involvement is often an unfamiliar concept to parents of those cultures. A more general explanation of feelings of inadequacy stems from the immediate life concerns that occupy the thoughts and actions of many families. Such necessities as food, shelter, child care, and medical care often take precedence over long-range goals of education. Teachers who are aware of individual family stresses can more realistically plan for acceptable levels of involvement (Horn, Cheng, & Joseph, 2004).

When parents are unable to assist or observe in the classroom, they are also unable to gain expertise from modeling the teacher's methods for working with children. This can be especially crucial in early childhood environments and special education classrooms where parents may lack confidence in handling children's behavioral and educational problems.

4. Barriers to parent involvement can also make it extremely difficult for parents to become active participants in school-related activities. Obstacles such as lack of child care for siblings, lack of transportation, and inability to afford to take time away from work to attend conferences or meetings are very real barriers for many parents. Employers who penalize absenteeism or withhold pay may cause a parent to miss an event scheduled during school hours. Participation may be limited by cost of transportation and distance to the school (special needs children, for instance, often must attend a school outside their neighborhood). Embarrassment over clothing or mastery of English can make a parent reluctant to enter the facility and meet with other parents.

A welcoming atmosphere begins at the door. *Courtesy of ECE Photo Library.*

5. There is a lack of a welcoming atmosphere in the schools. Staff members who are inconsiderate of language barriers or cultural differences can send the message that some families are not truly welcome in the school. Parents view the lack of adequate directions in locating various areas of the building, an absence of storage areas for personal items, and negative attitudes on the part of the office staff toward language barriers as conveying a less than welcoming atmosphere. Often classrooms have only one adult-sized chair—and it belongs to the teacher. Inflexible policies that make such routine tasks as registration and orientation difficult for single working parents, for example, also influence future relationships between home and school.

STRATEGIES USED TO OVERCOME BARRIERS TO PARENT INVOLVEMENT

The challenge that diversity presents to educators is amplified when one considers that for parent involvement across all educational levels there are generally few funds allocated for professionals to conduct quality parent involvement activities. New requirements under **Title I** legislation mandate that a percentage of Title I funds be allocated for parent involvement, but this often does not translate into support for individual classroom teachers. The classroom teacher and building principal generally are charged with the responsibility for devising strategies to improve communication and involvement to meet the needs of the school's families.

The following suggestions are meant to be starting points. To be successful, ideas and techniques should be tailored to individual needs. While there is no limit to the types of strategies that can be developed, some general categories bear attention.

Parenting

1. Information about parent education classes or workshops may assist families unfamiliar with a new community or whose children are having problems at school. Teachers can collaborate with each other to provide classes for parents. Many state-funded programs, such as prekindergartens, require linkages with existing programs in making such information available.

2. Teachers aware of the needs of member families can serve as resources for local parent support groups. These groups may be specific to a particular culture or may provide emotional support for single parents, teen parents, adoptive families, or blended families (Harry, 2002).

3. Schools should make an effort when the school year begins to offer workshops on topics of particular interest to parents, such as "A Day in the Life of Your Preschooler," "How to Help Your Child with Homework," or "Handling TV Superheroes." This may be the first time that parents have attended a school function. It is important that the first meeting be a positive one and generally on a neutral topic. Meeting about the school performance of a child often will create feelings of anxiety and concern; these are not the ideal conditions under which to begin a relationship.

4. Teachers need to become familiar with the customs of the various cultures represented in their classroom and develop some working knowledge about their students' situations at home.

5. Parent education in the workplace is an increasingly popular method for reaching parents who might otherwise have difficulty attending evening classes. Forging a link between employers, unions, and schools is an effective way to bring parenting information to parents and meet their needs for involvement.

6. Playgroups have been formed in communities with concentrations of families from a similar culture to assist with networking and reducing the isolation that can be caused by parenting young children in a situation where language barriers exist. In other communities, playgroups for adoptive parents of foreign-born children can be an effective way to link families with resource information and school services.

Communicating

1. School handbooks and policy statements should be examined to determine whether the information they give is complete. Families from different cultures may take offense at, or may misunderstand, the need for certain types of information and may feel that their privacy has been intruded upon (Flett & Conderman, 2001). Available services may not be fully explained and may go unused by qualifying families. Paperwork about common school policies, such as the free lunch program or speech and language services, may be difficult for a parent with low literacy skills. Often, feelings of embarrassment about a lack of understanding discourage the parent from seeking help.

2. Written communication from the school should be available in several languages, where necessary, in order to ensure the distribution of important news. School newsletters and notices should be monitored for readability.

Parents will stay informed if written communications are provided in their native language. *Courtesy of ECE Photo Library.*

3. For parents who cannot read, school calendar events can be broadcast on local radio stations. For non-English-speaking parents, use a radio station that broadcasts in their language.

4. A bilingual parent can serve as a liaison between the school and the home of new parents who may need assistance with registration, conferences, and so on. This liaison could serve as a mentor, accompanying parents to evening meetings to acquaint them with school groups such as the PTA or PTO. A mentor can serve in this capacity until a family's transition into the school allows its members to participate on their own.

5. Multimedia approaches are valuable in disseminating important information from the schools into the community. For an annual early childhood screening, for example, advertise on local stations that reflect the languages spoken in the community, print flyers in those languages, and ask local churches and day-care centers to contact parents.

6. Educational slang and jargon obstruct communication. Parents of all backgrounds and educational levels will feel intimidated if the school staff is unable to communicate in a way parents can understand (Flett & Conderman, 2001).

7. Consider alternate sites for parent conferences or home visits if a parent is reluctant to enter the school or have a staff member in the home. Local restaurants, churches, libraries, or the parent's workplace can serve as meeting spots. Indicating a willingness to accommodate parents may be the first step toward breaking down attitudinal barriers to school involvement and building a trusting relationship.

Volunteering

1. Parent involvement that is encouraged by "showcasing" families of diverse ethnic backgrounds could put unfair demands on a family's time and resources. English-speaking limitations or cultural beliefs about schools and teachers may inhibit a parent from speaking to the class. Do not assume that membership in a racial class imparts a great expertise in that culture. Family members may be third- or fourth-generation Americans with few ties to the original culture. Extend an open invitation for speakers and enlist the help of those who volunteer their services.

2. Parents who are experienced in classroom and school volunteering can be encouraged to serve as mentors for new parents unfamiliar with the concept of school volunteering. Because many cultures regard school as a place for the elite only and where teachers are the experts, parents may have to be convinced that they have something to contribute to the school. Lack of familiarity with the staff and school policies may make them unwilling to offer services. Again, an experienced volunteer or aide can provide assistance in understanding the routines and needs of the classroom teacher.

Learning at Home

1. Opportunities for parent–child interaction can come from parent meetings that focus on a specific curricular area. Modeling occurs when teachers demonstrate appropriate practice and materials with young children.

2. Take-home learning activities that emphasize a science, math, or literacy game or experience can be shared by the parent and child. Emphasis on books that depict children from multiple races and multiple family configurations will ensure that materials reflect more than just the Caucasian two-parent family.

3. Home visits can be excellent backdrops for individualized teaching experiences among the teacher, parent, and child. Building parent confidence in the role of first teacher will allow more interaction and will encourage the parent to participate in school functions. If parents are open to the idea of a home visit, this can be an excellent strategy for the teacher to observe the family in their own environment and meet other family members important in the life of the child.

4. It is helpful to send information home that explains new curriculum concepts and how they affect the children. For example, parents may be concerned about their child's ability to maintain native language skills and may have questions about an integrated curriculum and their child's chances for success. Share with parents material that will enable them to better understand the teaching philosophies of the school staff.

5. Teachers need to create an atmosphere of open communication so that concerns about the curriculum and any other area can be discussed. Parents who are mistrustful of the school or who are angry because their concerns are not heard will be less likely to participate.

Representing Other Parents

1. Advisory councils that are recruiting new members should seek to include a diverse group of parents. This "widening of the circle" ensures full representation when decisions are being made about organizing parent events, scheduling workshops, reviewing curriculum revisions, and other issues related to the school or center.

2. Mentoring programs that focus on developing leadership roles help bring parents into positions of governance. Ownership of a school begins when each parent feels included in the decision-making process on both large and small items.

CLASSROOM PRACTICES THAT SHOULD BE REVIEWED EACH YEAR

As teachers ready their classrooms each year, they should take care to familiarize themselves with the families of the students assigned to the class as early as possible. Some types of diversity may not readily be apparent from a class list or in a meeting with the child on the first day of school. The teacher may not be aware of a child parented by same-sex parents or a child from a specific religious background until the parent shares the information in a conference or as a result of a concern regarding an upcoming school activity or field trip. Other types of diversity are more readily apparent and may even precede the child's inclusion in the class. Parents with limited English skills may have worked with the principal, social worker, or director in a previous year, and plans may be in place to support communication between home and school. In other cases, a parent who must rely on a hearing interpreter, for example, in order to attend school functions may not initiate a request until the need arises. In the case of a family in which very little or no English is spoken, the teacher may represent the first contact to assess the need for services. Classroom practices, events, and activities should be adjusted annually to encompass the needs of the students. Areas to review and adjust include the following:

- The celebration of holidays and seasonal milestones
- The use of food in classroom parties and thematic units
- Art and music activities offered within the classroom

- Classroom decorations, including posters, calendars, and charts
- The selection of literature and poetry used in language arts
- Student plays and performances
- Field trips

While the classroom curricular content is generally prescribed at the school level, latitude usually exists for the types of literature, for example, used to convey a skill or concept. Similarly, art and music activities offer a wealth of focus areas that can and should be inclusive of the students' backgrounds whenever possible. Advance planning and the use of online resources can ensure that when an art concept is introduced, samples from a variety of cultures are available.

Other tips for educators have been developed from the positive experiences of teachers who have successfully bridged the communication and cultural barriers between parents and the school. These include the following:

1. Take the time to explore the parents' personal beliefs, values, and expectations that influence their interactions with others. Do not assume that someone from an Indian background, for example, will necessarily ascribe to any or all of the stereotypical beliefs about the culture. Time invested in developing individual relationships is well spent when attempting to build a positive partnership with a family (Flett & Conderman, 2001).

2. Learn about the family's culture to effectively build a trusting relationship with parents. After meeting parents and learning about the family's individual beliefs regarding customs and holidays, utilize resources to acknowledge their particular faith or cultural observance, where possible, in the room with holiday symbols, in music with representative selections of instrumental or vocal music, or in literature selected for read-aloud time.

3. Respect and recognize the family's culture and beliefs. Simple gestures such as learning common greetings of "good morning" and "good-bye" in a family's native language can show a new family that school staff has a welcoming intent.

4. When communicating with parents from culturally and linguistically diverse backgrounds, provide communication in many forms. Families may request an interpreter to a conference, for example, to help them understand the teacher's comments during a conference or an Individualized Education Plan (IEP) meeting. Similarly, newsletters may need to be translated into multiple languages in order to be read and understood by families with limited English proficiency.

5. Make use of casual contacts with parents. Parent drop-off and pickup times are excellent opportunities for brief conversations or for the delivery of the child's take-home folder or conference appointment notice. When teachers avoid parents due to language barriers but readily speak to English-speaking parents, an unintended barrier is erected by the school.

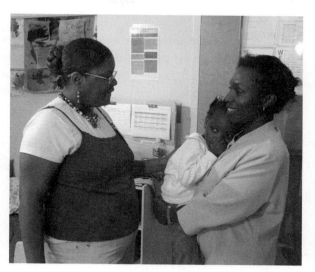

Students benefit when parents and teachers take the time for friendly conversation. *Courtesy of ECE Photo Library.*

6. Provide district-wide orientation sessions for families in their native languages. Important occasions such as kindergarten orientation, parent–teacher organization meetings, and other events are often inaccessible to parents with language barriers. Investing in presenters who can deliver the information to parents in a way they can understand establishes a commitment to partnership for everyone.

7. Encourage native-language parent groups. When neighborhoods have multiple families of similar origin, the school or child-care center can acknowledge all parents' needs to meet and discuss parenting issues by organizing support groups or parenting groups for speakers of different languages. Local resources for such groups include churches, universities, and local charities, which may employ staff who are bilingual and willing to conduct such activities for a fee (Stott & Halpern, 2003).

8. Recognize that the expectations for parental involvement in the United States are often very different from those in the home country. Parents adjusting to a new country may not be available or feel comfortable participating in the school. It may take time to help parents not familiar with working alongside a teacher as a classroom volunteer, for example, to feel ready for that role if that activity was not typical for parents in their native culture.

9. **Try to ensure that all written and oral communication is free of jargon, educational acronyms, and contemporary slang.** Families coping with language barriers may become frustrated when trying to interpret IEP, NCLB, pre-K, and other verbal shortcuts that are so prevalent in the vocabulary of teachers.

10. **Research the cultural differences in eye contact and physical space between people during conversations.** Cultural differences exist regarding both of these nonverbal cues, and parents who seem distant may be acting respectfully from a cultural point of view. Teachers who understand these critical cues will not take offense or invade a parent's comfort zone during conversations.

FOCUS FOR ADMINISTRATORS AND DIRECTORS

School principals and child-care center directors must be extremely conscious of the individual attitudes and biases of their staff members toward families with lifestyles or cultures different from their own. Discussion about working with all types of parents should occur within faculty meetings and staff in-services on a regular basis. The administrator's role is to facilitate meaningful conversation about challenges teachers are experiencing, identify resources needed to help all families access parent and classroom activities, and help all staff members hear the perspectives of their colleagues regarding strategies that are successful in involving families. It is the administrator's responsibility to establish a school culture of acceptance and a positive welcoming climate for all families.

In terms of curricular content, administrators should ensure that classroom materials reflect the backgrounds and heritages of enrolled students. This may involve an annual review of textbooks, library materials, and classroom libraries in order to update the collections that are used by students. Teachers in the early childhood and primary settings who have housekeeping centers will want to review the ethnic appearances of dolls, types of dress-up clothes, and other representations of typical life. An important element of a child's self-esteem is to be able to find similarities between his or her heritage and the representations in books and instructional materials used in the classroom.

Curricular approaches and classroom activities should never isolate a child or require a child to isolate a part of his or her background (Wardle, 2001). The administrator should review planned field trips and class projects with each teacher at the beginning of the year and review the possible impact on the children assigned to the class. Parents of certain religions, for example, may not be allowed to have their children visit a hospital for a field trip related to medical careers. The parent survey or questionnaire at the beginning of the year is an excellent method for obtaining parent input on concerns and limitations they might request during the year. While it may not be possible to eliminate all conflicts, advance planning and early communication can ensure that parents have input on decisions and are offered acceptable alternatives for their children.

The school or center administrator should also utilize appropriate labels for identification of children (such as multiracial, biracial, or mixed) depending on the parents' preferences. For too long, many states required parents and school offices to select from a list of ethnic backgrounds, ignoring the very real existence of children with mixed heritages. Fortunately, census data on student enrollment and other official forms, such as free lunch applications, are now providing parents with a way to report their child's heritage without compromise. Ensuring that all school-based surveys and forms allow parents to realistically indicate their children's ethnicity is yet another way schools can acknowledge acceptance of all families.

SUMMARY

Educators, administrators, and families will strengthen partnerships when each person feels valued and an integral part of a child's education. To be successful in meeting the challenges that all types of diversity present, teachers must first commit to setting goals for themselves. They need to learn more about today's complex family structures and stresses. Teachers, along with the help of administrators, should regularly examine school practices and policies that restrict full involvement. Practices such as daytime conferences, restrictive phone access to teachers, and volunteer opportunities that are limited to classroom hours must be reshaped to allow full participation from busy families. Lastly, educators and administrators need to be open, both philosophically and practically, to the changing complexities of today's American family. When educators view children and people as individuals with characteristics that include racial and ethnic diversity, rather than look at people as products of single-race or single-ethnicity reference groups, they are demonstrating genuine respect for the families schools serve (Wardle, 2001).

We know that children feel respected when their families are respected, and to achieve this, we as educators must reach across diverse cultural, lifestyle, and economic differences; use all of our resources outside the classroom; and include family life professionals to create linkages between family and school environments (Coleman, 1991).

ACTIVITIES FOR DISCUSSION, EXPANSION, AND APPLICATION

1. Interview an educator about his or her experiences with diversity in the classroom and in the school or center. Discuss the ways that diversity is addressed in the curriculum, holiday celebrations, socialization practices, and parent involvement strategies used in the facility.

2. Examine several textbooks used in elementary-level reading and social studies instruction to determine how diversity is presented to young students. Look at pictures, wording, and areas of emphasis.

3. Visit an elementary school library and the children's section of a public library to review children's literature from the perspective of multicultural balance.

4. Interview a school librarian and a children's librarian at your local library about recent trends in educational videos, programming, and children's books related to issues of diversity. How accurately do library holdings reflect the population being served? What attempts are made to include a balanced cultural viewpoint when purchasing new resources?

5. What personal qualities do you have that will help you establish a relationship with parents from other cultural groups? What personal qualities may be detrimental?

6. When you were growing up, what did your parents and other family members say about people who were different from your family?

CASE STUDY

Elizabeth is a fourth-grade teacher in a rural public school serving primarily Caucasian students. There has been little diversity among the families until three years ago, when migrant farm workers began permanently relocating to the neighboring towns. The Hispanic population in the school has increased from 2 percent to 15 percent, and Elizabeth and other teachers feel they must begin to review and revamp many of the school's communication methods and other practices in order to better serve the growing number of Spanish-speaking families enrolling each year.

1. How should the staff determine the needs of the new families?

2. What steps might the staff take to improve communication with the families?

3. What parent involvement strategies might need to be reviewed and revised?

4. What assumptions might the staff make that could be problematic for the students and parents?

USEFUL WEBSITES

csbchome.org

Center for the Study of Biracial Children. The Center for the Study of Biracial Children produces and disseminates materials for and about interracial families and biracial children. The Center provides advocacy, training and consulting. Its primary mission is to advocate for the rights of interracial families, biracial children, and multiracial people.

www.awaironline.org

Awair Online: Arab World and Islamic Resources. This site provides materials and services for educators who wish to teach about the Arab world and Islam.

www.cie.org

The Council on Islamic Education. This site gives general information about Islam.

www.clas.uiuc.edu

Culturally and Linguistically Appropriate Services, Early Childhood Research Institute. The CLAS Institute identifies, evaluates, and promotes effective and appropriate early intervention practices and preschool practices that are sensitive and respectful to children and families from culturally and linguistically diverse backgrounds.

www.ed.gov/admins/comm/parents/pntinv.html

U.S. Department of Education: Work with Parents and the Community. The information in this section is designed to assist local educational agencies, schools, and parents in meeting the requirements of parental involvement provisions required under Title I, Part A.

www.ed.gov/espanol/bienvenidos/es/index.html

U.S. Department of Education. This site is presented in Spanish and contains information for parents about No Child Left Behind regulations.

www.familyvillage.wisc.edu

Family Village: A Global Community of Disability-Related Resources. The Family Village is a global community that integrates information, resources, and communication opportunities on the Internet for persons with cognitive and other disabilities, their families, and those that provide them services and support.

www.fcsn.org

Federation for Children with Special Needs. The Federation is a center for parents and parent organizations to work together on behalf of children with special needs and their families.

www.interracialvoice.com

Interracial Voice. Interracial Voice is a networking news journal.

www.ncpie.org

National Coalition for Parent Involvement in Education. The NCPIE mission is to advocate the involvement of parents and families in their children's education and to foster relationships among home, school, and community to enhance the education of all our nation's young people.

www.nea.org/parents

National Education Association: Parents and Community. This site provides a wide range of resources for parents and teachers about helping children to have successful school experiences.

www.nichcy.org

National Dissemination Center for Children with Disabilities. The National Dissemination Center for Children with Disabilities serves as a central source of information on disabilities in infants, toddlers, children, and youth; IDEA, which is the law authorizing special education; No Child Left Behind (as it relates to children with disabilities); and research-based information on effective educational practices.

www.php.com

Parents Helping Parents. Parents Helping Parents (PHP) provides lifetime guidance, supports, and services to families of children with any special need and the professionals who serve them.

www.pta.org

National Parent Teacher Association. As the largest volunteer child advocacy association in the nation, the National Parent Teacher Association (PTA) reminds our country of its obligations to children and provides parents and families with a powerful voice to speak on behalf of every child while providing the best tools for parents to help their children be successful students.

REFERENCES

Berger, E. H. (2008). *Parents and teachers as partners: Families and schools working together* (7th ed). Upper Saddle River, NJ: Pearson/Merrill/Prentice Hall.

Coleman, M. (1991). Planning for the changing nature of family life in schools for young children. *Young Children, 46*(4), 15–20.

Federal Interagency Forum on Child and Family Statistics. (2007). America's children: Key national indicators of well-being. Washington, DC: U.S. Government Printing Office.

Flett, A., & Conderman, G. (2001). Enhance the involvement of parents from culturally and linguistically diverse backgrounds. *Intervention in School and Clinic, 37*(1), 53–55.

Harry, B. (1997). Learning forward or bending over backwards: Cultural reciprocity in working with families. *Journal of Early Intervention, 21*(1), 62–72.

Harry, B. (2002). Trends and issues in serving culturally diverse families of children with disabilities. *The Journal of Special Education, 36*(3), 131–138.

Hoot, J. L., Szecsi, T., & Moosa, S. (2003). What teachers of young children should know about Islam. *Early Childhood Intervention Journal, 31*(2), 85–90.

Horn, I. B., Cheng, T. L., & Joseph, J. (2004). Discipline in the African American community: The impact of socioeconomic status on beliefs and practices. *Pediatrics, 113,* 1236–1241.

Hosley, C. A., Gensheimer, L., & Yang, M. (2003). Building effective working relationships across culturally and ethnically diverse communities. *Child Welfare League of America 82*(2), 157–167.

Kliebard, H. M. (1987). *The struggle for the American curriculum: 1893–1958.* New York: Routledge.

Koeppel, J., & Mulrooney, M. (1992). The sister schools program: A way for children to learn about cultural diversity when there isn't any in their school. *Young Children, 48*(1), 44–47.

Mallory, B., & New, R. (1994). *Diversity & developmentally appropriate practices.* New York: Teachers College Press.

Nardine, E., & Morris, R. (1992). In A. Salerno and M. Fink (Eds.), *Home/school partnerships: Migrant parent involvement report.* Washington, DC: Office of Elementary and Secondary Education.

Norton, A., & Glick, P. (1986). One-parent families: A social and economic profile. *Journal of Family Relations, 35,* 9–17.

Pellegrini, A. D. (1991). A critique of the concept of at risk as applied to emergent literacy. *Language Arts, 68*(5), 380–385.

Randall-David, E. (1989). *Strategies for working with culturally diverse communities and clients.* Bethesda, MD: Association for the Care of Children's Health.

Spewock, T. (1991). Teaching parents of young children through learning packets. *Young Children, 47*(1), 28–31.

Stott, F., & Halpern, R. (2003). Listening to the voices of families: Thoughts, hopes, and fears in a Latino community. *Zero to Three, 23*(5), 16–21.

Tabors, P. L. (1998). What early childhood educators need to know: Development of effective parent involvement programs for linguistically and culturally diverse children and families. *Young Children, 53*(6), 20–26.

Van Deusen, J. (1991). Community schools: A vision of equity and excellence for young children. *Young Children, 46*(5), 58–60.

Walker-Dalhouse, D., (1993). Beginning reading and the African American child at risk. *Young Children, 49*(1), 24–29.

Walker-Dalhouse, D., & Dalhouse, A. D. (2001). Parent–school relations: Communicating more effectively with African-American parents. *Young Children, 56*(4), 75–80.

Wardle, F. (2001). Viewpoint. Supporting multiracial and multiethnic children and their families. *Young Children, 56*(6), 38–39.

Zager, R. (1989). Linking the home and school through the workplace. *Family Resource Coalition Report, 8*(2), 9–26.

KEY TERMS

Diversity—Refers to the differences between families, including racial differences and ethnic heritages, cultural differences, and differences in family structures (two-parent families, grandparent-headed families, single-parent families, etc.).

English as a Second Language (ESL) or English Language Learners (ELL)—Refers to children or adults whose native language is not English. Educational support services for children are often termed ESL or ELL programs.

Title I Legislation—A portion of the federal Elementary and Secondary Education Act (ESEA), which provides funds to school districts for reading and math support services based on the percentage of low-income students enrolled in the district.

Advisory Councils—Committees of citizens and/or parents who meet to review and present feedback to schools, child-care centers, or other entities.

Mentoring—Refers to the role of one adult helping a child or another adult learn a new role; a mentoring program might pair new parents with existing parents to provide answers to questions, train new parents on volunteering duties, and act as a resource of support for problems.

CHAPTER 4

Working with Parents of Children with Special Needs

STUDENT LEARNING OUTCOMES

After reading this chapter, you should be able to

- Recognize common responses, concerns, and issues of families of children with special needs.
- Describe the circumstances that may surround the identification of a child with special needs.
- Identify historical milestones of parent involvement in special education.
- Outline parent involvement required by special education law.
- Discuss the philosophy and practice of inclusion.
- Analyze particular challenges and concerns of families of children with special needs.
- Explain the special value of a family systems approach to parent involvement.
- Discuss the helping relationship between parents, teachers, and service providers.
- Identify unique barriers to parent involvement when the family includes a child with special needs.
- Outline strategies to enhance communication, support, and advocacy within special education service structures.

Why include a chapter on involving parents of young children with special needs? Previously, that information could only be found in materials geared toward special education teachers. Today, segregated educational opportunities, like other practices that insulate individuals with disabilities from their communities, are being challenged. No longer can teachers prepare to teach only "regular" kids.

Due to biotechnical and medical advances, infants and children are surviving the medical complications that accompany many developmental disabilities. Some disabilities, however, are related to complications from the very medical advances that save the lives of premature infants, and many disabilities are being diagnosed at younger ages than ever before. Due to this and other reasons, teachers almost certainly will have children with some degree of exceptionality in their classes and programs. Providing increased opportunities for children with special needs to be with other children their age brings everyone together—often for the first time. Exciting **inclusive** programs are developing in communities nationwide, and school and community programs are taking a lead in fulfilling the promise of legislative measures. Special education has promoted the development of many tenets of parent involvement, while research on children with exceptionalities and their families has supported many changes in all types of educational and social services. Much progress has been made since 1950 concerning parent involvement in special education, and the vision of continued change will shape the future of education for all children.

Throughout the country, inclusion is opening doors and providing new opportunities for children with special needs and their typically developing peers. *Courtesy of ECE Photo Library.*

First and foremost, it is vital to acknowledge that parents of children who have special needs respond to all the wonderful strategies explored in this book, just like any group of parents. A teacher who works with a child with special needs and successfully involves his or her family succeeds for the same reasons a teacher succeeds with any child and family. Parents who have a child with a disability may also have other children without disabilities. Although many teachers can relate to the parenting experience because they are parents themselves, fewer have had the experience of parenting a child with a disability. This chapter provides insight into the unique and sometimes invisible issues of parenting a child with special needs that are essential to developing positive parent involvement when special rights are protected by law. For, as the Little Prince said, "That which is essential, is invisible to the eye" (Saint-Exupéry, 1943).

CHILDREN WITH SPECIAL NEEDS: FAMILIES WITH SPECIAL NEEDS

The dynamic system we recognize as "family" is continually changing with life experiences and the development and maturity levels of its members. Yet, few changes impact family relationships as profoundly as the introduction of a child with special needs. Parent, sibling, and extended family relationships are uniquely influenced by the immediate and long-reaching implications that accompany the birth or adoption of such a child, or the change in a young child's development brought on by an accident, illness, or the diagnosis of a disability. Barraged with feelings and full of questions ("Why us?" "What was the cause of this?" "How will we cope?" "How close to normal will our child be?"), parents frequently struggle with intense emotions as they face new problems and make adjustments. This process frequently isolates families and may cause marital stress, modified family relationships, and the ongoing challenge of balancing the needs of each family member. Families enter a new world of professionals and services that may cause them to feel dependent for information, care, and developmental and educational interventions.

Familiar interactions with school systems often become transformed by the unique procedures of special education. In the midst of the disequilibrium, parents struggle to meet their individual needs and maintain some degree of hope for a sometimes uncertain future. For many mothers and fathers, their experiences border on the "twilight zone" of parenting, as the familiar typical parenting world becomes one filled with often unfamiliar medical, educational, and legal requirements. Despite this, children with special needs are children first and have strengths and needs common to all children. Likewise, their parents are parents *first*, and they are subject to all the strengths and foibles of any parent. Although the term "handicapped" was once used to describe children with disabilities, it is no longer acceptable in the vocabulary of "people first" language. Above all, families of children with disabilities are not "handicapped families."

Different Beginnings

Each family of a child with special needs has its own special story. The timing, circumstance, severity, and implications for each member vary with each family and become part of the history family members share with scores of professionals. With the frequency and sophistication of prenatal testing, parents may be aware of a potential difficulty before their child is born. Other parents learn at birth, or shortly thereafter, of a condition that threatens the expectation of a "normal" baby. Children with special needs may be born with a medical, physical, or developmental difficulty stemming from identifiable causes, such as prematurity, delivery complications, genetic deviations, intrauterine trauma, or prenatal exposure to substances (such as alcohol, drugs, or environmental toxins) that cause medical or developmental problems. Some children develop special needs as the result of a postnatal illness, injury, or environmental influence, such as lead poisoning. Chronic illnesses, diseases, or medical conditions also require some children to receive special services or programs.

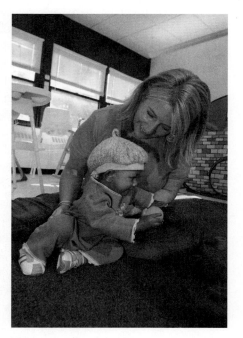

Early intervention can help children reach their potential. *Courtesy of ECE Photo Library.*

Several factors of our modern society have had a dramatic impact on special education. Sophisticated medical technology has allowed more infants who are premature, are at risk, or have severe disabilities to survive than in any other time in history. More babies are being born to mothers who have exposed them to drugs prenatally, and those babies often have disabilities. There has been an increase in the number of children diagnosed with disabilities, particularly those within the spectrum of pervasive developmental disorders, which includes autism. Other conditions, such as **attention deficit hyperactivity disorder (ADHD),** can impact a child's capacity to learn. These types of disabilities have become increasingly common in classrooms nationwide.

Parental Awareness of Early Disability

For many children, especially those with developmental delays, it is not always possible to determine the source or the long-term impact of the difficulty. Consequently, many parents' questions have answers that are hidden in the future. With so many potential origins and the variability in determining when or if a child's delay qualifies him or her for special services, parents may have limited awareness of a child's need for services. Parents may be unaware that children developing normally demonstrate particular skills at certain ages, or they may dismiss slow development (with speech and motor skills, for example) as a familial characteristic: "His Dad didn't talk until he was almost 3 years old, and neither did his cousin." In order to identify children who can benefit from special services and heighten public awareness of early intervention, an initiative called **Child Find** has been implemented throughout the country. Although it may have a different name locally, these efforts are mandated by federal law and require local educational agencies to advertise the availability of infant, toddler, and preschool developmental screenings and programs. Through these efforts, parents in large and small communities may become more sensitive to the ongoing development of their young children.

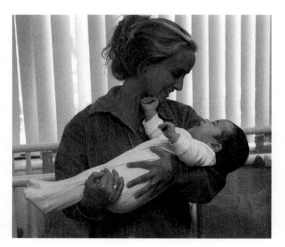

Parents may miss a developmental delay in their child because they are unaware of the typical ages at which children demonstrate particular skills. *Courtesy of ECE Photo Library.*

FAMILY INVOLVEMENT PROTECTED BY LAW

Each child with special needs is unique. A single diagnosis or the identification of a disability does not define a child's potential for development or the need for specific services or programs. There is a multifaceted spectrum of qualities to the concept of special needs. Whether it be cerebral palsy, mental retardation, hearing impairment, or **spina bifida,** there is no one prognosis or program placement. Specific programs are required to be individualized for each child, and, in early intervention, for the family's needs and abilities as well. When special education programming is needed, the rights of parents and those of the child are ensured by federal laws.

Historical Milestones of Parental Involvement in Special Education

Since the 1900s, there has been a dramatic and radical progression of philosophical changes toward involving children with special needs and their families. Although some states had visionary programs in place early on, until 1950 many parents who had children with developmental delays (if the children survived their early health crises) were encouraged to relinquish their roles as caregivers and have their children raised in institutions. In the 1950s and 1960s, more parents were encouraged to *not* institutionalize their children, because it was more commonly accepted that these children could learn and did deserve a right to enhanced educational opportunities. The National Association for Retarded Citizens was formed during this decade, and it began exerting pressure on the government to include children with special needs in educational policy decisions. It also increased support for research and training in special education. Parents were encouraged to help as "teacher" or "therapist" with their child's program, and training programs focused on helping them understand those roles. There also was a heightened interest in helping parents deal effectively with their feelings of grief that resulted from having a child with a disability. In 1968, the Handicapped Children's Early Education Program (HCEEP) began. HCEEP was a federally sponsored initiative to develop innovative models of early intervention and increase the availability of services. Parent involvement, a requirement for receiving one of the grants, was believed to improve the child's development. In this way, federal policy preceded the widespread practice of parent involvement in children's education.

The 1970s Usher in an Era of Change

The federal policy for HCEEP programs laid the foundation for the importance of parent involvement and the perception during the 1970s that parents should have knowledge of their child's disability, receive emotional support, and develop skills to cope with the demands of daily life. Parent meetings were typically designed by professionals and were based on the professionals' impressions of parent needs. As research from the HCEEP pilot programs emerged, the positive results of parent involvement provided new impetus for change in educators' views of families. Before 1975, there were no federal laws protecting the rights of children with disabilities to receive an education, although some states provided limited special services under whatever provisions the state legislatures designed. Most special education services were provided by independent agencies or private schools.

In the mid-1970s, parents were expected to carry out intervention actions designed by professionals. During this time, parents of school-age children had been asking for more educational services in the public schools and more participation in their children's program plans, including the right to help make decisions about their children's education. Significant legal victories were won in the courts as parents battled the states for legal rights to public education.

Parent involvement ultimately led to a major victory in 1975 with the Education for All Handicapped Children Act, also known as Public Law 94-142. This marked a fundamental shift in the teacher's view of the family. Previously, teachers and other professionals were in control of educational planning; with PL 94-142, that role had to be shared with parents in public schools. PL 94-142 gave individuals with disabilities aged 3 to 21 years access to a free, appropriate public education (FAPE). Over the years, reauthorizations of the law and amendments have added rights for children with special needs from birth to 21 and their families to the basic provisions of PL 94-142. The law in the latest reauthorization (2004) requires the following:

- An **individualized educational program** (IEP) written according to the child's particular educational needs when special education or related services are required. This must include an assessment and reporting of the child's educational performance, a statement of annual goals and short-term instructional objectives, a statement of specific special education and related services to be provided and the extent the child will be able to participate in regular education, a date for initiating services and the anticipated duration of the services, and objective criteria and evaluation procedures for determining the effectiveness of the program.

- Parent consent for initial evaluation; placement in special education; and changes in placement, eligibility, goals, or services. Parental rights must be provided in the parents' native language. Parents are also to participate in the development, approval, and evaluation of their child's IEP as a member of the IEP team. Parents also can participate in their child's educational program by carrying over instruction and therapies at home.

- Services are to be provided in the **least restrictive environment** necessary to meet the child's educational needs. Regular education must be considered before more restrictive placements, and the child's program needs to be modified as necessary for his or her success.

- **Related services** that help a child benefit from special education can include speech, physical, and occupational therapy; audiology; psychological services; diagnostic medical services; assistive technology; school health and social work services; early identification; and transportation. Parents also may receive counseling and training as a related service.

- Legal disciplinary action when students have an IEP is detailed in law, affecting alternate placements or suspensions, the number of days allowed for the disciplinary action, and a required behavioral intervention plan.

- Families have the right to examine all relevant records relating to their children's identification, evaluation, placement, and education, and parents can request copies of records and may challenge the information they contain.

This law also assured that schools must provide opportunities for parents to consent to or object to their child's educational identification, classification, program, or placement. The procedures to contest any of these provisions are collectively called due process. Later amendments and reauthorizations changed the language from "Education of the Handicapped" to the Individuals With Disabilities Education Act (IDEA); assured the legal right that all children were to receive a public education, regardless of the severity of their disability, until age 21; mandated strict confidentiality requirements for student records and notices; required that regular education teachers be part of the IEP team; and required that IEP goals and objectives be aligned with the state learning standards.

Although it is not a special education law, the Vocational Rehabilitation Act, Section 504, of 1973 does continue to have special implications for children and families in district schools. Its original focus related to nondiscrimination toward individuals with disabilities in employment. In its broader context, children who qualify may receive special accommodations and modifications (such as utilizing computers or assistive technology, modifying written materials, having extra time for tests, or using note takers) in their regular educational program even if they are not eligible under special education. The **504 plan** is based upon specific, individual needs and allows some special provisions for a child's educational success. Behavior and individualized health plans for children with specific medical needs can be accommodated under a 504 plan. A child with ADHD, for example, might not be eligible for special education but may have a 504 plan to require needed behavioral accommodations, and the plan for a child with diabetes may require that he or she receive medications or special nutrition breaks at school.

In the mid- to late 1970s, a new philosophical concept of human development and home interaction prompted investigation into the complexities of working with families of children with special needs. Because of early intervention pilots and parent research reported by Dunst, Trivette, and Deal (1988), Turnbull and Turnbull (2000), and Bricker (1989), there was a dramatic increase in knowledge about family-focused programming. Studies examined the effects of "parent as first teacher," mother–child interactions, child abuse, and parent stress. These and other studies propelled early intervention services into law in the 1986 passage of the Education of the Handicapped Act Amendments (Part H of Public Law 99-457). The law required that early interventionists from all disciplines view families as both planners and recipients of services, and that infants and toddlers with developmental delays and their families became eligible for special education services. While this law mandated services for 3- to 5-year-olds with disabilities in all states, it also allowed special provisions for children from birth to age 3 and their families. Infants who showed developmental delays (as defined by the state) or had a diagnosed physical or mental condition that had a high probability of resulting in a developmental delay were assured of services through an **Individualized Family Service Plan (IFSP).** The IFSP process is built upon the philosophy that families are systems, and no one member (that is, the infant or toddler) can be helped unless all members are involved. Services were selected in collaboration with parents, and coordinated, interagency programs of early intervention services were established. Services for infants and toddlers can be received in natural environments such as the home, day care, or community in which children without disabilities participate.

The changes in special education law reinforced the expectation that the general education classroom be considered first, before more restrictive placements are considered. The IEP must include in detail the extent that a child will participate in regular education and substantiate accommodations or modifications to state and local assessments.

The new IDEA law of 2004 builds upon previous laws, especially the educational reforms of the No Child Left Behind Act. Children whose educational needs or deficiencies result from "a lack of appropriate instruction in reading" are exempt from special education. It changes the requirements for learning disability eligibility and requires that a process to determine if a child responds to a research-based intervention become part of the child's evaluation. The response to intervention requirement may significantly change how regular education goes about teaching and evaluating students. It authorizes whole-school approaches for early reading and behavioral interventions that are scientifically based in order to prevent students from being too easily classified into special education. Teachers are to be "highly qualified," just as they are according to NCLB. Parent participation is clarified by IDEA 2004, which imposes restrictions on parent complaints, mediations, and due process.

The Americans With Disabilities Act of 1990 addressed the needs of adults with disabilities but also had some interesting implications for children. This piece of legislation heightened public awareness of the segregation and discrimination against people with disabilities in our society. The assurances of "equality of opportunity and full participation" affect the acceptance of children with disabilities into child-care facilities and community programs, and the accessibility of public facilities and services in general. This created a new push for the concept of including children with disabilities in regular preschool and school-age programs. Parents who themselves have disabilities now have increased opportunities to more fully participate in their communities and in their children's education. They can, for example, visit schools that are more accessible for the physically disabled and have increased access to interpreters and special accommodations for enhancing communication.

Just as laws for regular education are reauthorized from time to time, special education laws are also revisited and modified. Families, educators, administrators, and researchers continually advocate for change by lobbying legislators and appearing before committees to keep special education issues part of the national political agenda. Consequently, this reauthorization process does not proceed into law on an exact timetable, and amendments are added periodically. After a federal law is voted upon and approved, each state's special education administration must then review the law and design and approve the changes according to that particular state's special education rules and regulations. The critical message is that these legal protections and rights were not given but were earned by parents and professionals advocating for children's needs within the educational systems and philosophies of their times. Their successes were the result of angry confrontations and legal battles in attempts to underscore the importance of positive communication and partnerships between the educational system and families of children with special needs. In many ways, the research, legal definitions, and family-centered programs of special education are leading parent involvement into the next century.

Additional information on special education law can be found in Bauer and Shea (2003); Smith, Gartin, Murdick, and Hilton (2006); Turnbull and Turnbull (2000); and at various Internet sites listed under Useful Websites.

A Greater Parental Voice in Advocacy

The existence of special education law is largely due to the persistent efforts of parents who desired a better education for their children. Like parents of children with special needs before them, parents today are finding their voices and questioning the policies and practices of all aspects of education that impact their children. This creates new and better opportunities to develop partnerships and collaborations that can greatly enhance outcomes for each child and family. Although not all parents of children with disabilities have or need a strong voice, the empowerment of parents to participate in all aspects of their child's program and life within the community may more strongly impact other groups within the school or program. Parents of infants with special needs are sometimes coming to schools with the message "My child will be in your program in two or three years. I know this may take time, so I'm telling you now that this is what I want for him." Often these parents are telling schools and communities, "I want my child to belong here." As a result, children with special needs are increasingly included in regular child care, community preschools, recreation programs, sports teams, and other activities. Empowering parents to fully participate can have the added benefit of broadening their advocacy for children with disabilities from the local community to state legislatures and to Congress. Occasionally and unfortunately, schools and community programs are not proactive in complying fully with the law. Families can be motivated to be advocates for their children and become local change makers.

Opportunities for Inclusion: Realizing a Dream

Child by child, case by case, the vision of belonging not only in the family but also in a regular class in the neighborhood school and community has become a reality for American children in special education. The practice of considering the only appropriate programs for children with special needs to be segregated programs has brought parents, professionals, legislators, state boards of education, and the public to question policies that exclude children with special needs from regular school programs. Although inclusion is not mentioned in federal law, it is an interpretation of least restrictive environment that refers to placing children with disabilities in the school facility where they would typically be placed were there no disability, with their age and grade peers, for the full day. With inclusion, educational services are provided in the general education classroom, to the maximum extent possible, with appropriate classroom supports, such as a personal assistant or assistive technology devices. State and federal policies increasingly encourage the placement of children with disabilities in inclusive settings in compliance with the least restrictive environment mandate and require documentation of this on the IEP.

This requirement has been the focus of much debate and confusion among educators and parents alike. Although the federal law has required placement in the least restrictive environment since 1975, school districts have tended to segregate children who have special needs into isolated classes, programs, or buildings. In some rural areas, children with special needs must be bused out of district to receive their education. Increasingly, parents have disputed this placement in the courts. Because of the least restrictive environment requirement, many teachers in programs and schools will have children with special needs in their classrooms for all or part of their program day.

Including children with special needs in regular classes has benefits for all children. *Courtesy of ECE Photo Library.*

The concept of inclusion has spread like wildfire across the country, igniting controversy at federal, state, and local levels. Within the education community, inclusion has had inconsistent support among special educators. Teachers of self-contained special education classrooms or resource programs are concerned for the educational outcomes of their students in another setting as well as for their own job security in a changing system of educational services. Confusion surrounds the logistical and financial aspects of inclusion. The history and tradition of special education, pride in the expertise of being a special educator, and loss of control as many children are placed outside the segregated classrooms have contributed to "turf issues" that often surface in the inclusion face-off. Placement in "regular classrooms" requires that the IEP be fulfilled—including the maintenance of special services, therapies, and other supports. The inclusion of some children may require additional personnel to assist with the child's special requirements. Regular educators may fear that children will be "dumped" in regular classrooms, causing undue disruption of learning in the class, and they may fear that there will not be enough time to meet the needs of all students and that students will suffer. Regular education teachers who have not been professionally trained to work with children with disabilities are concerned about their abilities to do so and about receiving support from the school system. Many teachers, already challenged by the high numbers of children in their classes and the intensity of needs within "regular" education today, may not feel educationally, emotionally, or sometimes philosophically equipped to work with children with special needs.

Professionals aren't alone in objecting to inclusion. Some parents of regular education students may fear inclusion because it may disrupt their children's learning. Many families of children with special needs believe that a specialized class setting or even a residential placement is the most appropriate educational setting for their child, and that without the specialized attention and program, their child would not make sufficient progress. These concerns can be aired and considered at the staffing and IEP meetings concerning a child's placement and program (LRP, 1994b; Rose & Smith, 1993; Smith, Gartin, Murdick, & Hilton, 2006; Wilmore, 1994–95).

Likewise, many families have had opportunities to voice concerns about the implementation of IDEA when testifying before the National Council on Disability. They have voiced objections that schools fail to inform parents of their rights, act only under the threat of due process, and exclude children with disabilities from the regular classroom because the schools are not ready to include them or believe it to be too costly. As consumers of the special education system, these parents were invited to share their stories and suggest improvements in the law and its implementation. Surfacing in their testimony was the need for additional funding for special education, teacher and parent training, requirements for adequate supports in inclusive placements, and a clarification that least restrictive environment begins with the regular classroom (LRP, 1994b). These families were influential advocates who prompted change. Those who follow in their example are continuing to change special education.

Proponents of inclusion have had success in destroying barriers that keep children apart. The law stipulates that all placement options must be considered, beginning with regular classroom placement and proceeding toward more restrictive placements. During conferences, parents and profes-sionals revisit the concept of least restrictive environment and decide together as partners the most appropriate placement for each child. Many districts have made a sincere effort to accommodate children in regular classrooms. They have a strong philosophical belief that children belong together, that curriculum and methods can be adapted for the individual needs of all students, that students and staff can be successful with sufficient supports and in-service, and that an active partnership with parents is a priority. Many state initiatives, such as Project CHOICES and Early CHOICES in Illinois, provide a continuum of supports in planning for and implementing inclusion in district programs. Parents, along with regular and special educators, community members, administrators, students, and board of education representatives, may form a task force to initiate steps toward system change. Typically, this group will obtain technical assistance, conduct staff development activities, hold informational meetings for all parents, conduct building and classroom inventories, review individual student placements, and determine and provide necessary supports and aids. Successful inclusion doesn't just happen—it requires planning to put the key elements into place. These elements include effective instructional strategies, accommodations and support systems for students, administrative support, family involvement, planning time, professional development, vision and attitudes that support the goals, and teamwork and relationship building (Project CHOICES/Early CHOICES, 2007).

Benefits for all children are enhanced when inclusion begins during early childhood. Children with disabilities are valued as children with skills and abilities and have a healthier self-esteem; learn and use social skills; attend a typical early childhood program with their age-peers and feel less isolation; expand their language and communication skills in typical early childhood contexts; become more independent and better able to work, live, and play in an integrated society; have fun; and learn from and make new friends. Research findings support that children with disabilities perform academically as well in inclusive classes as they do in segregated classes (Taylor, 2000). Children without disabilities make new friends; develop an acceptance of diversity and individuality; learn when and how to help others; grow up accepting people with disabilities as valuable members of society; and accept others as friends and coworkers regardless of labels, abilities, or disabilities. Professionals, parents, and the community at large learn that children are more alike than different, all children should be appreciated for their strengths and special gifts, acceptance springs from a positive and optimistic attitude, life situations are the best learning opportunities, and diversity and individuality of all kinds are to be celebrated (Institute for Educational Research, 1992; LRP, 1994a; Project CHOICES/Early CHOICES, 2007).

The collaborations that create the best integrated programs, as with every other programmatic collaboration, are both parent–professional partnerships and collaborations among professionals. These are based on a shared vision of the family's hopes for the child's future and what professionals can do to help make that dream a reality. Professionals with expertise in special education share their knowledge with the family and other professionals to facilitate the child's success in diverse situations, whether it is in toilet training or augmented communication. Likewise, parents can offer information to teachers and staff about techniques that work well at home or that expand the professional's understanding of their child's abilities.

Parents may be faced with new challenges because of the inclusive experience and may need increased support from professionals as a result. Parents whose children are in inclusive settings are often as apprehensive as the teacher about their care, progress, and well-being. They may feel uncomfortable having to explain their child's disability to more people and may fear that their child will not be appreciated as part of this new group. The opposition from other parents, teachers, and administrators, as well as the need to work in a wider circle of partnerships, may prompt parental stress. Parents may need to be more active in the classroom, attend more meetings, and choose which support services are worth advocating for and what can be compromised.

On the other hand, parents may feel more a part of the school community and participate more fully in events at the school, such as holiday programs and fundraisers. Inclusion means having more people with whom to problem solve and share ideas. New hopes for a child to live and work in the community as an adult may develop as children take their place with others in neighborhood schools. Frequently, parents may not need extraordinary encouragement to attend IEP meetings or be active in a group such as the PTA. Often these parents have a clear concept of parent involvement and what it means for them and their children.

Many parents believe that if their dream of having their children be a true part of the community is to come true, all children should be educated together. At a time of stressed finances within society, few, if any, educational programs are funded sufficiently. Inclusion is not an automatic reduction of services, or of costs, since many special services increase the cost of educating a child. Yet throughout the nation, children with disabilities are being successfully included in community programs and schools. Researchers have compiled documentation that further substantiates that children with disabilities make significant advances in integrated settings and that their peers benefit as well. Having reasonable and high expectations for all, accountability, and integration of best practices in teaching will facilitate inclusionary success. It will take time, increased funding, and ongoing professional education to develop widespread administrative supports for inclusive programs, enhance teacher skills in classroom intervention strategies, and, overall, increase teacher comfort with accepting a child with exceptionality. Despite the obstacles, parents across the country are finding placements for their children in community programs, regular preschools, and public schools. The vision has become reality. The issues of inclusion will continue to be debated and decided at school board meetings and in the legal arena. The real issues, stated by Arnold and Dodge (1994), are based in tradition, values, and beliefs. Parents and professionals are reshaping those three dimensions in hopes of helping extraordinary children lead ordinary lives.

CHALLENGES AND CONCERNS FOR FAMILIES OF CHILDREN WITH SPECIAL NEEDS: IMPLICATIONS FOR TEACHERS

With the age of inclusion upon us, teachers are more likely to have children with special needs in their classrooms. With its emphasis on individual educational goals, many teachers believe that to meet the needs of all students, every child would benefit from an IEP. Best practice in teaching is best practice for all children, with or without disabilities. The best instructional practices take the individual child's strengths and needs into account and modify or adapt to the child's abilities in order to encourage skill growth and development. Likewise, best practices in parent involvement are the same for all parents; however, teachers and other professionals need to become more aware of the unique challenges and issues confronting the parents of these special children.

Confidentiality

Part of the ethical considerations in teaching all children is the matter of confidentiality. In working with children with special needs, it is critical for all who work with a child to maintain a strict personal watch on what is shared. Within the service team, information about the child's progress or situations that impact learning may need to be shared. Disclosing medical concerns, such as HIV or other conditions, may be subject to district or program policy for confidentiality. Parents may review school records about their child and question anything they find there. The informal guidelines are perhaps more difficult to monitor. Sensitive information about the family or child should have restricted access. This means conversations about children or families should be kept private as a matter of course and should not occur in the staff room. Not all staff members need to have sensitive information available to them. Care should be taken by all not to discuss specific situations or individuals by name at home or in public.

The Family Educational Rights and Privacy Act (FERPA) and the confidentiality stipulations of IDEA require protection for all paper and computerized records and that public schools have written policies in place regarding the release of student records. Parents have access to their child's school records, but they do not have access to personal notes about the child written by teachers or other school personnel, security police records, or the personnel records of school employees. Violations are considered quite serious, as they could mean jeopardized federal funding (Smith, Gartin, Murdick, & Hilton, 2006).

If parents do not trust teachers and staff to maintain confidentiality about personal information they share about their child, their family, or what they hear from the staff about other families, a significant gap in the home–school relationship occurs—one that may never be repaired.

Later Identification of a Suspected Disability

Not all disabilities or special education needs are identified early in childhood; some, such as ADHD, learning disabilities, or social-emotional disorders become evident as a child's academic and social situations become more challenging. Only then do differences move from suspicions to fact. Some disabilities, however, can occur suddenly during childhood, transforming the life of a typical child. Traumatic brain injury and subsequent variable disabilities (speech, motor, self-help, memory, learning, attention, seizure, etc.) for example, can occur as a result of an accident or other trauma.

Discovering that a child has special needs is often a confusing and painful process for parents, but sometimes they are relieved that their concerns can be identified with a specific name. Teachers in the regular classroom may be the first to notice the characteristics of a learning disability. In the case of **learning disorders or disabilities,** the indicators can be difficult to exactly pinpoint, because they can mimic other situations, such as a minor developmental delay, attention issues, or environmental effects. These subtleties can make it difficult for parents to know if they are "normal differences" or not. During early childhood, it is difficult to differentiate between a healthy, active child and a child with hyperactivity, especially with a first child. Diagnosis begins with questions, such as "Will the clumsiness be outgrown or does the child have a motor delay?" "Is the child's difficulty in listening and following directions distraction or disability?" It may take parents and teachers working together to complete the puzzle and determine what is in the picture.

Learning disabilities, however, are often not identified until the elementary years. This brief treatment of the subject highlights the complexities of this disorder and the complications in communicating with parents. Children with learning disabilities often have clusters of difficulties that contribute to low achievement. These problems may lie in the brain's dysfunction, creating a gap between what a child can do and what he or she is expected to be able to do, despite the child's concerted efforts. Despite being intelligent and knowing a great deal, the child may still have difficulty reading and writing. Sometimes, it may be a challenge to distinguish between a child who won't do something and one who can't do something. Sometimes, behaviors that appear to be problematic are actually clues that the child is having real difficulty. A child may withdraw from a task or say, "I hate reading!" when the area is difficult for them (Smith, 2002).

In learning disabilities or ADHD, a diagnosis only helps to some extent. Parents may have noticed problems at home or in community situations.

Mothers are often the first to recognize this difficulty. Treatment options or learning strategies vary and professionals may not agree. Parents may get conflicting information from the media as well. Together, parent and teacher become detectives, filtering clues and collecting evidence of what works, what doesn't, and how to tell when a child has reached his or her limit. Parental problem solving, like that in the classroom, requires parents to observe, analyze, and recognize their children's strengths, interests, and areas of difficulty, and develop plans for managing behaviors and supporting learning. If there are other siblings, the behavior issues can affect the entire family to a greater degree than what is typical. Because behaviors are unpredictable, inconsistent, and often quite noticeable to others, children with these challenges can be a family irritant. Children with learning disabilities or ADHD tend to be disorganized, easily distracted, and impulsive. Routine tasks like getting dressed or eating can cause explosions from the child, parent, or sibling. Sometimes, children do not understand or remember instructions; when corrected, they may get upset, fall apart, strike out, or withdraw. Since they have immature emotional development, they tend to personalize situations or communication that has nothing to do with them. If people are laughing, a child may be convinced that he or she is being laughed at and become upset. Significant mood swings and symptoms of depression are common. The constant challenges and unpredictability of the classroom and family life can make adults feel incompetent with these children. Teachers may need to help bolster parents' sense of confidence and competence in parenting a child with a disability. Teachers also may benefit from a supportive colleague or administrator, as progress can be slow, erratic, and discouraging. Teachers are well advised to keep aware of new teaching strategies and brain research to enhance their best instructional practices. Valuable print and media resources provide information that supports family and teachers alike.

Conferencing with Families: Discussing Suspicions

A teacher should utilize all tools to successful conferences discussed in Chapter 9; however, the prospect of discussing special concerns about a child's development and academic progress for the first time can be especially challenging. How do teachers broach the possibility that a child may have very serious learning difficulties and may need special education services?

Abbott and Gold (1991) include some suggestions for this meeting. Analyze the learning environment and teaching strategies that have been used. Is there anything that is working, or are there things that could be modified? Invite an administrator or other professional to observe the child and his or her behaviors. This can provide valuable information that, as the leader of instruction, the teacher may miss. Obtain information from the administrator about potential referral procedures or paperwork. Intensify anecdotal note taking and begin a portfolio of the child's work that provides clues to a difficulty, including the date and other observations. As you begin to suspect specific problems, bring the parents into the communication partnership. Contact the family on an informal basis to determine if they have noticed specific behaviors at home or if they have concerns similar to those of the teacher. Notify them of what strategies are being tried to address the concerns. Ask what the child has shared with them about the program or school recently and suggest a few ways they can specifically help their child at home. In addition, some screening tests can be administered in the classroom to provide more data. If concerns persist, the teacher needs to arrange a conference.

If possible, make contact in person or by telephone to set up the meeting. As the family has already been a part of the team in collecting information from home and recognize the teacher's concerns, the nature of the meeting may be clear. Invite the parents to a meeting to compare notes and determine how to continue. Explain that there are still some concerns and that meeting in person would be helpful. If there are two parents, try to arrange it so both of them can meet. Arrange the environment and prepare the information that is to be shared with care and sensitivity. Privacy, comfort, and an informal seating arrangement are important. Organize appropriate materials from the child's portfolio and his or her recent work. Review the anecdotal notes for supportive comments and clues. List specific modifications that have been used in attempts to help the child learn more effectively. Include the names of other professionals who may have been of assistance. Be prepared to help with the next step in providing information about resources they can use, in the program or school, in the community, or on the Internet.

Since the parents may be anxious about the meeting, carefully prepare how the conversation will begin. Carefully phrased questions may encourage parental input. Ask how the child has been doing at home and if there have been any changes in behavior, attention, skill development, homework interest, or other areas. How does this child compare with siblings or with other children of the same age? Talk about what the parents perceive the situation to be. Families usually know their children very well and may provide ideas on how to help them, but they may also corroborate the teacher's concerns. Keep the conversation simple and jargon free. Use reflective listening and clarify what you hear them saying. Phrase the suggestion to get additional testing in a basic manner: "Ms. Johnson, we seem to agree (or not agree) that Harry is showing delays, but I think we ought to get the help of some experts. I feel it is important that Harry be seen by someone who can assess his performance and tell us if there is a real problem, so we all can better help Harry." At this point there is no need to refer to special education or indicate a diagnosis. That is not the teacher's role at this meeting.

Be alert to parental verbal and nonverbal cues and body language as they share reactions or question. Panic or anxiety is common. A box of tissues nearby may be a consideration. Allow parents to express their feelings and thoughts and respect them. Assure them that there is no guarantee about the results of the assessment, only that there are concerns that need to be checked out further, and that it is in the best interest of the child to find out. Depending on the school or program, referral procedures may differ. Depending on the situation, a medical doctor, school psychologist, or social worker may be involved in the next steps. IDEA requires that a pre-assessment conference be held with the parents to inform them of what information is to be collected, why, and how it will be done. In schools, typically the psychologist arranges these meetings.

Occasionally, despite best intentions, the conversation may get a little heated. In this situation, the teacher may try the following suggestions from Boutte, Keepler, Tyler, and Terry (1992), Gorman (2004), and Kroth (1985). In a challenging meeting situation, remember these tactics:

- Be professional, pleasant, and welcoming. Provide refreshments.
- Be kind, respectful, and nonjudgmental.
- Remain calm and in control of your emotions. If parents' voices get louder, speak more softly.
- Listen. Maintain good eye contact and open body posture. Observe their nonverbal cues.
- Smile and use affirming language whenever possible.
- Use language the parents understand. Be specific on what you have observed about the child's difficulties and what interventions have been attempted.
- Write down parental concerns.
- Ask what else is bothering parents and let them exhaust their list of complaints.
- Ask them to clarify any comments that are too general.
- Show them your list and ask if it is complete.
- Ask them if they have suggestions for solving any of the problems they've listed. Brainstorm multiple solutions.
- Write down the suggestions.
- Make optimistic, realistic statements about problem solving.
- Select together the best options and agree on a next step or plan of action.
- Recognize positive parental attitudes and strengths. Provide positive feedback.

- Allow adequate time for responses.
- Stop the conversation for a break if necessary. Be prepared to get parents a drink of water to provide some time to rethink and regroup.
- If you suspect there could be a heated discussion or are concerned about safety, ask that another staff member join you, check in, or stop by to see you. Prearrange a cue word or phrase to indicate that you need assistance. Keep your door open or meet in a room near other staff members.
- If parents confront you with statements like "This is ridiculous. I can't believe this is happening," say, "I agree." Those two words can diffuse angry conversation.

When faced with a challenging situation, don't:

- Speak too quickly or loudly.
- Interrupt or dominate the conversation.
- Argue or raise your voice.
- Become defensive or angry.
- Promise things that are not possible.
- Own a problem that belongs to others.
- Deny or minimize the problem or parental concerns.

Parental Responses

How a child with a disability affects a family has historically been characterized in literature in many ways. During the 1800s and early 1900s, medical and educational professionals put the moral blame for childhood disability upon the parents. During the 19th century, reform schools, asylums, and residential schools for specific disabilities appeared to separate the child from the parents. From roughly 1920 until 1960, attention shifted to how children with disabilities damaged their birth families. Attitudes (such as guilt, denial, anger, and grief) or behaviors (role disruption, marital difficulties, and social isolation) assured researchers that there was parental damage due to the child's disability. Parental responses were explained by identifying the neurotic paths families followed. If parents were displeased with the doctor or teachers, it was displaced anger about their child who was not typical. If parents were too passive, it was due to their feelings of guilt or denial. During the 1960s and 1970s, some family research reflected a cause-and-effect connection between children with disabilities and their "damaged" families. The fact that there were few or virtually no supportive services or educational options for children with disabilities and their families was ignored.

Chronic sorrow became the popular description for the parental response to disability, since this was an understandable reaction to an unexpected and unwanted situation (Powers, 1993; Taylor, 2000). Readers should realize that studies conducted prior to 1980 were done before public education for children with disabilities was in place and before inclusion, family supports, and early intervention systems. These studies reflect the times in which they were done (Ferguson, 2002).

More recently, recognizing family stresses, coping, and resilience have been the focus of research. Researchers have recognized that many families cope effectively and positively with the experiences related to parenting a child with a disability. Family systems and the understanding of family life stages have targeted supports as a critical factor. Research has shown that these families have patterns of adjustment and well being similar to those of families with typically developing children. In fact, growing research supports positive outcomes for families who have children with disabilities. They include greater coping skills, family cohesiveness, spiritual growth, shared values, shared parenting roles, and better communication. Individual differences among families create the foundation to describe parent reactions to disability.

In 1969, Elizabeth Kubler-Ross proposed a four-stage description of the bereavement process for acceptance of life-threatening illnesses or death. Those four stages of mourning (denial, anger, depression, and acceptance) have also traditionally been applied to parental reactions to a child's disability. Medical professionals, counselors, and educators have taught parents these stages and encouraged them to categorize their emotions in relation to them. Teachers might be heard them to say, "They are in denial and can't accept that their child has a disability." According to Ulrich and Bauer (2003), this progression has not been supported by research. Many parents and educators also consider this simplistic emotional diagnosis to be condescending and patronizing, and one that results in a situation that hinders real communication and involvement. Families and members of parent organizations have shared that not all parents experience these stages. Through books and media, some have tried to help professionals and others better understand what they are experiencing.

If parental response is not neatly labeled by the four stages of grief, how can parental experiences be understood? Like all family situations, the identification of a child's disability can be viewed within the family system and the family life cycle. This changes the focus from a professional-centered model to a family-centered one. Instead of the "grief and tragedy" paradigm taught for so many years, the focus on the family affirms family strengths.

During these adjustments, families may indeed face a myriad of emotions: disbelief, shock, sorrow, self-pity, anger, irritability, denial, envy, self-recrimination, guilt, shame, fear, uncertainty, anxiety, depression, apathy, acknowledgment, and hope. All of them are common, sometimes recurring responses in adjusting to being a family with unique needs. Buscaglia (1983) and Powers (1993) both identify emotions that confront parents of children with disabilities as they experience the loss of their "original" child, whether that was the "perfect" baby or the child they knew "before." Initially, parents take in and evaluate what is happening to their child, themselves, and the rest of the family. Next, they search for answers from programs, professionals, and service providers to help them adjust to a different life with their child. They also develop an awareness of making some sense of the life events—at least in the interim.

In the family-focused view, each individual has his or her own level of awareness of the disability. This awareness is affected by feelings about the issues of disability; personal history; transformational experiences, knowledge, and learning about the issues; and the context or family framework created by personal culture and interactions with the world. The learning and growth process for parents and children includes transitional moments that prompt movement to a different level of truth or awareness. Individually, parents may be at different levels of awareness concerning their child, which may cause friction in their relationship. According to Ulrich and Bauer (2003), parents and professionals may have different opinions based upon their individual level of awareness. These differences can create tension and miscommunication about what is best for the child. Teachers can use the family-centered model to better understand the process that parents experience. Self-knowledge among all parties is important. Be alert for transformational experiences, and acknowledge their importance for parents and professionals to discover a shared meaning to build trust and communication. This family-focused perspective has four key levels of understanding disability that can help educators and families better recognize the complex emotions and motivations family members experience. Although the levels may occur sequentially over time, it is common for emotions and behaviors to fluctuate between levels depending on the issue or concern.

Level 1: A Lack of Awareness.
Parents who have little information about disabilities or useful vocabulary to describe their child's difficulties may pick up terms from the media or believe the teacher is incompetent or just wrong. They may explain away behavior with phrases like "He's just a boy" or "That is how my sister was at that age." In the grieving theory, parents would be labeled as "in denial," whereas the parent may not be denying the presence of a problem. Instead, they may be operating out of a lack of information or fear of what it could mean. They also may be quite content to be uninformed, so the apparent truth remains that nothing is wrong. They may blame the teachers, programs, or school for poor instruction. Extended family may criticize parents for not being strict enough. A transformational experience usually prompts the parents into level two and a deeper level of awareness. For parents of two daughters, such an experience occurred when the younger daughter began to

develop reading readiness and motor skills that surpassed the older child's abilities and interest in school.

Level 2: Recognition of a Disability.

Parents may acknowledge that there is a problem but that it can be fixed by professionals. They may believe that educational specialists can fix learning problems just as a doctor can treat an illness. Parents may seek out specialists, extensively research their child's diagnosis or educational eligibility for services, or insist that a particular service or program be included in their child's IEP. Their child now becomes "a special child" for whom "special services" are required. As they advocate for their child, parents may appear confrontational and insistent upon knowing exactly what professionals are planning to do to help. The transformational experience frequently has to do with the family's quality of life. Parents have recognized that with all the intensive focus on one child, their other children are being overlooked. They have no time for each other, and they may ask, "What are we doing? Do we want to live like this?"

Level 3: Minimizing the Differences and Normalizing the Child's Life.

At this point, parents want their child to fit in with his or her classmates and siblings and just do "normal" things. Parents may even request a reduction of services in favor of more typical school experiences. The transformational experiences may be related to what their child can or cannot do or to the child's move to a different educational environment or level.

Level 4: Realizing the Child Needs Support and Has Individual Opinions on How Needs Should Be Met.

Disability is a difference that comes with both challenges and benefits. For the child with a disability, celebrating diversity includes learning about oneself as well as about the disability. Professionals want to prepare the student to be a self-advocate. Talking with parents about dreams for their child becomes a discussion of reframing dreams into realities.

According to Powers (1993), there is no typical length of time for working through the feelings accompanying a disability, just as there is no predetermined pattern for all parents. There will be as great a diversity for acceptance as there are other diversities among families. Characteristics of a child's disability also impact the family's reaction to the exceptionality. The nature of the exceptionality, the severity, the time of onset, and the demands the child's needs place upon the family are all factors to consider in understanding the family's response (Seltzer, Greenberg, Floyd, Pettee, & Hong, 2001; Turnbull & Turnbull, 2000). Educators should remember that we serve children with special needs who live in families with unique and changing special needs as well.

Whether or not the disability is visible, whether it has a label of mild, moderate, or severe, or whether or not a precise diagnosis has been made, parents of children with special needs face unique emotional issues. Regardless of when parents learn of their child's condition or disability, the issues of acceptance of the disability are faced repeatedly as the child arrives at typical developmental milestones: the ages for walking, talking, starting kindergarten, beginning to read or ride a bike, getting a driver's license, going to a first dance, graduating, beginning a career or college, and so on.

For some families, there are increased tensions that may magnify any marital discord and feelings of inadequacy. Spouses and siblings alike may feel rejected or abandoned. Some statistics indicate that the divorce rate is higher when there is a child with a disability in the family (Alper, Schloss, & Schloss, 1994). Today, there are more single mothers parenting alone and a greater chance of blended families when there is a remarriage. Some children with special needs are in foster placements or adoptive families. There has been an increase in the number of children, many with medical or psychological problems, who do not find a lasting placement. Media attention has been drawn to the "boarder babies" left in hospitals by mothers incapable of assuming their care. These children, often HIV positive or substance exposed, are posing new challenges to the child welfare and educational systems. There are new concerns among social service providers that there will be a resurgence of residential placements, such as orphanages, for these and other hard-to-place children. In some districts, the special educational needs and behavioral concerns typical in this group of children have required rethinking classrooms and services.

Many families with children with special needs must carefully consider issues that are unique either in their nature or the timing of when they must be addressed. One of these issues is the guardianship and the support many children will inevitably need when they reach adulthood. Parents of young children may be troubled by these and similar concerns during their child's infancy, although the need for these types of supports is years into the future. These premature stressors are common to some parents of children with disabilities. Legal provisions for the children must span the lifetime of both the parents and the children.

Family Response Affects Involvement

It can be very valuable for the teacher to be aware of the various responses that have been identified, as this awareness opens new avenues of understanding in family–teacher communication. Regardless of which characteristics parents display, it is critical that the teacher recognize that each parent's response progression will be uniquely individual and impacted by adult developmental stages and life events that do not necessarily relate to the child. It is important for the teacher to understand and perhaps assist parents in understanding their feelings in regard to their child. These multiple, complex feelings can change character and intensity in response to the often turbulent internal emotions and external experiences parents encounter. Self-doubt, embarrassment, social isolation, fears, frustration, and confusion may thrust parents into periods of uninvolvement with the school or program. Because these periods may include the identification or diagnosis of a particular condition or disability, or present concerns of a potential difficulty, it is important for professionals to recognize that some families will need particular support and understanding.

Emotional Stress

Caring for any child can challenge the energy and patience of most adults. Families of children who have any type of special need, whether it be medical, physical, developmental, or social-emotional, all live with the stress and frustration of meeting the needs of one child while balancing (or compromising) the needs of the rest of the family. Many children with special needs do not develop on a typical schedule. Spoon-feeding a 5-year-old with swallowing difficulties, diapering a 10-year-old, or communicating with a nonverbal preschooler can cause endless modifications to a typical family routine. Sometimes the stress and fatigue of continuous care and the occasional crisis present unhealthy patterns for parents. They may not get enough sleep, or they may not have enough time for leisure activities or even to attend to personal needs.

Teachers should be aware of and be sensitive to parents' unmet needs and allow parents to utilize the child's program for respite time if necessary. And, when parents sometime resist the "homework" assignments given by teachers and therapists, teachers should understand that it may not be out of a lack of concern for the child's development. Parents of children with special needs are sometimes frustrated by the constant expectation to work with the child, instead of having the freedom to sometimes be "just" the mommy or daddy. The school program can be a unique support system for families beyond the educational realm.

Tragically, there is evidence that children with disabilities are more likely to be the target of family abuse (Allen, 1992). Infants and preschoolers with developmental disabilities may behave in ways that are upsetting to parents. Babies who have a high pitched, inconsolable crying pattern try the nerves of sleep-deprived parents. With some disabilities, and especially for infants prenatally exposed to drugs, this pattern of behavior is frequently coupled with other behaviors, such as rigidity, hypersensitivity, and sleep and feeding problems. Babies who have a difficult time retaining feedings may become failure-to-thrive or sick infants with caregivers who are distressed beyond their ability to cope. A normal child living in a stressful environment with an abuse-prone parent can become disabled because of injury from abuse. Without adequate supports, the family of a child with disabilities may incur enough stress to tempt some parents to become abusive. Adequate emotional support systems are a key factor for any family's well-being, but they are especially important for families of children with disabilities (Allen, 1992).

Social Isolation

Social isolation is a frequent concern of families with children who have special needs. Often the caretakers of children with medical or behavioral needs must have some special training, which may make respite care difficult to locate. Parents may be unwilling to entrust a young child with another person, yet, as the child grows and develops, this possessive sense of responsibility may ease, unveiling the obstacle of locating supplementary care. Child-care centers and even family members are sometimes reluctant to care for these children. Parents of children with disabilities also face isolation when they bring their children with them into the community. It can be difficult to face the stares or awkward questions from strangers and even family members. Restaurants, stores, and playgrounds can present emotional "tests" for the child and parent alike, not only for families of children with obvious disabilities but for those of children who have emotional or behavioral disabilities as well. Some disabilities are not immediately noticeable but can manifest in unexpected confrontations, loud emotional outbursts, and physical aggression in public, causing parental distress and embarrassment. Autism, attention deficit, developmental delays, or similar conditions can make it hard for the family to go out in public. Consequently, parents may limit their visibility in the community and shelter the child (and themselves) from the outside world.

When a child has limiting physical abilities, transportation can create extraordinary stress for the family once the child grows too large for his or her caregiver to physically carry him or her. Few older homes are wheelchair accessible inside and out. In addition to the more obvious ramps and door widths, furniture, fixtures, and other household features may need to be adapted as the child grows. Mobility issues in the home can initiate unanticipated remodeling or relocation for accessible housing. Vehicles adapted for wheelchair transport that allow a more typical family mobility style are extremely expensive. Consequently, families may alter their lifestyle and choices of activities in a way that limits participation by the whole family. Going to the movies or out to eat in a restaurant as a family, for example, may not be possible. If families must reduce their involvement in typical community and life experiences and are unable to overcome the restrictions, family morale and sibling experiences are likely to be affected.

Family acceptance of the child's disability mediates this issue but can test the tolerance of friends and associates. Families of children with disabilities are sometimes shunned or unintentionally ostracized in a neighborhood or community. Programs and schools, therefore, can offer a harbor of acceptance and understanding for the family as well as the child. Teachers can be sensitive to the need to be accepted by encouraging family involvement that includes social events and parent-to-parent contacts that meet the need for parental support and understanding in a special way (Powers, 1993).

Special Challenges Related to Medical and Physical Disabilities

Frequently the term "special needs" conjures up the image of a child who has a specific physical problem or one who requires special medical care. When a child is physically or medically disabled, there is the unique challenge of securing and adjusting to the medical recommendations for treatment. Although some conditions include anticipated surgeries (such as a child with Down syndrome who requires cardiac surgery, or the child with spina bifida who requires surgery to close the exposed section of spine or place a shunt to drain fluid from the brain), some encounters with the medical establishment are few and relatively minor. There also are children who need continual monitoring, as their condition may change dramatically from healthy to critical in a matter of minutes. The families of medically fragile children must adjust to new lifestyles that include and sometimes revolve around the particular medical needs of the child. Frequent medical appointments, endless hours in waiting rooms, extended travel and stays in distant cities to be seen by specialists, therapy sessions, hospitalizations, and surgeries all tax the physical, financial, and emotional reserves of the family.

Concerns about time, money, insurance, transportation, and the stress of home responsibilities and relationships place additional strain upon parents already anxious about the well-being of their child. Some parents of medically involved children have categorized their life in two ways: their routine while the child is hospitalized and their routine when the child is home again. Sometimes a child's hospitalization requires one parent to temporarily live near the medical facility and delegate home responsibilities and care of siblings to the other parent or support persons. These crisis periods may be concentrated during the early childhood years, when particular procedures are recommended for some conditions, or may be ongoing during childhood, as in the case of spina bifida and cancers like leukemia. When medically involved children are not hospitalized, they may require additional medical attention, medicines, special foods, or specialized equipment, care, or procedures that dramatically alter the home routine. Other children may be susceptible to chronic illnesses and may not be able to attend school regularly.

It is important for teachers to be flexible and understanding when the child is absent frequently or for long periods of time. Parents of these children may feel stressed by the past, present, or anticipated medical procedures or illnesses. Friendly contact from the teachers during these absences just to keep in touch and inquire how the child and the family are doing is typically appreciated. Teachers often visit their hospitalized students if it is possible and appropriate. Children with physical disabilities, including hearing and visual impairments, may require special training for skills such as signing or mobility, which usually involves family training as well. Life does go on, and both children and families often demonstrate remarkable resilience.

Apprehension over Program Transitions

Families that have built a relationship with the service team of the early intervention program will lose that support to a large degree when the child moves into another program. Transitions for children from preschool to kindergarten or for older children to middle school or junior high are stressful for children and families (Rosenkoetter, Hains, & Fowler, 1994). Concerns include changes in the focus of services (family to child), the types and location of services (home to program or school), eligibility and labeling, and personnel. Older children not only have new environments, transportation, therapists, teachers, and schoolmates but perhaps new eligibilities and service options as well. Families of children with special needs will continue to bring with them the complexities and challenges of their lives. Educators can continue to help families and children grow together, maintain focus on the vision of programs and schools by meeting each other's needs, and develop the skills and sensitivities the process demands.

New Opportunities via Technological Advances

Computers, microprocessors, and other electronic advances have brought many changes to the world of special education. Communicative and assistive devices, together with medical advances, have permitted many children and adults with special needs to more fully participate in life. Assistive technology can refer to low-technology adaptations (such as using a sipper top on a cup or using a padded support or footrest) or high-technology electronic devices (such as a portable computer with a speech synthesizer). Depending on a child's abilities and needs, the child will be evaluated by a team often composed of an occupational therapist, a physical therapist, a speech language pathologist, and/ or a specialist in assistive technology. This assessment will include reviewing medical and educational records and rating the child's language and cognitive abilities as well as skills in the sensory areas of motor, vision, and hearing. If a child will be using a computer or other electronic device, the team will carefully evaluate the child's range of motion, pointing accuracy, speed of pointing, and other response skills. Parents are often consulted in the assessment.

Assistive technology has enabled more children with special needs to be included in classrooms with their peers. *Courtesy of ECE Photo Library.*

Undoubtedly, computers and electronic technology have offered great promise to a great number of children. Many regular computers can be adapted with special internal cards or boards, adapted screens, or alternative keyboards. An assortment of internal adaptations permits the use of particular programs or peripherals. The variety of adapted touch screens or tablets and alternative keyboards permit children with physical limitations to utilize the attractive software programs available for young children as well as adapted programs. Alternative keyboards can be used instead of a mouse or joystick and may have specialized keys or switches to replace or supplement the standard microcomputer keyboard. Keys may be enlarged, have alternative stickers, or regulate particular keyboard functions. With special finger access software, a child can control the regular keyboard with a single finger, pointing device, or mouthstick. High-tech communication aids are basically computers with dedicated programs and special capabilities like synthesized speech. These utilize any number of pictographs, symbols, letters, or words to actualize prestored messages or individual words. Many toys can be adapted with activating switches (some actuated by an eye glance or a puff of air into a tube) to stimulate the attention and reinforce the attempts of young children to interact with their environment. Technological advances are offering increased opportunities to develop every child's potential. However, some of these high-tech aids are expensive, and locating sufficient funding for them may be a challenge. This, too, may be a focus of the family–teacher partnership.

Not all assistive technology involves such complex materials. Adaptives also include wheelchairs and **picture communication boards.** Parents and teachers can often use low-tech modifications to adapt regular toys to facilitate play and learning for children with disabilities. These adaptations may be physical supports that utilize strategies to stabilize materials to allow the child to play independently. Children with a limited grasp can use wristbands with toys attached to them or wear gloves with Velcro or magnets attached to them to assist the child in holding on to playthings. Play boards or toy bars can be used to affix toys to a surface so the toys won't move or fall off. Wheelchair trays can be lined with a special tacky-surfaced mat or have Velcro strips attached so that toys with Velcro at their base (such as toy dishes, dolls, or other smaller toys) can be more stable. Parts such as handles, knobs, or textured surfaces can be added to toys to make them more accessible. Markers, paintbrushes, and spoons can have foam-padded sleeves attached to the handle to make them larger and thereby promote an easier grasp. Larger toys and toys with clear, familiar features can be selected to enhance visual perception. Together, teachers and parents can create playthings and tools that allow children to more fully experience the world around them.

A FAMILY SYSTEMS PERSPECTIVE

The concept of family systems is crucial to understanding and effectively working with families with children who have special needs. The family is a unique system in which its members establish roles and relationships and grow, develop, and change in interaction with one another. Any change, like a wind gust upon a hanging mobile, will impact both its individual members and the family as a whole. Family systems have rules for affection, communication, and power as well as for ways of dealing with stress and problems. A child with a disability influences many aspects of the family system, from economics to social relationships to interpersonal relationships between the parents and other children. Understanding the family system framework requires an analysis of the family resources, family interactions, family functions, and the stage of family development.

The family itself is its single best resource. The characteristics of the exceptionality (age of child, sex, and type and severity of disability or condition) will prompt a different response from each parent. Other considerations, like the structural and personal characteristics of the family members, number of parents, ages, maturity levels, parenting and coping styles, physical and emotional health of family members, number and birth order of children, and family stability and harmony all factor into this life equation (Turnbull & Turnbull, 2000). The presence or absence of employment, financial security, and insurance coverage; the extensiveness and proximity of the extended support network of family and friends; and the family's religious beliefs also affect the impact a child with special needs has on the family. Many family characteristics affect the coping response to the adjustments that arise with the addition of a child with special needs and the professional family partnership. Family functions include who earns the family income, how affection is demonstrated, and to whom and to what degree members provide guidance to the family and pursue educational goals for the child (Turnbull & Turnbull, 2000). How family members secure rest and recuperation and how the domestic and health-care concerns of the home are handled are also factors of family functioning. Cultural differences may factor into how family is valued and how comfortable the family members are with outside service providers. Family traditions, values, and standards for raising children, as well as family preferences regarding when and to what degree they accept help from others, reflect the individual differences between each family system. Research has indicated that mothers tend to be more accepting than fathers, and that parents of lower socioeconomic class are more accepting than parents of higher status (Alper, Schloss, & Schloss, 1994). Geographic location may influence the proximity and variety of options a family has available to them. Families may choose to relocate (or remain in a particular location) because of the availability or quality of services. The value of specific opportunities a community can offer a child or young adult may also be a consideration. Family decisions made expressly for the child with a disability can greatly contribute to family stress. Sometimes the family lifestyle changes in response to financial or work–family issues: for example, if a mother stops working outside the home, she will have more time for child care but less income. Chronological changes occur as each member of the family grows older, and structural changes occur with births, deaths, marriages, and divorces.

Each parent will probably reevaluate his or her self-image and sense of self-worth. This process of reevaluation will occur in the husband–wife dyad as well and may prompt conscious and unconscious decisions for the couple. Relationships within the extended family may also face readjustment, depending upon the strength of those relationships and the frequency of family contact. The relationships among the family's children may be different and, in some ways, reflective of the attitudes and actions children observe in adults, peers, and others in the broader community (Powers, 1993; Stayton, Allred, Cooper, Kilbane, & Whitson, 1990).

Siblings: Special Relationships

Teachers may experience disabilities in the classroom through the eyes of a sibling of a child with a disability. Life for these siblings is often dramatically different from the lives of their classmates. Research supports that love, understanding, and encouragement strengthen sibling bonds, but negative messages are also imitated. The age and stage of development of the sibling in relation to his or her ability to understand the disability itself and its effect on the family is an important consideration.

Depending on the individual situation, siblings may be embarrassed, protective, aggravated, or tolerant in regard to their brother or sister with a disability. This is, of course, dependent on the extent and type of disability and, in general, follows the path of sibling interactions in typical families. Family stress impacts all members, including siblings. If a parent must be absent from home to be with a child in the hospital or spend time with him or her at the expense of time spent with other children, conflicts can arise. Extended family can help support not only the parents but also the entire family during stressful times. Nondisabled siblings may themselves supervise or care for their disabled sibling, and negative feelings can arise due to time taken away from their own recreational or educational activities (Taylor, 2000). Due to extraordinary expenses for the care of children with special needs, household budgets can be especially limited, which may curtail family activities and purchases.

Children typically want to be like their peers, and having a sibling with a disability makes them different. They may struggle with an emotional yo-yo that alternates from family pride and acceptance to anger and worry—with every emotional possibility in between. They can learn to take cues from others' responses to knowing about a sibling's disability and respond accordingly in social settings, or they may become the family advocate, educating others about their sibling's disability and standing up for the whole family. Some children may at times exhibit negative behaviors in an attempt to rebel or demand their share of attention in the family. Other times, they may try to become "the perfect child" to make up for their sibling's disability and to please their parents. This mission toward perfection creates a lot of stress for children, and it is reflected in many facets of their lives. Many support groups for families have special programs and conferences for children who have siblings with a disability. This provides them an opportunity to support and talk candidly with others who understand.

As an educator, it is important to be sensitive to these children and provide opportunities for them to be acknowledged as special individuals in their own right. There are a number of books that have been written from the sibling's perspective that may be helpful for them. It also may be helpful to allow them to keep a confidential journal. It is important for them to know that they are not alone.

Parent Involvement and the Helping Relationship

Many young children with special needs are involved in some type of early intervention or preschool program. Families frequently become involved with professionals, service providers, and educational programs and systems while their child is quite young. Consequently, early childhood teachers may expect to have children with some special needs (diagnosed or not) at some time. Often it is not until the child is in elementary school and not developing as he or she should that a disability becomes more evident. Recognizing that family stresses and emotions impact the relationship teachers have with parents helps teachers develop a sensitive partnership with these families. Parents bring heightened concerns for their child's physical care and development mixed with the need to keep some semblance of normalcy about their child's early years and their family life. Programs and schools often provide a much needed support and respite for these families. It is imperative that a trusting relationship is built between family and teacher. Partnerships can be built upon openness to information shared with the family and sensitivity to the changing needs and concerns within each family system.

The helping relationship between a parent and a professional is a powerful yet delicate relationship. The quality of that parent–professional relationship must be a concern to anyone working with children and families. These partnerships may have great meaning, reflect a range of emotions, and change over time as the child, parent, and professional grow and develop. Each partner wants to feel capable and effective, yet the pressure to "do something" is offset by the fear of not always knowing the right answer or being able to carry through. Some professionals want to control too completely or try too hard to fix the problems; in those cases, the ultimate objective of a partnership is forgotten.

In the helping relationship between parent and teacher, one goal is to increase family involvement and empower parents to become informed family members and effective service coordinators for their child. Despite the legal protection of parent involvement, many parents of children with disabilities do not become actively involved in their child's program. Participation in the IEP meeting is basic; however, like all parent involvement contacts, barriers and challenges exist for parents of children with special needs.

Dunst, Trivette, and Deal (1988), in recognizing this dilemma, offer suggestions from research. Working with families is a dynamic, fluid process that includes the art and craft of developing positive outcomes in the partnership. The relationship is the key, and every contact with the family counts toward establishing trust and respect. Confidentiality must be maintained and preserved at all times.

Honesty is critical, and effective help-giving requires an understanding of a family's concerns and interests. Emphasis should be placed on solutions, not causes. Effective interactions focus on positive, proactive strategies that promote the use of informal supports as the main method of meeting needs.

Family involvement is developmental, and parents may not be ready to begin a parent–professional helping relationship. Professionals may not yet be skillful in the craft of working with parents and should make a sincere effort in developing their communication skills. The following are suggestions for promoting positive relationships with parents:

- Allow the family to tell its own story and listen carefully to parents and family members. Respect their history. Don't minimize what they have to say.

- Help families to identify and process unresolved issues that are bothering them. Use reflective listening and effective questioning. Don't make premature judgments or moralize.

- Avoid hasty, patronizing attempts to solve problems, offer advice, or give information. Empathy, not advice, may be the real need.

- Provide accurate, honest information in response to parent queries, or assist parents in securing such information. Use language that parents and family members can understand. Avoid educational or medical jargon.

- Provide parents with many variations and individualized alternatives, including suggestions for functional skill building, for working appropriately with their child. Reflect the parent's goals.

- Do not attempt to produce or use guilt to motivate parents and family members. Don't threaten, ridicule, or place blame for their child's lack of progress.

- Inform parents and family members of community resources that may help them meet their child's or family's needs.

- Treat parents as adult partners who care about their child, and never assume that your training or experience has given you more knowledge than the parents have about their child.

- Assist families in recognizing that their needs will change over time, as will those of their child. Strive for realistic optimism.

- Be accepting of yourself and of the parents and family members with whom you work. Demonstrate warmth and sensitivity.

- Learn whatever family skills you need to work effectively, such as family assessments, home strategies for skill building, and so on.

- Be open to parents' questions and concerns and be available to talk with them. Don't be hesitant to say, "I don't know" and either provide a referral or seek answers and get back to the parents later.

- Examine your attitude toward children with disabilities. Remember, they are children first. Focus on their strengths, not on their weaknesses.
- Respect the parents' right to choose their level of involvement and participation.
- Find other parents who have children with disabilities who would be willing to talk with your student's family. Parent-to-parent networking is a great resource.

These suggestions have been gleaned from the works of Turnbull and Turnbull (2000), Simpson (1990), Linder (1983), and Fenichel and Eggbeer (1990).

Family-Centered Collaborations

Many of the developments regarding special education described in this chapter have served to create opportunities, and occasionally conflicts, for families of children with special needs. Legislation has brought families into focus as consumers of educational programs and services who have options to accept or challenge educational practices. As more families develop communication and advocacy skills from participation in early intervention programs and a general awareness of best practices, the programs and schools will see more families who are comfortable in the role of advocate and service coordinator for their children. Programs will be challenged to adapt and work with families as real partners in the process of education. Laws have challenged states and local communities to include recommended practices for family-centered involvement. As programs continue to develop and refine this concept, and as new programs are created based on family-centered and family-guided approaches, this philosophy continues to spread within the state and community social services. Agencies, once autonomous, are thrust together on interagency councils to determine how to achieve maximum outcomes with budget limitations. Collaborations that once were inconceivable are emerging with new energy, opening the door to more comprehensive services for families.

Increased Family Supports

The focus on comprehensive services has resulted in an increase in the services and supports offered to families with children who have special needs, often through collaborations at state and local levels. Many states have passed family support legislation, increasing the availability of respite and child care, adaptive assistance, transportation, financial assistance, and such family services as support groups, parent training, and information centers (Exceptional Parent, 1993). State agencies (such as those for education, mental health, and public health), local agencies, and programs are making information services about disabilities and parent-to-parent linkages more commonplace. Various disabilities, such as autism, benefit from special state research and training projects. James May (1991) reported an increase in awareness of men's needs in the parenting of children with disabilities and an increase in the number of support groups especially for fathers. To support the unique needs among fathers of children with special needs, he developed the Father's Network, which continues to reach men with similar concerns today. The PTA has a special division to encourage the involvement of parents who have children in special programs. Advocacy initiatives with varied state and local sponsorships are reaching out to families with questions and are heightening the awareness of disability issues. Both individual and group efforts have promoted family supports throughout the nation. However, even the best-constructed program is not without potential difficulties.

BARRIERS TO FAMILY INVOLVEMENT

Barriers Within the Service System

Many barriers to parent involvement for parents of children with special needs are identical to those identified in this book for all parents. Yet because special education interventions often take place during times of stress, professionals must have a heightened sensitivity to the possible origins, prevention, and resolution of any difficulties. The source of the problem may lie with the professional, with the system of services and how they are delivered to the family, or with the family system itself. Professionals may lack the experience or training to work with parents of children with special needs and may feel uncomfortable in that role. Different philosophies or a resistance to accepting the parent as a respected partner may present obstacles. Many colleges and universities fail to offer adequate coursework in family-centered approaches in their teacher preparation requirements. Parents may have suspected that their child had extraordinary difficulties in previous grades and may be harboring negative feelings as the result of a lack of action.

Systems themselves can create obstacles in policies, regulations, or procedures. Special education protocol is perhaps the most regimented system that parents will encounter within the educational setting. This can result in a lack of flexibility that is frequently coupled with a shortage of resources, including money for program extras like parent involvement, and a shortage of professional time to develop rapport with parents at meetings or build partnerships with families. Parent involvement in the form of active partnerships is a concept fostered through the family-centered programs in early intervention and by sensitive professionals and service providers. The current trends are a radical change from some past attitudes toward parents. Veteran service providers may experience difficulties in adopting a more family-friendly model of interaction. Family support services and parent advocacy may be the quantum leaps of philosophy for programs and schools. They formerly may have served only the child for their daily program, considered parent contact solely in terms of compliance with legal requirements for signatures and meetings, and viewed families who expressed their views with an advocate's voice as troublemakers. Times are changing.

Barriers Within the Family

The emotional and physical complexities of raising a child with special needs are often overwhelming for families. Yet, when the child becomes eligible for early intervention or special education services or programs, parents need to become aware of the variety of service providers, the language of special education, and their legal rights in a fairly complex educational system—all while continuing to function as a family during an often-turbulent childhood period. As professionals share knowledge of services, programs, and service systems with parents, parents typically increase their participation. Often parents do not desire to take on the responsibilities of active involvement because they are unclear about their child's needs, or because they believe there will be a time to become more involved as their child gets older. Until parents do become involved, it is important that the teacher concentrate on the child and attempt to overcome the problems. Parents can be so overwhelmed with survival issues and family responsibilities that they have no time or energy left to participate in meetings where they do not feel comfortable or necessary. There are enormous differences in parents, and some obstacles are within the dynamics of the particular family system.

Families may encounter barriers to participation in special education programs. These may include problems with communication, transportation, and child care; a lack of time; a lack of understanding of the system; feelings of inferiority; a perceived or real lack of respect; a feeling that problems won't be resolved; language and/or cultural differences; and difficulties in accepting the child's disability. While many potential solutions to these difficulties already have been proposed in previous chapters, there are many additional strategies to enhance communication, support, and advocacy within special education service structures.

STRATEGIES TO ENHANCE FAMILY COMMUNICATION, SUPPORT, AND ADVOCACY

Families who are stressed by life events and the circumstances that accompany caregiving, behavior management, and academic support for a child with special needs may be extremely sensitive to a professional's response to them or their child. They may feel vulnerable and anxious about situations in which major decisions are made about them and their child. Confronted with traditional authority figures, families may feel powerless, incompetent, or angry. It is of utmost importance, therefore, that teachers utilize strategies that create positive communication patterns, provide individualized supports, and empower families to become knowledgeable and active participants in their child's school or program.

Strategies to Enhance Communication

Most families have a strong need to be informed about their child's program and progress. Programs and schools frequently have large numbers of service providers interacting with the children. All members of the instructional team should make an effort to help families understand the roles of the educators and professionals who work with their child, including names, titles, and responsibilities. Communications that are sent home by various individuals should be coordinated, perhaps on a single "daily news" form, to provide an easy way to keep track of notes and requests.

Initial contacts with families should be as comfortable and as positive as possible. Parents should be informed about why information is needed, what procedures are ahead, and who will be involved. One of the best ways to enhance family participation is to help demystify the system. Parents may need help developing open communication skills when talking with professionals, practice in asking questions, and practice in sharing their knowledge, their experiences, and their hopes. Techniques for tracking observational data at home for health, behavior, or other concerns should be shared so that parents can become more active participants in their child's program.

Families may need assistance in deciphering the code of special education terminology. Acronyms and initials, names and functions of assessment instruments used with the child, and technical terminology used in the diagnosis or educational program should be explained. There are a wide variety of books and websites available to specifically help parents; however, the most helpful information may be in a handbook created by families for families. Teachers should offer to share explanations, materials, or reading material on particular aspects of a disability or program. Families may be interested in attending meetings on such topics as home therapy techniques and strategies, the IEP process, parent rights and responsibilities, advocacy training, or the program's assessments for children and families.

Some special education meetings can have many people in attendance; however, parents of children with special needs are valuable members of the service team for their child and should be helped to feel comfortable. *Courtesy of ECE Photo Library.*

Strategies to Enhance Support

During their involvement with their child's IEP team, parents determine what supports they feel are valuable. It is up to the teachers and support staff to provide access to and awareness of supports that make a "needs-fit" for the families. Family-needs inventories or other types of family assessments can assist individual families in identifying the issues that concern them most. With this information, the parent–teacher team can work together to identify resources, either within or outside the family system. For example, a family may express a need for child care. Several options would be an extended family member or friend, a student from the local college nursing or education program, the local child-care center that takes children with disabilities, or the child-care referral agency that could assist in locating a day-care home. Families should be empowered to actively pursue their own choices without undue assistance from the professional.

Conferences and meetings may cause extraordinary stress for the parents. This stress may overwhelm a parent to the point where he or she may not be able to respond to the suggestions during the meeting or accurately recall all the details to relate to the absent parent. An excellent support strategy is to suggest that both parents attend together, or that a parent ask a family member, friend, or advocate to attend with him or her. If there are two parents in the family structure, provide opportunities for both parents to have input in the child's program.

Professionals cannot assume that they know what a family is undergoing unless they themselves have a child with a disability, and even so, each family and situation is unique. Teachers can provide valuable assistance by helping families locate, through a parent network, other families that share a similar situation. Often these networks are sponsored by organizations for individuals with disabilities and are found through local or state agency programs. The state department of public health may offer special counseling and support services for families of children with genetic disorders. The National Organization for Rare Disorders (NORD) or a disability-specific organization at the national, state, or local level can be a valuable referral for a family. Community resource guides, available through social workers, service organizations, or community consortiums, can help families locate resources to meet other needs. The teacher can locate potentially helpful telephone numbers and agency contact names and share them with families. Many schools host a **parent-to-parent program,** which may be used as a support for all families or just those entering or leaving the program or school. Parent-to-parent programs offer an individualized and personal response from another parent who is familiar with the unique challenges these families face. These programs provide emotional support, information and education, social activities, and advocacy. They may also have a group structure that enhances the social supports for parents. Parent-to-parent programs may be organized through the school or program, a hospital, or another agency offering supports to families. Information on this type of program may be available through a state government office or through national organizations like the Beach Center on Families and Disability, the National Center on Parent-Directed Family Resource Centers, the Technical Assistance Alliance for Parent Centers, or the National Parent Network on Disabilities. Many websites on specific disabilities provide parent-to-parent support in chat rooms or via e-mail.

Strategies to Enhance Advocacy

Families have become empowered through the federal and state laws that protect their rights and establish responsibilities for involvement. Advocacy efforts on the behalf of children with special needs and their families are flourishing at the national, state, and local levels. Parents are coming to schools less passive and "humbly grateful," and they are more likely to advocate for the most effective services for their children. The means to achieving this involvement is not necessarily adversarial. In order for programs, schools, and parents to have a respectful and sensitive relationship, all parties must be knowledgeable of the facts, needs, rights, and options. Professionals should be aware of generalizations about parents of special needs children and focus on the individual relationship built as a team. Be alert for attitudes of defensiveness or intimidation within the relationship. Families may have the impression that the school or program staff is working against them or their child. This creates negative emotions that spill out into legal advocacy actions, such as due process. Strong family involvement and communication empower a working relationship in which differences can be mediated amiably. This problem-solving, communicative process develops from a consultative, helping relationship that is reflected in the intervention plan devised by the parent–professional team. (Specific information on parent conferencing can be found in Chapter 9.) Developing and practicing the positive partnership-building skills mentioned earlier can assist the teacher's (and the school's) link with nontraditional families and multicultural families. These skills contribute to the effectiveness of any advocacy efforts.

By monitoring the effectiveness of a child's program, teachers can be important allies in assisting families. Do the services meet the child's (or family's) needs? Would something else work better? Working within the system to ensure that quality programming is in place for the child and that parents are participating members of the team may avoid or reduce any future conflicts. This focus on the child—and the family—is at the core of the changing system of special education and is a vital piece of advocacy.

Good communication skills are basic to any advocacy effort. Through schools and programs, parents can learn social support advocacy skills, such as how to write and visit with their legislator or congressional representative, what legislation has been proposed that may affect families and children with special needs, and how to meet with local officials in order to positively impact community changes. Schools and programs also can provide parents with public relations skills that can be used when working with the community at large or with medical service providers, social service providers, and others. By sharing information and building skills within the system, there is a greater likelihood that parents will develop as allies, not adversaries (Alper, Schloss, & Schloss, 1994).

SUMMARY

Parenting a child with special needs is a unique parenting experience. Learning that one's child is not developing with typical skills and abilities is often a life-changing discovery. Each family system responds in its own way. Advances in genetic and brain research as well as other diagnostic procedures have given families and educators a better understanding of disabilities and more appropriate interventions. Despite improved knowledge, families respond with concern to the unknown and the inevitable parenting challenges they face.

Historically, families have played a pivotal role in the development of special education and have redefined parent involvement for the benefit of all families.

The magnitude of change in both the philosophies and practices of involvement for parents of children with special needs has created new and individualized strategies. Nationwide, programs are emerging that reflect these changes. Most visible are programs serving children from birth through 2 years of age and their families and inclusive programs that accept all children, regardless of ability. No longer are people complacent with the philosophy of isolating and segregating children who need special services, whether in the schools or in the community. New attempts at collaboration at the state and local levels are broadening the support networks into grassroots communities. Compliance with federal policies requires philosophies that view families as planners as well as recipients of services. Throughout a growing number of special education programs, parents are accepting the position of system-change agent by more fully exercising their rights under special education law. The government is developing family support policy with input from families, communities, businesses, educators, and social services and is discovering new collaborations to most effectively meet needs. It is an exciting time, and a challenging time, for families, service systems, and policy makers. Most exciting of all is that professionals working with children and their families are key facilitators of this change.

ACTIVITIES FOR DISCUSSION, EXPANSION, AND APPLICATION

1. Research and list public and private agencies, programs, schools, support groups, and other service providers in your area that provide assistance to parents of children with special needs in coping with the emotional and physical challenges of parenting. Create a resource list that includes the title of each resource, contact person, address, phone number, and type and cost of service.

2. Interview someone working in an early intervention program that serves infants and toddlers with disabilities and someone working with preschoolers or older children with disabilities. How does each view parent involvement in his or her program? Describe each worker's contacts with parents. Compare and contrast the following: frequency of contacts with parents, the nature of the interaction (typical location, length of contact, typical topics, support materials typically shared, etc.), and the type of parent education or advocacy programming provided. Compare your research with that of others in your group. Discuss the philosophies, services, and the impact upon parents.

3. Interview a parent of a child with special needs. Ask the parent's permission to share the responses with your group. Ask the parent to tell the story of parenting his or her child. What was the reaction when the child's difficulties were first realized? How did family and friends react? What were the parent's frustrations, sorrows, and joys? How is the parent involved in the child's program? What are the parent's dreams for the child? Share what you have learned with your group. What are the similarities and differences, and how can they be explained?

4. Interview a social worker, psychologist, therapist, teacher, or administrator for a special education program. What does the professional say are the challenges and rewards of working with parents of children with special needs? What are the most sensitive issues for professionals to discuss with parents? Why? What does he or she wish parents would do more or less of? What can teachers do to encourage parent involvement? Discuss your findings with your group.

5. Use ideas collected by your group in Activity 4 and other research to develop a usable resource, such as a checklist, article, or pamphlet, for teachers and other professionals. Include strategies, suggestions, and guidelines for working in partnership with parents of children with special needs.

6. Interview a parent of a child with special needs who is in elementary school or high school. If the child's disability was identified before age 6, ask how the parent feels services available to preschoolers with special needs have changed since his or her child was small. What were the issues the parent felt were important when the child was young? What issues does the parent perceive to be important for parents today? How and why are they different? Discuss with your group what you've learned.

7. Interview an adult with a disability. How is growing up now different for children with special needs than it was for him or her? In what ways is it the same? What are the critical differences for people with disabilities today? (Excellent contacts can be made through your area disability services organizations.)

8. Are young children with special needs being included in regular school and community programs in your area? Contact elementary schools, preschools, child-care centers, local YMCAs, library programs, sports organizations, churches, and so on. If you were a parent of a child with a disability, what would your response be? If possible, contact the parents of a child who is included in regular programs. Ask them to share their story of how their child was included. What have been the most difficult and the most rewarding aspects of the child's and family's experiences? What fears

did the parents have? What are their dreams for their child? Share with your group what you have learned. Discuss the school and community environments. Are they open to inclusion? Why or why not?

CASE STUDY

It is the first quarter of the school year. Ian, a first grader, has very poor reading skills and attention concerns that affect his overall school performance. He has begun to develop negative behaviors in the classroom to distract from his academic difficulties. Cathie Evans, his classroom teacher, believes it may be time to get special education assistance, but she is concerned about what she will say at the upcoming parent conference. His parents have already told her they don't want him put in any "class for retards."

1. What strategies can be implemented to help Ian?

2. What advice would you give Cathie as she prepares to discuss Ian's lack of progress with his parents?

3. What options can be available within the educational system both in regular and special education?

USEFUL WEBSITES

idea.ed.gov

U.S. Department of Education: Individuals with Disabilities Education Act. The site offers details on the 2004 reauthorization of IDEA for Part B (ages 3–21) and Part C (birth–2), a Question and Answer section, and an explanation of how IDEA aligns with the NCLB act.

www.dec-sped.org

Division for Early Childhood of CEC. This is the website of one of the divisions of CEC that focuses on children with special needs from birth through age 8 and their families. Includes publications and a professional-development focus on recommendations for best practices. The site also offers downloadable resources on topics like inclusion, developmental delay, behavior, and ethics as well as checklists for professionals, families, and administrators.

www.eparent.com

Exceptional Parent Magazine. This magazine offers information on disability and news for those interested in children with special needs from infant through adult. Areas include education, family, and community; financial planning; legal issues; healthcare; mobility; and technology.

www.fape.org

Families and Advocates Partnership for Education. This is a website for families, professionals, and advocates of children with special needs. It includes links to information on various aspects of IDEA and other resources to help individuals better understand the law.

www.partnersinpolicymaking.com

Partners in Policymaking. Partners in Policymaking is a national leadership project created in 1987 in Minnesota and now implemented in 45 states. It provides inclusion education, leadership development, and training.

www.wrightslaw.com

Wrightslaw. This site provides accurate, up-to-date information on legal issues in special education.

REFERENCES

Abbott, C., & Gold, S. (1991). Conferring with parents when you're concerned that their child needs special services. *Young Children, 46*(4), 10–14.

Allen, K. (1992). *The exceptional child: Mainstreaming in early childhood education.* Albany, NY: Delmar.

Alper, S., Schloss, P., & Schloss, C. (1994). *Families of students with disabilities: Consultation and advocacy.* Boston: Allyn & Bacon.

Arnold, J., & Dodge, H. (1994). Room for all. *American School Board Journal, 191* (10), 22–26.

Bauer, A., & Shea, T. (2003). *Parents and schools: Creating a successful partnership for students with special needs.* Upper Saddle River, NJ: Pearson Education.

Boutte, G., Keepler, D., Tyler, V., & Terry, B. (1992). Effective techniques for involving "difficult" parents. *Young Children, 47*(3), 19–22.

Bricker, D. (1989). *Early intervention for at-risk and handicapped infants, toddlers, and preschool children.* Palo Alto, CA: Vort.

Buscaglia, L. (1983). *The disabled and their parents: A counseling challenge.* Thorofare, NJ: Slack.

Dunst, C., Trivette, C., & Deal, A. (1988). *Enabling and empowering families: Principles and guidelines for practice.* Cambridge, MA: Brookline Books.

Exceptional Parent. (1993). Family support programs growing. *Exceptional Parent, 23*(6), 36–40.

Fenichel, E., & Eggbeer, L. (1990). *Preparing practitioners to work with infants, toddlers, and their families: Issues and recommendations for the professions.* Arlington, VA: National Center for Clinical Infant Programs.

Ferguson, P. (2002). A place in the family: An historical interpretation of research on parental reactions to having a child with a disability. *The Journal of Special Education, 36*(3), 124–130.

Gorman, J. (2004). *Working with challenging parents of students with special needs.* Thousand Oaks, CA: Corwin Press.

Institute for Educational Research. (1992). *Teacher Today, 8*(2), 2–6.

Kroth, R. (1985). *Communicating with parents of exceptional children: Improving parent–teacher relationships.* Denver: Love.

Kubler-Ross, E. (1969). *On Death and Dying*. Minneapolis, MN: Sagebrush Education Resources.

Linder, T. (1983). *Early childhood special education: Program development and administration*. Baltimore: Paul H. Brookes.

LRP Publications. (1994a). Developmental factors in preschool inclusion outcomes. *Early Childhood Report, 5*(11), 4–5.

LRP Publications. (1994b). Parents, advocates rail against programs that thwart education and inclusion. *Inclusive Education Programs, 1*(12), 5–7.

May, J. (1991). *Fathers of children with special needs: New horizons*. Bethesda, MD: Association for the Care of Children's Health.

Powers, L. (1993). Disability and grief. In G. Singer & L. Powers (Eds.), *Families, disability, and empowerment: Active coping skills and strategies for family interventions* (119–149). Baltimore: Paul H. Brookes.

Project CHOICES/Early CHOICES. (2007). Project CHOICES/Early CHOICES in-service materials. Springfield, IL: Illinois State Board of Education.

Rose, D., & Smith, B. (1993). Preschool mainstreaming: Attitude barriers and strategies for addressing them. *Young Children, 48*(4), 59–62.

Rosenkoetter, S., Hains, A., & Fowler, S. (1994). *Bridging early services for children with special needs and their families: A practical guide for transition planning*. Baltimore: Paul H. Brookes.

Saint-Exupéry, A. de. (1943). *The little prince*. New York: Harcourt Brace.

Seltzer, M., Greenberg, J., Floyd, F., Pettee, Y., & Hong, J. (2001). Life course impact on parenting a child with a disability. *American Journal on Mental Retardation, 103*(3), 265–286.

Simpson, R. (1990). *Conferencing parents of exceptional children*. Austin, TX: Pro-Ed.

Smith, S. (2002). What do parents of children with LD, ADHD, and related disorders deal with? *Pediatric Nursing, 22*(3), 254–257.

Smith, T., Gartin, B., Murdick, N., & Hilton, A. (2006). *Families and children with special needs*. Upper Saddle River, NJ: Pearson Education.

Stayton, V., Allred, K., Cooper, C., Kilbane, K., & Whitson, V. (1990). *A family systems approach for individualizing services*. Training module for Illinois Technical Assistance Project. Flossmoor, IL: South Metropolitan Association, Illinois State Board of Education.

Taylor, G. (2000). *Parental involvement: A practical guide for collaboration and teamwork for students with disabilities*. Springfield, IL: Charles Thomas.

Turnbull, A., & Turnbull, H. R. III. (2000). *Families, professionals, and exceptionality: A special partnership*. Columbus, OH: Merrill.

Ulrich, M., & Bauer, A. (2003). Levels of awareness: A closer look at communication between parents and professionals. *Teaching Exceptional Children, 35*(6), 20–24.

Wilmore, E. (1994–1995). When your child is special. *Educational Leadership, 52*(4), 60–62.

KEY TERMS

Inclusive—Refers to an educational environment in which all children—regardless of ability—learn together in a nonsegregated manner. Instruction is typically supported by several educators who team to provide appropriate instruction and services to all children.

Attention Deficit Hyperactivity Disorder (ADHD)—A developmental neurological disorder that involves a lag in development as evidenced by difficulty with attending, impulse control, and memory. It may be present with a high activity level, which is when the "H" is included.

Child Find—A federal requirement of local educational agencies (school districts) to advertise the availability of infant, toddler, and preschool developmental screenings and programs.

Spina Bifida—A developmental birth defect that involves an incomplete closure of the spine. Depending on the location on the spine and the severity of the deformity, a variety of symptoms occur. These can include partial paralysis, postural problems, bowl and bladder control issues, and cognitive difficulties.

Individualized Educational Program (IEP)—The legal document outlying a child's assessment and description of his or her educational performance, annual goals, short-term instructional objectives, specific special education, and related services to be provided. It also includes, among other information, the extent to which a child can participate in regular education and testing, any accommodations, and the dates the services are to begin and end.

Least Restrictive Environment—Refers to placement of children with special needs in a program or classroom that will meet their needs with the least amount of segregation from typically developing students. Placement options are determined by the IEP team (including parents) and range from the least restrictive (regular educational program) to the most restrictive (residential placement).

Related Services—Educationally related services that help a child benefit from special education, including such services as speech/language therapy, physical and occupational therapy, audiology, psychological services, social work services, assistive technology, and special mobility instruction.

504 Plan—A plan provided under the Vocational Rehabilitation Act, Section 504, to legally provide a child with accommodations and modifications to their regular education program. This can include such services and accommodations as assistive technology, additional time for test taking, modification of assignments, and so on for children not eligible for special education services.

Individualized Family Service Plan (IFSP)—Special education provisions for families and children ages birth to age 3 who show developmental delays or have had a physical or mental condition that puts them at risk for developmental delay.

Learning Disorder/Disability—A disability that affects a wide range of academic and functional skills, including reading, writing, mathematics, speaking, listening, motor planning, reasoning, and organizing information, which, despite appropriate interventions, negatively affects learning.

Picture Communication Board—An alternative communication device that has photos or images of various items, people, actions, and so on that an individual can touch or point to in order to communicate their wants, needs, and other expressions.

Parent-to-Parent Program—A program that typically provides informal information sharing and one-on-one emotional support to parents of children with special needs by other parents who have children with similar disabilities or have been in similar situations.

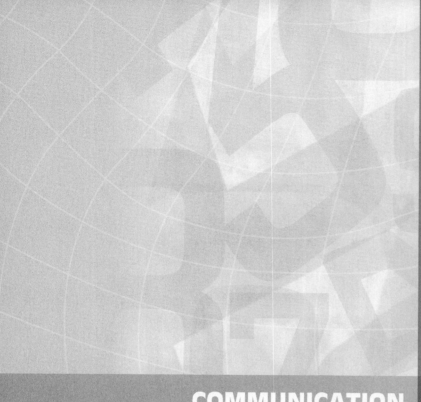

PART TWO

COMMUNICATION

CHAPTER 5
Written Correspondence

STUDENT LEARNING OUTCOMES

After reading this chapter, you should be able to

- Describe strategies and techniques utilizing written communication that facilitate home–school communication.

- Describe the roles that newsletters, passport systems, and technology-based communications play in improving communication between home and school.

- Evaluate strategies used to create a welcoming atmosphere for families in schools.

- Discuss methods used to collect information and opinions from parents.

- Identify the roles individual teacher communications and school-wide communications play in keeping parents involved and informed in their children's education.

Communication is a critical element in the formation and maintenance of successful partnerships. Clear, concise, and direct messages convey respect for the questions parents have about issues regarding their children. In this fast-paced decade, it has never been more important that parents and teachers understand each other's motives, feelings, and concerns. It is for this reason that educators need to approach each parent relationship with an open-minded attitude, the willingness to learn, and a spirit of cooperation (Caspe, Lopez, & Wolos, 2006–2007; Swick, 2003).

Educators taking that first step will find that there are numerous ways of conveying messages to the home. This chapter will detail the many written and technology-based communication strategies that are available for school-to-home use. Types of written communication include teachers' individual communications to parents and school-wide or group communications to parents, which are usually published under the leadership of a principal or director.

The following are the types of strategies described within the chapter:

notes	web pages
letters	shappy-grams
parent bulletin boards	newsletters
report cards	suggestion boxes
e-mails	surveys
passport systems	daily logs
parent contracts	parent handbooks
yearbooks	brochures
informational packets	

The impression made on families by the wording, timeliness, and subject matter of written materials chosen can influence their feelings toward the school or center, principal or director, and teachers. Some considerations to keep in mind are the following:

- Are printed materials sent home in enough time to allow parents to schedule and plan for upcoming events?
- Is everything spelled correctly? Check for good sentence structure and grammar.
- Is the wording readable and jargon free?
- Is feedback sought in a regular manner?
- Are the efforts at communication sporadic or regular and reliable?
- How is information communicated to parents with limited English proficiency or limited reading levels?

Creating true partnerships in education involves outreach to parents by the administrators and teachers. Some parents will participate by invitation alone; others will be more passive until they are comfortable enough with the personnel and building to take an active role. Whatever the level of involvement, communication is the cornerstone of each relationship.

BARRIERS TO EFFECTIVE WRITTEN COMMUNICATION

One of the greatest barriers for the individual teacher is time. Traditionally, the school or center schedule does not permit a true commitment to the purpose of communicating with families (Christensen & Sheridan, 2001). Teachers are given little, if any, planning time for curriculum tasks, and they have even less time for communicating with parents outside of the standard parent–teacher conference. Many early childhood teachers are on duty almost every hour the children are in the facility. Elementary school teachers frequently use breaks, lunch hours, and personal time after school to put together newsletters and notes. Understandably, many educators perceive the efforts spent on additional forms of communication as a burden, especially when administrators do not allocate appropriate amounts of time for that purpose. It is possible, then, that home–school communication could vary within a school, as it is dependent on the individual teacher's commitment to devote the time necessary for written dialogues with parents.

A second barrier is the lack of sufficient funds to maintain an ongoing publication, such as a newsletter. This lack of funds also contributes to the limited availability of office machines, such as printers and copiers. Teachers often are forced to choose between a weekly newsletter and a parent survey, for example, if paper supplies and copying access are severely restricted. While school- and teacher-based web pages and e-mail can greatly enhance communication for parents, centers and schools must have financial support in the forms of equipment and technology support staff with the expertise to maintain computers, servers, and web pages. Again, the lack of school commitment, in the form of time and money, toward improving home–school communication can complicate the efforts of motivated teachers.

Schools and teachers frequently fall into the trap of doing things the way tradition dictates—"It has always been done this way." The majority of today's families, however, have broken with tradition in many ways, and maintaining communication with them means finding and using innovative ways of keeping the channels open in both directions. Consider the ever-expanding variety of families that schools encounter each year: single-parent families, children under the guardianship of relatives, students in foster care, two-mother or two-father families, blended families, families with children who have special needs, and interracial families (Gestwicki, 2007). The need for flexibility and sensitivity becomes apparent. It is no longer desirable to think in terms of only mothers and fathers. For many children, there are other significant adults in their lives who desire a connection with the school. In order to feel involved in a child's education, the methods used to communicate should acknowledge parents' and other adults' commitments to the child (Prior & Gerard, 2007).

The following sections will describe specific techniques and strategies that will assist early childhood professionals in improving the quality of communications between home and school.

TEACHERS' INDIVIDUAL COMMUNICATIONS TO PARENTS

An important key to building successful relationships with parents is through frequent, positive kinds of communication (Hong, 2006). Each type of correspondence has specific applications depending on the topic and purpose. Examples of letters, notes, report cards, contracts, surveys, web pages, and e-mails will illustrate the variety and purpose of each type of communication.

Letters

Letters are an excellent vehicle for the transmission of lengthy or detailed information that parents need about their children, the school, or policies. A letter can serve the entire group of parents or be written for a specific few.

There are a variety of purposes for a parent letter. Often a teacher will send a letter to students in August as a method of introduction and perhaps to relay registration information or supply lists for the first day of school. This is especially appreciated by parents who are anxious over their young child's adjustment to a new school or program. A warm welcome from the teacher sets a positive tone for the year and is the first step toward creating a relationship with parents and children. See Figure 5.1.

Letters often accompany the explanation of a new or revised policy that applies to the students, such as library check-out policies, field trip procedures, homework policies, and parent–teacher conference formats. Other letters can be used to keep parents informed of what their children are learning at school. For example, one third-grade teacher who is introducing a new math program used in the school sends home an appropriate journal article reprint each Friday accompanied by a letter explaining how the various instructional strategies relate to his classroom and its students. In this way, he is hoping to increase parents' awareness of mathematical thinking and yet not overwhelm parents with too much information at any one time. Parent reactions are positive; they comment that they feel more confident when discussing their child's progress in school because the teacher has shared many of his practices with them as an ongoing project and has provided the necessary background information. Many publishers of instructional materials for young children now include information that can be sent home to parents at the beginning of a new unit to explain what children are learning and how parents can reinforce classroom

Dear _____,

Hello! My name is Mrs. Baker and I will be your kindergarten teacher this year. I am very excited about meeting you and your family when you come to Bradley East School for Orientation Day!

Please come to Room 100 on Monday, August 24th, at 9:30 a.m. for a tour of your new classroom, some delicious snacks, and the chance to meet all of the friendly faces here at your new school. You will meet the bus driver, Mr. Martin, and the principal, Mr. Garry.

Please bring your school supplies with you that morning so that we can put them in your cubbie and label it with your name.

* a large box of 64 crayons
* a large box of tissues
* six regular pencils
* one bottle of glue
* one roll of tape

I hope that you will enjoy the rest of your summer, and I will see you on Orientation Day!

Your friend,

Mrs. Baker

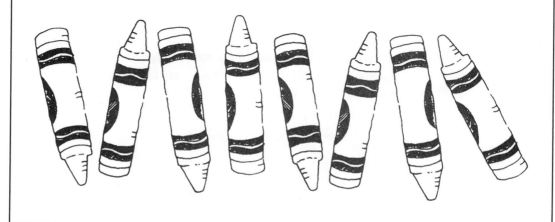

FIGURE 5.1 Welcome Letter

instruction. Everyday Math, for example, has developed Home Links, a section that outlines new strategies and the research behind the games and other classroom activities teachers implement with each new chapter.

Since time is in short supply for most teachers, prewritten parent letters can make it easier to communicate about a variety of topics. Sample letters can be found in books about parent communication, in educational clip-art books, and on teacher-resource websites. Often these letters can be modified to suit the individual teacher and thus save the time required to compose an original letter. Companies such as Good Apple and Gryphon House publish suitable model letters in books that are subject-specific and include graphics in a pleasing arrangement, ready for copying.

To make a letter effective and readable, care must be taken to use clear, jargon-free language that is concise and to the point. Limiting a letter to one page in length increases the chance that it will be read or, at the very least, skimmed. If it is any longer, busy parents are apt to put the letter aside for later reading (Arnold, 2005). If the content cannot fit on one page, consider breaking the topic into two or more separate communications to be distributed at different times. Have a colleague read the letter to ensure the clarity of the message and to act as a proofreader. Teachers and administrators also find that the regular use of a specific color of paper and an identifying program or school logo help letters from school stand out from other materials going home.

Spontaneous Notes

Spontaneous notes usually are written to convey less detailed, one-topic messages that involve daily activities in the classroom. Information such as conference time changes, field trip reminders, lost books, or humorous anecdotes often are handled through a quick note sent home with the student. Again, it is important to remain brief when communicating through notes, or the process will become impossible to maintain and an important means of communication lost. Clip-art books, CDs, and websites carry numerous short forms designed for spontaneous notes that are catchy and pleasing to the eye. Many carry headings, such as the following, to alert the parent to the primary message:

"Wanted you to know . . ."

"Dropping a line to remind you . . ."

"_____ is having a great day because . . ."

Teachers who make a point of staying in touch with parents on a regular basis usually keep a supply of notes on a clipboard handy for playground or recess time, snack times, or free-reading time when they can complete a few notes for daily distribution. Quick response to a parent note or question will greatly improve the communication between home and school and, in the process, strengthen the relationship between teachers and families.

When using notes to share interesting anecdotes about individual students, it is important to keep a checklist to be sure that notes are written for each child on a regular basis. In this way, recordkeeping is simplified and use of notes increases because it is convenient for the teacher. A note can be an effective substitute for a conversation, especially in schools where phone calls are difficult to complete due to a lack of private facilities or free time.

One Head Start program uses an observation log to help parents know what activities occupied their child during the day and to stimulate conversation between parent and child; see Figure 5.2 for an example of such a log. Parents accustomed to receiving good news will not regard communication from the school as a sign of a problem. When and if a problem does arise, the lines of communication and the establishment of a partnership will already be in place. Parents are more likely to work cooperatively with the school if they feel that the teacher has true respect and genuine concern for their child. Laying the groundwork early in the school year for a positive relationship will ultimately benefit everyone.

Happy-Grams

Happy-grams are very brief notes that generally have more graphics than words and convey a special message about improvement, good behavior, or cooperative acts. The happy-gram is a nice "pat on the back" for a student and lets parents see that small deeds or improvements are acknowledged and appreciated. Clip-art books, CDs, and websites often have several types of happy-grams that can be duplicated for use. A teacher can easily design her own using school logos, mascots, or student-drawn designs. As with spontaneous notes, a ready supply of these kept in a visible location make it fairly easy to complete a couple in just a minute or two. Generally, the simplest happy-grams require only that the child's name and date be filled in (see Figure 5.3). If a return response is desired, a space can be provided at the bottom of the happy-gram for that purpose. Make sure that happy-grams go home to all students periodically.

Websites

Increasingly, adults are relying on electronic forms of communication to stay in touch, to seek answers to questions, or obtain information. Schools and child-care centers that provide websites and e-mail access to employees find that families may prefer these methods of communication because they can be accessed from home or work, 24 hours a day, 7 days a week.

To help you talk
with your child about
his or her school day,
here is a brief description
of what your child did today.

CENTERS WHERE YOUR CHILD PLAYED: _____

_____

LANGUAGE: _____

_____

SPECIAL ACTIVITIES: _____

_____

_____

GYM: _____

_____

SNACKS WE ATE: _____

_____

MY JOB: _____

_____

_____

OTHER: _____

_____

FIGURE 5.2 Daily Activity Log

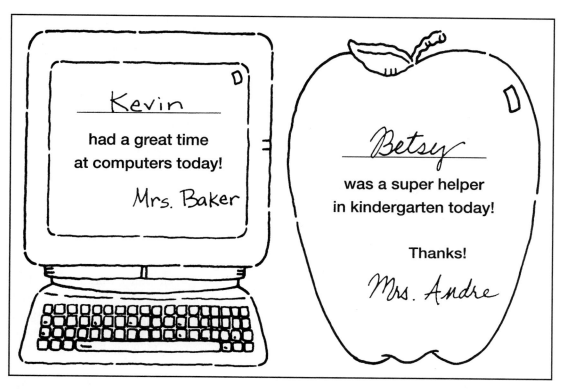

FIGURE 5.3 Happy-Grams

Basic school or center information should be posted and regularly updated on center and school websites to provide easy access for families regarding events such as registration, field trips, and hours of operation. In addition, photos from recent field trips and class parties can be posted and shared with family members who might not have been in attendance.

Websites should be organized by main pages and classroom or teacher pages so that family members can easily locate information. Generally, the principal or director is responsible for listing basic contact information, location, directions, and the principal's or center director's name, phone, and fax numbers, as well as a directory of e-mail addresses. Other basic information such as contact with parent–teacher organizations, bus schedules, and main offices is usually included on the main page.

Links to classroom pages provide easy access for families interested in viewing information about classroom activities. Teachers are usually responsible for updating individual pages, although procedures for doing this may vary depending on the school or center. News such as upcoming opportunities to volunteer, field trip notices, requests for donations of materials, and introductions of new staff can be posted on a teacher's web page. Family members who are unable to visit the center or school on a regular basis will feel included in the "information loop" and will be able to talk with their children about events important to them. This is critical for not only the noncustodial parent but also a parent who may be stationed in the military, a grandparent who does not drive, or working parents who are simply unavailable during the day (Sheldon, 2002).

E-mail

Electronic mail has emerged during the last decade as the communication method of choice among many people for both work and personal use. Teachers who elect to use e-mail may find that ongoing communication is more readily accessed than with phone communication. While nothing can replace a live conversation between two people, e-mail allows working parents to maintain a written conversation within the limitations of their schedules. Parents who cannot take personal phone calls at work can become frustrated by phone messages from a teacher that are retrieved after the center or school has closed. Similarly, teachers appreciate e-mail for the flexibility it affords them to contact parents during the evenings and on weekends, when phone calls might be intrusive (Prior & Gerard, 2007). E-mailing can also be more informative than a passport notebook or classroom journal, which requires teachers to compose comments during the day when they are also responsible for supervising the children. Additionally, e-mail can be more private and more expressive than a system of stars or check marks when communicating about behavioral concerns.

Care must be exercised when using e-mail to ensure that the message sent is the message the teacher intended to convey. By design, e-mail is meant to be quickly produced and sent; that is one of its primary advantages. However, the teacher should frequently check spelling and grammar so that a professional impression is maintained in all communications. It is sound practice for teachers to review each other's e-mails periodically to provide feedback on the tone of the messages. Written words have a lengthy lifespan, and a harsh or poorly written e-mail will likely be brought to the attention of the principal or director by a parent.

Another area of caution with the advent of e-mail involves confidentiality. Teachers should not use e-mail to relay sensitive information about a child to parents, as there can be no expectation of the receiver's privacy. In some circumstances, e-mail containing a child's name may also be considered an official student record and, therefore, could be subject to subpoena in the event of a due process hearing or litigation.

Parent Contracts

Home–school contracts demonstrate a commitment to parent involvement by requiring a planned promise of participation. Some schools or centers utilize a one-way contract, signed by parents, to agree to a minimum number of hours of volunteering, observation, attendance at conferences, or participation in parent education classes. Ideally, the contract would be a two-way document, signed by parents and school personnel, outlining each party's responsibilities toward the child's education. School personnel could agree to provide a range of resources for meeting a child's academic needs, use appropriate methods of reporting student progress, and provide opportunities for conferences. The use of contracts should not reflect a deficit approach. Emphasis should be on what will be done by all parties involved instead of consequences of negative actions should they occur. Contracts that specify punitive courses of action will not set a positive tone for the relationship.

Parent Compacts

One outgrowth of the No Child Left Behind (NCLB) Act was the school–parent compact. NCLB specifies that a compact should outline the means by which the school and parents will build and develop a partnership to help children achieve the state's high standards. The goal of the legislation is that educators work with families to develop a comprehensive plan for partnerships linked to school goals for student achievement and success. School districts who access Title I funds are required to adopt policies to ensure that the parent compact exists. Under the law, the following rules were developed for how school districts need to involve parents:

- Write parent involvement policies that are developed jointly with parents.
- Hold an annual meeting to explain parents' rights to be involved.
- Write school improvement plans that include strategies for parent involvement.
- Spend around 1 percent of district money on engaging families.
- Inform parents, in an understandable language, about the progress of their children and what they can do to help.
- Notify parents if a teacher does not meet the federal definition of "highly qualified."
- Distribute an annual report card on the performance of schools.
- Inform parents if a school is low-performing and provide options for transferring to a better-performing school as well as free tutoring the following year.
- Spread information about effective parent involvement practices and help schools with lagging parent involvement programs.

Parent Surveys and Questionnaires

Parent surveys and questionnaires are efficient ways of gathering information from large groups of people. There are a number of reasons to do a needs assessment or survey of a group of parents:

1. To determine what parents want to contribute to the school, center, or program

2. To determine what parents want to learn about or discuss

3. To determine what services or programs parents want the school to initiate

4. To determine what changes parents would like to make in existing programs and services

Considering these purposes may help to channel thinking and to narrow down the specific information that is needed. Decisions on the focus of the questions should be based on input from teachers, principals, and parents. Is the staff already investigating major program changes, an improved volunteer program, or the initiation of a new service? A needs assessment could provide valuable insights from future participants that would be helpful in shaping the activity. See Figure 5.4.

A teacher may devise his or her own survey to gain information about a child's home environment and previous experiences. A teacher may utilize a questionnaire, filled out by parents at orientation meetings, to provide background information about incoming students. These tools allow parents the opportunity to share their views of their child as a learner and describe any areas of concern. See Figure 5.5.

Utilizing Results. Kindergarten and early childhood teachers often survey parents about the literacy environment at home and the child's previous experience with books. Educators find that this information helps them design appropriate and realistic goals for incoming students and provides insight into how much support for literacy exists in the home.

When the survey deals with parent opinion, it is important to follow up with the survey results so that parents see that their opinions were read and tabulated. A general summary of the information gathered and ideas about the future use of the data will communicate to the parents an honest attempt on the part of the school to incorporate their opinions into the planning of new programs.

Once a program or service is instituted, it is wise to do an annual evaluation survey to generate feedback from participants. Again, publish the results in order to share findings with all parents. For example, in response to a survey of prekindergarten parents' interests in school-sponsored summer

INFORMATION QUESTIONNAIRE

CHILD'S NAME: _____

PARENTS' NAMES: _____

ADDRESS: _____

PHONE: _____

CHILD'S BIRTHDAY: _____

WILL YOUR CHILD RIDE A BUS? _____ NUMBER: _____

DID YOUR CHILD ATTEND PRESCHOOL? _____

NAME: _____

Does your child have any health problems of which the teacher should be aware?

Does your child require any special medicine?

Is your child allergic to anything? If yes, how does it affect the child?

Does your child have any speech problems?

Does your child have any vision problems? If yes, does the child wear glasses?

Does your child have any hearing problems or frequent ear infections?

What are any special interests of your child?

What do you see as your child's academic strengths?

What do you see as your child's academic weaknesses?

Would you be willing to help in the classroom?

Would you be willing to come to the classroom to share information?

___ Career (What?)_____

___ Hobbies or Interests (What?) _____

___ Other areas: _____

Specify other ways you might be interested in helping:

Would you be willing to help on projects at home if you are unavailable during the school day?

___ Cutting   ___ Sewing   ___ Donating Items

___ Other areas: (please specify) _____

LIST ANY AREAS OF CONCERN OR OTHER THINGS YOU WANT US
TO BE AWARE OF ON THE BACK OF THIS FORM.

FIGURE 5.4 Request for Basic Information about a Child

HELP ME KNOW YOUR CHILD

Date _____

Dear Parent/Guardian:

I invite you to share with me the talents, interests, and habits of your child, _____ , so that I may be prepared to teach in the best way possible. Please share concerns about your child so we can have a cooperative team approach to education. Call and let me know when you would like to visit our classroom or just talk about your child. The best time to reach me during the day is from _____ to _____ p.m. at _____ (telephone).

1. My child learns best by _____

   _____

2. Some things I do at home to help my child learn are _____

   _____

3. Right now my child's goal/dream is _____

   _____

4. You will know my child is having problems when _____

   _____

5. The thing my child likes best about school is _____

   _____

6. One difficulty my child has at school is _____

   _____

7. When my child is having difficulty learning something, I find it works best to

   _____

   _____

8. Questions I would like to discuss at a parent/teacher conference include

   _____

   _____

Please return this form to   Teacher_____

FIGURE 5.5 Request for Parent's Observations about a Child

activities, a school could follow up with parents: "We found that 68 percent of parents requested a parent–child story hour to be held weekly at the library during the summer vacation. We are investigating the feasibility of beginning such a program with the help of the local library."

Tips for Composing a Questionnaire or Survey

1. Determine what you need to know and why. Review question content carefully so that the data collected provides meaningful information. Answers to the survey questions should provide necessary facts to assist decision makers.

2. Identify who is conducting the survey, the purpose, and the goal of gathering the information. People are reluctant to take their time to fill out a survey without knowing the organization's name or the reason for doing the assessment. If the survey is to be sent to parents and community members instead of being filled out in a group, be certain that this information is clearly stated.

3. Keep the questionnaire or survey brief. One or two pages is the optimum length. Completion and return rates generally drop off if a survey is overly time-consuming. Consider an online survey, if possible, to allow parents to easily respond without the delay of mailing or sending back paper responses.

4. Write clear, jargon-free instructions. Have a test group of parents complete the survey, checking for technical wording or confusing directions.

5. If a rating scale is used, observe the following:
   - Limit the choices to no more than five. For example "excellent," "somewhat helpful," "fair," "not useful," and "did not apply" would be enough choices for parents filling out a workshop evaluation.
   - Ask only one question at a time.
   - Include an alternative indicating "don't know" or "does not apply."
   - Make sure sentence stems grammatically and semantically fit the choices.

6. Include blank space for respondent comments and encourage individuals to add personal remarks.

7. Consider grouping similar topic areas together to simplify survey completion.

8. Create a visually appealing, easy-to-read survey that is free of spelling and grammatical errors.

9. Clearly indicate when and where the completed survey should be returned.

Passport Systems

Passport systems and dialogue journals are two effective means of maintaining daily communication between home and school. Research has shown that daily communication improves the quality of the parent–teacher relationship. A passport can be as simple as a notebook that travels with a student to school each day and allows the teacher to carry on a written conversation about the child's behavior or academic progress. It can also be an ongoing e-mail conversation that takes place daily if the parent and teacher each have regular access to the Internet.

It is helpful to introduce the passport concept during a conference so that the method can be fully explained and a plan of action determined that is agreeable to both teacher and parents. It is important to the success of the passport system that the child be included in setting up this process. If a notebook is used, parents and teachers should explain the procedure and encourage the child's cooperation in transporting the notebook to and from school. Care should be taken to help the child understand that the messages are meant to help, not to exist as a source of punishment. Emphasis on a positive reward system instead of a punitive one will encourage the child to participate. If e-mail is used, the information shared can be kept confidential from the student and anyone else who might have access to a notebook during the child's day.

A passport system or journal can be as general or as focused as the situation requires. The teacher may wish to comment on the child's overall behavior during the course of the day or focus on one specific behavior. It is important to remember that examining one or two behaviors at a time will result in a higher rate of success for the child.

A planning session to begin the passport notebook should include the following:

1. **Discussion of goals for the child.** Keep goals short and attainable. Set short-term goals that move toward the desired result. Make sure that parents and the teacher are in agreement about the goals that are set.

2. **A description of the incentive and point systems being employed.** In order to gain the child's cooperation in delivering the passport, many teachers find that a point system tied to incentives ensures an acceptable level of compliance. During the planning conference, teachers and parents can collaborate on the number of points, as well as the frequency of rewards that seem appropriate for the age of the child.

3. **Discussion of the nature of feedback.** The teacher should model the type and length of the entries so that parents know what to expect and understand the kinds of comments that are most helpful to the teacher. Assurances to

parents that it is their input that is valued, rather than their spelling or handwriting, will go a long way toward gaining full cooperation. Teachers need to be sensitive to the concerns some parents may have about writing to the school, especially if their literacy level is low. Use informal language to make the entries as clear and as jargon free as possible.

4. Periodic conferences to discuss student progress in greater depth. Plan to meet periodically for in-depth discussions of the child's progress. Agree on a tentative schedule and then keep the appointments, even when things are going well. This will reinforce the concept that not all conferences are about problems.

Since the goal of the notebook is ongoing communication, it is important to bear in mind that positive references are more easily received by parents than are daily doses of negative comments or criticism. Emphasis on positive behaviors can be modeled for parents through use of the passport system. As an example, consider Mark, who is 6 years old and in first grade. He is generally disruptive during morning calendar time by using a very loud voice, talking out repeatedly when others are speaking, and teasing other students with silly names. His parents and his teacher have agreed to focus on Mark's disruptive speech first.

POSITIVE EXAMPLE:

> Mark exercised self-control during show-and-tell today and responded to the first reminder given to let others have their turns. He is still working on quiet behavior in the library during storytelling time.

NEGATIVE EXAMPLE:

> Mark had to be reminded three times during show-and-tell to stop yelling out. The librarian had to remove him from the group because of his loud talking.

As a teacher, try to imagine being on the receiving end of your comments from time to time to ensure that the focus of the passport has not lapsed into purely "bad news." It can be very discouraging for a parent as well as a student to be unsuccessful for long stretches of time. If there is little or no progress, it may be necessary to consider shorter intervals for reporting success or a modification of the reward system. As with all methods of written communication, care should be exercised to ensure that the message communicates the appropriate intent and tone and is not a reflection of frustration or anger on the part of the teacher.

Limitations of the passport or journal system include the possible unreliability of students bringing the passport home, potential privacy issues if the student attends child care after school, and daily time constraints that may limit the teacher from being able to take the time to adequately address the day's events. Loss of the notebook may also mean that weeks or months of records of student behavior are lost unless the teacher also has kept other notes. Teachers, principals, and directors may find this a topic worthy of staff discussion to identify the best method overall for their particular parent population.

Methods of Assessment and Reporting Progress to Parents

There is probably no single communication between home and school that is as emotionally charged and misunderstood as the report card. Parents expect to find a single grade that summarizes their child's progress and achievement in each content area. The traditional letter grading systems (A, B, C, D, and F) are often complicated by the use of pluses and minuses, which do little to clarify the status of the child's achievement in any given subject. Interpretation of the grading system and how individual grades are computed is further confused by the fact that grading scales and criteria for assigning grades vary not only from school to school and grade to grade but among individual teachers. Report cards often include the assignment of an effort grade, which is usually translated into a conduct grade by both parents and teachers. It is little wonder that many parents feel anxiety and tension when confronted with the report card four times each year.

One of the greatest drawbacks to the traditional report card is that it conveys very little specific information about grade level expectations relative to the child's performance and developmental level. Parents of even "A" students would find it difficult to compose a list of the skills and behaviors that comprise a reading, writing, or math grade. They should not be expected to do so. However, it *is* the responsibility of the educational system to provide parents with an accurate picture of the myriad of skills and behaviors that contribute to becoming an accomplished reader, writer, and problem solver. While the individual teacher likely has little control over the method required by the school for reporting academic and social progress to parents, he or she can ensure that an ample supply of support documentation is maintained to share with parents at conferences. This information may occur in the form of portfolios, classroom assessments, and other evidence-based work samples that have been collected over time and demonstrate a child's progress.

Improvements to the traditional report card have been developed as a result of the standards movement that has been implemented in every state since the late 1990s. Learning standards and benchmarks found in the Illinois Learning Standards, the North Carolina Extended Content Standards, and the State of Maine Learning Results, for example, provide statewide curricular frameworks that govern the content of state assessments. State standards also provide individual school districts with guidance regarding what students should know and be able to do as a result of a K–12 education, and all school districts are expected to implement curricula that are aligned to their state's specific goals and standards. In response, some schools now utilize a standards-based report card, which reports student achievement by standard and benchmark so that a single grade is not attempting to convey student academic progress in each content area. Many states are also now adopting early childhood standards that specifically outline how early childhood education links to elementary education, presenting a seamless curricular framework for prekindergarten through twelfth grade.

The Portfolio Approach. In the early childhood and elementary settings, portfolios present parents with a more complete and detailed picture of their child as a learner and thinker (NAEYC, 1988). Educators in early childhood and primary classrooms have included the **portfolio approach** as a method of charting student progress. A portfolio is a folder or file with individual work samples of both the child's and teacher's choosing that can be examined to assess growth and maturation in the learning process. Teachers select samples, date them, and often include an anecdote to describe the focus of the lesson at the time. Parents and teachers can then observe strengths, weaknesses, and areas of interest that reveal specific information about the child and his or her development level. Tape-recorded interviews of a child's reading, examples of a student's writing, examples of art projects, photos of a child participating in a science experiment, and copies of journal entries are all examples of portfolio contents. A teacher may add notes about writing and reading conferences held throughout the quarter as well as observations about the child's interest in books and listening behaviors, notations of story retellings, and descriptions of shared reading experiences. Portfolios also may include inventories, checklists, and rubrics that organize skills and information about particular content areas. A portfolio can be subject-specific, such as a language arts portfolio, or comprehensive for a quarter or semester, containing work samples in a range of subjects.

Advantages of Using Portfolios. One advantage of the portfolio method is that it can be adapted for use with any age or grade. On the early childhood level (birth through third grade), the portfolio approach can be a valuable aid in documenting the maturation through the developmental stages of writing, emergent literacy behaviors, and a variety of social skills. When a narrative is written for the report card or progress report, the teacher focuses on the whole child as a listener, speaker, beginning reader, writer, and thinker. Comments include the level of social-emotional development and fine and gross motor coordination. The use of multiple assessments allows a teacher to record more than just "paper and pencil" scores from standardized tests and screenings. Parents and teachers can more easily assess the impact each facet of development has on the whole child as a learner when all domains of development are fully examined. In this way, parents are also learning about the process of reading and writing, the expectations for the individual grade level, and the rate at which maturation and important developmental milestones can be expected to occur. See Figure 5.6 for an example of an observation form for language arts and Figure 5.7 for the related checklist.

Software that allows teachers and students to develop electronic portfolios is becoming more common in classrooms with access to technology. Students from early childhood levels to upper elementary grades can participate in the creation of their individual year's record of growth in any or all subject areas; the CD is easily and inexpensively copied and provided to the family at the end of the school year as a record of the child's growth in reading, writing, art, or math. The software is designed with formats that replicate album pages with spaces for photos or artwork to be added along with copies of essays and writing samples. Teachers from an early childhood special education class, for example, created such albums for the parents of their students. "A picture is worth a thousand words" comes to mind when trying to display how young children interact with hands-on activities at centers, and the albums provide parents with a wonderful keepsake of their child with their peers. Again, as a complement to narratives and checklists, photos enhance the parents' ability to "see" into the classroom. Such software is relatively inexpensive but requires access to a digital camera and computer.

Newsletters

Newsletters are extremely important channels of communication for parents and schools as well as community resources, hospitals, doctors' offices, and many other institutions. Newsletters are as diverse as the organizations that produce them. Newsletters from public libraries inform parents about upcoming children's events; newsletters from hospitals describe scheduled classes and support groups; and newsletters from community resources such as museums, zoos, and the YMCA keep parents in touch with programs for children and families. Child development and education researchers publish newsletters to reach an audience interested in current studies, trends, and legislation concerning children and families. Schools and day-care centers often publish newsletters about their programs in order to keep parents up-to-date on the latest events, policy and personnel changes, and general news pertaining to the class or center. As a source of information, newsletters are invaluable for keeping parents abreast of the things they need to know for and about their children (Krech, 1995).

Child's Work and Behavior in Language Arts
(cite specific indications of skills or knowledge)

Settings and Activities	Examples of Child's Activities
Story Time: Teacher reads to class (responses to story line, child's comments, questions, elaborations)	
Independent Reading: Book time (nature of books child chooses or brings in, process of selecting, quiet or social reading)	
Writing: (journal stories, alphabet, dictation)	
Reading, Group/Individual: (oral reading strategies, discussion of text, responses to instruction)	
Reading-Related Activities, Tasks: (responses to assignments or discussion focusing on word–letter properties, word games/experience charts)	
Informal Settings: (use of language in play, jokes, storytelling, conversation)	
Books and Print as Resource: (use of books for projects; attention to signs, labels, names; locating information)	
Other:	

FIGURE 5.6 Language Arts Observation Form

Kindergarten and First-Grade Language Arts Outcomes

Name_____ Date_____ Grade_____

Attitudes   The student:
1. Is comfortable speaking in front of others.
2. Values and respects what others have to say.

Concepts   The student:
1. Understands when it is important to listen.
2. Knows language is used to share ideas and feelings.

LISTENING/SPEAKING LEARNING INDICATORS The student:	Usually	Occasionally	Working On	Comments
1. begins to develop active listening skills (looks at speaker, responds appropriately)				
2. follows simple oral directions				
3. listens attentively while others read				
4. remembers ideas, characters, and events from stories				
5. expresses complete thoughts				
6. uses age-appropriate vocabulary				
7. participates in class discussions				
8. participates in chants, poetry, dramatizations, etc.				
9. retells familiar stories				
10. speaks audibly with accurate pronunciation and standard English				

FIGURE 5.7 Language Arts Checklist

Factors to Consider. There are several factors to consider before undertaking the publication of a newsletter; reviewing these may help a school or center determine whether a newsletter is the best method available. First, decide if the information to be delivered is already being presented to the target audience in another form (such as workshops, conferences, magazines, or websites). To be useful to the proposed audience, a newsletter must contain information that is timely and relevant. Teachers should avoid duplication of the efforts of another source, such as the school office, which may be doing an adequate job of conveying specific news for parents. The staff may decide that parent meetings or "make it and take it" workshops accomplish the stated purpose more effectively if curriculum information is the goal. When it is decided that a newsletter is the best vehicle for dispensing information, consideration of several factors can help create a focus for the publication.

In order to write a successful newsletter, an audience must be determined. In a school setting, for example, will the news be strictly for the parents, or is it also for other teachers in the school or center? Will the news be about a specific class, or will all classes be included in one general effort? The audience needs to be clearly defined so that the material will be relevant to the readers. It is also wise to consider the literacy level of the primary audience, ensuring that the publication is useful to those for whom it is intended.

The next task is to determine the overall purpose of the newsletter. Examine the following partial listing of purposes a school newsletter may adopt. Several may be worked into one publication; again, it is crucial to state the purpose in order to judge what is appropriate to print for a particular audience (Arnold, 2005). An editor of a school newsletter for example, could consider the following purposes:

- To keep parents informed about classroom activities
- To educate parents with information on child development
- To provide insight into the educational purposes of classroom activities
- To keep teachers informed about events in other classrooms
- To act as a "clearinghouse" for parenting books, videos, parent education classes, and events in the community designed to appeal to families
- To assist in the recruitment of volunteer help
- To acknowledge donations of time, materials, and money

A school or center may choose a single purpose as a primary focus or use a combination of these to achieve the correct balance of information (Couchenour & Chrisman 2008).

Another factor to be considered is the choice of an editor and writer for the newsletter. Some publications come from a director's office and are totally under his or her control, while others have submissions from classroom teachers, parents, and students. Another type of newsletter is one that is published by the individual teacher for and about his or her students. If the objective is to be the source of a variety of information, it may be wise to include many people on the staff and appoint one person as the editor. Special care should be taken to choose someone who has excellent writing and grammar skills and who is conscientious about details and deadlines. If the purpose is solely to educate parents, it may be wise to leave all editorial choices to the newsletter originator, who will be responsible for the entire content.

Time must be allocated to research, write, edit, and produce a good newsletter. If there is the possibility of release time for handling the duties of writing and editing, be certain it will be of an ongoing nature. If it is to be the sole responsibility of a classroom teacher (and therefore added to an already-long list of tasks), then careful consideration will need to be given to the length and frequency of publication.

Content Areas. There are a variety of content ideas that can be included in the publication of a newsletter. Some are regular features, appearing in every issue, while others appear when appropriate. It is important to have regular features that parents can anticipate reading; if specific types of information are routinely included, the newsletter will develop a good readership.

General Classroom News. A section containing general news about the class is especially effective when specific children's names are included (as long as each child can be mentioned during the year). Be certain to include special projects or productions that students may be involved in; parents are always interested in reading about the wide range of activities that take place in a busy classroom. See Figure 5.8 for an example of a newsletter containing general news.

Description of Upcoming Units. This section is used to explain to parents the educational goals of planned activities. This can help parents in reviewing classroom routines or in understanding changes to be made in regular scheduling. It can also be a method of soliciting the donation of particular items needed for a unit or requesting volunteer help from parents who may have a talent or skill in the topic area being covered.

Parenting Ideas. A section covering suggestions for parenting is another content area often covered in a newsletter. A particular area of interest can be featured in each issue, perhaps at the suggestion of parents. This type of content can enable the director or editor to describe examples of developmentally sound activities that parents and children can share. It can also be an excellent chance for the editor to elaborate on elements of child development and how they relate to classroom incidents. A teacher may find that an article on separation anxiety in young children, for example, will give a more detailed explanation for

Baker's Bulletin

March 30

Easter Hat Parade!

Thursday, April 5 at 1:30 is the annual 1st Grade Spring Hat Parade at Bradley East. The children need to have their hats at school by 8:30 on this day. The judging begins in each classroom at that time. Please come and watch the parade and the awards given to 3 hats in each classroom this Thursday!

Spring vacation begins at 2:30 on April 5th following the Spring Hat Parade.

Thanks to all the families who came out and cheered on the teachers and Bradley Police in a friendly (?) game of basketball last Tuesday Night. It was a lot of fun and for a good cause.

Bag Books
Please have your child return their bag books at least once a week. They can return them more often if they finish reading them and would like new ones.

Snack
The snack calendar is on the back side of this newsletter.

Teacher Assistants this week were . . . Grant, Clayton, Beth, Cameron, and Daejaunte

Check out the Grapevine Newspaper at: BradleySchools.com

Have a safe and wonderful Spring Vacation. School resumes on April 16th.

FIGURE 5.8 Teacher's Newsletter

behavior occurring in the classroom. Similarly, the sharing of information will aid parents and teachers in choosing a consistent method of handling the numerous incidents that require tact and understanding, both in the classroom and at home. The editor can research (and credit) parenting information from the many available resources or write original material.

Clearinghouse. This popular content area contains information about and reviews of many types of resources for parents, such as magazines, books, videos, speakers, parent education programs, or local library story hours. A well-organized and accurate listing of events is a great service for busy families and will encourage attendance at quality programs for children.

Children's Art and Stories. Samples of student work are featured in many newsletters as a way to highlight ongoing activities. Even the simplest newsletter can employ this technique, using a copier to reduce drawings. The newsletter will be eagerly anticipated if parents see their children's efforts being publicly recognized. Again, it is important to include examples from all classes and/or students on a rotating basis. A simple checklist can be maintained to ensure that all children are included during the year.

Calendar of Events. Providing parents with a simple calendar (see Figure 5.9) is an efficient way to let them know what to expect in the coming weeks and may reduce the need for a steady stream of notes and reminders. For a broader-based newsletter, a calendar can chart upcoming community events of interest to parents and children, important deadlines about screenings, immunization dates, and registrations of class dates and times. For a classroom, the calendar is an easy method of preparing parents for all upcoming activities, deadlines, messy art or playground days, snack contributions, or volunteer obligations. Encouraging parents to use and refer to the calendar will increase the chances that the newsletter will be regularly read.

Want Ads. Advertisements of items or services for sale and wanted, especially for baby equipment, winter clothing, and babysitting, can be a popular feature. Parents can begin to network with other parents for exchange of goods and services within a similar group of families. A simple request for ads to be included in each issue could be posted on the parent bulletin board.

Publicity and Public Relations. These needs of the school or center can be handled through the newsletter. Highlighting an exceptional teacher, student, special event, or achievement can be a way of creating local interest in the school or center. This feature can also be a place to thank parents for donations of time, money, or materials. It is important to remember that volunteers need recognition, and this is an excellent way to show appreciation to those who contribute.

A Yearlong Theme. Information on a theme such as family literacy, family math, or cooking with children can also be a regular feature in the newsletter. An editor could choose useful information from a book or magazine and share it

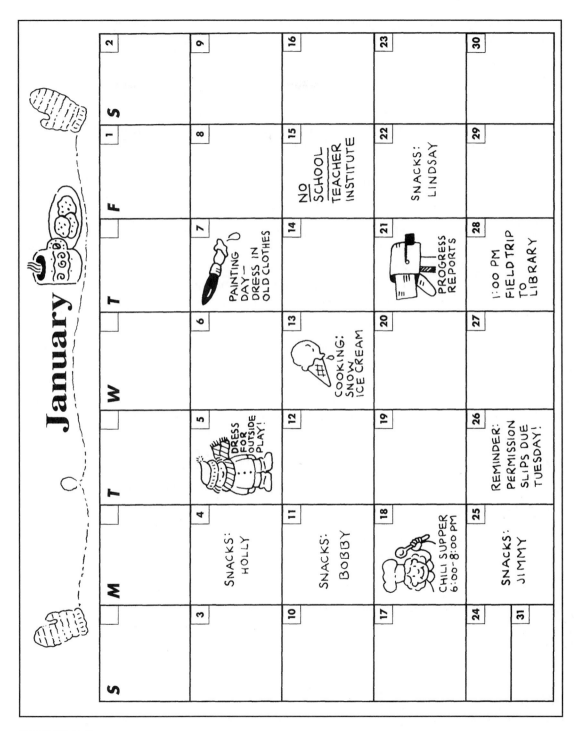

FIGURE 5.9 Activity Calendar

with parents in an effort to promote parent–child interaction at home. Remember that copyrighted material should be credited each time it appears.

Staff Biographies. Including engaging information about school or program staff is another way to familiarize parents with teachers, administrators, and other support employees. Short descriptions of interests, goals, or talents help parents see staff members as interesting people.

Membership News. Any parent–teacher or home–school organization operating in the school or agency may desire space in the newsletter for reporting recent activity and news. A regular feature ensures greater exposure, which could result in increased participation in fundraisers or at meetings.

Children's Page. A section of simple activities helps ensure that children will deliver the newsletter to their parents. A first-grade teacher solved the problem of newsletters "missing in transit" by including a clip-art pattern of shapes along the bottom of the first page. After their parents were finished with the newsletter, students were to color a pattern similar to patterns being explored in math class. Readership improved dramatically when students had a chance to demonstrate their newly acquired skills.

Newsletter Formats.

A format can be created through the use of lines, boxes, blank spaces, graphics, and type size. Consider the overall appearance desired when deciding on a format. A newsletter with columns unbroken by lines and boxes creates a scholarly, academic appearance. Boxes and clip art used strategically will evoke a more informal appearance that is easy on the eyes and simple to read and absorb. See Figure 5.10 for an example of a newsletter format that is simple, effective, and fun.

The use of identifying logos is a good way to add graphic interest to each page. Decide on a logo and use related artwork to denote article beginnings and endings, important sections of information, and so on. For example, a school district parent education program that features a baby tiger (the district sports mascot) as a key part of its logo uses small paw prints as lead-in graphics for each article. This method helps guide the reader's eyes to specific blocks of information and also provides relief from columns of print. The use of logos also helps the reader connect the newsletter to the school or agency.

To increase readability, experiment with page layouts, blank space, graphics, and print to find a combination pleasing to the eye. Time spent organizing and arranging in the beginning stages of production is time well spent. When an easy-to-write, appealing-to-read newsletter has been designed, the staff will be proud to share it with administrators, parents, and prospective families.

Types of Newsletters.

There are primarily three types of newsletters a school or center may wish to consider: teacher-generated, prepublished, and professionally printed. There are also combinations of the three that may be adapted to suit individual needs.

FIGURE 5.10 Shape Format Newsletter

The easiest and most personal type is the teacher-generated newsletter that is often handwritten and photocopied in school. The teacher has complete control over the content and total responsibility for distribution to the parents. This type of newsletter is always well received because individual children are named and specific activities described. A simple page with seasonal graphics and a few rules or boxes can be an easy method of organizing information. Newsletters of this type can be photocopied at school on colorful paper. There are numerous school-related clip-art books and software programs available at teacher-supply stores and libraries that cover every imaginable content area, fundraiser, theme, or holiday. Uncomplicated letterhead forms can be found in many clip-art books, and computer software packages are published for virtually all levels of computer expertise. Either method can help create an interesting format that will save time and be simple to use. For minimal investment, this type of newsletter can be within reach of the tightest budgets.

A middle-of-the-road approach could be to purchase a newsletter from a publishing company and personalize it with a school address and logo. This is an easy way to dispense parenting information and articles related to child development without placing undue strain on any single teacher or the director. Companies sell newsletters intended for every age, with each covering topics relevant to the families of a specific group of children. This is a costlier method than the teacher-generated publication, but it requires far less investment of time, research, materials, and labor. Preschools and day-care centers may distribute a prepublished newsletter, possibly from the corporate office, that has a space for a handwritten note from individual teachers.

A professionally printed newsletter will undoubtedly be too costly for most classrooms and groups, although a center or elementary school could ask a staff member with desktop publishing experience for a comparable effect. There are numerous software programs available that produce newsletters with extremely professional results. A professionally printed newsletter has an almost unlimited range of color combinations, photographs, graphics, and paper quality. Design and layout services generally are included in the cost of printing in order to assure a superior product.

Parent Bulletin Board and Posted Announcements

In addition to the newsletters, handouts, and notes that go home with students on a regular basis, many teachers find that a parent bulletin board is an efficient way of dispensing information to families and caregivers. Located near pickup and drop-off areas or in the classroom, the parent bulletin board serves several useful purposes. Many teachers routinely post the snack schedule, school calendar, lunch and breakfast menus, volunteer schedules, recent newsletters, book orders, and other distributed material in order to inform parents of upcoming activities or for those who may have misplaced the information. Last-minute reminders about deadlines for book orders, fundraiser money, or permission slips are apt to be read and acted upon, especially while the parent is in the building. Unclaimed articles of clothing can also be posted for parent identification. A bulletin board can instantly communicate an outbreak of chicken pox, for example, hours before individual notes can be sent home.

Parent bulletin boards can also be a vehicle for parents who want to share information with each other about parent–teacher news, room-parent responsibilities, parent advisory group minutes or decisions, and community events. This dedicated bulletin board can be of special interest at orientation meetings or registration times.

Creation of a special place where parents can share and receive information is a way of indicating respect for families and their value to the school. The parent bulletin board should be easy to spot and updated regularly to attract an audience. See Figure 5.11.

A preschool parent board is an excellent way to convey information to hurried parents. *Courtesy of ECE Photo Library.*

THE ROLE OF THE PRINCIPAL OR DIRECTOR IN FAMILY INVOLVEMENT

Critical to the development of a strong parent involvement component in a school or child-care center is the administrator. Often overlooked in textbooks and training programs, the administrator not only plays a key role in establishing the expectation

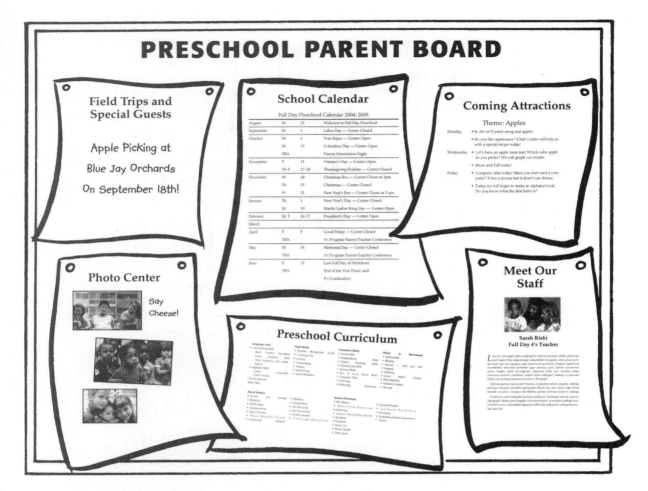

FIGURE 5.11 Informational Bulletin Board

of regular communication between faculty and the families they serve but is usually the person responsible for producing school handbooks, informational brochures, and school newsletters. The attitude, philosophy, and skills of the principal or director will, in large part, determine whether or not the school or center is a family-friendly place. A principal or director who values family involvement will support written communication strategies by providing tech support for web page development and staff e-mail; assistance with publication of school handbooks, informational packets, brochures, and yearbooks; and space for parent bulletin boards and informational boards.

The principal or director's role in assessing the level of parent communication can begin by conducting an analysis, such as the Home–School Communication Assessment, to determine the types of communication strategies already in place. This assessment can be a positive experience to review together as a staff. Once the chart has been completed, the faculty can begin discussions of targeted areas for increasing parent involvement efforts. In some instances, a staff may decide to select one or two strategies on which to focus for the year. Increasing written communication from each individual classroom might be the goal, with the strategies of newsletters and happy-grams as the methods each teacher will employ. In other instances, staff from one grade level may find deficits in certain types of verbal communications, such as positive phone calls, that they can address, while those from another grade level identify increasing parent conferences as their target strategy. As a result of these staff discussions, several positive outcomes will likely occur: teachers will hear what colleagues believe is valuable in developing partnerships with families, reluctant teachers will find support and "resident experts" who can assist them with the implementation of strategies, and the director will have an up-to-date, working knowledge about the efforts underway to involve parents. This information can form the foundation on which to build a stronger, more comprehensive parent involvement program at the school.

One suburban elementary school found that, while areas for improvement certainly existed at all grade levels, overall, families in the school enjoyed a fairly comprehensive communication plan and parents were active in advocacy and governance roles within the school parent–teacher organization and on community-wide committees. This information served to recharge the staff by providing confirmation of a highly involved family base. In this situation, a director or principal can use the positive information to refocus a staff overly stressed by the problems some families present that occupy a large percentage of a teacher's time and energy to address. In many public schools, identification of such data is necessary for the completion of school improvement plans, both at the school level and those remedial plans required under NCLB.

SCHOOL- OR CENTER-BASED WRITTEN COMMUNICATION STRATEGIES: PARENT HANDBOOKS, YEARBOOKS, INFORMATIONAL PACKETS, AND BROCHURES

The administrator will often initiate the publication of complex types of written communication, such as the parent handbook, a yearbook, and informational brochures. When developed in concert with staff, these documents serve specific purposes in reaching families and communicating about the many events, activities, services, and milestones that occur during the year. Most of these publications are revised and republished annually; therefore, financial resources must be allocated for this purpose.

Parent Handbooks

Parent handbooks are an efficient way to convey the basic policies and requirements of a school or center. Pertinent information is readily available when questions arise, eliminating the common misunderstandings that often result from poorly communicated policies. Parents are more likely to keep a handbook for future reference than a stack of individual handouts on topics ranging from illness to holiday schedules. An effective handbook will communicate to both prospective parents and those currently enrolled in a program. The information presented in a handbook can be divided into four categories: school philosophy, basic operating information, school policies, and general information.

School Philosophy. Central to a parent handbook is the school philosophy. The parent handbook serves as an excellent vehicle for stating the basic philosophy guiding the school and its curriculum. Attitudes about children's learning, classroom environment, and discipline should be outlined in a concise, jargon-free statement. This working philosophy should be reviewed periodically to ensure that it accurately reflects the curriculum and instructional methods.

Basic Operating Information. Basic operating information consists of information unique to a specific school or center, such as:

- name of school
- address and map
- phone numbers
- employees' names and titles
- hours of operation
- calendar of school days
- list of holidays when the school or center is closed
- pickup and drop-off locations and routines
- bad weather and emergency procedures
- tuition amount, date due, method of payment, and consequences of late payment
- absence notification procedures
- immunization requirements for school entrance

This information also is important as a quick reference for relatives and babysitters in need of phone numbers or emergency information.

General School Policies. General school policies are formulated by the director or principal with input from staff. Policies should be modified periodically to reflect the changing needs of the families served. For example, some schools concerned about the increased interest in action cartoons have banned certain toys brought from home for show-and-tell or have limited the children's free time because of aggressive, disruptive play. Diversity in the school population also may necessitate modification of holiday celebrations to eliminate some traditional festivities, such as Halloween and Christmas, and include new observances, such as Fall Festival, Harvest Time, and Friends and Family. These policies should be responsive to the needs of the participating families, and policies should respect the backgrounds of the families represented in the school.

Health guidelines are often described in the handbook. Timetables for returning to school after illnesses such as the chicken pox, flu, fever, and common colds are crucial to the well-being of the staff and students. Educating parents about basic health rules at school is a function of the staff. For many parents, this is their first introduction to practical methods of dealing with childhood illnesses and their transmission. It is also important to specify under what conditions a student must immediately be picked up from school (i.e., injury or acute illness) and how emergency numbers will be utilized. Medication policies should be outlined in this section so that parents have clear-cut answers about which medications are permitted to be given by staff and which are not. Keep in mind that it is far easier to enforce stated health practices when parents have been informed prior to school or program entry.

Discipline is a major concern of parents, teachers, principals, and directors of facilities that provide care for young children. It is essential that the staff members explore various methods of discipline and develop a philosophy about classroom management. Each staff member should be able to articulate the specific steps that will be taken to maintain an environment that encourages respect for all participants. All teachers and aides need to have a thorough understanding of how to handle the many day-to-day situations that arise in the classroom in order to ensure consistent, fair treatment of all children. This is especially important in full-day programs where staff changes may occur two or more times during the day. Behavior modification, reward systems, token economies, and assertive discipline are just a few of the classroom management techniques available to teachers. Educators at a well-run school or center will have spent considerable time researching and exploring various options, as well as sharing input with one another, before choosing a workable method. The discipline philosophy should then be described in clear, understandable terms so that parents know what the expectations are for their child's behavior at school.

Parent involvement policies are necessary to educate and inform parents about their rights and responsibilities concerning participation in their child's education. A comprehensive list of ways to involve parents, both in and out of school, may encourage even reluctant parents to participate. Tasks or responsibilities should cover a broad range of levels of commitment and complexity to appeal to parents with a variety of talents, interests, and schedules. A school or center may wish to include a list of the types of volunteer help needed and the staff members to be contacted for more information. This section also should include any requirements of parents who want to participate in the classroom or in a special program. For example, some districts require TB tests and background checks for all volunteers. Emphasis should be not only on required hours of time spent but also on the numerous benefits parents gain when they are involved in a program (Gestwicki, 2007).

School policies concerning the methods of reporting student progress can also be addressed in the handbook. Schools and centers vary greatly in the type and frequency of progress reports and parent–teacher conferences. Early childhood classrooms, including kindergartens, rely on the parent–teacher conference, which is an opportunity for parents and teachers to have an uninterrupted, face-to-face conversation about the emotional, social, and academic progress of the individual child. Conference frequencies can vary from one to four or more times per year. The progress report is a written summary of work habits, academic skills, and social behaviors described in narrative, symbol, or checklist form. Placing a blank copy of this report in the handbook gives parents a clear picture of the evaluation methods used and the topics to be discussed. This also allows parents time to formulate questions and comments before they receive their child's assessment.

Financial assistance criteria for free breakfast or lunch programs can be described in this section to help parents determine whether or not their child qualifies for services. If scholarships or tuition assistance programs are available, a contact person and phone numbers could be listed along with a confidentiality statement regarding inquiries or referrals.

Other policies that may be included are registration procedures, school facilities, supplemental programs available to students, birthday party and invitation procedures, and preschool screening locations and dates.

General Information. The fourth section of a parent handbook serves as an overview of miscellaneous information of interest to families. Included may be a list of ongoing fundraising projects, their goal for the school or center, and to what degree each family is expected to participate. If a school relies heavily upon the fundraising efforts of its member families for revenue, it is wise to list the projects, their approximate duration, and the timing of commitments to ensure good participation. This section could spotlight previous moneymaking projects and describe how they benefited the children. Programs or materials in existence (i.e., water safety lessons, computers and software, cultural events, or foreign language programs) that were funded by these projects should be mentioned so that prospective and incoming parents understand the need for cooperation and support.

Descriptions of school facilities such as outdoor play areas, computer labs, gymnasiums, and the cafeteria help parents become better acquainted with the entire campus. A clearly labeled map of the school and grounds with areas of interest to parents—the office, main entrances, visitors' parking spaces, conference rooms, auditoriums, and gyms—will be helpful when a parent visits the school to volunteer in the classroom or attend a school function.

Supplemental programs available to students can be listed in this section. Preschools and day-care centers often provide transportation to local facilities offering swimming or gymnastic lessons and will supervise children who wish to enroll. An elementary school may offer a before- and after-school care program for the supervision of children during non-school hours. Programs open to families, such as parent education classes, parent–child activity classes, and other meetings may have short program descriptions and enrollment information listed.

Staff biographies are an excellent way to help parents become acquainted with the many teachers, administrators, and support staff in a school or center. Parents appreciate reading about the people who interact daily with their children.

Parent–teacher organizations and parent advisory boards that exist in a school or program are often described in the handbook. Membership information, a list of contact people and current board members, and schedules of regular meetings may increase interest in these groups and attendance at their functions. Information can be updated from year to year as the handbook is revised.

Publishing the Parent Handbook.

A parent handbook is generally published for distribution at the school or center. Many schools and centers rely on the school logo and assorted reproductions of children's art work to illustrate the handbook. Each grade level may include a page that gives specific information relevant to it, such as immunization requirements, special fees, extra supplies, and so on.

The simplest, most economical method of publication is through the use of a computer, copier, and assorted clip art. It is fairly easy to produce a readable, personalized handbook that can be collated and assembled by parent volunteers before the start of school.

There are several inexpensive methods of binding the handbook. Depending on its length and the tools available, the handbook can be stapled with a colorful cover and distributed in a large envelope with other paperwork during registration. A spiral binding machine that uses plastic combs creates a workbook-like appearance that can be produced assembly-line style with volunteers and a relatively small investment in materials. Some programs put the handbook in a folder that can also be used to store other school forms and notices sent home during the year.

Budget restrictions generally determine the type of handbook that is to be produced. Experimentation with format will result in a product that suits the needs of the individual program or school. Do not overlook fundraising revenues or the resources of a parent–teacher organization as a source of dollars to cover the cost of the handbook. Many organizations are interested in specific ways to contribute and may have volunteers willing to assist in the assembly of the handbook as well.

Yearbooks

A lasting way to establish a school or classroom identity is through a yearbook. Yearbooks may be as simple or as elaborate as the teacher or staff desires; it is the message—"We had a great year; we learned about each other and grew as a group"—that counts. A yearbook is a valuable keepsake for students and parents alike; it allows teachers to highlight special events and student milestones. Prospective and newly enrolled families can readily see the day-to-day workings of a classroom by skimming through this collection of photographs, drawings, quotes, and awards.

Publishing a Yearbook. A yearbook may be a published school-wide effort that is made available to families for a fee. Occasionally, a portion of the cost is underwritten by a parent–teacher organization or a booster club. When a yearbook is to be professionally printed and bound, a committee should oversee its production. Tasks include collecting news from all classrooms, arranging for photographs to be taken, contacting companies for printing prices, and gathering content information. The selection of graphics, proofreading, and order tabulation are additional tasks that can be handled by parent volunteers. Some schools offer a stipend to the teacher who agrees to lend expertise and leadership to such an endeavor.

Frequently a classroom will create a single album to document the year's events. When new topics need to be chronicled, working on the album can be a choice at the writing center. As an ongoing project in an early childhood classroom, the yearbook is often handled by a parent volunteer working at school or at home. Events covered include classroom parties, field trips, special visitors, events, musical programs, unusual centers, new students, student teachers, and new siblings or families. As a class project, older students can exercise almost total control over the editorial content of their yearbook. This project can be an excellent vehicle for allowing students to experience the entire writing-editing-rewriting-publishing process associated with current language arts curricula. One elementary school was fortunate enough to have a former newspaper reporter among its parents, and he was willing to supervise the entire project. The parent volunteered one hour per week assisting children as they selected material, cut and pasted photographs, and illustrated written accounts of classroom events.

Lasting Use. As a tool for communication, yearbooks from previous years can be circulated during registration and orientation meetings to help new parents envision the myriad of activities that will take place in the coming year. Pictures convey significant amounts of information about the children, classroom environment, staff involvement, and kinds of experiences the children enjoy.

Parent Suggestion Box

Communication among parents, teachers, and administrators is often encouraged through personal meetings and conferences. However, due to time restrictions or fear of confrontation, a parent may prefer to voice an opinion in writing. A parent suggestion box placed in a well-marked, centrally located spot in the school can provide a way for parents to share comments or make suggestions. Care should be taken to respond to all suggestions so that participants feel that their opinions were received and acknowledged. It is usually school policy to request a parent's name and phone number on any suggestion so that further comments or information can be obtained, if necessary. Suggestions that may have wide appeal to other families, such as the addition of a new fundraiser, a social event for the school, or ways to improve an existing extracurricular program, could be added to the school newsletter to begin an open discussion. The suggestion box also can serve as the receptacle for parent evaluation forms following parent–teacher conferences, workshops, or parent meetings.

Informational Packets

When a school or program has numerous applications, brochures, fact sheets, and handbooks about a variety of services, it is useful to package them together in an informational packet. Creating a packet simplifies enrollment when a new student arrives midyear or when a family requests information about eligibility for a supplemental program such as prekindergarten, Parents as Teachers, or Title I. Volunteers can assemble necessary literature to make distribution more efficient and complete. Outreach programs often will package materials in this manner because they rely on professionals outside the district to make parent contacts. Churches, preschools, day-care centers, hospitals, greeter services, physicians' offices, and visiting nurses may provide this service because they deal with a wide spectrum of families. Tapping these resources for outreach, as well as using in-district channels, increases the service visibility in the community.

Brochures

Computer software has made the process of creating a unique and personalized brochure quick and easy to do. A brochure can describe the features of a program or a service. Using colorful paper and clip-art graphics, a simple brochure can be an inexpensive way to publicize important resources for parents. The following are examples of programs or services that can be advertised:

- Toy or book lending libraries
- Parent resource libraries
- Parent rooms
- Home visiting services
- Early childhood screenings
- Parent education series
- Prekindergarten classes
- Speech and languages services
- Psychological testing services
- Tuition scholarships
- Before- and after-school child-care programs
- Local social service agencies
- Special education services and parents' rights

Brochures are tools for communicating with parents who may be difficult to reach or reluctant to consider a particular program suggested during a conference or staffing. Brochures may open the door to dialogue by giving parents "food for thought"; they also provide a measure of outreach for parents to share with other parents who may have limited contact with the school.

SUMMARY

Central to parent involvement, whether at a school, day-care center, or community organization, is the communication between the organization and the parents of its students. Planned communication reassures parents that they will be routinely informed about events, upcoming news, and important policies that may affect them or their children.

Communication is also the key to initiating and maintaining positive relationships between parents, teachers, administrators, and the community. This chapter has described a number of methods of written communications, including notes, letters, happy-grams, invitations, bulletin boards, and news-letters—all of which convey important information from schools to families. Other methods of one-way communication, such as report cards, often initiate further contact and are critical in laying the groundwork for positive relationships in future meetings. Passport systems and e-mails represent written conversations that encourage parents' broader level of ongoing participation and input in their child's day-to-day school experiences.

Implementation of new techniques, followed with evaluation by both schools and families, ensures meaningful communication that will create a climate for increased levels of parent involvement. Educators and administrators need to be aware of the changing communication needs of the broad spectrum of families that schools serve today.

ACTIVITIES FOR DISCUSSION, EXPANSION, AND APPLICATION

1. Discuss strategies available to the individual teacher for increasing the level of communication between his or her classroom and students' families.

2. Discuss strategies that could be implemented collaboratively among a group of teachers or an entire school to facilitate improved home–school communication.

3. Develop a comprehensive, one-way communication plan for a specific type of program: Head Start, prekindergarten, or a primary grade. Describe how the methods chosen will serve the parents' need for information and encourage participation in their child's education.

4. Develop a typical school newsletter that would incorporate goals, purposes, and content areas appropriate for a specific population of parents (for example, Head Start, day-care center, or kindergarten class).

5. Initiate a passport book with a student (or hypothetical student), and model responses appropriate to a specific situation (i.e., aggressive behavior in the classroom, difficulty getting assignments completed, or lack of respect for classroom materials).

6. Write an example of a welcome letter, a note requesting a parent conference, and a happy-gram.

7. Design an elementary school or child-care center's web page or a classroom teacher's web page.

8. Create a beginning-of-the-year welcome letter from a teacher to the parents of the children in the class.

CASE STUDY

Lindsay Bennington is a second-year kindergarten teacher who is committed to sending home a monthly newsletter to her students' parents. She has determined that she will cover classroom news, previews of upcoming units, a monthly article about a curricular issue in early childhood education, parenting suggestions, and want ads for used clothing. Her principal is impressed by the scope of the project but cautions Mrs. Bennington about meeting other required deadlines for paperwork and planning responsibilities. In November, Lindsay is behind schedule by several weeks while attempting to prepare for parent–teacher conferences. She decides to reduce the scope of the newsletter in order to meet her end-of-the-month deadline. In December, Lindsay is once again behind due to numerous after-school rehearsals for the holiday concert. She decides to only use the areas that she had deleted in November in order to get the newsletter out before the holiday break. In January, Lindsay sends home a parent survey to gain feedback on the newsletter and is surprised to learn that few parents are reading the letter at all and none have used the want ads section. She is disappointed but is determined to continue with her plan.

1. What are some of the reasons Lindsay's newsletter has not been useful to parents?
2. Should Lindsay proceed with her newsletter? Why?
3. What areas might Lindsay delete from her newsletter and why?
4. If Lindsay still believes that this type of comprehensive newsletter can be useful to parents, what changes will be needed in order to ensure that the project is completed on time each month?

USEFUL WEBSITES

atozteacherstuff.com/pages/1743.shtml
A to Z Teacher Stuff. This teacher resource website contains many helpful ideas for teachers to use in their classrooms and with parent communication.

www.cyfc.umn.edu/publications/seeds/series2v2/key.html
Children, Youth, and Family Consortium. The Consortium was established to build the capacity of the University of Minnesota and Minnesota communities to use research, influence policy, and enhance practice to improve the well-being of Minnesota's children, youth, and families.

www.disabilitysolutions.org/newsletters/files/four/4-2.pdf
Disability Solutions. This online newsletter is for parents of children with disabilities who want to improve relationships and communication between home and school.

www.educationoasis.com/instruction/bt/home-school_communication.htm

Education Oasis. This teacher resource site offers many tips and ideas for improving home–school communication.

REFERENCES

Arnold, M. (2005). *Effective communication techniques for child care.* New York: Thomson.

Caspe, M., Lopez, N., & Wolos, C. (2006–2007). *Family involvement in elementary school children's education* (Family Involvement Make a Difference Research Brief No. 2). Cambridge, MA: Harvard Family Research Project.

Christensen, S. L., & Sheridan, S. M. (2001). *Schools and families: Creating essential connections for learning.* New York: Guilford.

Couchenour, D., & Chrisman, K. (2008). *Families, schools, and communities: Together for young children.* New York: Delmar Learning.

Gestwicki, C. (2007). *Home, school, and community relations.* New York: Thomson.

Hong, S. (2006). Building school–community partnerships: Collaboration for student success. *Harvard Educational Review, 76*(2), 22–34.

Krech, B. (1995). Improve parent communication with a newsletter. *Instructor, 105*(2), 67–73.

National Association for the Education of Young Children. (1988). Position statement on standardized testing of young children 3 through 8 years of age. *Young Children, 43*(3), 42–47.

NCLB rules for parent involvement. (2000). *Gifted Child Today, 30*(1), 6–8.

Prior, J., & Gerard, M. (2007). *Family involvement in early childhood education: research into practice.* New York: Thomson.

Sheldon, S. (2002). Use technology to increase communications, but ensure equity in family involvement. *Type 2: Communicating to improve partnerships for student success, 12.* National Network of Partnership Schools: Johns Hopkins University.

Swick, K. J. (2003). Communication concepts for strengthening family–school–community partnerships. *Early Childhood Education Journal, 30*(4), 275–280.

KEY TERMS

Portfolio Approach—Portfolios are folders of work samples saved over a period of time. For each child, a teacher develops a portfolio that can be shared with parents, reviewed as report cards are prepared, and used to document long-term academic progress.

CHAPTER 6
Verbal Communication

STUDENT LEARNING OUTCOMES

After reading this chapter, you should be able to

- Identify important factors to consider in choosing a published parent education program.

- Define the qualities necessary for an effective parenting group leader.

- Explain the role of incidental contacts, social events, websites, and the mass media in involving parents.

- Describe the purposes and key factors involved in open houses and orientation meetings.

- Identify types of toy and book lending libraries and guidelines for their operation.

- Discuss the importance of telephone calls, e-mails, and daily contacts in developing and maintaining home–school relationships.

- Describe strategies and techniques for encouraging parent attendance at various school events.

Two-way verbal communication strategies involve a wide range of contacts that occur among parents, administrators, and teachers. These contacts can range from incidental meetings in the school or community to shared participation in a parent education series lasting six or more weeks. Each type of contact adds to the collection of impressions that families have of the school and staff; together, they form the basis of a relationship. When positive contacts outweigh negative ones, either in number or depth, the teacher's chances of building a partnership with a child's family are increased—which is to the child's ultimate advantage.

Central to open communication is the belief that interaction between home and school is valued. An open-door policy is usually interpreted as teachers and administrators welcoming parent involvement, parents as decision makers, and parents as advocates for their children's education.

This chapter describes the concept of parent education in published programs, discusses the characteristics of effective group leaders, lists strategies for encouraging parent attendance at groups, and offers alternative formats for presenting parenting programs. Orientation meetings, open houses, social events, telephone calls, parent spaces, and support groups also are examined.

TYPES OF PARENT CONTACT

Daily and Incidental Contacts

Daily contacts are generally limited to those parents who drop off and pick up their children from a school or center. Parents often like to share information about the child's mood or behavior, state of health, or concerns that may surface during the day at drop-off or pickup time. Teachers who develop a good rapport with parents through short, frequent conversations find that they are better able to cope with children's needs, both academically and socially. These contacts provide the opportunity to deal with questions or problems immediately, rather than through letters or journals, and may lead to faster resolution of problems. Incidental contacts occur frequently when teachers and students reside in the same community. It is not unusual for students and their parents to have chance meetings with teachers in the supermarket, at the mall, in church, or at restaurants. It can sometimes be difficult to limit conversation to nonschool issues, and it will not always be possible to avoid discussing, for example, why Susie is having trouble sitting still during group time. Most experienced teachers have developed some ready phrases to ward off serious discussions that would be better off held in private. Explanations such as "I'd like to discuss this with you when I have Susie's portfolio in front of us; why don't you call me on Monday so we can set up a conference?" usually let a parent know that the teacher's interest in continuing the discussion later is genuine.

Social Events

The strategies used to involve parents in school through social events are limited only by the imagination and interest of the staff. There are numerous types of get-togethers that can enhance the home–school relationship. Listed below are ideas for social events that encourage participation.

- **Breakfasts for parents.** Invite parents to share a light breakfast together to discuss common concerns, interests, school improvements, and so on.
- **Volunteer teas or luncheons.** Teachers can prepare lunch or snacks and serve them to their parent volunteers in recognition of their efforts during the school year.
- **Potluck suppers.** A school, grade level, or class can set aside regular times throughout the year for potluck suppers. Parents can enjoy a ready-made meal with their families and relax with teachers and other staff members.
- **Picnics.** A picnic held at the beginning or end of the school year can help staff members and students' families become acquainted and renew old friendships.
- **Lunch with the principal or director.** Inviting parents to share lunch at school is a proven way to maintain open lines of communication.
- **Grade-level sessions.** Similar to the open house, a grade-level session can familiarize parents with the typical schedule and materials that their children experience each day.

The key to conducting successful social events is to gain the cooperation and commitment of the teachers and administrators involved. Genuine interest in spending time with families is an absolute necessity. A less-than-enthusiastic staff will convey a poor attitude to parents and reinforce negative biases that some parents have toward educators and schools. The effort to plan such gatherings must be a joint commitment on the part of parents and teachers. When successful, families and staff begin to view each other as real people, with common interests and concerns. Trust and meaningful relationships can build on this type of foundation. The benefit to the child is realized when parents and teachers work together in a partnership for the child's best interests.

Open Houses

Open houses or back-to-school nights are important strategies for the creation of a welcoming atmosphere for parents and families in the school. Parents feel more connected to their child's school experience when they can see the classroom, examine books and materials, and meet with staff members face-to-face. Open houses are most successful when scheduled at the beginning of the school year because they allow parents and teachers to meet on a positive note before any problems appear (Nicholson & Myhan, 2002).

The following are some tips for a successful open house:

- Display the papers and artwork of all children if you prepare such a display.
- Send home invitations and flyers well in advance of the scheduled date so that parents with varied work schedules can plan to attend.

- Inform parents on the invitation that one-to-one conferencing will not be held at the open house but can be arranged for another time.
- Provide nametags for parents—perhaps illustrated with their child's picture— to facilitate conversation among parents and to assist the teacher in connecting with the families.
- Hang a poster or a chart outlining the schedule of a typical school day.
- Have extra copies of school handbooks, forms, and paperwork on hand for new parents who may not have received them.
- Consider staggering families' arrival times, perhaps alphabetically by last name, so that not all families are present at one time. This method frees the teacher to talk with more parents and avoids overcrowding.

Generally, open houses are meant to be relaxed and informal meetings between teachers and families. It is difficult, then, when a parent seizes the opportunity for a detailed, personal conversation with the teacher about one child's progress. This not only places the teacher in an awkward position but is unfair to the parents. Privacy and access to the child's records are important components of a conference, and the open house provides neither. Experienced teachers are prepared with suggestions for scheduling the conference at another time, and they know how to close off discussions about personal matters.

Another popular style of open house structures the parents' visit so that they experience a shortened version of their child's schedule. In this format, teachers explain curriculum, materials, methods, and evaluation systems in place in the classroom. Parents follow the class schedule in an abbreviated form that omits specialist times (such as PE, music, and art) and lunchtime. Parents gain invaluable information about classroom expectations for behavior and academics and become familiar with the materials appropriate for the age or grade level of their child. They also gain a sense of the rhythm of their child's day and the variety of adults with whom the children have daily contact.

Orientation Meetings

The transition to a new grade is often accompanied by an orientation meeting for both parents and students. Preschool, kindergarten, junior high, and high school are typical new beginnings that are marked by a formal orientation meeting. The purpose of the orientation meeting is to provide parents and children the opportunity to visit the new building, meet the staff, and learn about the policies and schedules for the upcoming year. Orientation meetings are an efficient way to relay new information and answer questions.

Resources that are helpful to have at such meetings include parent handbooks, volunteer information, medical forms, supply lists, permission slips, parent surveys or questionnaires, emergency information cards, and any other district requirements for the grade or classroom. Parents also appreciate hearing a description of the curriculum and materials their children will be using, specific information about discipline policies, and the teacher's general philosophy of education (Henderson, Johnson, Mapp, & Davies, 2006).

Tips for conducting a successful orientation meeting include:

- Consider limiting the number of parents attending any one session (if more than one session can be arranged) so that individual questions can be answered and time can be spent getting to know parents.
- Print nametags with both the parents' and the children's names to help the teacher begin to associate names and faces.
- Keep the meeting flowing and stick to the predetermined time schedule. If individual parents need more time to discuss special situations, suggest a conference for sharing information in private. Don't allow one or two parents to dominate the meeting.
- Have quiet activities planned for children (if invited) that will occupy them during the adult portion of the meeting.
- Have extra materials available for newly registered students or for noncustodial parents who may wish to have separate sets of school packets. Prepare several packets to have on hand for students who enroll midyear.

Field Trips and Room Parties

Field trips and room parties are time-honored ways for parents to participate in schools. Parents feel comfortable with these familiar roles and may become interested in pursuing greater levels of involvement after establishing relationships with teachers and other parents. Field trips and room parties may, therefore, serve as a springboard for involvement for many families.

In order to facilitate positive experiences with these strategies, teachers should provide parents with specific information in advance of an event. Details about school policies and procedures, methods of handling discipline and behavior problems, beginning and ending times of the event, and clear descriptions of the schedule and all activities expected of the parent should be shared in advance of the trip or party. This information may be covered at an orientation meeting, in a handout, or in the parent handbook.

Planning will ensure a safe and pleasant experience for all involved. Future volunteer commitments may be gleaned from parents who feel their help was needed and appreciated and believe they made a difference.

Parents often volunteer to assist on field trips. *Courtesy of ECE Photo Library.*

The Role of the Teacher

Classroom teachers in child-care centers, preschools, and elementary schools have the opportunity to make the greatest impact on families through their formal and informal contacts with parents. Simple gestures such as greeting each family member by name, welcoming them into the school and classroom, and sharing positive comments about their child will go a long way toward developing a positive home–school partnership. It is often these early and initial contacts that set the tone for future meetings, calls, and conferences, and they should not be underestimated in their importance. While a teacher's responsibilities are broad, excellent teachers ensure that if they have not had conversations with or met parents and families face-to-face, they reach out to all parents via phone, e-mail, or notes early in the year.

The Role of the Director or Principal

Administrators can ensure the development of home–school communication by discussing the various methods and strategies they expect to be used in the school or center throughout the year. Training and support should be offered to staff members who are not familiar with parent involvement strategies, and ongoing conversation within the staff or faculty about such endeavors will help all teachers become more effective communicators. When considering holding an open house or an orientation meeting, the administrator will play a key role in determining the schedule, assisting with advance information about the event to parents, securing necessary permissions to use the facility after hours, and obtaining the resources, both material and financial, needed to conduct the event. While teachers and staff members are key elements of successful open houses, orientation meetings, and social events, it is the administrator's role to organize, motivate, and facilitate such school- or center-wide events.

PARENT EDUCATION

Parent education is not a single concept that comes in one easy-to-identify package. Rather, it is a group of strategies that can assume a number of directions and formats. Parent education is the parent meeting that a teacher holds to demonstrate math concepts and manipulatives used in her first-grade classroom. It is also the guest speaker hired to address an auditorium full of parents. Parent education is the home-based teacher who models the use of developmentally appropriate books and fine motor activities for the parent of a 3-year-old. It is the information shared on a "warm line" that links a neonatal nurse to the distraught parent of a newborn. Parent education is instruction that focuses on the parent's role in supporting the child's development and personal growth, and on understanding the learning process and how children's educational programs function (Gestwicki, 2007; Wright, Stegelin, & Hartle, 2007). A significant portion of this learning process should engage parents in forming new images of how their new status as parents influences the need for new roles, new resources, and new skills (Swick, 2004).

This section will examine published parent education programs, describe the characteristics of an effective group leader, present strategies that encourage parent attendance, and suggest alternative formats of program design.

Published Parent Education Programs

Parent education often takes the form of a series of group meetings that focus on the development of specific techniques for managing and understanding behavior, child development stages, and discipline. A variety of parent education programs developed by psychologists and educators are readily available through training workshops or in prepackaged curricula.

Three successful **published parent education programs**—Parent Effectiveness Training (PET), the early childhood Systematic Training for Effective Parenting (STEP), and Active Parenting—share several common theories about discipline and parent–child communication. Key concepts include "I" messages, "you" messages, no-lose methods of conflict resolution, natural and logical consequences, and active and reflective listening techniques. Based largely on the works of renowned psychologists Rudolph Dreikurs and Adolph Adler, these programs draw heavily on the strength of parent participation and the benefits of group discussion. Both STEP and Active Parenting, which are video- and discussion-based, use a group facilitator; PET requires its leaders to participate in a one-week training workshop.

Additional programs are the ADVANCE parenting curriculum and the curricula from the Center for the Improvement of Child Caring. The ADVANCE Parenting Education Curriculum was developed as a result of that agency's work with parents from poor, predominantly Hispanic neighborhoods. It has become a model as one of the first family support programs to target high-risk Latino populations. The parenting curriculum includes a nine-month series of parenting classes. Topics include an overview of parenting, prenatal care, infant needs, physical needs of young children, childhood illnesses, nutrition, child behavior, cognitive and linguistic development, emotional needs, self-awareness, and goal setting. For additional information, contact the Family Support and Education Program, Hasbro National Family Resource Center, Mercedes Perez de Colon, 301 S. Frio, Suite 310, San Antonio, TX, 78207; (210) 270-4630.

The Center for the Improvement of Child Caring has developed two parenting programs that are specifically designed for minority parents. Effective Black Parenting is described as a "culturally relevant skill-building program for raising proud and confident African American children." The curriculum has 15 three-hour sessions teaching parenting skills that respect African American patterns of communication and recognize the roots of the extended black family.

Los Niños Bien Educados is a parent education program developed specifically for Spanish-speaking and Latino-origin parents. It deals specifically with traditions and customs in child rearing and with adjustments that are made as families acculturate to life in the United States. Both of these programs are available through the Center for the Improvement of Child Caring, 11331 Ventura Boulevard, Suite 103, Studio City, CA, 91604-3147; (818) 980-0903.

The Role of the Director or Principal: Factors to Consider When Selecting a Parent Education Program

When considering a particular parent education series, it is important to research the authors and their programs to determine what style of discipline is advocated and which psychological theorists' ideas they support. Scan the materials to determine if the content and advice correspond to program goals and beliefs. Each program differs in its methodology and philosophy; it will be necessary to match the needs of your parent population, the philosophy of the school, and the published curriculum to find a compatible match. Other factors to be considered include the cost of the program, availability of specialized leader training, cost of additional materials necessary to facilitate a group, and the feasibility of reusing the materials.

Programs that require leader training may pose a problem in schools or centers with high staff turnover. Materials-based curricula make it easier to share leader responsibility but may require equipment in order to present the program. Determine whether purchasing parent manuals would be a financial burden for parents; also, compare the reading level of the text to the literacy level of the parents being served. Does the book resemble a textbook, and is it likely to be read only by better-educated and highly motivated parents? Is it an easy-to-read manual that, when given a quick glance by a busy mother, will convey some substance? Is the information presented in such a manner that parents who have difficulty reading will be able to understand it? Have a parent advisory board or parent council review the material and program delivery, including length, to ensure that it will be effective for participating parents. A careful examination of these factors will maximize the dollars spent on parent education programs.

Choosing a Leader for a Parenting Group

It is often assumed that teachers are best suited to lead parenting groups. Unfortunately, many teachers, even early childhood educators, have had little, if any, training in working with parents (Greenberg, 1989). Many parenting programs draw group leaders from the "helping" professions: nursing, education, social work, counseling, and the clergy. The following qualities are instrumental to the success of a parenting group.

Child Development Background. The group leader should have a solid background in child development in order to credibly and accurately educate parents about the growth and development of children. While experiences with children and families may take many forms, there is no substitute for a working knowledge of child development. A parent educator's expertise will be called upon when questions arise about discipline, parent expectations, and developmental timetables (Cataldo, 1983). An effective leader needs to be able to relate anecdotal experiences to accepted practice.

Rapport-Building Ability. Consider the abilities of the potential leader for building rapport with many kinds of people. An effective leader is not only sensitive to cultural diversity among families but is able to deal with parents from a wide range of socioeconomic backgrounds, often blending the two within a single group. This may require research about a variety of cultural norms and customs in order to provide a meaningful experience for all parents. Differences in socioeconomic levels can be minimized by promoting casual attire for meetings and placing minimal emphasis on careers or job titles during mixers and introductions. All parents have the right to feel welcomed and respected, regardless of their profession or level of education.

Parenting Experience. Firsthand experience as a parent is not required but can certainly be a positive factor in gaining credibility with a group of parents. Curran (1989) suggests that educators who are not themselves parents should emphasize their experience with children on the job and in volunteer work.

Organization Skills. Select a professional with good organizational skills because there are numerous details that ensure the success of the group's progress: mailings, up-to-date social service information, the ability to make referrals to local agencies, and follow-ups on requests for additional information, to name a few. It is also critical for a leader to be well prepared for each session and to have done the necessary background work so that each session will flow smoothly. This includes such details as ensuring a comfortable room arrangement, availability of proper equipment, and appropriate handouts for each session, as well as making adequate preparation for the subject matter of each session.

Communication Skills. An effective leader will have good communication and public speaking skills and the ability to create a relaxed, nonthreatening atmosphere for all participants. A leader should become familiar with a variety of strategies and techniques for group dynamics in order to more effectively lead and focus discussions.

Enlist Two Leaders. First-time leaders uncertain of their skills may find the dual-leader format an excellent way to ease into the role of parent educator while gaining valuable experience working with groups. There are advantages to having members of complementary professions work together, for they bring to the group a wider range of expertise. Consider these pairings:

- For an infant development class: a pediatric nurse and an early childhood educator.
- For a group of parents whose children experience developmental delays and are part of a kindergarten class through inclusion: an early childhood special educator and an early childhood teacher.

Other Considerations. Most parenting programs either train parents in a group or offer training manuals for self-study. Fees for training and materials vary widely; if there is a limited budget, sponsoring agencies might decide to invest in personnel training or reusable materials.

The overall success of any parent education program usually rests on the personality and professionalism of the group leader (Curran, 1989). Consideration of these factors will ensure that parents who attend an introductory session will complete the entire series.

Strategies and Techniques to Encourage Parent Attendance

1. Find out what topics interest parents. A significant factor in the success of any program is to determine what parents want to know. It is difficult, if not impossible, to maintain attendance at meetings that do not address relevant concerns of the parents involved (Swick, 2004).

There are several ways to find out what parents want. One way is to form a committee to canvass all parents with either a written or a phone survey (Swap, 1993). In this way, each parent has the opportunity to voice an opinion or make a suggestion about the focus of upcoming meetings. While the survey method can be time-consuming, it does allow a realistic profile of all parents involved and may lead to other valuable information about needed events or services.

Another method for obtaining information is to request that an existing advisory board or council review suitable programs and decide what is in the best interests of the group (Curran, 1989; Swap, 1993). There is a strong relationship among the anticipated outcomes of the parent education program, the location, and the nature of the population it serves. Whether the community is rural or urban, whether parents are married or single, and whether mothers are adults or adolescents are all factors that will test the effectiveness of a particular program. Advisory boards and parent councils should develop a clear picture of the population they hope to serve and match the program to the needs of the group (Gestwicki, 2007).

2. Be sensitive about wording when choosing a title. The title chosen for the series may have a great effect on the level of interest. Use positive words or concepts—"Those Terrific Two's" instead of "Surviving Toddlerhood," for example. Few parents will wish to attend sessions with a negative title or about topics that imply a deficiency in their parenting skills. Humor can relay the message of the program without making the topic seem overbearing or heavy (Rockwell & Kniepkamp, 2003). The term "parent education" itself might offend parents who are less than confident about their skills. Consider wording that conveys the content but does not label attendees in a negative manner. Educators have found that labels, which can be devastating for children, have an equally negative effect on parents.

3. Explore many avenues for advertising. In order to reach a wide group of parents, it is helpful to look at a number of options for advertising. If the budget allows it, consider ads on local radio and community access television. If your group is a not-for-profit organization, you may qualify for free public service announcements. Often, local newspapers publish a calendar of community events as a public service. Teachers may request space in their school or district newsletter. Flyers, bulletin board signs, and report card enclosures also provide wide coverage for a minimal investment of paper and time.

4. Choose a site that is centrally located. The choice of the site may determine how many people attend the program. If evening sessions are planned, consider the neighborhood; the safety of the building; the amount of adequate, lighted parking; and accessibility to public transportation. Try to arrange for a quiet room whose dimensions suit the anticipated number of parents. A large cafeteria for a group of 10 will not be conducive to a warm, sharing environment, just as a preschool room with child-sized furniture won't be adequate for 30 adults.

5. Determine whether or not to offer child care and transportation. The makeup of the school population can help determine what services to offer. If lack of reliable child care would be a major impediment to parent attendance, then it might be worth the expense to arrange for this service (Rockwell & Kniepkamp, 2003). On-site child care could be provided by a paid babysitter or by volunteers such as other parents, high school students, Girl Scouts, church youth groups, and so on. Other options include purchasing child-care slots from a family day-care home or local center for use during meetings, or reimbursing parents for an in-home sitter.

Transportation costs often include public transportation or taxi service, or the expenses of volunteer drivers from the school or an outside program. These costs may add significantly to the overhead of the classes; however, the participation of many parents may depend on their availability. The parent survey can give an idea of whether transportation is needed and its probable cost.

6. Arrange the room to promote comfort and a willingness to share.
When a room has been selected for parent education classes, allow ample time
to inspect it for several important features. Check the number and condition of
chairs and tables to ensure the comfort of adults. Be certain that the room can
be arranged in such a manner that conversation and group sharing can be
facilitated easily and that each member of the group can see each other with
ease. A semicircle, large square, or large circle is effective at engaging all seated
adults with equal visibility (Berger, 2008). If tables are needed for note taking,
check that there is enough space between tables and chairs to accommodate all
sizes of adults. Role-playing activities may require extra chairs or space in front
of the group; the room should be arranged accordingly before the start of the
meeting.

Locate and examine the temperature controls; keep the room comfortable
and well ventilated, especially if it is closed during the day or on weekends.
Determine whether there are adequate lighting, restroom facilities, and kitchen or
sink space for serving refreshments. Place projectors and screens so that they do
not block anyone's view yet are near electrical outlets. A group leader who
suddenly finds that there is no outlet for a planned video will suffer needless
embarrassment over an unchecked detail and may hold up the meeting.

7. Be flexible about scheduling. Depending on the group leader's availability,
sessions should be offered at a variety of times to allow maximum participation
from all interested parents. If the school is hiring an outside leader, there may not
be much control over the times and dates the classes can be offered; if a teacher or
other school employee is the group leader, there may be more flexibility.
Information can be gathered through a written or phone survey to determine the
most convenient times for the majority of parents.

Be aware of local customs when scheduling a series of ongoing classes. For
example, in many communities, Wednesday evenings are unofficially reserved for
choir, religious classes, or church services. In other towns or neighborhoods,
there may be a long-standing tradition for sports leagues to practice or school
functions to be held on a particular evening. Be alert to school holiday schedules
and try not to compete with fundraisers, parent–teacher conferences, or three-day
weekends. Attendance at the classes is bound to suffer if parents have too many
responsibilities in one night.

Alternative Formats

In addition to traditional parenting class formats, parenting information can be
distributed in ways that are tailored to fit today's tightly scheduled lifestyles. For
many mothers and fathers, attendance at an evening series would be difficult to
sustain over a period of 6 to 8 weeks. To accommodate families with two working

parents, single parents, or parents with complicated home situations, educators have experimented with alternative formats that make parenting classes more accessible.

1. Consider a flexible time and format. Parents may prefer to attend a lunch-hour seminar instead of an evening class. Some employers offer brown-bag seminars for employees who wish to participate in parenting skills classes but lack the time outside of the office. A once-a-week or once-a-month format could be arranged to cover topics chosen by the employees.

After-school classes might appeal to teachers, shift workers, and stay-at-home mothers who want to be at home in the evenings with their families. A latchkey program at the school could provide child care at a nominal cost. For parents with behavioral or academic questions about their child, consider a "warm line" staffed by teachers, social workers, nurses, or school psychologists.

2. Tie parent education material to a social function. Some programs have found increased attendance for special speakers or topics if a social event is offered at the same time. For example, a potluck supper could be preceded with a 30-minute talk by a guest speaker or could occur while children are being entertained by a storyteller or busy with a hands-on art activity. A coffee or lunch at school could serve as the starting point for the distribution of materials related to a parenting topic; a more formal series of classes could come later.

3. Tie the classes to necessary resources. One day-care center chose the dinner hour for parent education classes, promising extended, no-cost child care for parents who participated. Directors also offered the opportunity to newer staff members, who also benefited from the material presented. Discussion between staff and parents proved valuable in helping each group understand the other's point of view in handling children.

In another example, a school district took advantage of a new park to provide supervised outdoor play while parents took part in informal classes. Parents whose children were enrolled in a morning preschool program decided to take part in parent education classes that were offered simultaneously in the same facility.

Toy and Book Lending Libraries

Another type of parent contact occurs through the use of **toy and book lending libraries.** Many programs that serve young children use the toy or book library as a method of extending developmentally appropriate activities and books from the classroom to the home. A library may consist of a room within a school or center that has a wide range of developmentally appropriate toys, books, and games that are available to families for checkout. Teachers also develop in-class libraries that may feature read-aloud books and activity bags that students may take home to share with parents or caregivers.

Play is a central theme to most early childhood programs and has long been recognized by educators and child development specialists as critical to healthy growth (Frost, Wortham, & Reifel, 2001; Pica, 2006). Toys, then, are the tools through which children learn and practice social skills, develop critical thinking processes, use their imagination, and increase visual, gross, and fine motor abilities (Morris, 1991). Lack of access to a wide range of developmentally appropriate toys can hamper these critical elements of development for many children. The first toy library was created to fill this need and provide resources for parents to supply necessary toys for their children.

A Brief History of the Toy Lending Movement. Toy libraries originated in England more than 50 years ago, and the idea spread to most European countries. In 1935, the first toy lending library in the United States was established in California (Jackson, Robey, Watjus, & Chadwick, 1991). Currently there are two basic models of toy libraries in operation throughout the United States and Europe. The first, termed the British model, is usually located in a public institution such as a school, hospital, church, or library and is staffed by paraprofessional volunteers. Often privately funded, these libraries serve low-income, at-risk families as well as the general population (Jackson, Robey, Watjus, & Chadwick, 1991). Under the guidance of a volunteer, parents visit the library to choose a toy that will suit the age and developmental level of their child. In some programs, the parents have access to training sessions that demonstrate the many ways a toy can be used to facilitate language and fine and gross motor skills and show how to match toys to the child's individual needs (Nimnicht & Brown, 1972).

Variations on the British model enable the toy library to reach a wide range of parents. The *early education stationary library* is usually housed at a preschool, church, or other facility for use through that building. The *early education mobile unit* is taken to families, often through a home visiting program on a rotating basis. The *therapeutic toy library* may be limited to the families enrolled in a special education program and designed to promote learning at a particular stage or for a specific disability.

The second model is the Lekotek toy library, which was developed in Scandinavia and specifically designed for children with disabilities (Juul, 1984). The primary components of Lekotek are family support, sharing of play techniques, monthly family visits, and parent support groups. Lekoteks were created because, during the 1960s, children with special needs were without services until the age of 4. Karen Stenland Junker and Evy Blid, themselves parents of children with special needs, desired intervention that would reduce the loneliness and isolation felt by these families. They also wished to promote information and intervention during the first year of life, a critical determiner of future development. Today, Lekoteks serve children with special needs—mental as well as physical—and are an important part of the team of professionals who provide services to the child and family, but they are also available to families with children who have other risk factors. Lekoteks provide assistance to preschools in promoting the successful integration of children with special needs into mainstream classrooms. Funding is obtained through corporation grants, foundations, private donations, user fees, fundraisers, and the United Way.

Setting Up a Toy Lending Library. Community-based organizations, schools, and teachers interested in setting up a toy lending library can do so by following some basic guidelines. Adaptations and modifications can enable a large facility (such as a hospital or church) or an individual teacher to create a similar service for parents and children (Stone, 1983).

1. **Locate appropriate storage space for toys and materials.**
2. **Develop a catalog system for labeling and classifying toys.** Label toys by their age appropriateness, such as *infant, toddler, preschooler,* and so on, or by their functional use, such as *promotes fine motor development* or *provides practice in specific concept learning.*
3. **Develop an inventory system.** Keep records for each toy that include the place and date of purchase, price paid, availability of replacement parts, address of manufacturer, and directions for use.
4. **Establish a circulation process.** Develop policies about checkout, renewal, overdue materials, replacement of broken toys, eligibility, and family registration.
5. **Set aside a play area for demonstrating toys.** In a school setting, this may not be necessary. A place for volunteers to sort, store, and check out materials may be the only requirement for space. In a facility where parents may want to be shown how to use a toy or have a child examine it, space may need to be allocated.
6. **Establish an intake file to record family registrations.** Information such as name, address, phone numbers (home and work), ages and names of children, children's developmental ability if a disability is involved, and any other relevant facts could be filed on an index card or registration sheet.
7. **Survey parents periodically to evaluate the library services.** Surveys and questionnaires can be helpful when making decisions about additional purchases, expansion of hours and services, and so on.

8. **Develop ways to publicize the toy library.** Brochures, pamphlets, flyers, and newsletter articles can inform local parents about the library and its services. Provide a list of the policies, procedures, and responsibilities of the library.

Examples of School-Based Toy and Book Lending Libraries.

Teresa Harris, a kindergarten teacher in O'Fallon, Illinois, took the concept of the toy lending library and adapted it to suit her individual parent population. Her program has been designed and modified as a result of experience, use, and parent input. The result is a unique program that fulfills the specific objectives she has for her families.

"Loveable Bags" and "Fun with Boxes." Teresa Harris developed her bags and boxes to enrich her students and extend kindergarten learning activities to their homes. Over several years, Teresa has developed 60 take-home activity bags that allow families to work with materials, games, and books that are developmentally appropriate. Each activity consists of the following:

- one or two books
- a laminated sheet of instructions for parents
- various manipulatives to facilitate a game or a learning experience
- a parent evaluation sheet
- a list of the ways the activity supplements learning and which skills are being enhanced

Activity bag and box checkout is handled by parent volunteers each morning and afternoon. They record the child's name and bag number, as well as any items that need to be replaced or repaired in any of the bags or boxes, on a clipboard. Bag and box distribution is initiated at a parent meeting where the concept is shared and parents are allowed to preview the contents. One bag is circulated among all students first (one per school night) until all students have experienced the activity and returned it to class on time. Gradually, Teresa adds to the number of bags traveling to students' homes each week.

Activity bags can be filled with yard sale toys, discount store party favors, wholesale club merchandise, and items from teacher supply stores. Student book clubs can be a source of inexpensive, easy-to-replace books, keeping the cost of each unit to a minimum. See Figures 6.1, 6.2, and 6.3 for examples of an activity and the checkout grid.

Parent–Infant Activity Bags. Kathy Gary, a parent educator in Belleville, Illinois, looking for a way to provide home activities for her parents and infants, adapted the toy lending library concepts for her Parents as Partners home visiting program. Her interest was in sharing developmentally appropriate, inexpensive

FIGURE 6.1 Activities for Children to Check Out and Take Home

Book: If You Give a Mouse a Cookie
by Laura Joffe Numeroff

Contents: small paperplates, crayons, pipe cleaners, scissors, holepunch, yarn, construction paper.

Activities

1. After reading the story, share a paperplate and the ear pattern with your child.

2. Together create a mouse mask by helping your child trace the ear patterns onto their choice of paper.

3. Allow your child to glue their ears, add whiskers or other features on their mask.

4. Help your child punch a hole on each side of the plate. Place a piece of yarn through the holes and tie to fit around their head.

5. Encourage your child to act out the parts of the mouse as you re-read the story.

6. Review the order of the story by asking your child what happened first, next, next and last?

Bag Activity Page 1

—filled together times...

yons and a piece of paper with your
when finished, be sure they sign
ke the mouse. Then display their
gerator.

take part in making chocolate
t child use the mouse shape cookie
n to the cookies. Be sure to top
lass of milk!

make playdough with your child
hare the cookie cutter. have a glass of milk while
creating with the playdough.

Skills that will meet specific developmental areas: sequencing, fine motor, gluing skills, tying skills, eye-hand coordination.

Bag Activity Page 2

FIGURE 6.2 Take-Home Activity Explanation Sheet

Fun in a Box Loveable Bag	1	2	3	4	5	6	7	8	9	10	11	
Amanda		×										
Brian			×									
Joshua	×											
Dimitri				×								
Keneesha					×							
Ling								×				
Miguel						×						

FIGURE 6.3 Take-Home Activity Checklist

toys, books, and games with parents of infants. Kathy found that when parents engaged in one-to-one activities with their infants, they were helping them develop important language and motor skills. Parents can check out materials during the home visit and exchange bags at subsequent meetings. Each activity is created to suit a particular age and stage of growth and development.

PARENT SPACES, ROOMS, AND RESOURCE LIBRARIES

A common barrier to parent involvement is that schools are obviously designed for their traditional residents: students and teachers. One way to overcome this barrier is to create a **parent room** for visitors and volunteers. A parent room is a visible indication of the importance the school places on the parents' presence in the school or program. The function of the parent space is twofold: It acknowledges the need of parents for a place to meet informally with other parents and volunteers, and it serves as a central location for resource information (Berger, 2008).

Consider the following scenarios with School A and School B. Picture yourself as a parent in each facility and visualize the difference a parent room can make to the atmosphere in the school.

Imagine entering School A, perhaps to volunteer or to speak to a class, and discovering that there is nowhere to hang your coat or make a phone call to your sitter. You are early for your volunteer shift so you wait, standing, in the hall. How welcome do you feel?

Now picture yourself in School B, where you've come to volunteer in the media center. You arrive 30 minutes early to enjoy coffee with fellow PTO members and make phone calls to recruit extra help for the school book fair. You examine several new articles on helping children improve peer and sibling relationships; you consider checking them out. How welcome do you feel in this school?

Setting Up a Parent Room

The physical requirements of a parent room or space are relatively simple, and many items can be obtained by donation from families and businesses. A comfortable sofa, several chairs, small tables, a telephone, a coffeepot, bookshelves, magazines, and a bulletin board for posted announcements would adequately serve the purpose. If school space does not permit an entire room, consider making a portion of a workroom into a parent space (Davies, 1991).

The key point is that a specific place is designated as a "home base" and communications center for parents who spend time in the school (Swap, 1993). The presence of such an area sends a positive message to parents and other adults who volunteer their time: The teachers and administrators welcome them as partners in education and value their efforts by making them feel a part of the school (Becker & Epstein, 1982).

Setting Up a Parent Resource Library

The **parent resource library,** often located within the parent room, contains materials to assist families in their many roles. Topics are almost limitless, provided they serve the needs of the families of the school population. Examples are:

child health and wellness   stress management

pregnancy and childbirth   sibling rivalry

birthday party ideas   breastfeeding

positive discipline   family finances

choosing and making toys   infant care

family vacation information   general parenting

finding child care   toilet training

children's games   television limitation

family fitness

Parents enjoy using the resource library. *Courtesy of ECE Photo Library.*

In addition to books and parenting magazines, DVDs on related topics also are a significant part of the library. These enable parents who are visually impaired or who have poor reading skills to have access to parenting information. Depending on its size and the availability of volunteers, the resource library could be staffed during specific hours of the day or evening by a parent or other community volunteer. A simple file card system to organize checkout procedures is quick and inexpensive. Parents using the library could fill out a registration form similar to the one in Figure 6.4.

FAMILY MATTERS!
PARENT RESOURCE
LIBRARY REGISTRATION

Name:_____

Address: _____

Phone: _____

Names of Child(ren) at this School:_____

_____

THANK YOU!

FIGURE 6.4 Parent Resource Registration Form

Once registered, the adult family members receive a list of all materials available for checkout, the library's operating hours, and guidelines for using the facility. See also the discussion on toy lending libraries beginning on page 218.

Funding Sources

Sources of funding are as varied as the materials housed in the library. The following sources could be investigated:

- Business or private donations of money or materials
- Mini-grants from local businesses or foundations
- Fundraising proceeds from the PTO/PTA
- Community college family literacy programs or grants
- Local adult education or literacy programs
- Collaboration with other district services such as Title I programs
- Prekindergartens, at-risk programs, special education cooperatives or districts, Even Start programs, parenting programs (Parents as Teachers, etc.), local PTA/PTO organizations, and district media/library services

CONTACTS THROUGH TECHNOLOGY

Websites and Web Pages

Increasingly, schools and child-care centers are joining businesses and other organizations in utilizing the Internet for communicating with their constituents. Websites and web pages offer opportunities to communicate everything that's happening in the school or center using formats such as event calendars, school or room schedules, news releases, lunch menus, school policies, and directories that include staff names as well as school phone numbers and e-mail addresses.

Telephone Calls

The telephone offers an opportunity for personal conversation. *Courtesy of ECE Photo Library.*

Telephone calls from the school have earned a dubious reputation. Generally, a phone call is connected with discipline problems, illnesses, accidents, incomplete work, tardiness, or requests for help (Berger, 2008). It is no wonder that parents steel themselves for unpleasantness when a teacher or principal phones them at home or at work. This situation is unfortunate, because the telephone also can be used to relay positive information to parents (Gestwicki, 2007). Consider the reaction of a parent to a congratulatory phone call by a child's teacher on a recent accomplishment:

> Elizabeth was able to participate in a playground game for the entire PE session today.

Kevin made the longest Unifix cube chain the class had ever seen, and his group counted each block.

In less time than it takes to write a note, the phone call lends a warm, personal touch to communication between home and school.

However, scheduling phone time can be troublesome if the only access is located in a busy school office. The following suggestions may help facilitate teacher phone time in a practical way:

1. Try to locate a phone in a private area so that background noise and other people are not part of the conversation.

2. Request additional phone lines if access to an open line is a chronic problem. This may require a commitment of money to install; however, it is a feature that benefits all teachers in the school.

3. Be realistic about time allotments for phone use. If scheduling daily or weekly phone calls to parents cannot be accommodated within the regular teaching day, consider phoning just one family per week. At the end of the typical school year, this method would reach 36 families.

Some districts have successfully improved access to teachers by utilizing the advanced technology afforded by computers working with the telephone system. One district in Tennessee pioneered the use of voice mail to promote better communication between teachers and parents. Each teacher was given an electronic voice mailbox and 1 to 3 minutes of message time, and parents simply called a designated number to play the message from a specific teacher (Bauch, 1989). Possibilities for message content include homework information or general tips supporting literacy at home. Phone calls from parents at schools implementing this system increased by more than 500 percent without significantly increasing personnel time (Bauch, 1989).

Other schools have employed a computer calling system that forwards to specific parents or groups of parents phone calls with information supplied by the administrators or teachers. Content varies from attendance information to school schedule changes.

While administrative support is critical to the success of any new parent–teacher effort, the planning must be a joint effort to ensure commitment (Gestwicki, 2007). One way to realize the effectiveness of the program is to maintain a record of positive phone calls made. Parents and teachers will be encouraged to continue the program when the log of positive contacts grows and teachers begin to reap the rewards of improved relationships with their students' families.

Mass Media

Educators often overlook using the mass media as a source of communication to parents and families. They assume it is too costly and difficult to arrange. There are, however, a number of strategies that can make radio, television, and newspapers powerful tools and often free sources of publicity for a school or program.

Radio and Television. Local radio and television programming often is geared toward discussions of interesting events in and around the community. Interview and phone-in program formats offer the opportunity for a teacher or administrator to publicize upcoming events that would be of interest to local families. Free radio and television time can often be arranged by requesting public service announcement time. A parent education series, homework hotline, or upcoming speaker could be advertised to reach parents not affiliated with the school or who have difficulty reading printed materials sent home with students.

Local cable community access stations are able to air longer video segments to promote parent programs or display an interesting presentation by students. Information about specific time and tape requirements can be requested in advance. In some instances, a staff member from the station may record a class performance for future airing. This is an effective way to include all families in the enjoyment of a play, concert, or holiday presentation by students.

Newspapers. Newspapers can serve a dual role in bringing students and programs to the attention of the general public. Most newspapers have a community calendar section that heralds upcoming area events. Activities such as parent education series, open houses, workshops, and informational meetings can be included free of charge and will reach a wide audience.

Newspapers also are interested in publishing human interest stories and pictures of children participating in interesting activities. Notify the local paper of special events the class is planning and arrange for a visit by the photographer. It is exciting for students to gain recognition for their efforts in this manner, and the coverage allows the community to see the positive things occurring in schools.

SUMMARY

There are a number of levels of verbal communication that can occur between parents and teachers. Some, such as telephone calls and incidental contacts, are relatively short and infrequent. Others, such as family workshops, field trips, open houses, and orientation meetings, provide greater opportunities for parents and teachers to interact and begin to develop a relationship based on mutual trust. The parent education strategy provides parents with meaningful dialogue and the chance to relate as parents and adults who share common struggles and successes.

Some parents feel comfortable enough to quickly build a relationship with their child's teachers; others move slowly as confidence and trust replace fear and suspicion. It is well worth the effort on everyone's part to attempt to reach all families and extend opportunities to work together.

ACTIVITIES FOR DISCUSSION, EXPANSION, AND APPLICATION

1. Create an outline for a kindergarten orientation meeting. Include a short description of all information presented to parents and written materials distributed.

2. Imagine you are the director of a child-care or preschool facility serving 80 families. Parents and staff have expressed strong interest in parenting classes that could be offered at the center. Create a schedule of parent education offerings in combination with other strategies presented in this chapter that would represent the overall plan for one school year.

3. An early childhood center housing grades prekindergarten through second would like to request funding for a toy lending library. Write a rationale for this request including information about the population to be served, staffing, and benefits to families.

4. As an early childhood professional, you have decided to increase the verbal communication between your families and the school or center. Describe strategies that might be employed to address the needs of all parents involved. Specify the age and grade of the students and the type and location of the school or center (rural, urban, private, suburban, public, etc.).

5. A school or center located in a culturally diverse neighborhood is evaluating the strengths and weaknesses of the verbal communication strategies currently in use. Discuss the implications such a population might have on new techniques to be added and on modifications to those already in place.

CASE STUDY

Mr. and Mrs. Rozewell are attending an open house at their daughter Susan's elementary school. Susan proudly leads them to her kindergarten classroom to meet her teacher, Mrs. Frantor. Upon entering the room, they see an abundance of children's artwork hanging on walls. They ask Susan to show them her drawings. Susan takes them by hand and they search the many items that are on display. Susan can't find any of her work and is very hurt and disappointed as so many of her classmates' items are displayed. The Rozewells are angered that Susan's work is not displayed. They feel that Mrs. Frantor has only displayed what she feels is the best of the best.

1. Do you feel that Mrs. Frantor was correct by displaying only what she interpreted as the best artwork?

2. Do you feel that the Rozewells are entitled to be upset?

3. What can you suggest that might help Mrs. Frantor to avoid this situation in the future?

USEFUL WEBSITES

www.activeparenting.com

Active Parenting. This program provides parents with the skills that will help them develop their children's cooperation skills, sense of responsibility, and self-esteem.

www.ciccparenting.org

Center for the Improvement of Child Caring. The CICC is a private, nonprofit community service, training, and research corporation. The organization is a major supporter and participant in the nationwide effective parenting movement to improve the overall quality of child rearing and child caring in the United States.

www.familysupportamerica.org

Family Support America. This site identifies resource centers throughout the United States that help parents by providing information, support, and connections that families need to survive. Child abuse, alcoholism, disciplining children, divorce, and other topics are addressed.

www.gordontraining.com/parent-effectiveness-training.html

Parent Effectiveness Training. The mission of this program is to provide people worldwide with the communication and conflict resolution skills necessary for creating effective and lasting relationships in the workplace, in families, and in schools.

www.parenteducationnetwork.ca

Parent Education Network. This site has information about online parenting skills courses and workshops for parents, referrals, and community linkages.

REFERENCES

Bauch, J. (1989). The transparent school model: New technology for parent involvement. *Educational Leadership, (47)*2, 32–34.

Becker, H. J., & Epstein, J. L. (1982). Parent involvement: A study of teacher practices. *Elementary School Journal, 3,* 85–102.

Berger, E. H. (2008). *Parents as partners in education: Families and schools working together* (7th ed.). Upper Saddle River, NJ: Merrill/Prentice Hall.

Cataldo, C. (1982). *Infant and toddler programs.* Reading, MA: Addison-Wesley.

Curran, D. (1989). *Working with parents.* Circle Pines, MN: American Guidance Service.

Davies, D. (January 1991). Schools reaching out: Family, school, and community partnerships for student success. *Phi Delta Kappan, 72,* 378–380.

Frost, J., Wortham, S., & Reifel, S. (2001). *Play and child development.* Upper Saddle River, NJ: Merrill/Prentice Hall.

Gestwicki, C. (2007). *Home, school, and community relations* (6th ed.). Clifton Park, NY: Thomson Delmar Learning.

Greenberg, P. (1989). Parents as partners in young children's development and education: A new American fad? Why does it matter? *Young Children, 44*(4), 61–74.

Henderson, A. T., Johnson, V., Mapp, K. L., & Davies, D. (2006). *Beyond the bake sale: The essential guide to family/school partnerships.* New York: New Press.

Jackson, S., Robey, L., Watjus, M., & Chadwick, E. (1991). Play for all children. *Childhood Education, 68*(1), 27–30.

Juul, K. (April 1984). Toy libraries for the handicapped: An international survey. Paper presented at the Annual Convention of the Council for Exceptional Children. Washington, DC.

Morris, B. (September 1991). The child's right to play. Paper presented at the 5th Early Childhood Convention. Dunedine, New Zealand.

Nicholson, J. L., & Myhan, J. G. (2002). Twenty practical parent involvement tips. *Issues in Education, Journal of Early Education and Family Review, 10*(2), 13–17.

Nimnicht, G., & Brown, E. (1972). The toy library: Parents and children learning with toys. *Young Children, 28*(2), 110–116.

Pica, R. (2006). *A running start: How play, physical activity, and free time create a successful child.* Center Barnstead, NH: Marlow and Company.

Rockwell, B., & Kniepkamp, J. R. (2003). *Partnering with parents: Easy programs to involve parents in the early learning process.* Beltsville, MD: Gryphon House.

Stone, M. (1983). *Enhancing parent involvement in schools.* New York: Teachers College Press.

Swap, S. M. (1993). *Developing home–school partnerships.* New York: Teachers College Press.

Swick, K. (2004). *Empowering parents, families, schools, and communities during the early years.* Champaign, IL: Stipes Publishing.

Waxman, P. L. (1991). Children in the world of adults—onsite child care. *Young Children, 46*(5), 16–21.

Wright, K., Stegelin, D., & Hartle, L. (2007) *Building family, school, and community partnerships* (3rd ed.). Upper Saddle River, New Jersey: Pearson/Merrill/Prentice Hall.

KEY TERMS

Two-Way Verbal Communication—Communication designed to elicit verbal dialogue between two or more persons.

Published Parent Education Programs—Published programs, developed by psychologists and educators, which focus on the development of specific techniques for managing and understanding behavior, child development stages, and discipline.

Toy and Book Lending Library—A library in a school, center, or other location that has a wide range of developmentally appropriate toys, books, and games that are available on loan to families.

Parent Room—A space designated for parents who spend time in the school or center as volunteers to set up a "home base" and communications center.

Parent Resource Library—An area where families can browse through and check out books, parenting magazines, and DVDs relating to family needs.

CHAPTER 7
Home Visits

STUDENT LEARNING OUTCOMES

After reading this chapter, you should be able to

- Identify model programs that have home visits as a major component.

- Defend the necessity of having a purpose when making a home visit.

- Explain the key components of a successful home visit.

- Describe the criteria that can be used to select a home visitor.

- Identify behaviors that should be avoided by home visitors.

Home visits by early childhood, elementary, and secondary school teachers are becoming increasingly common. More and more, boards of education and school administrators are supporting school personnel in this effective strategy, which enhances family–school relationships. In this chapter, we examine how home visits have been utilized since the turn of the century as a means of involving families in the education of their children. The advantages and disadvantages of this strategy are presented. Procedures to follow when making home visits as well as practices to avoid are covered. Model programs—both traditional school-based visits and home-based visit programs—that have home visits as a major component are described and referenced.

HISTORICAL PERSPECTIVES

Home visiting has been practiced for years in Europe and in this country as a method of working with needy families. At the turn of the nineteenth century, it was common to see doctors, nurses, and teachers making home visits. Home visiting was one way to meet medical needs, teach parenting skills, and provide support for high-risk families (Miller, 1987). Seefeldt (1980) reported that even before the time of Margaret McMillan, the founder of nursery education early in the nineteenth century, teachers of young children visited homes as a means of involving parents in the educational progress of their children.

Home visits are becoming increasingly common. *Courtesy of ECE Photo Library.*

Hendrick (2003) suggests that as the home visitor interacts with the child, the goal is to also draw in the parents so that they can gradually add to their own repertoire of ideas and activities that will enhance their child's growth. As the parents begin to understand how important it is to develop language competence in young children, and as they learn simple and practical ways to foster this ability, a positive, continuing influence has been built into the child's life.

During the 1960s and 1970s, numerous intervention programs incorporated home visits in response to the needs of children who were developmentally delayed, economically disadvantaged, socially constrained, or in some way disabled as learners. These programs placed a heavy emphasis on involving parents in the enhancement of their children's health as well as social–emotional and cognitive development.

In more recent years, home visiting has moved from primarily being an **intervention** to that of being a strategy of reaching people before problems develop. This emerging discipline is called **prevention.** Prevention efforts strive to promote positive qualities and strengths in people and families to empower them to function in healthy ways. The following are models of programs currently operating; they offer training and/or materials that can assist educators who wish to initiate home visiting.

MODEL HOME VISITING INTERVENTION PROGRAMS

High/Scope

The High/Scope Perry Preschool Project began in 1962 as an intervention program that consisted of 2½ hours of preschool five days a week for 7½ months each year for two years. In addition, teachers made weekly 90-minute home visits to the families of all the children enrolled in the program. This program has been duplicated in this country and overseas. The longitudinal effects on the children initially enrolled have been favorable throughout their childhood and into their adult years (Roopnarine & Johnson, 2005).

Head Start

Head Start is a federally funded, comprehensive child development program that has mandated home visiting since its inception in 1965. One of the major components of the program is parent involvement, in such areas as parent education, program planning, and facility operation. Many parents serve on policy advisory councils and committees to provide input on administrative and managerial situations. The program requires that every family in center-based programs receive at least two home visits a year. In addition to teacher visits, the program also employs social service staff members to make home visits and provide services that include community social service referrals, family needs assessments, information on available services, recruitment and enrollment of children, and emergency assistance and crisis intervention. Early Head Start, Home Start, Migrant Head Start, and American Indian–Alaskan Native Head

Start extend the operations of the center-based Head Start programs and also offer extensive home-based services that include home visiting (Couchenour & Chrisman, 2008; Gestwicki, 2007; Prior & Gerard, 2007).

Mother–Child Home Program

The Mother–Child Home Program (MCHP), developed by the Verbal Interaction Project in 1965 under the direction of Phyllis Levenstein, is an example of a home-based intervention model in which home visitors, called toy demonstrators, visit homes twice a week over two years to families with children aged 2 to 4 years. Following the school calendar, a total of 92 visits are made. During the visits, parents are given instruction on how to introduce toys and books to their children as well as how to model positive language interaction in play situations. In 1982, the program was incorporated as the National Center for the Mother–Child Home Program and changed its name to the Parent–Child Home Program. By 1998, there were 29 replications of this program in the United States and 10 other countries (Berger, 2008; Gestwicki, 2007).

Portage Project

The Portage Project, established in 1969 in Portage, Wisconsin, serves children between the ages of birth and 6 years who have diagnosed disabilities or who are developmentally delayed or economically disadvantaged. Visitors make weekly, 90-minute home visits, during which they work with parents to plan and implement strategies for addressing the needs of the child as identified through an initial assessment process. These strategies are incorporated into the family's daily routine to help family members become involved in the child's developmental program. The home visitor also works with parents to develop or strengthen their support network, develop action plans for addressing broader family concerns, and access community resources. The materials utilized in the program include a developmental checklist of 580 developmentally sequenced behaviors divided into six areas: infant stimulation, self-help, language, cognition, motor skills, and socialization. A set of 580 cards describes activities for the parents to use to help their children develop specific behaviors in the six areas. A manual of instruction provides detailed directions on how to implement the Portage Project. This home visiting model has been replicated in private schools, public schools, and Head Start programs throughout the United States. Several countries, including the United Kingdom and Japan, also have incorporated the program. The materials are available in 30 languages (Berger, 2008; Roopnarine & Johnson, 2005).

Home Instruction Program for Preschool Youngsters

The Home Instruction Program for Preschool Youngsters (HIPPY) began in Israel in 1969 and was introduced to the United States in 1984 with the assistance of the National Council for Jewish Women. This model targets parents with limited formal education and their 4- and 5-year-old children. Paraprofessionals make biweekly home visits to provide parents with books and activity sheets. They teach parents how to use the materials with their children; parents and children then work together for 15 to 20 minutes each day. During each of two years, the program provides 30 weeks of activities for parents, scheduled to generally coincide with the school year. The activities include basic reading skills, such as tactile, auditory, visual, and conceptual discrimination; language development; verbal expression; eye-hand coordination; pre-math concepts; logical thinking; self-concept; and creativity. On alternate weeks, the parents, home visitors, and program coordinator meet to role-play the week's assigned activities and discuss parenting issues of concern. The paraprofessional home visitors are members of the participating communities and often are recruited from families who have participated in the program. In 1999, there were 121 programs serving 15,000 families in 28 states, Guam, and the District of Columbia (Couchenour & Chrisman, 2008; Gomby, Culross, & Behrman, 1999).

MODEL HOME VISITING PREVENTION PROGRAMS

New Parents as Teachers

The New Parents as Teachers (NPAT) program, which focuses on first-time parents, is a model prevention effort. The program began in 1981 as an adaptation of the parent education model developed by Burton White. In this program, there are two forms of contact with the parents: home visits and group meetings. During the home visits, curriculum materials relevant to the child's age as well as to upcoming stages of development are distributed and discussed. Home visits are scheduled once every 6 weeks and last an hour. Along with home visits are group meetings in which seven to eight families come together to discuss child development topics. These meetings are held once a month and serve the dual functions of social support and increasing the parents' knowledge base. In 1999, there were 2,197 NAPT programs in 49 states, the District of Columbia, and six other countries serving over 500,000 children (Couchenour & Chrisman, 2008; Gomby, Culross, & Behrman, 1999).

Developmentally appropriate curriculum materials are used and discussed. *Courtesy of ECE Photo Library.*

Hawaii Healthy Start

The Hawaii Healthy Start program is another model prevention approach. It was started in 1985 by the Hawaii Family Stress Center as a federal demonstration project to prevent child abuse and neglect. The program has evolved into a statewide program funded by the Maternal and Child Health division of the Hawaii State Department of Health.

The following are the goals of the program:

1. Assure that all families have a primary health-care provider.
2. Assure that there is proper use of community resources.
3. Promote positive parenting.
4. Enhance parent–child interaction.
5. Enhance child health and development.
6. Prevent child abuse and neglect.

Home visits are conducted by paraprofessionals. Services begin at the birth of a child and continue until age 5. If a hospital-recorded review suggests the possible need for service, the family is interviewed in the hospital shortly after the birth of the child. Home visits are offered to families who exhibit the need for such assistance based on their scores on a family-stress inventory administered during the hospital visit. At first, visits are conducted weekly, with their frequency reduced as families resolve specific problems. The program receives funding from both public and private agencies.

THE PURPOSE OF THE HOME VISIT

The appeal of the home visit as a strategy for parent involvement is based on the opportunity that it provides for the school to work with individuals within the context of the family. The home visit provides an avenue for the teacher to get to know the child's family, environment, and culture in order to serve both the child and the parents more effectively (Bauer & Shea, 2003).

A home visitor should never make a visit without having a specific, planned purpose. Watson (1991) cites the following purposes:

- To get parents involved with their child's learning.
- To use parents' skills and knowledge, family interests, and resources to teach children.
- To teach parents developmentally appropriate ways to reach specific objectives.
- To get families involved in the program, the school, and the community.
- To determine and address needs of children and their families.
- To provide information about community resources.
- To provide guidance for families in getting the help they need (and to strengthen parents by encouraging them to meet their own needs).
- To broaden the experiences of children.
- To increase the self-esteem of children and parents.

Bundy (1991), on the other hand, concludes that the express purpose of the home visit is to introduce the children to their teachers and other staff members in familiar surroundings.

THE EFFECTIVENESS OF HOME VISITS

The home visit as a strategy for involving parents as partners is becoming more prevalent as schools and agencies that receive state and federal funds are mandated to visit the homes of the children enrolled in their programs. The programs that utilize home visiting are widely diverse. Their structures, goals, and the families they serve limit to some extent the lessons we can draw from research about their effectiveness. Gestwicki (2007) reports that home visiting in and of itself has never been an effective cure-all in addressing the complicated needs of families. Still, research suggests that the most effective programs are comprehensive, continuous, and family-focused. The evaluation of effectiveness is further complicated because home visiting programs offer different curricula and different frequency of visits and employ staff members with different backgrounds and skills—all of which can be strong variables in program effectiveness. Despite these problems, some programs have demonstrated positive health and/or developmental outcomes for children. Many also have found positive effects on mothers' personal development measured in terms of higher self-esteem, continuing education, and movement toward self-sufficiency.

Cataldo (1987) suggests that home visits offer a sense of support in assuring parents that somebody cares, and such caring helps socially isolated families feel more important. Powell (1990) reports that early studies of home visiting uncovered positive effects of home-based early intervention on the children's cognitive and social development as well as on adult development. He further indicates that recent studies have shown positive effects on improving child and maternal health. Wasik (1993) notes that the home visit offers benefits that increase the ability of the program staff to help the families they serve. These benefits include (1) gaining access to information about the conditions in which the family lives, (2) learning about family interaction patterns, (3) discovering family values and beliefs, and (4) finding out about the social and material resources that are available to support the family. The information collected can serve to prompt intervention efforts that are more family-centered and sensitive to each family's environment.

Gestwicki (2007) indicates that home visits provide a setting that fosters increased trust among the parents, child, and teacher. The visit also affords the teacher with firsthand insights into how the parents and child interact in their home environment. The teacher uses this information to meet the child's needs and to utilize the parents' resources, which are learned about during the visit. Bauer and Shea (2003) suggest the home visit helps the teacher get to know the child's family environment and culture better; this knowledge helps in serving the child and parents more effectively. The visit is an occasion for the teacher to meet the other members of the child's family and become acquainted with the child's learning context. Home visits provide opportunities to get to know the family, give an explanation of the representative program, gather information, report the child's school progress, problem solve, and obtain parental input for additional parent involvement strategies.

Successes

At a home visitor training conference, trainees whose home visiting experience ranged from 2 to 22 years were asked to list the successes of this strategy (Rockwell, 1993). Their responses were as follows:

- Family attitudes change.
- The family's ability to work with the child improves.
- Families increase their utilization of outside resources.

- The visitor gets to know the family.
- The gap between home and school is bridged.
- Collaboration skills are improved.
- Positive relationships are created.
- Parents and children gain increased self-esteem.
- The visitor develops an understanding of the child's environment.
- The child exhibits positive behavior changes.
- Parents become involved in school activities.
- Parents become a resource for the teacher.
- Fathers become involved.
- Families are empowered: Parents set up their own support group, returned to school to obtain a GED, and found employment.
- Families give positive feedback about what visitors have done or suggested.
- Success stories are shared.
- Parents see children in a positive light (learn how to enjoy them).
- Teamwork is increased.
- Friendships are created and respect is gained.
- Attitudes change (from negative to positive).
- Parents view school and staff as partners rather than foes.
- Parents support the child's attendance in the program.
- Parents view themselves as the child's first teachers.
- There is a positive overall change in the family's life.
- Real change or progress is observed.
- Families want home visitors to return.
- Notes and phone calls between the family and teacher increase.

Disadvantages

Home visits do have some disadvantages. The time required to plan, schedule, and conduct the visit is the most frequently mentioned disadvantage. Presuppositions that both the parents and the home visitor bring to the setting also can be a problem. Negative past experiences often pose a barrier that stalls all efforts of involving the parents. It is critical that the initial home visit be used to eradicate any negative experiences that might serve to derail the future involvement of the family.

Home visits to high-crime neighborhoods or to isolated rural areas can be dangerous. The Michigan Department of Education (1999) suggests the following safety tips for home visitors.

- Stay alert.
- Dress appropriately.
- Leave jewelry at home.
- Leave your purse at the office or in the trunk.
- Carry necessary identification and keys on your person.
- Remove yourself from dangerous situations.
- Travel in pairs when possible.
- Survey and make yourself familiar with the neighborhood.
- Identify safe areas (for example, restaurants, telephones, restrooms, and police stations).
- Trust your instincts.
- Consider a neutral meeting location (for example, in a library or at a restaurant) if the visit cannot be made safely or if the family prefers it.
- Ask the family to come outside to meet you if you are uncomfortable with the area.
- Keep your car in good repair.
- Keep emergency supplies in your car, including all-weather gear.
- Ask the family to secure all pets before your arrival.
- Attend safety seminars.
- Always carry a cellular phone in case of emergency.

DIVERSITY IN HOME VISITING PROGRAMS

Home visiting programs can be quite different in content and methods. The practice itself is a generic label representing a service delivery system. Programs vary considerably as to whether the substance of the home visit is focused primarily on the child (single focus) or includes attention to the parent and family function (multiple focus). Regardless of the type of program—school-based, home-based, single-focused, multiple-focused, intervention, or prevention—the home visitor will be working with the entire family. When issues arise that are out of the parameter of services offered by a specific program, the home visitor should respond by assisting the parent in making contact with an appropriate community resource.

CULTURAL SENSITIVITY

Cultural background lays a foundation of values and perspectives of the world that help family members define who they are. A family's values and practices often will differ from those of the home visitor. This implies that the home visitor must cultivate rapport and trust with families that may view the world very differently. If home visitors are to develop a sensitivity and respect for the **cultural mores** of the families with whom they work, they must be given training that focuses on the fundamental values, beliefs, customs, practices, and traditions of those families. The understanding that will be gained through such training will enrich the home visit and promote a more supportive partnership between the home and the school. (See Chapter 3 for additional information.)

QUALIFICATIONS FOR HOME VISITORS

Training

Unless a staff member has had some training in social work, it is doubtful that he or she will have had any experience or background in planning or conducting a home visit. Training will help avoid problems that could jeopardize all future parent involvement strategies. A study by Wasik and Roberts (1993) involved a national survey of home visitor characteristics, training, and supervision. The respondents represented public or private health, education, social service, and Head Start programs. The findings revealed that the percentage of home visiting programs that offered training ranged from 40 percent for private education to more than 70 percent for Head Start programs. The programs using a written curriculum for training ranged from 12 to 30 percent. The wide diversity of programs within given communities offers an excellent opportunity for the various programs to work collaboratively, not only in developing home visiting training materials but also in offering joint training opportunities.

Coordination of training efforts also can provide those who are new to this strategy an opportunity to learn from those who have had more experience. An example of a home visitor training program that brings both experienced and novice trainees together is shown in Box 7.1.

Personal Traits

The U.S. Department of Health, Education, and Welfare (1993), through its Office of Child Development, discusses several personality traits that will serve home visitors well as they attempt to convince parents to open the doors not only to their homes but to their lives.

Home visitors should be warm, outgoing, energetic, enthusiastic, and dignified. They should be able to adapt their personality to meet varying needs. Home visitors must relate well with both adults and children and be able to listen well and communicate effectively. Home visitors have learned that there is no single right or wrong way to approach all the situations they will face. They must be sensitive to the actions and reactions of others and be able to change strategies

BOX 7.1

Home Visitor Training Program

1. As an introduction, list three things that describe how you felt when you made your first home visit. Each participant then gives his or her name and agency and shares feelings. (Mixer)

2. Give an overview of and tell about the history of home visiting. (Mini-lecture)

3. Break into small groups and write down the problems that individuals in the group have had in making home visits. (Brainstorming and small-group discussion)

4. Write the success experiences that individuals in the same small groups have had in making home visits. (Brainstorming and small-group discussion)

5. Post the problems and the success experiences on the wall. Choose one of the problems and prepare a 2- to 3-minute role-play that demonstrates the problem. The small group also should be prepared to offer its collaborative decision as to how this problem might be resolved. (Small-group discussion and role-playing preparation)

6. Have each group role-play its problem and solicit audience reaction and feedback about how audience members might resolve or have resolved the problem. The group may also share its solution. The experience of group members should be capitalized on here. (Role-playing and large-group discussion)

7. Allow each group to share its success experiences. (Large group)

8. Break for 10 to 15 minutes.

9. Give the rationale and philosophy for home visiting. Programs represented can share their rationale and philosophy. (Large group)

10. Discuss the personal traits required of the home visitor. (Brainstorming, large group)

11. Describe how to conduct a home visit. Step-by-step, share the components that are part of all home visits. (Transparencies and overhead projector, mini-lecture, and large-group discussion)

12. Ask small groups to compile a list of do's and don'ts for home visitors. (Small-group discussion)

13. Post lists of do's and don'ts. Compare and develop a master list as a collaborative effort by the entire audience. Record the list and share it by mail with all participants. (Large and small groups)

14. Stress the importance of communication skills. Classify listening skills and do active-listening exercises. (Large and small groups)

15. Close.

easily when subtle signals indicate resistance or nonacceptance. Home visitors must be able to see the other person's point of view and want to work out solutions that are not only "right" but also acceptable for each family. Home visitors should have an eager interest in the job and the motivation to work long and hard hours.

Whatever the culture or background of the families to be served, home visitors must be able to win their confidence quickly in order to be accepted and trusted. Trust does not come automatically—it must be earned. Home visitors should have the ability to converse with each family using the family's native language. If necessary, an interpreter should accompany the home visitor. Home visitors should be able to respond to families' needs as they arise. Some visits may need to be made on weekends or during the evening, but such visitation should have the family's approval. Home visitors also must keep privileged information confidential and must respect each family's privacy.

MAKING THE HOME VISIT

Regardless of how much training a person has received, making the first home visit is never easy. The first-time visitor is usually nervous, fearful, unsure of what to expect, afraid that something might be said that will offend the family, and—even despite training—a bit uncertain of what to say or do. The best antidote for these emotions is to realize that they are very common and that after making a few visits, they begin to disappear.

Here are some important points to consider arranged in order:

1. Plan the visit. Why are you making the visit? What will you try to accomplish? Gather information regarding the child in question. If presenting a lesson or an activity, collect your materials and organize them.

2. Schedule the visit. Inform the parents that you are coming. This can be accomplished by telephoning or sending a note or letter to the home indicating the purpose, date, time, and expected length of your visit. This allows the parents to let you know whether the time is convenient and to suggest an alternative time or place. Some families would rather meet in a neutral site such as a restaurant or church; this request should be honored.

3. Arrive at the home on time.

4. Establish rapport. When you ask for the person or persons being visited, use full names. Introduce yourself and explain the purpose of your visit. Open the conversation by briefly telling something about yourself, your background, and your relationship to the school. Be open to discussing problems that might be foremost on the parents' minds. Attempt to deal with problems if possible. Be positive, pleasant, sincere, and caring.

5. Convey a genuine interest. Interest is the key word, particularly an interest in the child or children. Review the last contact, whether at school or at a previous home visit. What were the recommendations at that time? Gather and record information about the accomplishments that pertain to previous recommendations. Identify strengths and weaknesses. Reinforce accomplishments and efforts. If dealing with a lesson or a specific activity that was discussed during the previous visit, be prepared to reteach if necessary.

6. Conduct the planned activities. Follow your objectives, yet be prepared to adjust and modify them to fit the circumstances. No matter how well prepared you are, there will be an untold list of situations that will distract you and the parents. Always try to focus on the parent, child, or both, according to your program plan.

7. Review the activities that were presented. Allow time for and encourage parents to ask clarification questions. Have the parents demonstrate any new activities.

8. Make announcements regarding future parent–child activities at school and in the community. Distribute the materials you plan to leave. Gather the materials you plan to take with you. Make an appointment for the next visit.

9. Conclude the visit. Remind the parents of important things to do. Say goodbye to everyone.

Everyone enjoyed this visit. *Courtesy of ECE Photo Library.*

10. **Evaluate yourself after the visit.** Ask these questions:

- Was I prepared?
- Was I successful in establishing rapport?
- Did I engage in a two-way dialogue?
- Did I utilize active-listening skills?
- Did I respond to parent concerns?
- Were the materials adequate?
- Did I explain the activities in an understandable manner?
- How did the child react?
- How did the parents react?
- What was the highlight of the visit?
- What problems were there?
- How could I improve?
- What changes were observed in the child? In the parents?
- What can I do to expand on today's learning?

SPECIFIC BEHAVIORS TO AVOID WHEN WORKING WITH FAMILIES

1. **Avoid pushing your values on the families.** We all have our own values and must appreciate and allow others the right to have theirs.

2. **Avoid doing for the family what its members are capable of doing for themselves.** Help empower them to become competent in meeting the specific needs of their child and family.

3. **Avoid diagnosing and prescribing for families and telling them what to do.** You can assist as they assess their own needs and interject your own observations if necessary.

4. **Do not stereotype families.** Each family is unique, with its own strengths and weaknesses.

5. **Do not assume the role of Mr. or Ms. Fix-it.** You cannot resolve all the world's problems with an instantaneous cure-all. It is critical that home visitors be knowledgeable of community agencies that can assist families in obtaining needed services. Networking with agencies within your community will increase your effectiveness when needs occur.

6. **Be consistent.** It is imperative that you keep appointments and follow through with all commitments. The family must be able to trust that you are being honest and acting in the best interests of the child and family.

7. **Do not expect too much too soon.** Habits and ways of relating to people and situations have been formed over years and do not change overnight. It is perfectly OK to expect change, but expecting it too quickly can be frustrating and self-defeating for everyone involved.

8. **Avoid letting the family become dependent upon you.** Do be a professional helper. Do not offer to lend money or provide transportation for personal activities. The home–visitor relationship must be a friendly one, but keeping it on a professional level will assist you in preventing it from becoming counterproductive.

9. **Do not violate confidentiality.** What families tell you is to be held in confidence. Never discuss these families with your own family or friends. Families should be told that the information and data you collect while in their home will be held in strict confidence.

SUMMARY

Home visiting is a parent involvement strategy that, if employed successfully, can be the foundation for future involvement of the family in the education of the child. It is a strategy that provides unique access to families and extensive information about their home situation. The primary aim is to encourage parents to take an active interest in the education of their children and to work as partners with school personnel in meeting goals that will be beneficial to all.

ACTIVITIES FOR DISCUSSION, EXPANSION, AND APPLICATION

1. Divide the class into two groups. Have one group discuss and list what it believes are the advantages of home visits. Have the second group list disadvantages. Post the two lists and discuss the pros and cons of home visits.

2. Divide the class into groups. Have each group select a problem from one of the following hypothetical situations that one might encounter when making a home visit. Follow these steps:
   - Choose a group recorder.
   - Read the problem situation.
   - Discuss the strategies that the group might use to resolve the problem.
   - Prepare a dramatization to demonstrate the problem or situation.
   - Role-play the problem or situation.

- Solicit class reaction and feedback on how to resolve the problem.
- Share the group's consensus on how the problem was resolved.

SITUATION 1

The family is never home when you visit.

SITUATION 2

The home is infested with roaches and rats.

SITUATION 3

You are to visit and work with one child, yet there are three other children in the family and they are always there when you arrive.

SITUATION 4

The parent spanks the child or children in your presence.

SITUATION 5

You arrive for the visit and the only one home is the mother's boyfriend.

SITUATION 6

While visiting the home, there is constant interruption from telephone calls and from people you do not know who are coming and going in and out of the house.

SITUATION 7

The family speaks a language that you are unable to understand. Furthermore, the family cannot read or understand English.

SITUATION 8

There is a power struggle between the parents about how to best raise the child.

SITUATION 9

The child (5 years old) is being raised by grandparents, and they are at their wits' end regarding his quite-normal restlessness. "He just can't sit still for more than five minutes!" they complain.

SITUATION 10

You can never find the homes of the children. You seem to always get lost and end up driving in circles.

SITUATION 11

Every time you visit, the mother watches the television soaps while you work with the child.

SITUATION 12

You are confronted by families' friendly and not-so-friendly pets.

SITUATION 13

While interviewing the mother, you see evidence that she has been abused.

SITUATION 14

While visiting, you see evidence of child abuse.

SITUATION 15

You have made numerous visits, and the family never follows through with suggestions you have made for working with the child.

SITUATION 16

During the home visit, the parents dominate the conversation with issues that are not related to the child.

SITUATION 17

You fear for your physical safety when visiting a family's neighborhood.

SITUATION 18

The parents have a negative attitude toward the school.

SITUATION 19

The parents provide food and a drink when you really don't want them.

SITUATION 20

You arrive at the home and find the child or children home alone.

SITUATION 21

A parent answers the door unclothed.

SITUATION 22

The parents are sleeping when you arrive.

SITUATION 23

During the visit, you observe weapons under the sofa.

SITUATION 24

The parents refuse to let you enter the home.

SITUATION 25

A parent asks you to sit on the sofa, and as you do, you discover that it's wet.

SITUATION 26

The parent tells you that she is considering suicide, because she is so fed up and stressed with her life.

3. Discuss the problems your personal values could present as you make a home visit. How might this issue be resolved?

4. Discuss the basic guidelines for making a home visit.

5. Would you feel comfortable making a home visit? Explain your answer.

6. You are the director of a prekindergarten program that serves 200 families. Staff members have never made home visits, nor have they received training. Outline what you believe should be included in a home visitor training program for your staff.

7. Should teachers make home visits, or should they only be made by people specifically hired to do them? Explain your position.

8. Contact a representative from one of the home visitor models mentioned in this chapter. Prepare a detailed report of the model, and share it with the class.

9. How would you react to a home visit made to your home? Share with class members both positive and negative reactions.

CASE STUDY

You arrive at the door for a home visit just as the mother is leaving. She asks you to stay with the child until she gets back. "It's only for a minute. I'll be right back," she says.

1. Do you stay with the child?

2. What will you say if the mother does not return for an hour or more?

3. What steps can you suggest to avoid this situation in the future?

USEFUL WEBSITES

eclkc.ohs.acf.hhs.gov/hslc
The Early Childhood Learning and Knowledge Center. This website offers information regarding all Head Start programs. The benefits of home visits and how they can strengthen families are presented.

www.ehsnrc.org/AboutUs/ehs.htm
Early Head Start. This website provides detailed information regarding the framework of the Early Head Start program, which features home visits, especially for families with newborns.

www.hippyusa.org
Home Instruction Program for Preschool Youngsters (HIPPY). At the heart of the HIPPY model is the home visit. How the visit is utilized as a vehicle that allows parents to empower themselves is detailed at this website.

www.parent-child.org
The Parent–Child Home Program. Formerly the Verbal Interaction Project, one of the first home-based visitation programs. This organization is

committed to helping families challenged by poverty, low levels of education, language barriers, and other obstacles to educational success guide their children to school success by stimulating parent–child verbal interaction and developing critical language and literacy skills.

www.patnc.org

Parents as Teachers (PAT). PAT is an international early childhood parent education and child support program serving families from pregnancy until their children enter kindergarten. The program is designed to enhance child development and school achievement through parent education that is accessible to all families. It is a universal access model that utilizes home visits.

www.portageproject.org

The Portage Project. This organization is committed to creating and enhancing quality programs that promote development and education of all children through services, materials, and advocacy. This is one of the original home-based programs.

REFERENCES

Bauer, A. M., & Shea, T. M. (2003). *Parents and schools: Creating a successful partnership for students with special needs.* Upper Saddle River, New Jersey: Pearson/Merrill/Prentice Hall.

Berger, E. H. (2008). *Parents as partners in education: Families and schools working together* (7th ed.). Upper Saddle River, NJ: Pearson Education.

Bundy, B. F. (1991). Fostering communication between parents and schools. *Young Children, 46*(2), 12–17.

Cataldo, C. Z. (1983). *Infant and toddler programs.* Reading, MA: Addison-Wesley.

Cataldo, C. Z. (1987). *Parent education for early childhood.* New York: Teachers College Press.

Couchenour, D., & Chrisman, K. (2008). *Families, schools, and communities together for young children* (2nd ed.). Clifton Park, NY: Thomson Delmar Learning.

Gestwicki, C. (2007). *Home, school, and community relations* (6th ed.). Clifton Park, NY: Thomson Delmar Learning.

Gomby, D., Culross, P. L., & Behrman, R. E. (1999). Home visiting: Recent program evaluations—analysis and recommendations. In R. E. Berhman (Ed.), *The future of children 9*(1), 4–6.

Hendrick, J. (2003). *Total learning: Developmental curriculum for the young child* (6th ed). Upper Saddle River, NJ: Merrill/Prentice Hall.

Michigan Department of Education Early Childhood Programs. (1999). *A guide to home visits.* Michigan Department of Education Government Documents.

Miller, A. C. (1987). *Maternal health and infant survival.* Washington, DC: National Center for Clinical Infant Programs.

Powell, D. R. (1990). Research in review: Home visiting in the early years: Policy and program design decisions. *Young Children, 46*(2), 66–73.

Prior, J., & Gerard, M. R. (2007). *Family involvement in early childhood education: Research into practice.* Clifton Park, NY: Thomson Delmar Learning.

Rockwell, R. E. (April 30, 1993). Project Apples. Home visits workshop. Moline, IL: Western Illinois University.

Roopnarine, J. L., & Johnson, J. E. (2005). *Approaches to early childhood education* (4th ed.). Upper Saddle River, NJ: Prentice Hall.

Seefeldt, C. (1980). *A curriculum for preschool.* Columbus, OH: Merrill.

U.S. Department of Health, Education, and Welfare, Office of Child Development. (1993). *A guide for operating the Head Start home-based option.* Washington, DC: U.S. Government Printing Office.

Wasik, H. B. (1993). Staffing issues for home visiting programs. In R. E. Berhman (Ed.), *Home visiting: The future of young children, 3*(3), 140–157. Center for the Future of Young Children, The David and Lucile Packard Foundation.

Wasik, H. B., & Roberts, R. N. (1993). Home visitor characteristics, training, and supervision: Results of a national survey. In R. E. Berhman (Ed.), *Home visiting: The future of young children, 3*(3), 150. Center for the Future of Young Children, The David and Lucile Packard Foundation.

Watson, S. D. (1991). *Handbook for home visits.* Greenville, IL: Bond County Community Unit No. 2.

KEY TERMS

Intervention—A strategy developed in response to the needs of children who are developmentally delayed, economically disadvantaged, socially constrained, or in some way disabled as learners.

Prevention—A strategy of reaching families before problems develop. Prevention efforts strive to promote positive qualities and strengths in people and families to empower them to function in healthy ways.

Cultural Mores—Customs and beliefs associated with a particular culture.

CHAPTER 8
Parent Group Meetings

STUDENT LEARNING OUTCOMES

After reading this chapter, you should be able to

- Establish a rationale for conducting parent group meetings.

- Discuss a variety of parent group meeting formats.

- Identify the most common reasons that parents give for not attending group meetings.

- Describe how to plan, prepare for, conduct, and evaluate a parent group meeting.

The **parent group meeting** as a parent involvement strategy can be a beneficial and productive form of parent–teacher collaboration. In this chapter, we examine formats of parent group meetings from small to large. A common reason that school personnel give for not utilizing this strategy is that parents do not attend. We have interviewed parents throughout the country and will present their side of the story. Ways to overcome the barriers that keep parents from being involved in this way are addressed. General issues in planning and conducting large and small parent group meetings are discussed. A detailed model for planning, conducting, and evaluating parent group meetings is given. A sample meeting schedule is also provided.

RATIONALE FOR THE PARENT GROUP MEETING APPROACH

Meeting with parents in a group setting offers the teacher yet another strategy to work with parents as partners. People feel more comfortable and relaxed in group settings. Group settings provide a supportive and friendly environment in which learning activities can be optimally presented. There may be an initial hesitation to discuss feelings and unspoken thoughts, but after getting acquainted in an informal setting, participants often can overcome social anxiety and speak openly. As the group develops a history of positive interaction, the interest and excitement of the participants will build and be reflected in greater initiative and a feeling of *esprit de corps*.

Bauer and Shea (2002) indicate that parents and teachers meet in groups for three major purposes: to transfer information, to teach and learn behavior management or interpersonal communication techniques, and to give and receive social and emotional support. Whatever the primary purpose, every group will, to some extent, include all three elements.

Rockwell and Kniepkamp (2003) suggest that there are nine potential advantages to parents working with teachers in group meetings.

1. Families develop new friendships.
2. Parents learn from other parents and families.
3. Individual parents and guardians become involved.
4. Parents gain new insights about and understanding of the curriculum.
5. Parents develop an awareness of developmentally appropriate teaching and learning practices and how they are helpful both at school and at home.
6. Parents gain an appreciation for teachers' efforts.
7. Parents are better able to define appropriate levels of expectations for their children's developing abilities and skills.
8. Parents feel more comfortable in their interactions with teachers.
9. Parents develop an appreciation of their own abilities.

WHY PARENTS FAIL TO ATTEND GROUP MEETINGS

In many schools, parent involvement is synonymous with group meetings. If parents are invited to attend group meetings, then the school considers its obligation to parent involvement fulfilled (Cook, Tessier, & Klein, 2000). When parents don't attend, they often are labeled as uninvested in the school or their children. However, little or no attention may have been given to whether the planned meetings address the needs of those invited. These meetings usually are large in size and are designed to give educational information in a lecture format. The speakers often use vocabulary that is either difficult for parents to understand or is patronizing to them. Many parents avoid asking clarifying questions at such meetings because they feel intimidated and don't want to risk looking foolish. As a result, they may attend one meeting, but they do not return.

In an attempt to identify the factors that cause parents to avoid this involvement strategy, we have made extensive inquiries over the past 45 years with parents in 35 states. The following factors that discourage parents from attending group meetings have been reported. Some suggestions for ameliorating these problems are also provided.

1. Parents receive late notification. Send home an invitation to the meeting at least two weeks in advance. Send home one or more reminder notes during the week of the meeting.

2. Meetings are not held at convenient times. Do not schedule all meetings in the same time slot. Try a variety of meeting times: in the morning, before school, during school, after school, and on weekends. Do this in consideration of parents who have work schedules that prohibit them from attending afternoon or evening meetings.

3. No child care is provided. Child care should always be provided by competent caregivers in a safe environment. Care providers should be more than just a few years older than the children they are caring for. The room where care is provided should be well equipped with cribs and toys that are appropriate for a wide range of ages.

4. Parents are not included in planning topics of interest to them. Parents should be given numerous opportunities to identify meeting topics and presenters they are interested in. Do not ask for this input until the parents are acquainted with each other and the staff members. Usually by the second or third meeting, trust has been established and the parents feel their input does matter.

5. Meetings often do not start or finish on time. It is critical that all meetings begin and end as scheduled. This is appreciated by both parents and teachers.

6. Meetings are usually too long. A good time frame for a parent group meeting is 1 to 1½ hours in length.

7. Teachers complain when parent attendance is low. It's normal to be disappointed when only a few parents show up for a meeting. However, do not complain; present the meeting as planned with the same enthusiasm you would have had if 50 parents had come. The word will spread about the great meeting that so many missed. The next few meetings should show an increase in attendance. This may take more than one meeting to achieve, as parents have good recall of past unproductive meetings.

8. Meetings are too formal. Informal or casual is the most popular dress for meetings. However, it is important to let parents know. Notification can be accomplished via the meeting invitation and the reminder notice.

9. No refreshments are served. Refreshments are a critical component of a meeting. They do not have to be expensive or elaborate. Cookies, coffee, and soft drinks can contribute to a relaxed atmosphere that is more conducive to sharing and working together as partners.

10. No transportation is provided. Many parents have no way to get to meetings. This is a problem that should not be ignored. Some programs offer bus service, while others offer rides with other parents and teachers who have cars.

11. There is a small clique of parents who dominate sessions. This is a problem that cannot be tolerated. We need to be assertive in conducting meetings in a way that allows all present to participate.

12. Parents are not given an opportunity to evaluate meetings. All meetings should be evaluated by parents and staff members. The results should be used to plan future meeting topics and speakers of interest to the families served by the program.

To maximize the value of the parent group meeting strategy, staff members need to keep in mind the potential problems just listed as they plan and conduct meetings.

TYPES OF PARENT GROUP MEETINGS

Parent group meetings occur in a variety of sizes and range from formal lectures to informal workshops. Numerous formats are used in programs serving children from birth through high school.

Berger (2008), Click and Karkos (2008), and Couchenour and Chrisman (2004) designate these meeting formats:

1. Roundtable discussion: All participants sit in a circle or around a table. A topic is chosen when the meeting is scheduled. A parent, teacher, or guest serves as the moderator. A good moderator can prevent a few parents from dominating the discussion. The discussion is limited to the preselected topic or topics.

2. Concentric circle: This approach is similar to the roundtable. There are two circles, one inside the other, with all participants facing the center. The group in the smaller, inside circle discusses the chosen topic for a given period of time, usually 10 to 15 minutes. The larger group, in the outside circle, listens and prepares questions and reactions. When the time runs out, the entire group is free to interact and further discuss the topic.

3. Buzz sessions: Participants are divided into groups of two to eight people. The ideal size is four, as this allows everyone to have input. The buzz session allows participants to share their feelings on an issue that is to be discussed later in the meeting by the entire audience. Each group chooses a leader and a recorder. The groups are placed around the room as far away from each other as possible to avoid distraction. After a given time period (20 to 30 minutes) the large group reassembles and everyone discusses the topic at hand.

4. Brainstorming: When using this form of participation, it is critical to accept all of the audience's contributions. Everyone is encouraged to speak up; there are no wrong suggestions. Participants may add to, combine, or modify ideas. Encouraging and accepting all ideas from the group stimulates an abundance of diversified thought.

5. Workshops: This strategy has proven the most effective for the authors of this book. When parents are asked, "How do you learn best?" the response usually given is "By doing." The workshop format enables the participants to capitalize on this learning style. The major component of a workshop is the active involvement of the participants, which can often involve all family members. See Figure 8.1 for an example of an informal workshop format that allows the parents to be actively involved as they interact with their children.

6. Role-playing: Role-playing is the dramatization of a hypothetical yet realistic situation in which participants place themselves in designated roles. This strategy is often received reluctantly by participants. However, after practicing, their hesitancy and reluctance to participate begins to disappear.

7. Panel discussion: Information on a topic or issue of concern is given by four presenters. A panel moderator introduces the speakers and the topic. Each presenter is allowed 10 minutes to share his or her thoughts. Following the presentations, the panel moderator asks for questions from the audience. All panel members respond, if appropriate. The moderator summarizes the major points discussed and the conclusions reached.

8. Colloquy: This is a form of panel discussion that allows the audience to interject questions or make comments throughout the presentation rather than waiting until the speakers have finished.

9. Debate: A controversial issue is chosen as a topic, and two teams of five to six members each are formed to present both sides of the issue. The audience listens as each speaker is allowed 2 to 4 minutes to present a point of view. The teams

Family Book Worms!

INVITATION

Reading fun and activities for the whole family!

Enjoy literacy activities that promote a lifelong interest in reading.

Please Come!

Date:

Time:

Place:

Dress casually.

Refreshments will be served.

Please complete and detach the form below by _____ to reserve a space for your family.

_____ Yes, we will attend the "Family Bookworms" family meeting.
_____ Sorry, we are unable to attend the meeting.

Child's name _____
Number of adults attending _____ Number of children attending _____

If you have any questions or need transportation, please call _____

Name _____ Phone _____
Email address _____

FIGURE 8.1 Family Book Worms Workshop Materials

Family Book Worms!

REMINDER

Join us for reading fun for the whole family.

Please Come!

Date:

Time:

Place:

Who's Invited: The whole family

Dress for fun!

Refreshments will be served.

Call _____ and reserve a spot today. If you
need transportation, let us know.

FIGURE 8.1 Continued

Content Areas
Art
Dramatic Play
Language
Literacy
Motor Skills

Purpose
To promote literacy awareness and provide families with literature and
literacy activities to promote a lifelong interest in reading.

Nametags

Materials
Green, yellow, red, and orange construction paper
Black markers
Scissors
Bookworm nametag pattern (see below)

- Use the bookworm nametag pattern (see below) to make nametags in
  four colors.
- Assign one color per family.
- Different colored nametags will be used to assign families to one of
  four activity stations.
- Make an extra set of nametags in each of the four colors to post at the
  activity stations.

FIGURE 8.1 Continued

Mixer—Bookworm Hunt

- As families arrive, distribute the bookworm nametags.
- Ask each family member to write his or her name on the nametag and use masking tape to attach it to his or her clothing.
- Be sure all members of each family have the same color nametag so they can work together at each activity station.
- After families have arrived, give each family a copy of the "Find a Bookworm" Hunt.
- Ask them to move about the room and interact with other families while trying to complete their bookworm hunt.

Introduction

Reading aloud to children is one of the most significant parent/child activities that supports improved literacy. Reading aloud to children builds their understanding of concepts, develops oral language and vocabulary, promotes the joy and pleasure of reading, and develops a sense of the importance of literacy learning. There is a strong correlation between being read to at home and children's later success with reading.

Tell families they can proceed to the bookworm activity station that has the same color as their nametag. They will stay at that station until a bell rings as a signal to move clockwise to the next station. The activity stations are:

1. My Very Own Book (green bookworm)
2. The World of Print (yellow bookworm)
3. Let's Make a Puppet (red bookworm)
4. Time to Browse and Read to Your Child (orange bookworm)

FIGURE 8.1 Continued

alternate with pro and con views. A moderator keeps time for the presentations and keeps the debate moving. After all team members have spoken, the moderator asks for questions from the audience to be directed to the debate team members.

10. Symposium: Several speakers give a formal presentation on various aspects of a topic chosen in advance. Each speaker is allowed 5 to 15 minutes. After the presentations, a moderator directs questions from the audience to each speaker. The moderator summarizes and closes the meeting.

Family Meeting Activities

Station #1: My Very Own Book
(green bookworm nametag)

Use inexpensive materials to make books that are easy to read.

Materials
8 ½" x 11" sheets of white paper
Colored yarn
Scissors
Crayons
Paper punch
Paste
Large variety of magazines with photos (collected
    from families prior to meeting)
Family photos

What to Do
1. Fold two sheets of paper in half.
2. Place folded sheets of paper together to
   make an eight-page booklet.
3. Make two holes in the fold of the sheets
   of paper with the paper punch.
4. Thread the yarn through the two holes
   and tie.
5. Ideas for book titles:

- Things I Like to Eat
- My Animal Book
- Things I Do Not Like
- Things I Like
- My Family

6. Write the title on the cover and let your child
   decorate it.
7. Help your child cut pictures from the magazines
   and place one or two pictures on each page.
8. Your child can also draw pictures and dictate
   captions.

FIGURE 8.1 Continued

Station #2: The World of Print

(yellow bookworm nametag)

Learn about the many forms of print in the everyday environment, including signs, labels, logos, and symbols.

Materials
Examples of environmental print, such as store logos,
   cereal boxes, and so on
Poster board
Markers
Crayons
Scissors

What to Do
At this station, display a definition of environmental print: Print that is encountered outside of books and is a pervasive part of everyday living. Before this family meeting, draw a traffic light on poster board. Color each light with the appropriate markers. Write the word "stop" under the red light, "caution" under the yellow light, and "go" under the green light.

1. Show your child the poster board traffic light. Ask him or her what each of the lights signifies. If they do not know, explain what each color means.
2. Play "Red Light, Yellow Light, Green Light." Explain how traffic lights work and what the signals mean. Emphasize that the green light means "go" and the red light means "stop." Show the stoplight with the three words and colors.
3. Explain that when all the children in the group see the green light, they are to clap as fast as they can. When they see the yellow light, they should clap slowly, and when they see the red light, they should stop clapping.
4. One person uses his or her hands to cover up two lights, so only one light is visible.
5. Try this again with jumping, walking, or hopping.
6. Continue playing, which will help children associate the printed word "go" with the green light and the printed word "stop" with the red light.
7. Look at other everyday signs and logos and discover which ones the children can "read." For example, McDonald's, Hardee's, Target, Home Depot, Pizza, Pepsi, Coke, Dairy Queen, Kentucky Fried Chicken, Taco Bell, Subway, and so on.

FIGURE 8.1 Continued

Station #3: Let's Make a Puppet

(red bookworm nametag)

Make a puppet that can be used to reenact the motions of a story character as they listen to a favorite story.

Materials
Fabric scraps
Colored construction paper
Colored pipe cleaners
Crayons
Scissors
Yarn
Glue or stapler
Paper cylinders (toilet tissue or paper towel rolls)
Assortment of storybooks or books of nursery rhymes

What to Do
1. Glue or staple a piece of construction paper into a cylinder.
2. Decorate the paper cylinder with available materials.
3. Select a storybook or nursery rhyme that features a central character, such as *Where Can It Be?* by Ann Jones.
4. Encourage your child to act out the story with his or her puppets as you read the story or say the nursery rhyme.

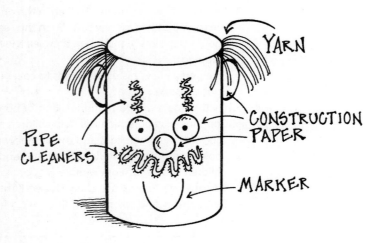

FIGURE 8.1 Continued

Station #4: Time to Browse and Read to Your Child

(orange bookworm nametag)

Share old tried-and-true children's storybook favorites as well as some of the newer books that appear to be destined to become future classics.

Materials
Children's books (about 3-5 per family)
Comfortable chairs on a large rug in the book corner
Handouts of suggested titles for children aged three through five years

What to Do
1. Take time to look at the books at this station. Many of the books may be familiar to you and your child and others may be new to you.
2. If possible, look at all of the books at this activity station. There may be time to browse further after the meeting.
3. Take a copy of the handouts that list recommended book titles and authors.

Thank everyone for coming and invite them to share a snack of seasonal fruit and crackers.

FIGURE 8.1 Continued

11. **Lecture:** A speaker is chosen to lecture on a given subject for 30 to 45 minutes. The speaker should be chosen not only for his or her knowledge of the subject, but also for the ability to relate to the parent audience.

12. **Video/DVD presentations:** There is an abundance of good videos and DVDs that deal with a wide range of parent and child issues. Local and state film libraries often will provide films at no cost. You might also make a video of class activities to share with parents.

EVALUATION

Family Bookworms

Family Meeting Evaluation

We would like to know what you thought about the "Family Bookworms" meeting. Please circle the picture that best describes your feelings. We appreciate your feedback, so feel free to make comments. Thank you.

Good apple   So-so   Rotten apple

Comments and Suggestions

_____
_____
_____
_____
_____
_____
_____

Thank you for coming!

FIGURE 8.1 Continued

Parents should have input in planning future meeting topics. *Courtesy of ECE Photo Library.*

Bauer and Shea (2002) report that parent–teacher collaboration groups can choose specific models that are appropriate in fulfilling the group's specific purposes. They can consider informational meetings, orientation meetings, open houses, commercial programs such as Parent Effectiveness Training (PET) and Systematic Training for Effective Parenting (STEP), problem-solving groups, discussion groups, and training groups.

Berger (2008), Click and Karkos (2008), and Couchenour and Chrisman (2004) suggest the following popular formats: school meetings, classroom meetings, courses for parents, mother and baby groups, and self-help groups.

This list is not intended to be exhaustive, but it does capture the great diversity of approaches available to parent–teacher groups. It is important to remember that no single approach will meet all the needs of a group. Therefore, the teacher must use professional judgment in matching group processes to parents' stated needs, strengths, personal characteristics, and cultures.

GUIDELINES FOR PLANNING PARENT GROUP MEETINGS

Regardless of the type of meeting format, the teacher should follow a guideline when planning the meeting, if only to avoid some of the pitfalls that have kept parents away.

Developing a Purpose

All meetings should have a purpose. Educators need to ask themselves—and the parents—what they wish to accomplish by conducting a meeting. Whether the purpose is to introduce parents to the program, get acquainted, or recruit parent volunteers, leaders should never proceed without collaborating with parents on why the meeting is being held.

This teacher is explaining the meeting's purpose. *Courtesy of ECE Photo Library.*

Choosing a Topic or Title

A group is a collection of people with a common denominator. Teachers should ask themselves, "What is the common denominator for the parents with whom I am working?" The most effective way to get an answer is to ask the parents. When making home visits, doing intake interviews, sending home questionnaires, or conversing informally with parents, ask what they'd like to have information about and what would interest them if a parent group was formed. Once the group is started and a trusting relationship has been established between parents and the teacher, real personal and family needs will begin to surface. Be alert to these needs as they are shared, and plan future meeting topics accordingly (Prior & Gerard, 2007).

The title of the meeting is important. To help persuade parents to come, it should be catchy and upbeat rather than negative. For example, the title

"Healthful Snacks" can be upgraded to "Dealing With Snack Attacks—Some Tasty and Healthful Alternatives." The title "Developing Physical Skills" might be more inviting if revised as "Get Ready, Get Set, Move!" (Kniepkamp, 2005).

Delivering Advance Information to Parents

It is important to inform parents about the meeting well ahead of time. This can be accomplished by sending an invitation home. The invitation should describe the meeting and include such information as who, what, where, when, why, dress (informal or formal), child care availability, refreshments, and a phone number or an e-mail address so families can RSVP and obtain further information. The invitation should be sent home with the children, e-mailed, or mailed at least two weeks before the meeting. A meeting reminder can be sent three days before the meeting and again on the day of the meeting (Rockwell & Kniepkamp, 2003). See Figure 8.1 to see meeting invitation and reminder examples.

Invitations and reminders describe future meeting details. *Courtesy of ECE Photo Library.*

Additional strategies that can be used to publicize meetings are a formal letter mailed to the home and word of mouth. Word of mouth is the most effective approach, but it requires people who can share information about the meeting and the importance of attending. Some programs have computer-based calling from the school and use electronic mailboxes so that parents can call and hear a message from the teacher every day (Lunts, 2003; McNabb, Valdez, Nowakowski, & Hawkes, 1999). The messages provide parents with homework pointers, information, and reminders of upcoming events. A telephone committee can make reminder calls. The children are an excellent source of publicity as well. Tell them about the invitation they are taking home. They can deliver the written message plus encourage their parents to attend. This strategy is most effective when the children are going to be part of the meeting. Obviously, however, do not exploit the children into pressuring their parents to attend.

Developing a Planning Schedule

An important component of a parent meeting is a planning schedule that will assist the teacher in planning and conducting the sessions. When meetings are not planned, problems can occur that result in chaos and wasted time. Table 8.1 is an example of a planning schedule for a parent group meeting.

Table 8.1 Planning Schedule

One month before the meeting:
1. Decide on a topic that fits program and stated parent needs.
2. Clear and then set a date and time.
3. Reserve a room or outdoor space.
4. Contact the personnel involved (volunteers, speakers, coworkers, etc.).

Two weeks before the meeting:
1. Send out flyers and invitations.
2. Arrange for transportation and child care, if needed.
3. List supplies needed and begin to collect them.
4. Reaffirm the date, time, and place.

One week before the meeting:
1. Duplicate handout materials.
2. Make nametags.
3. Organize supplies.

Three days before the meeting:
1. Send out a reminder of the meeting.
2. Check with the janitor to arrange for extra chairs, tables, a key, etc.
3. Buy refreshments.

Day of the meeting:
1. Ask the children to remind their parents about the meeting.
2. Arrange the room and set up stations, if needed.
3. Make sure you have all of the necessary materials.
4. Prepare the refreshments.
5. Arrive early.

Developing a Meeting Agenda

A meeting agenda will assist the teacher in starting the meeting on time and conducting it as planned.

- **Registration:** Greet parents as they arrive. Make them feel welcome. Distribute nametags.

The teacher greets a parent as she arrives at the meeting. *Courtesy of ECE Photo Library.*

- **Mixer:** Develop an activity that will help the participants feel welcome, get acquainted with each other, and set a fun, relaxing tone for the meeting. The activity should also correspond to the meeting content. See Figure 8.1 for a mixer example.
- **Opening:** Give a general welcome. Introduce yourself and staff members.
- **Purpose:** Explain the purpose of the meeting and any special procedures that are to be followed.
- **Content:** Conduct the meeting.
- **Closing:** Briefly summarize the session and state what was accomplished.
- **Evaluation:** Distribute evaluation forms and explain where to leave them when completed. See Figure 8.1 for a meeting evaluation example.
- **Refreshments:** Serve refreshments.
- **Closing:** Say good-bye to parents and clean up.

This sample agenda for planning, conducting, and evaluating a parent meeting can be followed regardless of the meeting theme. See Figure 8.1 to see how these steps were applied to a family meeting with a Family Bookworms theme.

SUMMARY

The parent group meeting is an involvement strategy that has been used for decades. A meeting at the school is often difficult to fit into parents' already crowded schedules. For that reason, we should not be upset with parents who cannot attend every meeting. Meetings should cover topics that address the stated needs of families. They should be carefully planned and utilize meeting formats that vary according to topic and group size. They should be held at a variety of times in order to reach all parents. The length of the meetings should rarely exceed 1½ hours. Child care should be provided by competent care providers. At the end of the meeting, distribute evaluation forms so participants can give feedback on the meeting. Keep it simple; for example, have them circle a character (such as a smiling face or frowning face) to show what they thought. Also, provide a space for additional comments should participants wish to elaborate. Use these evaluations to improve future meetings.

ACTIVITIES FOR DISCUSSION, EXPANSION, AND APPLICATION

1. Develop a rationale for incorporating a parent involvement program into an elementary school, grades K–5.
2. Prepare and present a simulated preschool or elementary parent group meeting utilizing a workshop station format.
3. List and share reasons parents might give for not attending meetings.
4. Invite a group of parents to the class to discuss the problems—and successes—they have had with meetings held at school. Include both preschool and elementary experiences.
5. Discuss the meeting formats that class members would feel most comfortable with as they initiate parent group meetings in their respective programs.
6. Generate some group mixers that might be used at meetings as icebreakers to make parents feel welcome.
7. Attend a parent group meeting in your community. Critique the meeting and share your findings with the class.

CASE STUDY

Mr. and Mrs. Kyle arrived at 6:45 p.m. for the parent meeting that was scheduled to begin at 7:00 p.m. and end at 8:00 p.m. Other parents were arriving as well. However, the meeting did not begin at 7:00, as the teacher wanted to wait until more parents arrived. Finally, after waiting 20 minutes, she started the meeting. After introductions and an explanation of the purpose of the meeting, four more parents arrived. Rather than continue with the meeting, the teacher stopped her remarks, introduced the new arrivals, and began to fill them in on what had been previously covered. The meeting continued and ended at 8:30 p.m., thirty minutes past the time it had been scheduled to end. Many of the parents were not happy with the delayed start and the late ending of the meeting.

1. Do you agree with the teacher's decision to start late to await the arrival of the late attendees?

2. Do you feel that the teacher was correct in stopping the meeting to greet and introduce the late arrivals?

3. How do you think the parents that arrived on time felt about waiting so long for the meeting to begin?

4. What suggestions can you make that would help the teacher avoid this problem in the future?

USEFUL WEBSITES

www.csos.jhu.edu/P2000/center.htm
Center on School, Family, & Community Partnerships. The center's website has many articles and programs concerning family and school partnerships.

www.familysupportamerica.org
Family Support America. This website includes links to resource centers throughout the United States that reach out to help parents.

www.reading.org
International Reading Association. Literacy development is frequently a topic that is addressed in parent meetings. This site provides excellent tips to promote family/teacher involvement in early literacy development.

REFERENCES

Bauer, A. M., & Shea, T. M. (2002). *Parents and schools: Creating a successful partnership for students with special needs.* Upper Saddle River, New Jersey: Pearson/Merrill/Prentice Hall.

Berger, E. H. (2008). *Parents as partners in education: Families and schools working together* (6th ed.). Upper Saddle River, New Jersey: Pearson/Merrill/Prentice Hall.

Click, P., & Karkos, K. A. (2008). *Administration of programs for young children* (7th ed.). Clifton Park, NY: Thomson Delmar Learning.

Cook, R. E., Tessier, A., & Klein, M. (2000). *Adapting early childhood curricula for children in inclusive settings* (5th ed.). Upper Saddle River, NJ: Merrill/Prentice Hall.

Couchenour, D., & Chrisman, K. (2004). *Families, schools, and communities: Together for young children* (2nd ed.). Clifton Park, NY: Thomson Delmar Learning.

Kniepkamp, J. (2005). Calling all parents . . . Successful methods of involving parents in the educational process. *Connections, 34*(1), 16–18.

Lunts, E. (2003). Parental involvement in children's education: Connecting family and school by using telecommunication technologies. *Meridian, 6*(1). Retrieved February 1, 2006, from http://www.ncsu.edu/meridian/win2003/involvement/index.html.

McNabb, M. L., Valdez, G., Nowakowski, J., & Hawkes, M. (1999). *Technology connections for school improvement: Planners' handbook.* Washington, DC: U.S. Department of Education.

Prior, J., & Gerard, M. R. (2007). *Family involvement in early childhood education: Research into practice.* Clifton Park, NY: Thomson Delmar Learning.

Rockwell, R. E., & Kniepkamp, J. R. (2003). *Partnering with parents: Easy programs to involve parents in the early learning process.* Beltsville, MD: Gryphon House.

KEY TERMS

Parent Group Meeting—A parent involvement strategy that promotes parent–teacher collaboration to help children succeed academically.

Mixer—An activity designed to help meeting participants feel welcome, help participants get acquainted with each other, and set a relaxing tone for the forthcoming meeting content.

CHAPTER 9

Parent–Teacher Conferences

STUDENT LEARNING OUTCOMES

After reading this chapter, you should be able to

- Explain a rationale for the parent–teacher conference.

- Describe a procedure to follow in planning and conducting an effective parent–teacher conference.

- Define reflecting, paraphrasing, clarifying, drawing out, and active listening.

- Identify negative listening responses.

- Explain parent–teacher conference follow-up strategies.

- Compile a list of the benefits of parent–teacher conferences for all involved.

The process of communicating with parents is an essential component of being an effective teacher. Research in the area of teacher education has revealed that an effective teacher must exhibit competence in human relations and planning skills (Prior & Gerard, 2007). One of the most common challenges to communication is the parent–teacher conference, which most schools schedule once or twice a year (Wright, Stegelin, & Hartle, 2007). Because this strategy for communicating with parents is the one most often used by teachers, it is important that conferences be productive and enlightening for all concerned.

Unfortunately, many parents and teachers look upon the conference with tension, anxiety, or fear. Parents sometimes feel afraid that they will be criticized, blamed for their child's behavior, or made to feel inferior because they do not understand education **jargon.** Teachers frequently worry that they will be held responsible for the child's lack of progress. They do not want to give negative information or be misunderstood (Gestwicki, 2007; Stevens & Tollafield, 2003). Yet, the parent–teacher conference is the one event in the teaching profession for which teachers have received little or no training (Million, 2005). It is no wonder that it is often approached with fear and trepidation.

To be productive, parent–teacher conferences must be recognized as one of the necessary ingredients of a successful parent–teacher partnership. Conducted on a regular basis, they provide an ideal forum to facilitate the exchange of information about children (Sciarra & Dorsey, 2007). This chapter presents suggestions for conducting effective conferences and utilizing the information shared for the benefit of the child.

Parent–teacher communication should be an ongoing process. *Courtesy of ECE Photo Library.*

PURPOSE OF THE CONFERENCE

Parents are their children's first and most influential teachers. Their influence does not stop once their children are enrolled in an educational setting. The pressures of parenting and teaching have much in common; both parents and teachers play a vital role in children's growth and development. They both create and structure a learning environment in which the child is the major focus. The home and the

BOX 9.1

Benefits for Teachers

Teachers will:

- Understand parents' impressions and expectations of the school program.
- Gain a better understanding of the program's effect on the child.
- Obtain additional information about the child.
- Encourage parents' understanding and support of the program.
- Communicate the child's school progress and offer ideas and activities that can stimulate development.
- Develop a working partnership with the parents.

school need each other, and the child needs both. Parent–teacher communication should be an ongoing process throughout the child's school experience. Parent–teacher conferences can be beneficial for parents, teachers, and children alike as they share bits of information which, when integrated with current educational practices and standards, can then be acted upon (Rich, 1987).

Parent–teacher conferences provide an excellent avenue to encouraging parent involvement in the school. While the most important beneficiary is the child, teachers and parents both benefit from working together. Benefits of the conferences for both teachers and parents are shown in Boxes 9.1 and 9.2.

BOX 9.2

Benefits for Parents

Parents will:

- Gain a better understanding of their child's school program.
- Learn strategies that can enhance the child's development.
- Understand their child's personal growth.
- Obtain information on the school's philosophy on teaching and learning styles.
- Communicate concerns, questions, and suggestions that can lead to a better school experience for their child.
- Provide experiences that contribute to their child's physical, emotional, and intellectual growth.

PREPARING FOR THE CONFERENCE

The process of preparing for a conference should be as complete and detailed as possible. Positive parent–teacher communication should be established and conference materials prepared in advance (Click & Karkos, 2008; Sciarra & Dorsey, 2007). This initial positive communication can be facilitated by inviting and encouraging parents to visit and observe the classroom, placing "warm" telephone calls, sending welcoming letters and happy-grams, setting up a school open house, and soliciting home profile sheets.

The **home profile sheet** is a list of nonthreatening questions that the children use to "interview" their parents (custodial or noncustodial) or others who will be coming to the conference. The questions should be developed with input from the children. They might include questions about the adults' favorite songs, foods, colors, animals, books, and hobbies; questions about the parents' birthplace or hometown; and questions such as "What would you like to know about my school?" When the profile sheets are returned, the children draw pictures of the people they have interviewed. The drawings may be mounted on construction paper and posted in the classroom with a sign that reads "Welcome Families" (see Figure 9.1). Parents will enjoy seeing their children's drawings. The process serves to welcome parents and stimulate conversation. After some form of positive communication has occurred, parents are more likely to be receptive to the conference (Bauer & Shea, 2003; Click & Karkos, 2008; Gestwicki, 2007; Sciarra & Dorsey, 2007).

The teacher should begin collecting samples of the children's work at the start of the school year. Keeping anecdotal records and samples of children's work, noting special interests and abilities, shows parents the time and attention the teacher has given their child. The records should reflect the child's growth in self-esteem, language mastery, social skills, and personal relationships as well as progress in academic subjects, if applicable. A **portfolio** is an excellent means of organizing each child's materials. The portfolio offers the teacher a means of individualizing a child's progress over time. It consists of a collection of the child's work and gives the parent and teacher an opportunity to share accurate and current information about how the child is functioning in the classroom (Click & Karkos, 2008; Hendrick, 2003). Allow the children to help decide what goes into their portfolio; this gives them the opportunity to be involved in the conference. Children may even wish to include their own thoughts about their progress.

A teacher reviews a portfolio as she prepares for a conference with a parent. *Courtesy of ECE Photo Library.*

Plan a conference agenda that will prevent or limit conference anxiety. Some elements to consider are the establishment of rapport, a statement of the meeting's purpose, the communication of specific information, an opportunity for parent input and information exchange (strategies for parents and strategies for teachers), recommendations, plans for follow-up contacts, a conference summarization, and the conference termination (Couchenour & Chrisman, 2004; Gestwicki, 2007; Prior & Gerard, 2007). An easy rule of thumb to remember as you plan is to make the conference like a sandwich: Start on a positive note, move on to points that need improvement, and return to a positive idea to end the conversation.

Mail a conference invitation to the home. It is important that this written communication is translated into the native language of the parents (Warner & Sower, 2005). The invitation should ask the parents to select an available conference date and time that is convenient for them. The invitation should indicate the length of the conference, its location, and its agenda. Special consideration should be given to parents who have more than one child enrolled in the school. If possible, back-to-back conferences should be made available to them (Gestwicki, 2007; Sciarra & Dorsey, 2007).

The invitation also should encourage the parents to prepare a list of questions. Suggest that they prioritize the questions, as there may not be time to answer them all. If parents bring more questions than can be answered during the conference, arrange for an additional conference or perhaps a telephone call to continue the discussion and provide closure.

Some sample questions that parents might want to ask the teacher are shown in Box 9.3.

Interviewer: Lexi Touchette

Parent's Name: Becky Touchette

Occupation: teacher

Favorites:
    Animal~ cat
    Song~ Every Day
    Foods~ french fries
    Colors~ blue
    Books~ Water for Elephants

What would you like to know about my first grade class? What are you going to learn in math

FIGURE 9.1 Children's Interview with a Parent

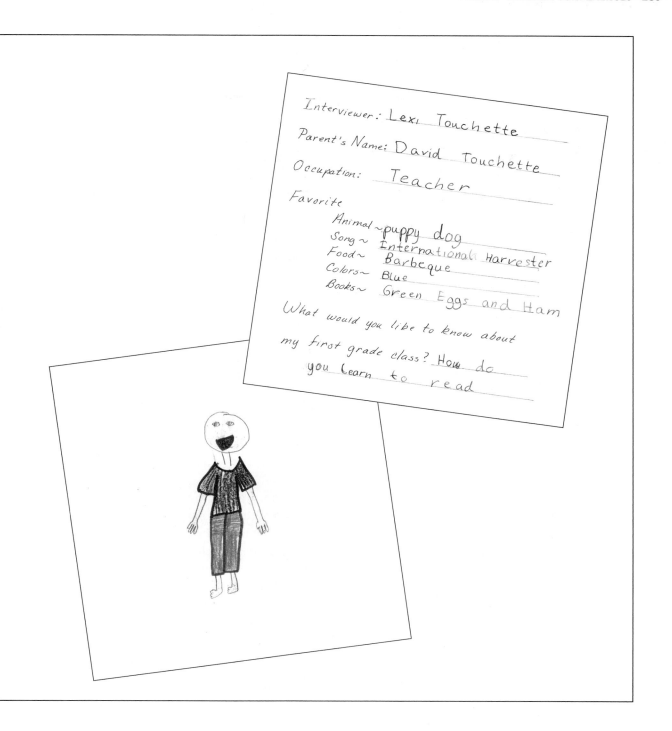

Interviewer: Lexi Touchette

Parent's Name: David Touchette

Occupation: Teacher

Favorite

Animal~ puppy dog
Song~ International Harvester
Food~ Barbeque
Colors~ Blue
Books~ Green Eggs and Ham

What would you libe to know about my first grade class? How do you learn to read

BOX 9.3

Parent Questions For Teachers

- What are my child's strengths and weaknesses?
- Is my child involved in any special instruction?
- What is your policy on homework?
- How is my child doing with the various subjects?
- How can I better help my child at home? What specific things can I do?
- Are there any special problems relating to discipline or socialization?
- How well does my child communicate?
- Is my child motivated?

A few days before the conference, a confirmation letter should be sent to the home reminding the parents of the meeting date and time. Be sure to enclose the school telephone number and request that they call immediately and reschedule if they are unable to keep the appointment.

Also prepare for the conference by considering its physical environment. Proper lighting, temperature, and privacy help make the surroundings more comfortable (Gestwicki, 2007). The environment must help parents feel more relaxed and less intimidated. Having adult-sized furniture and seating arranged so that parents and the teacher can sit side by side will help parents feel welcome. Provide paper and pencils for note taking (Stevens & Tollafield, 2003).

Be considerate of the parents who are waiting for their appointments. Arrange for a waiting area. Prepare the area with information regarding the school and the special services it provides. Include a newsletter and information on the school's volunteer program, curriculum, philosophy, and homework and grading policies; suggestions on how parents can help at home; and invitations to various school events. Make a "Conference in Progress" sign that can be hung on the door to prevent interruptions. A final step of preparation is to take a minute before each conference to look over the objectives of the meeting, anecdotal notes, records, reports, samples of work, child's name, parents' names, and any other information pertinent to the child.

CONDUCTING THE CONFERENCE

It is important to remember that many parents are apprehensive about the conference. The teacher must work at putting parents at ease. One of the most effective ways of doing this is to greet each parent at the door in a friendly way.

Know and use the parent's name; do not assume that the parent has the same last name as the child. State your own name clearly, and in the next sentence, refer to the child. After this initial exchange, refer to the agenda and begin the conference. A successful conference includes the following.

Building Rapport

To many parents, the school environment is intimidating. This may be due to negative experiences that might even date back to their own childhoods. Regardless, the teacher must work at putting parents at ease, encouraging them to feel welcome and assuring them that they have not wandered into enemy territory. An initial bit of small talk related to the weather or another neutral topic might help. The child–parent interview is a perfect icebreaker. Avoid emotionally laden topics such as religion or politics (Stevens & Tollafield, 2003). Some parents may only want to engage in small talk, as it provides a way to avoid discussing the issues at hand. Always begin with a positive remark and make sure that everyone present knows that the purpose of the conference is to share information and work together to help the child (Gestwicki, 2007).

Teachers must demonstrate an acceptance of parents' different viewpoints and opinions. *Courtesy of ECE Photo Library.*

Obtaining Information from the Parent

Eliciting information from the parent is key to the success of the conference. The teacher must be a sensitive, active listener. Begin with general, open-ended questions such as "What does Donna say about her school activities?" or "What did she share about our field trip to the orchard?" Avoid negative questions such as "Does Donna still refuse to do her homework?" Instead, try "How does Donna feel about doing her homework?" Structure questions so they encourage the parents to share perceptions about the topic and give the teacher an opportunity to provide suggestions. This process allows the teacher to obtain information before providing suggestions. It also gives the parents an opportunity to share their knowledge about the child.

The teacher also can gain insight into parental expectations, which can have instant benefits during the conference as well as in future work with the child.

Providing Information

The teacher must express openness to questions and advice about the child. Indicate an understanding of the parents' views by making brief comments and asking clarifying questions. Be truthful about problem areas, but present them in a way that makes your concern for the child evident. This is the opportune time to examine a portfolio of the child's work in order to share both progress and concerns. Be prepared to give the parents specific ideas, activities, and strategies that they can use at home to help their child.

SKILLS THAT MAXIMIZE ACTIVE LISTENING

Effective communication is the most essential ingredient to the success of the parent–teacher conference. If a conference is to be effective, the teacher must employ skills in **active listening.** Being a good listener requires concentration, effort, and a willingness to give credence to what another is saying (Couchenour & Chrisman, 2004); all efforts are fruitless unless the teacher wants to hear what the family has to say. Active listening literally means being active in the listening process. A listener can use four basic skills to make sure that he or she clearly understands what the speaker has stated. These skills are reflecting, paraphrasing, clarifying, and drawing out.

Reflecting

Reflecting is the ability to restate as exactly as possible what another person has said. Keep in mind the example of a mirror reflecting exactly the image that appears before it.

The importance of reflecting as a basic communication skill is that the ability to say back to a speaker what you heard lets the speaker know that your interpretations, judgments, or meanings have not slanted or loaded what was stated. Reflecting does not imply that you agree with what was said, only that you heard it and know what words the speaker used to convey the message. For example:

Speaker: *"I don't want to talk with you right now. I'm angry with my son for forgetting to bring his homework home last night."*

Listener: *"You don't want to talk with me now because you are upset with your son for forgetting to bring his homework home last night."*

When using reflective listening, it is important that the listener reflect the sender's message without adding emotional inflections, which could indicate judgment, to the response.

Paraphrasing

When **paraphrasing**, the listener attempts to restate the important elements of a speaker's lengthy or complex statement in his or her words because it would be difficult to repeat the statement word for word.

Try to use some of the speaker's words, but, more importantly, focus on the meaning and the points he or she makes that you believe are the most significant to him or her. For example:

Speaker: *"I can't talk with you now. I'm so angry with my son for forgetting to bring his homework home last night. I've given him reminders each day before he leaves for school, and he always promises, but he never remembers. I'm the kind of parent who can't relax when I know how important it is for my child to do his homework. How can I work effectively with my other children when he makes me so upset?"*

Listener: *"You don't want to talk right now because you have had an argument with your son, and you want to wait to talk with me after you have resolved this issue with him."*

The ability to listen, and to demonstrate that you have heard what the speaker has said by reflecting or paraphrasing, is a valuable skill because it promotes the feeling that the speaker and listener are at the same level of understanding in their communication.

Clarifying

The **clarifying** question seeks to elaborate on what the speaker has said. The clarification can be in two areas. One area that may need clarification is definition: What the words mean to the speaker may not be the same as what they mean to the listener. The clarifying question can be used to establish a working definition of a word or phrase. The intent is to clarify meanings, not to nitpick on dictionary definitions or shades of meanings. The intent is also to avoid the kind of arguments that occur when the listener tries to convince the speaker that he or she "doesn't mean that." The listener tries to accept the definition offered by the speaker as the operational definition for the discussion they are having. For example:

Speaker: *"I'll tell you what the problem is—it's violence and crime in the streets. It's getting so a decent citizen isn't safe anymore. We need more law and order to control the lawless element in this society."*

Listener: *"I understand that you think violence and crime is a problem and that we need more law and order in our society. Can you tell me what law and order means to you?"*

The other type of clarifying question seeks to find out why the speaker has placed value and importance on certain concepts or words. For example:

Speaker: *"I think kids in school should be allowed more freedom than they have now. They should be free to inquire into all kinds of things. Instead, they are locked into a system that tells them what to learn and when to learn about it."*

Listener: *"You think kids in school should be free to learn and explore. What specific things do you feel they should be free to explore?"*

The key to this skill is that the listener is attempting to understand the importance and value that the speaker places on the statements made during the conversation. The listener may be in total disagreement with the speaker, but this skill permits him or her to begin with a common understanding of the idea they disagree on. It helps to prevent the kinds of arguments that sometimes occur when both parties are close to agreement but the words they use in communicating their positions continue to keep them apart. There are times, however, when thoughts and feelings are not expressed clearly or fully. Even though the listener may have heard the speaker accurately, he or she may not understand what the speaker means, or there may be a sense that there is more to the message than what was said. In these instances, it may be necessary to clarify ideas and draw out the speaker.

Drawing Out

Drawing out is a skill that is used to allow the speaker the opportunity to expand upon what has been stated. It is used to clarify parts of the message that may not be in the original statement but still are a part of the total context of the communication interaction.

There are several situations in which a drawing-out question can be useful. If the speaker is focusing the majority of the message in the past, ask about the present. If it seems necessary for the listener's understanding to find out how the speaker came to his or her present position, ask about past events and how they relate to what is being said. For example:

Speaker: *"This is really a poor place to work. Why, when I worked for Smedly Midlap and Sons, we had coffee breaks, lunch in the buildings, an exercise program, bowling leagues and . . . and . . . and . . ."*

Listener: *"I hear you talking about what it was like at the other place where you worked, but can you tell me what makes this a poor place to work?"*

Additional examples of drawing-out questions are:

- Are there other factors that caused you to arrive at that decision?
- Have you considered other ways of handling that problem?
- Is this generally how you feel about things like this?

Negative Listening Responses

An awareness of **negative listening responses** helps to alert the teacher that the message that is being communicated has not been heard or fully understood by the listener. There are two types of responses that are considered negative responses.

The first type of negative response is called an asyndetic response. This response is evident when the listener gives a response that has nothing to do with the message the speaker made. For example, the teacher may be talking about the child's behavior, but the parent responds with a statement about how nice the classroom looks. When these types of responses occur, the teacher wonders if the parent is even paying attention to anything that has been said. Asyndetic responses may also sidetrack the conversation to a different subject, and the teacher must find a way to get back to the topic.

The second type of negative listening response is called a tangential response. This occurs when the parent responds to the teacher, but only to a certain part of what has been said. The teacher may be talking to the parent about the child's behavior and how the child throws objects around the room. The parent responds that someone threw an object through the family's window last week. Once again, the teacher does not know if the parent heard the whole message. The only thing the teacher knows is that the parent heard part of the message and is relating this to some other event.

Nonverbal Communication

Communication is generally thought of as being verbal, but nonverbal communication is just as important. We communicate not only with spoken words but with gestures, postures, eye contact, facial expressions, and different levels of voice volume and intonation to reveal our thoughts, feelings, intentions, and personalities. Close attention to nonverbal communication will enhance the perception of what is being said by all participants as messages are sent and received (Couchenour & Chrisman, 2004).

CONCLUDING THE CONFERENCE

Summarize the areas of strength and weakness. Be sure you and the parent are in agreement about how you will work together to reach the goals that have been set. Establish timelines for completing the planned activities. Clear up any misinterpretations. If another conference is needed, schedule it at this time. Close the conference on a positive note by inviting the parents to call, write, or stop in to express any concerns. Stand up and see them to the door.

FOLLOW-UP STRATEGIES

Within one week after the conference, the teacher should send home a note or letter thanking the parents for their participation. Again, it is critical that the message is written in the native language of the parents. This letter should include a conference summary that highlights what was discussed and planned. Include such details as the goals of the conference, information presented, information gained, and agreements made. A telephone call is a helpful follow-up, especially if the family needs another conference or a referral for other services.

SUMMARY

A successful parent–teacher conference should provide parents with new information about their child and practical suggestions on how they can work as partners with the teacher for the benefit of the child. To accomplish this, the teacher must employ active-listening skills and be prepared to offer parents realistic approaches for working with their children at home. An awareness of skills that maximize active listening as well as an awareness of negative listening responses will result in benefits for both parties; however, the ultimate beneficiary is the child.

ACTIVITIES FOR DISCUSSION, EXPANSION, AND APPLICATION

1. Why is it necessary to prepare portfolios of children's work prior to the parent–teacher conference?
2. What is the value of involving the child in obtaining family information via the home profile?

3. Interview a preschool teacher and a teacher in grades K–3. Compile a list of each teacher's parent conference strategies and compare. What are the similarities? What are the differences?

4. What can the teacher do to create a comfortable environment for the parent–teacher conference?

5. List some strategies for building rapport with the parents before the conference begins.

6. Compile a checklist of questions that the teacher might ask parents and questions that parents might ask the teacher. Using these questions, role-play a parent–teacher conference.

7. What is the necessity of sending written information regarding the conference in the parents' native language?

8. Why should the teacher have an awareness of negative listening responses?

CASE STUDY

The mother of Ramon, Ms. Ramirez, whose native language is Spanish, has been invited to a parent–teacher conference by Ms. Jones, Ramon's teacher, via an invitation written in English. Ms. Ramirez never arrives for the conference. Ms. Jones cannot understand why Ramon's mother wouldn't attend, as this is the first conference of the school year.

1. What do you think is the problem in this situation?

2. What would you suggest that Ms. Jones do to resolve the problem?

USEFUL WEBSITES

teacher.scholastic.com
   Scholastic. This website has many resources for teachers, including information about ways to communicate with families effectively.

www.cpirc.org
   The Colorado Parent Information and Resource Center. This website includes articles about parent–teacher communication.

www.fen.com
   Family Education Network. This site is a leading source of educational content, resources, and products for parents, teachers, and kids. It includes sections for parents and teachers, articles about parent–teacher communication, and advice from veteran teachers.

www.nea.org

National Education Association. The website of this organization provides helpful information for teachers and parents. Resources and guidelines for organizing and conducting successful parent–teacher conferences are presented.

REFERENCES

Bauer, A. M., & Shea, T. M. (2003). *Parents and schools: Creating a successful partnership for students with special needs.* Upper Saddle River, NJ: Pearson/Merrill/Prentice Hall.

Click, P., & Karkos, K. A. (2008). *Administration of programs for young children* (7th ed.). Clifton Park, NY: Thomson Delmar Learning.

Couchenour, D., & Chrisman, K. (2008). *Families, schools, and community together for young children* (2nd ed.). Clifton Park, NY: Thomson Delmar Learning.

Gestwicki, C. (2007). *Home, school, and community relations* (6th ed.). Clifton Park, NY: Thomson Delmar Learning.

Hendrick, J. (2003). *Total learning: Developmental curriculum for the young child* (6th ed). Upper Saddle River, NJ: Merrill/Prentice Hall.

Million, J. (2005). Getting teachers set for parent conferences. *The Education Digest, 70*(8), 54–56.

Prior, J., & Gerard, M. R. (2007). *Family involvement in early childhood education: Research into practice.* Clifton Park, NY: Thomson Delmar Learning.

Rich, D. (1987). *Teachers and parents: An adult to adult approach.* Washington, DC: National Education Association, The Home School Institute.

Sciarra, D. J., & Dorsey, A. G. (2007). *Developing and administering a child care and education program* (6th ed.). Clifton Park, NY: Thomson Delmar Learning.

Stevens, B. A., & Tollafield, A. (2003). Creating comfortable and productive parent/teacher conferences. *Phi Delta Kappen, 84*(7), 521–524.

Warner, L., & Sower, J. (2005). *Educating young children.* Boston: Pearson/Allyn & Bacon.

Wright, K., Stegelin, D. A., & Hartle, L. (2007). *Building family, school, and community partnerships* (3rd ed.). Upper Saddle River, NJ: Pearson/Merrill/Prentice Hall.

KEY TERMS

Jargon—Vocabulary specific to a particular profession or group.

Home Profile Sheet—A list of nonthreatening questions that children use to interview their parents (custodial or noncustodial) or others who will be coming to the conference.

Portfolio—A purposeful compilation of children's work samples, products, and teacher observations collected over time.

Active Listening—Technique of sensitively picking up on a speaker's verbal and nonverbal messages and asking clarifying questions to ensure full comprehension.

Reflecting—Restating as exactly as possible what another person has said.

Paraphrasing—Restating in slightly different words what another has said.

Clarifying—Seeking to elaborate on what the speaker has said.

Drawing Out—A skill used to allow the speaker the opportunity to expand on what he or she said.

Negative Listening Response—A verbal response from the listener that indicates to the speaker that the message stated has not been heard.

PART THREE

SUPPORT

CHAPTER 10

Parent and Community Volunteers

STUDENT LEARNING OUTCOMES

After reading this chapter, you should be able to

- Provide a rationale for the utilization of parent and community volunteers.

- Describe the steps that must be taken to organize and conduct a preschool or elementary school volunteer program.

- Discuss the necessity for interviewing and background screening of potential school volunteers.

- Identify procedures to be followed in determining needed volunteer services.

- Explain the value of recognizing volunteers for the services they provide.

A valuable strategy for involving parents in the education of their child is to involve them as volunteers. Because every school volunteer program will have unique needs that will require unique solutions, there is no one way to conduct a volunteer program. However, in this chapter we provide some specific steps and procedures that will assist in avoiding some of the problems that can occur when initiating a volunteer program.

THE BEGINNINGS OF VOLUNTEERISM

Volunteerism is not new to the United States, and it is not new to educational programs that serve children from birth through high school. Parents and community members have volunteered services to schools since they began. In the early days of the nation, farmers cut wood and gave it to the schoolmaster to use in heating the schoolhouse. Later, immigrants who had learned English assisted in teaching newly arrived immigrants. Following World War I, when communities were establishing high schools, volunteers often built the outdoor athletic fields, baseball diamonds, and running tracks. During the Great Depression of the 1930s, many school hot lunch programs depended on volunteer labor.

Volunteers build a community partnership in the school. *Courtesy of ECE Photo Library.*

Today, parents, teenagers, college students, carpenters, lawyers, secretaries, teachers, and retirees—males and females covering the occupational range from professional to semiskilled—all participate in volunteer activities. While the roots of volunteer services are deep, the concept of organized, coordinated volunteerism in schools is a phenomenon that has gained in popularity only over the past four decades.

Many school volunteer programs have been initiated primarily to solve some of the problems that schools have faced for many years. Some of these problems are overcrowded classrooms, children who need individual attention, the need for individualized tutoring and small group teaching, the need to bring into the classroom a broad base of talent that no single teacher can provide, and the need to develop a positive public relations system that, in the long run, will result in additional public support for the schools.

A great impetus to involve parents and community in the schools has come from the federal government. The last five U.S. presidents have devoted time to make rather lengthy public service announcements that have stressed the vast number of volunteer efforts that take place daily in this country. In 1968, the federal interagency requirements of the Department of Health, Education, and Welfare stated that all federally funded programs must show some form of parent and community representation in participation and in an advisory capacity. These guidelines have greatly influenced schools' use of volunteers and the reception of volunteers once they have agreed to help in the schools or at home. **School volunteers** are unpaid personnel who usually work on a part-time basis and who perform important tasks that supplement but do not replace the work of employed staff members within the school.

When starting a volunteer program, use caution. It is easy to get carried away with a good idea and attempt to do too much too fast. Many successful programs have started with one teacher or one classroom and gradually expanded. In reviewing the various steps that are essential to a successful program, we hope that those using this book will recognize that each step needs to be taken with care.

As with any new program, the concept and procedures for implementing it must be presented to the board of education or board of directors for approval. The question of cost will certainly arise. Although volunteers do not receive money for their time and effort, there are costs involved. The amount of money needed will depend on the scope and size of the program. Funds will be needed for office supplies, equipment, telephone service, and postage. These initial costs are often underwritten by local citizens, foundation or program grants, and, in some instances, the school boards. The adoption of a volunteer program frequently depends on how detailed the planning is and the projected speed with which the program will progress.

THE NEED FOR A VOLUNTEER PROGRAM

There is a need to bring volunteers into the schools to enrich the learning process and expand the learning environment of the children. For example, a great need exists to assist teachers so they can provide more individualized instruction in their classes; this can be accomplished by relieving them of some of their nonteaching duties.

There is also a need to provide our schools with resource people who are able to share special talents, skills, and expertise normally not available in schools and early childhood settings. This is especially true at the elementary level, where the teacher is expected to teach a wide range of subject matter. Additionally, there is a need to provide opportunities for concerned members of the community to participate effectively, improving the educational program of the schools. There is also a need for volunteers to help stimulate greater citizen understanding and support of school programs through their participation and work in the program. Finally, there is a need for the school to obtain valuable ideas from the community as well as relevant information about the problems and needs of the community.

This father shares his special talent with the children. *Courtesy of ECE Photo Library.*

Volunteers working within a school system can obtain insights into and get a more valid view of the problems facing the schools. Volunteers frequently become the most ardent supporters of the public schools. However, volunteers should not be used to help a school district save money. Volunteers should never be used in lieu of teaching assistants or other certified personnel. Such uses are an abuse of the volunteer concept and only result in the underrating of the expert services that trained, professionally certified staff can provide. A well-planned and well-organized volunteer program will provide enrichment and expand the learning opportunities for children. The use of volunteers should complement and enhance the role of professional educators rather than supplant or undermine that role.

Not all volunteer programs have been successful. Some school personnel look upon volunteers as more trouble than they are worth. Others scratch their heads in bewilderment, saying, "I don't know why they volunteered; they don't intend to stay." Volunteers who come in good faith often feel they are not wanted and wouldn't be missed if they were absent. Often they ask, "What is my role?" School volunteer coordinators, teachers, and other school personnel who utilize volunteers may also ask, "What is my role?" Once the choice is made to use volunteers, they must be looked upon as a vital part of the total school operation and must be given continuous consideration. To do less will increase the possibility of failure.

WHAT JOBS WILL THE VOLUNTEERS DO?

There are many potential jobs for volunteers, ranging from routine tasks to fairly sophisticated levels of responsibility. Some common volunteer roles are members of advisory councils; assistants in classrooms and in tutorial and special programs; translators; library and office helpers; and clerical assistants. Volunteers also may help with arts and crafts, skilled recreation, group guidance, neighborhood work, public relations, and community education.

Housekeeping jobs are sometimes assigned to volunteers to relieve teachers and other professionals of routine and drudgery. Giving volunteers these kinds of assignments is less threatening to staff members because these simple jobs are easy to manage. However, limiting volunteer duties to these kinds of tasks is harmful to volunteers who are serious about their work and want to do meaningful, responsible tasks. However, it is erroneous to assume that volunteers represent a free source of labor that can fill roles that should be held by paid employees. Even though volunteers may have the proper qualifications, staff jobs must be done by people who can be held accountable.

Frequently, once volunteers arrive at the school, they are assigned jobs that are not thought out, planned, or even needed. Volunteers who have come to the school eager to give their time and utilize their talents sometimes find they are given only minimal tasks, and when those tasks are completed, they are left to sit and watch the activities that are going on around them. For that reason, some volunteers will choose not to return. If teachers have not been properly oriented to a volunteer program or have not been given the opportunity to indicate what volunteer services they need in their classroom or the total school program, it can be predicted that volunteers will not be used effectively. To avoid this possibility, teachers must be given an opportunity to determine the kinds of volunteer assistance they need. The following seven-step process can be used to get input from teachers about their specific needs (Rockwell, 1993).

Determining Needed Services

1. Examine the total program to determine volunteer needs for specific roles and responsibilities. The entire staff can meet with the volunteer coordinator to make a list of jobs volunteers could do. It is critical that no limits are put on the ideas and services they feel are needed. All ideas should be listed.

2. Review the inventory of needs and identify the services on the list that are currently available from regular staff at the school. In most schools, an existing pool of talent can provide some of the services requested.

3. Determine which services requested are available from existing local agencies by referral. Beware of the long waiting lists that often occur for some agency services.

4. Subtract the number of list items in Steps 2 and 3 from the number in Step 1 to get the remainder of services that volunteers might provide. If the initial inventory in Step 1 was complete, the remainder will include services that no paid source or agency could provide.

5. Determine which of the remaining services could be provided by volunteers.

6. Translate the lists of needed services into a list of volunteers.

7. Write clear and concise job descriptions for each service a volunteer could provide.

A first-grade teacher's list of volunteer needs is shown in Box 10.1.

Frequently, teachers and other school personnel want to use volunteers in school activities that are not directly connected with the academic program.

BOX 10.1

First-Grade Teacher's Volunteer Needs

- Person to read to the children.
- Someone with knowledge of carpentry who can make simple and inexpensive materials for my room.
- A clerical assistant.
- Helper on field trips.
- Resource people for careers.
- Someone to make paint smocks.
- Someone to help create and decorate bulletin boards.
- A gardener (and some land).
- Musicians.
- Someone to make videos of special classroom events.

Generally, state regulations and contractual agreements between teachers' organizations and boards of education permit the use of volunteers in supportive services. Here are examples of supportive activities:

1. **Attendance clerk:** Checks and records student attendance.
2. **Library aide:** Shelves books; makes simple repairs on damaged books.
3. **Media aide:** Keeps instructional and media equipment in working order.
4. **Lunchroom monitor:** Helps monitor lunchroom conduct.
5. **Playground monitor:** Helps on the playground during free play (but not during physical education classes).
6. **Classroom assistant:** Collects materials for and helps prepare class displays and bulletin boards.
7. **Chaperone:** Assists the teacher on field trips.
8. **General aide:** Catalogs and files instructional materials; helps construct educational games and kits.

Volunteers with extra knowledge, exciting experiences, and specialized skills should be utilized in the classroom. In most states, only the approval of the local school administration is required in order to have special resource people in the classroom. Police officers and firefighters frequently are used in a "Community Helper" unit in the primary grades, and local government officials are used in high school social studies classes. The following are some examples of special resource volunteers:

1. **A carpenter:** Demonstrates the use of his or her tools.
2. **An artist:** Explains a famous masterpiece.
3. **A parent who has spent the summer in another country:** Gives a slide presentation.
4. **An attorney who has worked as a public defender:** Tells of his or her experiences.
5. **An automotive factory worker:** Explains the automated assembly line.
6. **A registered nurse:** Discusses the training, skills, and tasks involved in professional nursing.
7. **A farmer:** Describes how recent flooding has affected crop production.
8. **A native of Mexico:** Models traditional garments and teaches the children a song in Spanish.
9. **A local musician:** Demonstrates various styles of music on the piano.
10. **A parent:** Conducts a storytelling session during the lunch hour.

Occasionally, school volunteers will be needed to provide specialized help on an ongoing basis, such as two or three times a week for a semester or more. Also, it may be appropriate to have a volunteer assist during an entire unit of instruction. The volunteer mentioned in Number 8 above could be used during the entire unit on Mexico. If this type of relationship is desired, the teacher should carefully outline the duties of the volunteer, the specific instruction the volunteer is to provide, and the beginning and ending dates of such instruction. Generally, it is a good idea to provide this information in writing to the proper school administrator. Of course, any instruction, whether on a onetime or continuing basis, should be closely supervised by certified personnel.

One area of school volunteer work frequently overlooked is activities that can be done at home or in the community. Following are some examples of volunteer positions that utilize home or community work:

- A parent who serves as a liaison between neighborhood groups and the school
- A group of volunteers trained to conduct a community-wide survey for the school
- Volunteers who help disseminate information to the community regarding the importance of impending bond issues
- Volunteers who collect recycled materials to be used by the teacher in a classroom activity
- A parent who sews and decorates cloth bags to be used by the teacher with a toy or book lending library
- A volunteer who prepares and distributes a weekly calendar of school and community activities that take place in school facilities

Legal Concerns

Generally, there are few legal concerns related to this kind of volunteer service because such help is not directly related to the academic program or the instructional process.

Legal regulations regarding the use of volunteers will vary from state to state. Most programs require criminal background checks and health papers. Those considering using volunteers for parent and community involvement should seek information from local and state authorities.

Job Descriptions

Accurate job descriptions are needed so that volunteers will know what is expected of them. **Volunteer job descriptions** should identify specific details for each service provided, list the skills required, and describe the time commitment needed to provide the service. Box 10.2 illustrates an example of a job description form.

When teachers write job descriptions, they have an opportunity to thoroughly think through the task for the volunteer. After the job descriptions

BOX 10.2

School Volunteer Job Description

SCHOOL: Franklin   TEACHER: Ms. Janet Kniepkamp
POSITION: Playhouse Builder   GRADE LEVEL: Kindergarten

JOB DESCRIPTION: Assist a team of volunteers to plan and build a playhouse for the
                         kindergarten classroom.

TIME NEEDED: Day: 3 Saturdays   Time: 9:00 a.m.–12:00 p.m.
                 Start: September   Finish: September

SPECIAL REQUIREMENTS: Construction and/or decorating skills preferred but not required.

are written, they should be assembled in a job description catalog for distribution by classroom and grade level to each teacher, secretary, and principal in the district.

WHERE WILL THE VOLUNTEERS COME FROM?

Community Sources

Volunteers can be drawn from all segments of the community. A wide range of occupations and economic and social roles enrich a school volunteer program (Barclay, 2005; Henderson, Johnson, Mapp, & Davies, 2006). The most abundant source of volunteers will be parents of the children served by the program (Berger, 2008). Another excellent source will be friends and acquaintances of staff members or of other volunteers. Certain volunteer tasks can be accomplished by upper elementary, junior high, or high school students. College students can provide a variety of useful services.

Most volunteers are mature or middle-aged adults. The U.S. Bureau of Labor Statistics indicates that 34.5 percent of volunteers are between 35 to 44 years old, closely followed by 45- to 54-year-olds, who make up 32.7 percent. Teenagers also have a relatively high volunteer rate of 30.4 percent, which perhaps reflects an emphasis on volunteer activities in schools (U.S. Department of Labor, 2005). Retirees become excellent volunteers because they usually are devoted and loyal in their service. In addition, a person who has spent 30 or more years on a job or a series of jobs has accumulated a wealth of information and skills that can be extremely helpful to the school. Retirees also can provide a link to an older generation that many children do not have because their grandparents are deceased or live far away. According to the Bureau of Labor Statistics, 32.2 percent of all baby boomers—25.8 million people born between 1946 and 1964—volunteered in formal organizations in 2005. This statistic represents a potentially rich resource of retiree volunteers for educational programs for the next two decades (U.S. Department of Labor, 2005).

Retirees may be loyal and devoted volunteers. *Courtesy of ECE Photo Library.*

Recruitment

The recruitment of volunteers can and should cut across the categories of age (from elementary school students to retired adults); sex (both males and females); occupation (professional to semiskilled); economics (all income levels); racial, ethnic, and religious backgrounds; and education.

The method of recruiting will depend on the size of the program and the available volunteer pool in the community. In general, recruitment is not too difficult after the recruitment targets have been identified. Parents, naturally, are the major source of volunteers; in a program that emphasizes parent involvement, this source is readily identified. When recruiting community volunteers, talks given to local civic groups are effective (Barclay, 2005). Speakers appearing before local groups should stress the need for volunteers and be prepared to answer questions about the goals and purposes of the program. Community understanding and support are vital in providing a quality program.

Other approaches are school websites, tours, brochures, or letters mailed to target groups. These should describe the need for volunteer services as well as give examples of jobs that need to be filled by volunteers. Volunteers who already work in the program can potentially be the most effective recruiters.

THE VOLUNTEER COORDINATOR

The volunteer program will be different in each school depending on the number of children, the size of the community, public transportation facilities, and other community resources. In establishing guidelines for a school volunteer program, it is necessary to plan carefully.

First, designate an individual or individuals who will be responsible for the direction and supervision of volunteer services. A full-time coordinator will be needed for larger programs. Smaller programs might be able to combine this position with another assignment. For example, in some small elementary schools, the building principal is the **volunteer coordinator.** In an early childhood setting, the position often is assumed by the director. In Head Start programs, the coordinator of parent involvement usually fills the role. In some situations, the position might be filled by a qualified volunteer who is willing to serve as the coordinator.

The job of the volunteer coordinator is a multifaceted one. Success or failure of the program depends on a coordinator's ability to manage the many factors involved. The coordinator must be proficient in human relations, communications, and managerial skills. The coordinator also must have the time, interest, and skills necessary for the following:

1. Understand the policies and procedures of the school.
2. Make school personnel aware of the benefits of volunteer service.
3. Explore and determine the level of support and cooperation the school will provide the volunteer program.
4. Provide an important link between the school and the community.
5. Orient volunteers to the value and goals of the program.
6. Maintain regular communication with all volunteers.
7. Stimulate continuing community support and interest in the program.
8. Exemplify the kind of model that volunteers can imitate in the performance of their duties.
9. Constantly evaluate the efforts of the volunteers and of the entire school volunteer program in an effort to improve it.

Although not all volunteer coordinators will perform these duties, they illustrate the range of duties a coordinator might be asked to perform.

It is the job of the volunteer coordinator, working under the direction of the principal, the director, or a designated assistant and in cooperation with the teachers and staff, to develop clear answers to the following questions:

- What kinds of volunteer services are needed?
- How many volunteers are desired?
- When are these volunteer services needed and for how long?
- What performance objectives are required?
- For which age or grade levels are volunteer tutors needed?
- What special problems are involved?
- What facilities and resources will be available?

After questions such as these are answered, you're ready to get a program under way. Here are the steps to follow; the order can be changed, depending on the circumstances. All the items listed need to be given some attention during the operation of a program (Rockwell & Comer, 1978).

1. Publicize the volunteer program. News stories in the local paper, public service announcements on radio and cable television stations, posters in grocery stores and Laundromats, and notes and letters sent home with the children are all effective.
2. Speak to groups such as the PTA, PTO, civic organizations, and so on.
3. Recruit volunteers.
4. Interview and screen volunteer prospects. Screening means performing a thorough **background check**, which includes reference checks (by phone or mail), a criminal record check, a child abuse registry check, and a driving record check.
5. Process teachers' requests for volunteer assistance.
6. Assign volunteers to situations that best match the needs of teachers.
7. Develop and maintain schedules.
8. Keep an information file on regular and substitute volunteers.
9. Orient the volunteers in the following areas:
   a. Goals of the program
   b. Needs of the school staff
   c. School regulations
   d. Physical arrangement of the school
   e. Location of materials and supplies
   f. Existing school programs and services
   g. Neighborhood recreational help and supporting social services

10. Provide preservice training for volunteers. This training will vary depending on where the volunteers are to be placed and what training the teachers, and the volunteers themselves, think they need. Training also should cover general skills and duties of the volunteers, child development, appropriate developmental practices, and human relations skills, including self-image and effective communication.

11. Introduce volunteers to the school staff.

12. Secure and be responsible for the use of inventory and necessary supplies.

13. Maintain volunteer records and supplies.

14. Notify volunteers in advance if their services are not needed on a particular day.

15. Follow up on absences and their causes. Make adjustments to remove the cause, if possible. For example, if the volunteer is not able to attend because of a lack of transportation, perhaps the coordinator can arrange transportation.

16. Secure substitutes or alternate volunteers if necessary.

17. Observe volunteers and be prepared to make constructive suggestions to help them improve in the volunteer role.

18. Guide and counsel volunteers with individual conferences and group meetings. In-service training programs should be ongoing, depending on volunteer and teacher needs.

19. Continually investigate and search for school and community resources that might offer services to the volunteer program.

20. Confer regularly with volunteers, school officials, and teachers to maintain morale.

21. Provide continuous formal recognition of volunteers throughout their service. Publicity in the news media and the school newsletter, letters of appreciation, trophies, pins, certificates, and recognition dinners are all widely used methods of recognizing volunteers. A coordinator generally knows of the assistance that the volunteers have provided, but formal recognition provides an opportunity for awareness at the community level.

22. Evaluate the volunteer program and offer recommendations for strengthening it.

It is a challenging task to find a volunteer coordinator who can effectively carry out all of these duties. However, the volunteer coordinator may well be the key to the success of the entire program and must be selected with great care.

VOLUNTEER INTERVIEWING, BACKGROUND SCREENING, AND JOB PLACEMENT

Each volunteer should be interviewed and screened before being accepted. The interview should take place at the school or center and be conducted by the volunteer coordinator, the principal, or the center director. The purpose of the interview is to judge the individual's motivation, assess his or her skills, and determine where the volunteer should be placed in order to make the greatest contribution to the program (Bauer & Shea, 2002).

An interview is an important early step in volunteer selection. *Courtesy of ECE Photo Library.*

A crucial component of the volunteer interview process is thorough background screening. This screening is rapidly becoming a standard practice with agencies, organizations and schools that serve children. Screening usually takes place before a volunteer begins his or her work in a program. However, with proper supervision, some schools may allow the volunteer to work while the screening process is taking place, with the understanding that the volunteer's continued involvement with the school or program will depend on the results of the check.

All applicants that apply should complete a Volunteer Application (Figure 10.1) and a Volunteer Background Investigation Permission and Release Form (Figure 10.2). The signed release form allows the school or the day care center to complete a criminal record check, including a child abuse registry check and a driving record check. Many schools and centers are now requiring this screening. It is important to explain that these checks are performed for the well-being and safety of the children. Parents and community volunteers should welcome and support these security measures. Your local police department, in most cases, will be able to check an applicant's record with the National Crime Information Center within 24 hours.

Franklin Elementary School
215 W. Main St. • Anoka, MN 55303

Volunteer Application Form
School Year 2007-2008

Last Name (legal)_____ First _____ M.I. _____ Nickname _____

Address _____

City_____ State _____ Zip _____ Home Phone (   ) _____

Best ways to contact me during school hours: *(Check all that apply.)*

❏ Home Phone *(see above)*   ❏ Work Phone (   ) _____   ❏ Cell Phone (   ) _____

❏ E-Mail _____   ❏ Other _____

May we share your name and contact information with the project chairs for the opportunities you select? ❏ Yes ❏ No

Please indicate days and times most convenient for you to volunteer:

❏ Monday   Times: _____   ❏ Thursday   Times: _____

❏ Tuesday   Times: _____   ❏ Friday   Times: _____

❏ Wednesday   Times: _____   ❏ Weekends   Times: _____

❏ Available for at home projects: _____

Additional information:_____

I need notice in advance of: ❏ 1 day   ❏ 2 days   ❏ 1 week   ❏ more than a week _____

Student Information: Name: *(first & last)* _____ Grade ____ Teacher _____

Name: *(first & last)* _____ Grade ____ Teacher _____

Name: *(first & last)* _____ Grade ____ Teacher _____

Relationship to student(s): ❏ Parent ❏ Grandparent ❏ Community member ❏ Other _____

We will provide reasonable accommodations with advance notice to persons with disabilities upon request.

Accommodations request: _____

Office Use
Date Rec'd _____
CRHR Form Returned _____
Other _____

✔ _____   ✔ _____
SIGNATURE   **DATE**

Criminal Record History Release Form - Volunteers: The Anoka-Hennepin Volunteer Program requires volunteers 18 years and older to complete a Criminal Record History Release Form to protect our volunteers and students. Every volunteer 18 years and older must sign a form each year at each building where they will volunteer. The level of risk in a volunteer situation will determine whether a check will be done.

In case of a medical emergency, please give the name and contact information of a person you would like us to contact.

Name (optional)_____ Relationship_____ Phone _____

VOLUNTEER OPPORTUNITIES

Please check the opportunities that interest you. This does not commit you to helping, but it does give us permission to contact you when these opportunities arise. **You will not be contacted about opportunities that you have not checked.** NOTE: Opportunities that are sponsored by Franklin's PTO are indicated with "(PTO)". All other opportunities are school-sponsored/related.

DECISION MAKING

❏ **PTO Meetings:** Attendance at PTO meetings is considered volunteer time. Meetings are held on the 3rd Thursday of the month at 6:30 p.m. in the Media Center and include updates on current projects, reports from the principal, volunteer services coordinator and community education programmer.

❏ **Parent Legislative Team (PLT):** Parents work with the Legislature as a nonpartisan group to encourage action and advocacy for improved education funding for Anoka-Hennepin students. Meetings typically in the evening.

❏ **Parent Legislative Network (PLN):** Parents in the network receive nonpartisan email updates from the Parent Legislative Team (PLT) regarding legislation that affects students in Anoka-Hennepin. The PLT may occasionally request assistance from the PLN in the form of phone calls or emails to legislators on these matters. Your email address:

_____.

(over)

FIGURE 10.1 Volunteer Application

Please check the opportunities that interest you:

❏ **Building or District Level Committees:** Occasionally there is need for a parent to serve on a committee regarding various issues (playgrounds, curriculum development, boundaries, etc.) These meetings may be held during the school day or in the evenings.

TALENT DEVELOPMENT

❏ **Literacy Circles:** Lead a group of 6-9 students in a literature discussion group once per week. A required training takes place in the fall.

❏ **Challenge Math:** A math enrichment class of 8-10 students meets once per week. Volunteers facilitate a unique problem-solving curriculum. Training provided in the fall.

❏ **Destination Imagination:** Lead a group of students in creative problem solving. Training required and provided.

❏ **Picture People:** An art enrichment program through the Minneapolis Art Institute. Volunteers attend a training session and learn about a group of art works. They take the art into classrooms and share it with the children.

FAMILY SUPPORT / COMMUNITY

❏ **Franklin Skating Party (PTO):** Skate at Sorenson Park while enjoying socializing, cookies and hot cocoa. This event typically takes place in late January or early February, weather and ice conditions permitting.
  ❏ Rink attendant.   ❏ Serve refreshments

❏ **Bingo for Books:** Students get free books by winning at Bingo! This is an evening event during the winter.
  ❏ Setup (approximately 3-5 p.m.)
  ❏ Cleanup (approximately 7-9 p.m.)

❏ **Teacher Appreciation Suppers (PTO):** Thank our teachers for their hard work! Meals take place during fall and winter conferences and in May during Staff Appreciation Week.
  ❏ Provide a salad bar item, bread, dessert or homemade soup.
  ❏ Call volunteers and arrange donations.
  ❏ Setup during conference meals at 3:30 p.m.
  ❏ Cleanup during conference meals at 8:00 p.m.
  ❏ Setup and/or cleanup during the school day for May meal.

❏ **Vision & Hearing Screening:** Typically in October, the health para needs people to help test the vision and hearing of students during school hours.

❏ **Gardening:** Volunteers provide most of the maintenance of Franklin's gardens. Work is done primarily in spring and summer.

FUNDRAISING

❏ **AHEF Certificates (PTO):** Help is needed with the sale and advertising of AHEF gift certificates.

❏ **Annual fundraiser (PTO):**
  ❏ Processing: Tally order forms, check for errors.
  ❏ Distribution: Help distribute pre-packed orders.

❏ **Book Fairs, fall & winter (PTO):**
  ❏ Cashier, daytime   ❏ Setup (afternoon)
  ❏ Cashier, evening   ❏ Takedown (evening)

❏ **Halloween Dance (PTO):**
  ❏ Planning committee   ❏ Ticket/concession sales (2 shifts)
  ❏ Costume contest   ❏ Decorating
  ❏ Concessions/food coordinators

❏ **Family Fun Nite (PTO carnival):**
  ❏ Planning committee   ❏ Ticket Sales
  ❏ Setup   ❏ Prizes   ❏ Games Coordinator
  ❏ Cleanup   ❏ Advertising/Silent Auction/Raffle
  ❏ Run game or work event   ❏ Concessions coordinator

❏ **Campbell's Labels, General Mills Box Tops, Kemps & Land-O-Lakes Milk Caps (PTO):** Trim, bundle and count labels, caps, etc. for shipping. This can be an at-home project.

❏ **Calligraphy:** A few times a year we need people to do lettering on certificates.

TEACHER SUPPORT IN THE CLASSROOM

❏ **Field Trip Chaperone.** ❏ **Classroom Party Helper.**

❏ **5th Grade Wolf Ridge Field Trip:** Chaperone this overnight field trip.

❏ **Halloween Parade Supervisors:** Help supervise students during the annual Anoka Halloween Parade (field trip).

❏ **Kindergarten Data Collectors:** Interview kindergarten students five times during the school year—Sept., Oct., Jan., March, and May—to identify the students' understanding of Letter Identification, Rhyming, Syllables and Concepts about Print. Training is required and provided in September.

❏ **Science Fair Judges:** Evaluate science projects of students participating in the Science Fair. Typically held in late March. Judging takes approximately 2-3 hours during the morning of the event.

STAFF SUPPORT OUTSIDE THE CLASSROOM

❏ **Fifth Grade Recognition:** 4th grade parents usually plan this event that takes place on the last day of school.
  ❏ Calligraphy (names on certificates)   ❏ Decorations
  ❏ Serve cake & ice cream   ❏ Cleanup

❏ **Arts & Academics Night:** Volunteers are crucial to this event, typically held in late March:
  ❏ Setup during the day of the event
  ❏ Cleanup after the event closes in the evening
  ❏ Exhibit monitoring during the evening

❏ **Wednesday Handouts:** Count flyers and materials and distribute to classroom mailboxes. Help is needed every Wednesday morning, from approximately 10:30-noon. Help once a year, once a month, or periodically.

❏ **Workroom Assistance:** Teachers and/or office staff may have work to be done that may include photocopying, stapling, die cutting, collating, preparing bulletin boards, etc.

❏ **At Home Work:** Occasionally there is classroom prep work that can be done at home.

❏ **Recess Helpers:** Assist the staff supervising recess.

❏ **Media Center helper:** Shelve books.

❏ **Art Helper:** Come in, as needed, to hang art projects in the hallways and assist with other art room tasks.

❏ **MCA Hallway Monitor:** Monitor the hallways during MCA testing days.

❏ **Yearbook:** Photographers and creative people needed to prepare the yearbook.

MISCELLANEOUS / HELP AS NEEDED

There are times when we need volunteers for unplanned activities.
  ❏ Available to help at school during the day
  ❏ Will work on projects at home

Please have your child return this form along with the criminal record history release form or mail to:

Volunteer Services Coordinator
Franklin Elementary School
215 W. Main St.
Anoka, MN 55303

Voicemail: (763) 506-2630
Fax: (763) 506-2603
School Phone: (763) 506-2600
School TTY: (763) 506-2619

ANOKA-HENNEPIN
SCHOOLS
A future without limit

Please indicate your interests and dislikes.	
I enjoy doing:	**No!** I don't want to:

Volunteer Programs are supported by Anoka-Hennepin Parent Involvement Website: www.anoka.k12.mn.us

FIGURE 10.1 Continued

CRIMINAL RECORD HISTORY RELEASE FORM - Volunteers

ANOKA-HENNEPIN INDEPENDENT SCHOOL DISTRICT #11
EMPLOYEE SERVICES 763-506-1100
11299 HANSON BOULEVARD NW, COON RAPIDS, MN 55433-3799

The following named individual has made application with this School District for volunteering:

Last Name: _____ Home Phone: (_____) _____

First Name: _____ Work Phone: (_____) _____

Middle (full): _____ Date of Birth: _____

Maiden, Alias or Former: _____ Sex: (M or F) _____

Address: _____

City, State, Zip_____

Are you currently an Anoka-Hennepin District #11 employee?   No ❑   Yes ❑

✔ Have you lived in another state or country within the last 5 years?   No ❑   Yes ❑

✔ If you answered "yes", list the state(s) or countries in which you have resided and/or worked and **when**:

    state/country_____ date _____

    state/country_____ date _____

    state/country_____ date _____

If you have lived in another state, it may be necessary for AHISD #11 to complete a record history check from that state or the FBI.

✔ **HAVE YOU EVER BEEN CONVICTED** of any crime or offense against the law, or are there any charges pending, including felonies and misdemeanors (with the exception of speeding and parking tickets)?

  No ❑   Yes ❑

✔ If yes, please provide information for each offense:

    charge(s) convicted of: _____

    date of conviction(s): _____

    court and location: _____

    action taken: _____

•••• CRIMINAL RECORD HISTORY RELEASE ••••

The Anoka-Hennepin School District requires a Criminal Record History Release Form to be completed for all volunteers 18 years and older. Every volunteer 18 years and older must sign a new form every school year at the building where they volunteer. The $15 fee is currently being waived for volunteers. Volunteering in schools is conditional upon the determination by the District that an individual's criminal history does not preclude the individual from volunteering for the District.

This release and authorization acknowledges that Anoka-Hennepin Independent School District #11 may conduct a search and obtain any criminal or civil history record information pertaining to me which may be in the files of any Federal, State or Local criminal justice agency in any state or province or any information as deemed necessary to fulfill the volunteer requirements.

I authorize Minnesota Bureau of Criminal Apprehension (BCA - **MS 123B.03**) and any of its agents, to disclose criminal history record information to the Anoka-Hennepin Independent School District #11 for the purpose of volunteering with this School District.

I do hereby agree to forever release and discharge Anoka-Hennepin Independent School District #11, its agent, BCA, and their associates to the full extent permitted by law from claims, damages, costs, and expenses, for any errors, omissions or any other charge or complaint filed with any agency arising from the retrieving and reporting of information.

✔ _____ ✔ _____
SIGNATURE OF VOLUNTEER   DATE

❑ We are also requesting a federal check pursuant to Minnesota State Statute 299C.62 on this individual.

RETURN THIS FORM TO THE VOLUNTEER SERVICES COORDINATOR AT:
Franklin Elementary • 215 W. Main St. • Anoka, MN 55303-2089

Office Use
CRHR Rec'd _____
App. Rec'd_____
❑ _____

Rev. 4/06

FIGURE 10.2 Volunteer Background Investigation Permission and Release Form

The volunteer should be disqualified from holding a position that involves direct contact with children if his or her criminal records include past history of child abuse, convictions where children were involved, or a history of violence or sexually abusive behavior.

For additional information relating to types of abuse and neglect, the teacher's role, and reporting procedures, see pages 160–168 of Gestwicki's *Home, School, and Community Relations Professional Enhancement* text that accompanies this book.

From the interview, the volunteers learn the purpose of the program, why they are needed, and what is expected of them. The interview should be carefully planned so that the prospective volunteer fully understands the satisfactions that can be gained through service as well as the obligations that must be met. Volunteers should not be seen as free labor and therefore exempt from conforming to expectations (such as preparing adequately for the task, being regular and punctual, writing records, attending training meetings, etc.) that must be met in order to conduct an efficient, high-quality program (Cook, Tessier, & Klein, 2000).

When describing the program to a prospective volunteer, the interviewer should review the lists of tasks or job descriptions developed from the aforementioned inventory of needs. While the responsibility for the assignment of volunteers based on an assessment of their abilities and competencies rests with the staff, assignments must be mutually agreeable to both staff and volunteers.

The most important qualifications for a volunteer are a dedication to the welfare of children and a willingness to commit time and energy on their behalf. Some volunteers may possess an intellectual and emotional commitment but not an aptitude for working directly with children. A well-conducted interview will help determine where volunteers of this nature may serve best. It is important that an alternative be available for these volunteers. An appropriate activity might include soliciting funds, equipment, and materials from community groups. These volunteers also could aid in interpreting the program to the community, serve on a newsletter publication staff, or prepare teaching materials in their homes.

People to be avoided as volunteers are those who cannot discipline themselves to accept the school program. If they can't keep appointments or complete training, they are going to bring more confusion than help to the children and the staff. Desirable traits that the interviewer should look for in prospective volunteers are helpfulness, sincerity, creativity, dependability, reliability, confidentiality, and responsibility. The interviewer should have knowledge of the volunteer needs of other community agencies, as it might not be possible to use everyone who offers to help; an applicant may possess skills that could be better utilized by another agency. Cross-referral by local groups can be beneficial to all involved.

SELECTION OF AN ADVISORY COMMITTEE

An advisory committee for volunteer services is essential to a volunteer program. Such a committee should represent a broad spectrum of community agencies and organizations as well as the teachers and parents of the children who will be the beneficiaries of the services provided. Examples of agencies that might be invited to serve include the local volunteer bureau, Boy Scouts, Girl Scouts, Urban League, YMCA, YWCA, Council of Churches, County Homemakers, Junior League, PTA, PTO, Council of Negro Women, Council of Jewish Women, labor groups, and student organizations. It is also important to contact groups that have traditionally supported child-related programs, such as the American Legion, Shriners, Kiwanis, Lions, local teacher organizations, and the American Association of University Women.

The advisory committee should meet well in advance of the initiation of the program to approve the general plan and to help formulate a presentation to the board of education or other funding agency or both. In some communities, the program is funded by one of the service organizations previously mentioned, while formal approval of the program to operate in the schools is granted by the board of education. The advisory committee also should continually monitor and evaluate the program.

ESTABLISHING POLICY

Developing a Guiding Philosophy

It is important that a guiding philosophy be developed for the program. This philosophy will vary from program to program. If developed with care, the philosophy will serve the school well in the recruitment and orientation stages as well as throughout the life span of the program.

The following are examples of guiding philosophies:

1. The volunteer program is an integral part of our program.
2. Volunteers are viewed as partners of the staff and are members of the school team.
3. Volunteers should complement rather than replace the existing staff.
4. Volunteers are not paid. They donate their time and talents and therefore have special meaning and value to children.
5. Volunteers bring richness in the variety of talents, skills, and interests they contribute. They invest time and energy to meet the regular and special needs of children on an individualized and group basis.

6. Volunteers relieve school professionals so that their time and energy may be directed to areas of greatest need and concern.

The statement of philosophy for the program should be general in nature and be tailored to each individual program. However, a clearly stated written philosophy is the key to all successful school volunteer programs. It should touch on matters of crucial importance, such as the intended role and function of the volunteer and the relationship of volunteers to the staff.

Setting Goals and Objectives

The goal of a program is a broad description of what the program is to accomplish over a period of time, usually one school year. The objective of a program is a specific statement of a step toward the goal and must be measurable in some way.

The writing of a philosophy and the selection of goals for the program should involve the school administration, the advisory committee, and all staff members. Generally, goals are determined first, and then specific, measurable objectives are developed to meet each goal. This step cannot be omitted. At the end of the program, it is essential to be able to measure the degree to which the program did or did not accomplish its goals.

For example, a community might think that home–school relations could be improved by increasing the number of parents working at the school and becoming familiar with the school program. This goal might be stated as follows: The volunteer program will strengthen home–community–school relations. An objective for the goal could be that during the school year, 50 parents will participate in a parent volunteer program. Another goal could be that parents will provide enrichment activities for the students. An objective for this goal might be that 25 percent of the students will participate in an enrichment activity presented by a parent. Enrichment activities are defined as experiences that broaden student understanding of the topics the teacher has already introduced.

WORKING WITH VOLUNTEERS

Orientation

At least one formal orientation session should be held for all volunteers before any volunteer work begins. It should cover the most important details that volunteers should know before they begin working (Olsen & Fuller, 2003). Include the goals and purposes of the school, the school's philosophy as it relates to volunteer services, specific duties and responsibilities of volunteers, the relationship of the volunteers to the staff, and an overview of specific do's and don'ts.

One useful method of further conveying the information covered in the orientation is to prepare a volunteer handbook (Gestwicki, 2007). This handbook, which can be given to all volunteers, includes the detailed information presented at the orientation and provides a handy reference for volunteers throughout their contact with the program.

Volunteer training is crucial. *Courtesy of ECE Photo Library.*

Training

Orientation should be followed by training. The training program should be perceived as an ongoing process involving on-the-job training as well as informal small group and individual preplacement sessions. As many staff members as possible should participate in these sessions with the volunteers. This eliminates communication problems between the professional staff and the volunteers. Staff involvement in training also helps increase the volunteers' awareness of the professionals' roles and provides an opportunity for professionals to become aware of the problems and concerns of the volunteers. Training sessions can contribute to the development of harmony and a cooperative spirit for the volunteer program.

The training program's format should be varied. Informality should prevail. Videos and demonstrations are useful training tools; lengthy formal lectures should be de-emphasized. If possible, new volunteers should have opportunities to hear from experienced volunteers. The training session's content depends on what jobs the staff has decided it needs volunteers to do.

Obviously, the training should fit the job. Classroom volunteers will need to understand their role in the classroom. If possible, the teacher who has requested the help will assist in or conduct the training sessions. If the job is clerical, the volunteer should be trained to use the computer, the laminating machine, and any other office equipment the school may possess. It is discouraging to volunteers to receive training that is not relevant to the job they have volunteered to do (Prior & Gerard, 2007).

Supervision

Supervision, whether group or individual, must be regular. Volunteers need and are entitled to have their performance assessed on a regular basis. They need to share successes and also be supported during periods of frustration and feelings of inadequacy. If supervision or opportunities for volunteer feedback are omitted, a high turnover rate can be predicted (Sciarra & Dorsey, 2007). Volunteers desire guidance in their work and can be distressed by a lack of direction. A good program of supervision and support will help volunteers be accountable for their commitments, show up on time, do their work in a thorough fashion, and be valuable contributing members of the school or center team.

Evaluation

A vital component of the volunteer program is evaluation. Evaluation serves as a systematic, constructive form of feedback to help a program improve. If changes are called for as a result of evaluations—whether they are performed by the volunteers, teacher, coordinator, principal, director, or total program—then those changes should be made. Evaluation information should be sought from all who have participated in the program. All volunteers should engage in a self-evaluation of their contributions (Little, 1999). Staff members who utilize volunteer services also should evaluate the volunteers.

Obviously, evaluation helps those in charge of a volunteer program see whether volunteers have been doing what they were expected to do. Matching the evaluation results with the overall objectives of the program will provide the volunteer coordinator and the advisory committee with information about the goals of the program. If the objectives have been met, then the program has done what it set out to do. If some of the objectives have not been met, then the program needs to be adjusted so those objectives can be met in the future, or perhaps the objectives need to be modified. It is possible that a thorough evaluation process will discover that totally new objectives need to be formulated and considered by the advisory board. If the volunteer program is to be viable and ongoing, then evaluations, whether constructive or critical, must be heeded (Endres, Rockwell, & Mense, 2004).

Recognition

Every volunteer, regardless of the time devoted to the program, should receive frequent praise and encouragement for their services. Volunteers gain satisfaction when they feel they have been accepted as colleagues by their coworkers. Another form of satisfaction results from their contributions to the progress and growth of an individual child or group of children.

Staff members must make a continual effort to express their acceptance of volunteers and the skills they contribute. In addition to this effort, a dinner, reception, or some type of recognition ceremony should be held near the end of the school year to publicly recognize the volunteers for their services (Endres, Rockwell, & Mense, 2004; Olsen & Fuller, 2003).

SUMMARY

Volunteers are some of the most important members of the education team. They are the extra hands, eyes, and legs that teachers frequently need for a successful day. It is a wonderful feeling to know that there are people who are willing to give freely of their time and talent to serve in this capacity. Volunteers have many responsibilities. They should be dependable and show maturity, cooperation, and the ability to accept suggestions and instructions willingly. They must be eager to learn and to do assigned duties; and they must feel free to consult with staff members when they have questions about the program. They also need to genuinely care for children. A good program, well conceived, can help volunteers achieve all of these qualities.

ACTIVITIES FOR DISCUSSION, EXPANSION, AND APPLICATION

1. Identify barriers that might be present when a school volunteer program is attempted.

2. Discuss possible issues that might occur should thorough background screening of prospective volunteers be omitted.

3. What are the volunteer resources in your community?

4. What major topics should be addressed in a volunteer orientation session?

5. What volunteer services do you think are needed for your program?

6. What are some ways that volunteers can be recognized for their services?

7. Do a survey of the volunteer training programs that are conducted in the early childhood centers of your community. Do a similar survey for training programs conducted in the elementary schools.

8. Design a classified ad, website, or newsletter inviting parents to become volunteers in an early childhood or elementary school program.

9. Contact and interview two parents, two teachers, and two administrators, and ask their opinion on the use of volunteers in school settings. Share the interviews in class.

CASE STUDY

Ms. Johnson has volunteered to work in Ms. Jones's Head Start classroom. When she arrives, she is acknowledged by a head nod from Ms. Jones and asked to take a seat in the rear of the room. After waiting patiently for 20 minutes, Ms. Johnson asks if she can be of any help. Ms. Jones responds, "Why don't you clean the bathroom, and then perhaps you might empty the trash. I'm really not sure what to give you to do today. I didn't know you were coming, so I really don't think there's anything else." Ms. Johnson is quite upset. She thinks, "My time is too valuable for this. I thought I was going to do something with the children. If this is what happens when one volunteers, I won't be returning."

1. What suggestions do you have regarding Ms. Jones's acknowledgement of Ms. Johnson?

2. Do you feel the work Ms. Johnson was asked to perform was appropriate?

3. What steps could be taken to remedy this situation?

USEFUL WEBSITES

www.anoka.k12.mn.us
Anoka-Hennepin School District. This website provides extensive information regarding a wide variety of volunteer opportunities for parents, grandparents, and community volunteers.

www.ncpie.org
The National Coalition for Parent Involvement in Education. NCPIE is a coalition of major education, community, public service, and advocacy organizations working to create meaningful family–school partnerships in every school in America.

www.pta.org
The National Parent Teacher Association. The National PTA is the largest volunteer child advocacy association in the nation. This site provides resources and guidelines for families, schools, and volunteers.

REFERENCES

Barclay, K. H. (2005). *Together we can: Uniting families, schools, and communities to help all children learn.* Dubuque, Iowa: Kendall/Hunt.

Bauer, A. M., & Shea, T. M. (2002). *Parents and schools: Creating a successful partnership for students with special needs.* Upper Saddle River, New Jersey: Pearson/Merrill/Prentice Hall.

Berger, E. H. (2008). *Parents as partners in education: Families and schools working together* (7th ed.). Upper Saddle River, NJ: Pearson/Merrill/Prentice Hall.

Cook, R. E., Tessier, A., & Klein, M. (2000). *Adapting early childhood curricula for children in inclusive settings* (5th ed.). Upper Saddle River, NJ: Pearson/Merrill/Prentice Hall.

Endres, J. B., Rockwell, R. E., & Mense, C. G. (2004). *Food, nutrition, and the young child* (5th ed.). Upper Saddle River, NJ: Merrill/Prentice Hall.

Gestwicki, C. (2007). *Home, school, and community relations* (6th ed.). Clifton Park, NY: Thomson Delmar Learning.

Henderson, A. T., Johnson, V., Mapp, K. L., & Davies, D. (2006). *Beyond the bake sale: The essential guide to family/school partnerships.* New York: New Press.

Little, H. (1999). *Volunteers: How to get them, how to keep them.* Naperville, IL: Panacea Press.

Olsen, G., & Fuller, M. L. (2003). *Home–school relations: Working successfully with parents and families.* New York: Pearson Education.

Prior, J., & Gerard, R. (2007). *Family involvement in early childhood education: Research into practice.* Clifton Park, NY: Thomson Delmar.

Rockwell, R. E. (1993). Parent involvement. In B. J. Howery (Ed.), *Early childhood handbook.* Springfield, IL: Illinois State Board of Education.

Rockwell, R. E., & Comer, J. C. (1978). *School volunteer programs: A manual for coordinators.* Athens, OH: Midwestern Teacher Corps Network, Ohio University.

Sciarra, D. J., & Dorsey, A. G. (2007). *Developing and administering a child care education program* (6th ed.). Clifton Park, NY: Thomson Delmar Learning.

U.S. Department of Labor, Bureau of Labor Statistics. (2005). *Volunteering in the United States.* Washington, DC: National Committee for Citizens in Education.

KEY TERMS

School Volunteers—Adults or students who assist teachers, administrators, or other staff members in schools or early childhood centers without receiving monetary compensation for their time and talent.

Volunteer Job Description—A detailed description of the job for which volunteer service is requested. Includes the skills required and the time commitment needed to provide the service.

Volunteer Coordinator—The individual who is responsible for the direction and supervision of volunteer services.

Background Check—A background check, including a criminal record check, child abuse registry check, and driving record check, required of all potential volunteers before their participation in a school or early childhood center volunteer program.

CHAPTER 11

Parents as Decision Makers: Empowerment in Process

STUDENT LEARNING OUTCOMES

After reading this chapter, you should be able to

- Analyze the historical and legislative evolution of involved parents as decision makers in regular and special education movements.

- Outline parental rights and responsibilities for involvement.

- Discuss levels of family empowerment in program or school relationships and how they apply to educational programs.

- Identify trends for parental decision making in educational programs.

- Explain how teachers and parents can promote meaningful parent involvement in leadership roles.

If educators believe that one goal of parent involvement is to empower parents to be more effective as their children's first teachers and partners in their children's education, the acceptance of parents as decision makers is a test of that conviction. Parents already possess the right and power to make decisions concerning their child and to choose their degree of parental participation. Since the role of participant inherently includes choice making, parents exert their right as decision maker when they choose to have their child attend a particular program or school, when they participate in parent meetings and conferences, or when they accept a visit from the teacher.

Over time, the parental role as program and policy decision maker has broadened. More early childhood centers and elementary schools than ever before now recognize that the power of parents to assist programs and enhance outcomes for children is generated by a program philosophy of authentic partnership and from the opportunities provided parents to undertake real responsibilities, not token tasks.

PARENT INVOLVEMENT: A HISTORICAL EVOLUTION

In the United States, the parents' role in education has been an evolving one. During the 18th and 19th centuries, parents and schools had a cooperative partnership: The schools taught some reading, writing, and arithmetic; parents taught (or arranged for others to teach) the craft skills needed to earn a living as well as the social, religious, and moral foundations they valued. Parents formerly did more than just select the local schoolmaster. Because the teacher often lived on a rotating basis with local families who had children in the school, the parents strictly monitored the teacher's behavior and activities. Parents paid for their child's schooling and often decided the curriculum; to them, the school and teacher were in their employ.

The industrial revolution and the change from a rural, agricultural lifestyle meant that families could no longer prepare their children for the varied jobs available to them. The influx of immigrant families necessitated education in the language and learning traditions of their new country. Schools quickly took over the preparation of children for adult work as well as some of the family responsibilities for child health and well-being. Children were required to be vaccinated before entering school, and school lunches and physical education became part of many school programs. During the late 19th and early 20th centuries, teacher-training requirements increased; previously, anyone who was literate, studious, and willing to teach children could be an educator, but now teaching became a distinct profession. As colleges and universities began developing programs to educate teachers, they were also conducting research about the best methods for child development. The influence of John Dewey, a leading twentieth-century philosopher, psychiatrist, and educational reformer, was felt in education and in programs available to the public. **Nursery schools** and parent cooperatives began to spring up across the country. To facilitate parent participation in children's school lives, local and national Parent Teacher Associations were soon visible in schools across the country. At that time, however, their activities were restricted to hosting social events, supervising field trips, and fundraising. Instead of trying to merely increase parent attendance at school-sponsored activities, schools were enlisting family support in activities outside of school to enhance children's learning. In order to be successful, schools and families needed to develop a more meaningful partnership.

Legislation Impacts Policies

Depending on the individual state, children are now required by law to begin school between ages 5 and 7 and to attend until ages 16 to 18. Parents have established the right to choose where this education will take place: in public, parochial, or private schools or even at home. Over time, other legal protection has been won for parental rights. For example, parents worked to secure the Family Educational Rights and Privacy Act, passed in 1974, which assured parents the right to review their child's school records, to correct incorrect or misleading information, and to be assured of privacy regarding the information held in school files.

Important changes in parent involvement can be traced to the legislation, policy making, and research generated during the 1960s. The passage of the Civil Rights Act of 1964 increased the awareness of the rights of all individuals. Throughout the country, students in high schools and colleges demanded a voice in decisions that affected their lives. Programs were initiated during the **War on Poverty** that assured the involvement of program participants—the poor—in the planning and delivery of services.

Head Start, the national model preschool program for low-income children and families, was developed during this time as part of the War on Poverty. It was the first program to comprehensively involve parents in the education of their children. It has maintained the expectation that parents should be active participants in their children's classrooms and "owners" of the program through active involvement on advisory boards and policy councils, and as paid classroom assistants. These involvement strategies provided researchers with documentation from which to substantiate the value of parent involvement in early childhood programs and the longitudinal value of early childhood education.

Parent Action and other parenting groups throughout the country have joined the PTA in promoting advocacy for family policy making. Parents in these groups have organized to ensure that they will have a voice in public policies that affect them and their children.

The Elementary and Secondary Education Act of 1965 granted federal money into local schools with the goal of eliminating the educational disadvantages of poor children in the public schools. A series of Title programs were developed under this legislation. The primary focus was on young learners and included parent involvement, in an effort to enrich school resources for supplementary educational programs (Title I), or home visits for preschoolers and working with parents (Title IV-C). Parents are required to be involved in Title I planning and decision making as well as in developing the school plan. In order to help parents assume these roles, the law requires that parents receive assistance and support, if necessary.

Special Education Laws Secure Parent and Family Rights

The quest for appropriate educational opportunities for all children has led program policy makers and parents to a shared decision-making process. During the late 1950s and 1960s, parents of children with disabilities became actively involved in developing services for their children. In the era when public schools did not welcome children with disabilities, parents often developed their own special education programs outside of the public system. Active as fundraisers, teachers, administrators, and advocates, parents undertook the legal challenges to acquire rights and opportunities for their children. Parents developed into an organized group of political advocates who contributed to a series of successful litigations, ultimately leading to the congressional passage of Public Law 94-142 (Education for All Handicapped Children Act of 1975) and Public Law 99-457 of 1986. Regular reauthorizations of the Individuals with Disabilities Education Act (IDEA) credit parental advocacy in promoting family-friendly changes.

As public schools assumed the responsibility for educating all children, many parents were given a passive role. They were often expected to accept the professionals' decisions for their children's placement and programming and remain outside the school unless needed as room mother or fundraiser. As the full impact of PL 94-142 began to be felt, some parents began to assume the empowered role of partner in educational decision making for their children and themselves via the Individualized Educational Program (IEP) for children aged 3 to 21 and, with PL 99-457, the Individualized Family Service Plan (IFSP) for younger children and their families.

Although this role as a decision-making partner has been outlined and protected by law, parents do not always exercise it for a variety of reasons. In response, many organizations (often with broad-based parental support and membership) offer special legal rights awareness publications, websites, and classes to educate parents with children in special education. Parents also may form support groups to share advocacy and other information.

When parental partnership expectations are not met, and as communication at the local level breaks down, parents with children in special education may initiate legal action, called due process, against the special services provider. Individuals are encouraged to avert due process through mediation; however, parents have this power protected by federal legislation. In 1992, amendments to IDEA took effect, requiring updated terminology and expanded and affirmed services for all individuals with disabilities. In 1997, the reauthorization increased the participation possibilities for parents in the education of children with special needs. The gains made by these parents have been influential in developing increased opportunities for all parents. (See Chapter 4 for additional information on involving families of children with special needs.)

PARENT RIGHTS AND RESPONSIBILITIES FOR INVOLVEMENT

A popular focus of education has been the right of all children to a successful learning experience. Parents frequently have taken action to defend this right, battling such issues as segregation, gender equity, and restrictions on homeschooling.

Although the emphasis in education often appears as children's rights, parental rights exist as well. According to Henniger (1987), these parental rights and corresponding responsibilities in the educational process include the following:

- **The right** to personal feelings about education.
- **The responsibility** to be knowledgeable about educational goals, techniques, and principles.
- **The right** to personal feelings about a child's place in the educational system.
- **The responsibility** to listen carefully and openly to professionals.
- **The right** to meaningful communication with the child's teacher.
- **The responsibility** to ensure that communication flows two ways.
- **The right** to plan and maintain parent groups.
- **The responsibility** to support and develop leadership capabilities in themselves and in others.
- **The right** to know the school's policies and program plans.
- **The responsibility** to be supportive of the plan or to take an active role in changing the policies.
- **The right** to be represented in policy-making decisions.
- **The responsibility** to get involved and participate when possible.

It is because of the need to be represented in policy decisions that affect their children that parents develop into decision makers. Through the developmental process of building a supportive parent involvement policy and practice, positive energy and momentum emerge. The momentum grows within families and professionals as they realize that their efforts can produce results. For example, parent conferences with relaxed communication and genuine rapport may result in a new classroom volunteer with numerous ideas and resources, or a major contributor to the advisory committee. The resulting positive feelings can build a progression of enhanced self-esteem, satisfaction, a desire for additional interaction, and a willingness to assume new responsibilities and face new challenges (Long, 2007). For many families, this will be a gradual process; for others, it is an exciting invitation.

LEVELS OF PARENT EMPOWERMENT

Of course, not all parents begin their involvement with their child's program as empowered child advocates. Rasinski and Fredericks (1989) recognized four levels of home–school relationships that correspond to a degree of empowerment for families that are valid today. These tiers of involvement are parent as monitor, parent as information source, parent as participant, and the empowered parent.

The most simple and basic level open to nearly all parents is that of *monitor*. Parents can take an interest in what is going on in the program through the child ("What did you do today?"), or by reading newsletters and other one-way communications sent home by the teacher. In the next tier, the parent is an *information source*. Parents maintain the lines of communication via two-way communication strategies such as phone calls, notes, and parent–teacher conferences. Parents move to the next level of involvement—*participant*—by participating in such activities as meetings and special events and by being a program volunteer.

The highest level of involvement is that of *empowerment*. Empowerment involves parents and teachers working together for the good of many children and families. This may involve jointly developing program plans, advising staff and administration, and taking leadership in coordinating program efforts such as supervising the parent space, organizing the parent library, or coordinating the program volunteer effort. This level of collaboration emerges from a strong personal commitment to the success of the program goals and requires mutual trust and cooperation between parents and program staff. Unlike the lower levels of involvement, many aspects of empowered decision making may not actively involve all parents, because there typically are a limited number of positions available and limited participation potential for parents. Likewise, parents may be not only interested but also ready and able to assume leadership roles in a parent involvement program. Their life experiences in their careers, businesses, or organizations may have empowered them to join educators in an active partnership.

Empowerment is not an "add it on later" idea but an important element in planning parent involvement opportunities, especially for families that may be considered at risk, are poor, belong to a minority racial group, or have non-mainstream culture and language. According to Family Matters at Cornell

University, empowerment is one of the keys to overcoming social class and cultural barriers as they relate to involvement in schools. Low-income parents who feel excluded and powerless have responded well to decision-making opportunities in Head Start and other school programs promoting parent participation. It is imperative, therefore, that parent representatives reflect the school population in regard to race, culture, and socioeconomic groups.

Parent involvement in decision making is evident when parents join school committees that make decisions on curriculum policies, parent involvement activities, school budgets, and reform initiatives. Teachers and administrators keep parents informed about the programs and guidelines, allowing parents to effectively provide input on documents like the Title I plan and school–parent compacts. Parents sometimes move on to assume roles in state and national groups (Funkhouser, Gonzales, & Policy Studies Associates, 2005).

Empowerment means that parents can support their child's learning in partnership with the school. *Courtesy of ECE Photo Library.*

Not only must opportunities for parent involvement exist at all levels but also parents and professionals alike must be sensitive to the ability of parents to respond. A family system viewpoint takes into consideration the variables of unique family characteristics, interactions, and life stages. Consequently, the level of parent involvement is reflective of the particular values, strengths, and needs of each family. For some parents, the role of decision maker, active team member, or child advocate will be realistic and achievable. For others, many aspects of these roles will be beyond their ability or capacity to respond.

Parent involvement upholds the belief that parents should share the rights and responsibilities of decision making and be a part of the educational process. These assumptions, however, may be in conflict with parental needs or preferences. Not all parents may be interested in or able to make a commitment to higher levels of involvement. Although a parent may be a capable decision maker or an excellent leader, the parent's personal need to set limits on outside activities and preserve a sense of balance within the family must be respected. Professionals must recognize that parent involvement is a dynamic activity that will develop (or fluctuate) with the rest of life's experiences.

CURRENT TRENDS IN FAMILY DECISION MAKING

It is evident that parent involvement in decision making can take many forms. Some programmatic options for young children may be determined by parents, such as enrollment in a particular preschool program or the choice of a graded or ungraded classroom. Parents can assist with the "teacher tasks" of decision making, such as collecting informal assessment data to document their child's progress. Evaluative reviews for many center and school programs often include self-study evaluations as a significant component of that process. Families typically are asked to participate in this type of program review. Since the 1970s, federal grant initiatives have responded to the need for parental input in programs by supporting programs that emphasize parent empowerment components. Partners in Policymaking, a model empowerment and self-advocacy training program from Minnesota, originated in this manner. The National Association for the Education of Young Children (NAEYC) also promotes a quality accreditation procedure for early childhood programs that requires considerable parental input in the evaluation process. Family involvement is sought from local to state levels as school improvement becomes a priority for families, communities, states, and the country at large. The Council of Chief State School Officers' 1998 report on state policies to support school reform stated: "Executive officials and state legislatures know that they must have the knowledgeable support of parents and all members of the community if they are to succeed in transforming public education to meet the demands of the twenty-first century. Education is no longer left solely to the educators." Families entered the policy-making arena as recognized partners in the process.

Parent Advisers

As programs for children continue to seek more effective and family-friendly strategies, family members are often asked to serve as advisers, both formally or informally, to ensure that the parental perspective is represented and parental expertise is utilized. The **parent adviser** may actually assist in developing policy through an advisory committee, parent or faculty board, or focus group. Many community and federal preschool programs, such as Head Start and Title I, utilize parents in this way. Table 11.1 illustrates recommendations for successful participation by parents on a committee, board, or focus group.

Parents who have been consulted have a heightened sense of ownership. When their agenda is similar to the professionals' agenda, true partnerships emerge. Planning parent meeting topics, agendas, and formats, for example, without consulting parents about their interests and without exploring options with them is likely to result in low or fluctuating attendance at meetings.

A parent advisory committee may be developed for a particular short-term purpose, or it may be ongoing. A classroom advisory committee might, for example, select materials for the parent space or books on families for the classroom library. A committee on after-school child care could serve the larger school and community. Parent advisory committee activities may include such objectives as organizing parent volunteer projects; selecting criteria for the selection of personnel; initiating suggestions for program improvements; assisting

Table 11.1 Guidelines for Successful Parent Advisory Participation

1. Parents are involved in significant school-related areas, such as curriculum, allocation of funds, personnel, or parent activities.

2. Advisory groups meet regularly to discuss issues and make recommendations. Regular meetings build a sense of purpose, trust, and partnership.

3. Parent involvement has real, not token, impact. Recommendations are listened to and have real effects on decision making.

4. Parents should be representative of the school's families in regard to race, culture, age, socioeconomic status, and so on.

5. All advisory group members should receive some training on the group's function, policies, specific focus areas (such as district budget or curriculum), effective group process, and related skills, as needed.

6. Parents may benefit from leadership training in parliamentary procedure, communication and group management skills, or problem-solving techniques.

7. All advisory group members should have an opportunity to exchange information with veteran advisory members in groups with similar functions. Technical assistance from consultants or workshops offers these opportunities.

8. The needs of all members should be considered. Child care during meetings should be provided for those who need it. Assistance with transportation or reimbursement for mileage may be critical for parent participation in advisory activities. Clerical services and office supplies should be available to all advisory members.

9. Printed materials (guidelines and regulations, program summaries, handbooks, etc.) should be available to all members.

10. Meetings should be arranged with consideration for all members and run efficiently and purposefully with respect to time and responsibilities.

11. Advisory group members should be recognized for their contribution to the group in a tangible way, such as with an annual dinner, an award, or coverage by the local media.

Adapted from Lyons, Robbins, & Smith, 1982.

in selecting and organizing parent activities; providing input from other parents and encouraging their participation; representing and linking other private and public organizations, clubs, and agencies in the area; and monitoring and evaluating the program. Utilizing parents as advisers establishes both a vital trust and a respect for their concerns, which help to bring lasting benefits to programs.

Families in Organizations

Parent advisory committees can play a major role in parent–school partnerships.
Courtesy of ECE Photo Library.

Parent Teacher Associations and similar organizations frequently provide opportunities for parents to support programs and to speak on behalf of children and youth in the schools, in the community, and before governmental agencies and other organizations that make decisions affecting children and families. PTAs have broadened the expectations of parent involvement in schools and programs beyond fundraising. Families have banded together to form building or program organizations, such as the Preschool PTA, when they are not already established for the entire program or school. Other initiatives have encompassed the unique needs of particular groups, such as fathers or immigrant families. It is important to realize that some families may bring educational or business expertise to a group's leadership, while others may be more suited to become actively involved with the group by taking on a parent mentor position. This type of assistance is available from the state or local PTA or through parent resource websites and books. Parent groups also invite professionals as guest speakers to describe their work and answer questions. Parent organizations share successful activities that exemplify family–school partnerships and make suggestions about actions that might be taken locally.

Parent involvement at this level can have unexpected positive outcomes for programs and staff. In some communities, families have developed a resource team of parents willing to share their interests and talents as they relate to school activities. In many locales, groups have played a major role in restoring funding for class activities such as field trips or supplemental educational programs. Parent advocacy can help schools by improving the working conditions of teachers, supporting decreased class sizes, improving parent–teacher relationships, increasing school attendance, improving facilities, and acquiring learning materials and resources.

Parents on Councils and Task Forces

Opportunities for genuine parent involvement are increasing in many communities. In an effort to better solve local problems and address concerns (from playground planning to neighborhood violence and gangs), strategies such as problem-solving teams or task forces are being adopted in the educational sector. These groups provide social support for the school system and empower the parents who serve on them. Increasingly, state law requires parents to become participants on school site councils and intends for parents to have actual decision-making authority.

These **task forces** or councils may be composed of a community coalition of educational programs, organizations, government, and business interests focusing on a particular issue. This type of involvement has been an important requirement of federal special education, compensatory education, and school programs and a key component in school restructuring efforts (Council of Chief State School Officers, 1998).

In the effort to guide state implementation of legislation (PL 99-457) affecting the development of program policy for children from birth through 2 years of age and their families, many states have included parents and professionals on interagency coordinating councils and created local councils with similar membership. Although this effort continues in state-level planning councils, many local interagency councils provide an opportunity for grassroots parental input and offer support for many parents to participate in council activities. These same local councils provide the professionals and families with information on family services available within the council area. Champaign County, in Illinois, has a Birth to Five Council organization that assists families and professionals with information about services available within the county. Through the organization's website, http://ccbirthto5.org, individuals can locate support groups and services, playgroups, early childhood programs, special needs services, and family resources such as child care and prenatal and parenting education resources.

Websites and service directories can help families and educators locate community support groups and services for children. *Courtesy of ECE Photo Library.*

Parents as Advocates

Parents also can participate in this empowerment stage of involvement as advocates, individually or in groups. Parents may assume decision-making roles regarding school issues, problems, and programs. Not all parental advocacy efforts, however, are connected directly to the school or program. Parents often take the initiative to meet a need with a grassroots effort and provide leadership for continuation of the group as long as the need exists. Parents have assumed responsibility for action through support groups founded across the nation in response to a need—from Preemie Parent Support to Mothers Against Drunk Driving. Mother's Centers, part of a national movement begun at the grassroots level, are designed for the support, training, and nurturing of adults and children in the local community.

In Denver, an organization called the Family Star Community Center has been working with neighborhood residents to strengthen and revitalize the community. Family Star grew out of a 1988 meeting of 60 neighborhood residents concerned about a crack house located across the street from an elementary school. Families built the collaboration, now an incorporated nonprofit organization, and have been successful in attracting financial support from a variety of sources to develop many initiatives that strengthen families and provide a better start for the neighborhood children. An Infant–Parent Education Center, which employs formally trained neighborhood residents, also includes parent participation in the center's management (Children's Defense Fund, 1992). Family Star continues to effect change for families and is an outstanding example of grassroots advocacy.

Parents have effected change by assuming leadership roles on school boards, by lobbying members of congress at town meetings, by organizing letter-writing campaigns, by speaking on forums, and by giving testimony at public hearings. Although there may be limited opportunities for parents to participate in some of the above activities (such as school board leadership), many parents could help with mailings or jot a note on a postcard to let their position be known on such topics as budget cuts and availability of preschool programs, both of which are advocacy activities.

PARENTS ON THE TEAM: SHARED POWER

Nationally, parent empowerment has grown through multilevel, progressive changes. Yet those changes have not been uniform, and the challenge of including parents as active team members remains. In 1987, Oliver Moles, a prominent researcher and author, pointed to documented surveys that affirm parental interest in the roles of advocate and decision maker and that show that education agencies support parents as such. At the local level, however, teachers, principals, superintendents, and school board presidents did not necessarily value parents as decision makers. Power sharing may be difficult when parent representatives from diverse groups need to interact with officials from programs and schools (Kugler, 2002). Challenges still exists in areas; however, the changes in requirements for Title I, No Child Left Behind, and other initiatives have promoted changes in involving parents.

Any change in the traditional school structure or organizational pattern may be threatening. The controversy over giving parents any true power challenges the paradigm of school as we have known it. Yet the burgeoning school reform movement in the United States involved new collaborations, including those with businesses and parents. In 1989, Davies suggested that external forces such as mandates, laws, citizen protests, and citizen organizations demanding change may be necessary to change traditional school systems. "Without public dissatisfaction," Davies emphasizes, "politicians are unlikely to make substantial shifts in the allocation of public resources. This points to the need for . . . work outside the schools by grassroots parent and community organizations to press for school reform and improved results" (Davies, 1989).

Parents in some areas of the United States have the opportunity to instigate services using private and/or government monies and to employ professionals directly for their children's services. Magnet, charter, and alternative schools approximate this concept. In some areas, it is possible for parents to choose early intervention services for their child from a variety of providers. Instead of funds going to a particular program, funding and services follow the child according to state guidelines. If families are not satisfied, they can change providers.

In order to provide programs that respond to local concerns and needs, parents can be involved in assessment of family needs and the evaluation of existing services. They can participate as committee members in local partnerships that decide how to spend funds that are earmarked for families and children. Parents can also participate in providing information that supports research for grant writing and other fund-seeking initiatives. In order to effectively participate in local partnerships, parents need to be fully informed members of the team. Table 11.2 outlines possible areas that need to be disclosed. By providing opportunities for families to address concerns through decision making, individuals can be encouraged to maintain active involvement at the local level (Council of Chief State School Officers, 2002).

In many communities, barriers exist that significantly affect the actualization of parent involvement at the decision-maker level. They can be legitimate concerns or generalizations about all parents based on a negative philosophy or negative interactions with a few parents in the past. These concerns may relate to a threat to power or control, or a fear of the untried. When some parents have a new opportunity to work with professionals, some tension on both sides may exist.

Table 11.2 Information and Skills for Decision Making

In order to be effective contributors to any decision-making effort, parents need to possess appropriate and equivalent background information common to others in the group. This may include the following:
- Knowledge about the program, school, district, community, local leadership, and past and current priorities that will affect their actions.
- Information about past activities that impact the current situation and/or information about other groups with a similar focus.
- Knowledge of laws, rules, regulations, policies, and guidelines that pertain to the situation.
- Information on model programs, curricula, or best practices that would give valuable perspective.
- Information about organizational finances that would influence suggestions or impact the potential outcomes.

Appropriate skills are necessary to function as part of a decision-making group. Parents and other team members may need to have or acquire the following:
- Listening and communication skills
- Team-building skills
- Documentation skills (such as note taking and letter writing)
- Research skills (locating information)
- Telephone skills
- Interpersonal or political networking skills
- Assertiveness and advocacy skills

Professionals may have caused issues for parents that were not addressed or reconciled. Parents likewise may have caused similar situations for professionals. These feelings and issues may be "brought to the table" during the forum. Anger and frustration with the system or with parents should be openly recognized. Respecting the individuals involved may require giving time to an open discussion between parents and professionals in order to share perspectives and experiences, which can build empathy and understanding (Zipper, Hinton, Weil, & Rounds, 1993). Parents and other team members also may need to acquire information or develop team-building skills related to working on a committee.

Building an empathetic and understanding relationship between parents and educators requires giving time to open discussions. *Courtesy of ECE Photo Library.*

OPPORTUNITIES FOR TODAY AND TOMORROW

Despite the difficulties or discomfort that may be experienced by many schools and programs at the launch of a parent involvement program, it is time to seriously consider working together with parents. Today, as factors threaten the existence of many human services and school supports, there is an increased need for parent–school partnership. Programs for families and children are frequently underfunded or abolished in difficult times, thwarting the goals to create the best community program possible.

In 1991, David Elkind pointed out, "The humanitarian needs of young children are today in conflict with other economic demands upon public budgets and the profitability of private companies. There are no simple answers to these questions. Both sides have solid arguments. Unlike retired persons, however, who have effectively organized to have their financial and medical needs recognized, young children cannot organize, and parents and early childhood educators must advocate for them." This remains true today in many areas. School conditions, large class sizes, reduced opportunities for fine arts classes and extracurricular opportunities (such as field trips), and inadequate materials for activities frustrate parents and professionals alike. Schools are stymied by educational accountability issues that are impacted by societal factors outside the school. As change agents, taxpayers, and voters, parents have proven themselves to be a formidable force.

Teachers must remember that parents aren't "just parents." They may be connected to local businesses, religious organizations, and civic groups. In these capacities, parents can be helpful in a variety of ways. Parents can use their influence with businesses to encourage them to donate services, such as taxicab rides to parent meetings, furniture and equipment, or space for meetings. Parents who are active in local clubs and organizations can encourage those groups to sponsor fundraising events to benefit the family education program, collect used clothing, or sponsor a parent education course in partnership with the school. (See Chapter 12 for more information on community networks and collaborations.)

A CALL TO ACTION

Education professionals and schools provide a logical, nurturing connection with which parents can recognize their power to promote change. By providing opportunities for parents to develop authentic decision-making skills at the local level, and by assisting parents to network with local support groups and national associations, schools and programs can help parents empower themselves. Educators can share critical legislative and educational information acquired through their professional organizations with parents and model advocacy activities on behalf of their programs and parents. Many professional organizations have parent membership divisions and can assist parents through educational materials, websites, and programs to become involved with their schools and governmental agencies.

Teachers can facilitate other empowering opportunities for parents through their class or program involvement strategies. Classroom parent advisers can select books and enrichment materials for the school–home lending library, review audiovisual and print materials for parenting programs, distribute surveys to other families, and select activities that parents would respond to most favorably for publication in home activity calendars. When parent involvement strategies are successful, teachers can share these experiences with others via local newspapers, professional newsletters, journals, or magazines, or at meetings and conferences. The impact of these media articles and meeting presentations can be strengthened dramatically by planning or developing them in collaboration with parents.

Providing parents with opportunities and skills at the local level can empower them to work for appropriate change and improvement in education and in their communities (Henderson, Mapp, Johnson, & Davies, 2007). Professionals can provide general guidelines for writing legislators to enable parents to feel more comfortable with this type of advocacy, or parents can host a meeting with the school principal to expand the preschool parent lending library into a parent resource center for the whole school. Legislators and other leaders in government, business, and civic organizations can be invited to visit the school to learn firsthand the importance of their efforts. Teachers can provide valuable opportunities for parents to actualize the goals of their advocacy efforts.

SUMMARY

Parents and programs are dynamic and ever changing. The historical and legislative evolution of families in the decision-making role has involved both regular and special education. Empowerment has been recognized as a purposeful developmental process that aims to help families gain mastery over their lives and environments; parental decision making is a function of the empowerment evolution that takes place within each parent (Turnbull, 1992). Families maintain rights and responsibilities to be involved in their children's lives. The scope of parental decision making also can be a function of the program's parent involvement philosophy. The process of parent involvement utilizes the natural resources at hand—in people, environments, and organizations—and builds on internal skills for communication, coordination, and leadership. The process nurtures motivation through encouragement, guidance, and an opportunity to promote positive changes in the lives of the children, the family, the professionals, and within the program itself.

Involving parents in decision making is part of the natural progression of parent involvement strategies. In allowing parents to take part in decision making, educators do not give them any rights they do not already possess. It is important to remember that involvement at this level of empowerment is dependent on personal variables (such as personality, values, and opportunities), external supports, and a system in which incentives outweigh deterrents. Because of this, program administration and professional support are critical. Parent involvement at this level can be challenging to achieve. It is therefore important for educators to realize that parent decision making has had an erratic historical evolution and that history is still ongoing. It is up to each teacher and each program to decide how parental contributions will be valued.

ACTIVITIES FOR DISCUSSION, EXPANSION, AND APPLICATION

1. What evidence of the current trends toward increased parent decision making is found in programs and schools in your community or area? Interview personnel from several sites to learn what leadership roles are available to parents and what strategies are being employed to include parents in decision making. What factors contribute to the quality of involvement in this area? What would cause positive changes? Did you notice any negative observations?

2. Identify five strategies one could suggest to the programs or schools to promote meaningful parent involvement in decision making. If things were changed in this manner, what would be the positive and negative perceptions from the staff perspective? From the parent perspective?

3. What aspects of the historical evolution in parental decision making described in this chapter (for regular and special education) are recognizable in the schools and programs you studied? Is this a linear evolution? Who or what prompted the development of parents' involvement?

4. Interview a parent with a child in a school or center program. What types of opportunities and what levels of involvement are available to the parent within or as an extension of the program? What is available outside the program?

5. Interview a teacher or administrator involved with a Title I or Head Start program. What types of opportunities are available for parents to participate in decision-making processes? What does the teacher or administrator do to ensure parents can participate effectively? What can he or she share about the successes or challenges in the process?

6. Discuss current concerns and issues facing educational programs and families in your community. Which do you feel most strongly about? Identify the most appropriate individual to contact regarding your biggest concern. The individual could be a federal or state legislator; a school board president; a state, regional, or local superintendent of education; or a mayor, alderman, or ombudsman. Write a letter describing your views on the issues and what actions you would like to see taken to produce the desired outcomes. Share your response from this individual with your group.

CASE STUDY

Parent involvement in decision-making roles varies greatly throughout a community or state. Even when mandated by law, as with Title I programs, the quality of interpersonal interaction will be influenced by the attitudes of the school personnel. Consider the information shared in this chapter about parents as decision makers. Use it to suggest guidelines for parent involvement in decision making at the early childhood or elementary school level.

1. What factors should the program or school seriously consider to promote successful interactions?

2. What might need to be arranged in order to ensure the effective participation of families in decision-making roles?

3. Select one type of family participation role (such as adviser, organization member, council or task force member, or advocate). Presume that you are in charge of facilitating parent participation. Identify four specific practices that you would incorporate into the process to ensure successful involvement and discuss why each is important.

USEFUL WEBSITES

www.ascd.org

Association for Supervision and Curriculum Development. In addition to its other services and resources, ASCD has developed a comprehensive Advocacy Kit that provides guidance and tools for planning an advocacy campaign.

www.childrensdefense.org

Children's Defense Fund. The Children's Defense Fund provides advocacy information to use at the grassroots level, including data on federal legislators' voting records on issues involving children. The information is updated each year.

www.essentialschools.org

Coalition of Essential Schools. The Coalition focuses on improving school design, practices, and community partnerships. It offers to participating schools mentoring, resources, and information on current issues. Resources for school and community partnerships are available under the Community Connections menu in the Resources tab.

www.everyday-democracy.org

Everyday Democracy. Everyday Democracy, founded in 1989 as Study Circles Resource Center, is a national organization that offers ideas and tools for community change for individuals and organizations. It is focused on helping people think and talk together to solve challenges to education and other societal concerns. Use the Education menu for resources and articles affecting schools, families, and communities.

www.nea.org

National Education Association. The National Education Association is one of several national teachers' unions that provide additional resources for working with parents.

www.parentactionforhealthykids.org

Parent Action for Healthy Kids. This program is designed to help connect parents, communities, and schools to improve the health and well-being of children and youth. It strives to provide the best resources available so individuals can advocate for improved health initiatives in communities and schools.

www.partnersinpolicymaking.com

Partners in Policymaking. This site offers online courses to educate individuals to be effective and active partners with those who make public policy.

REFERENCES

Children's Defense Fund. (1992). *The state of America's children yearbook.* Washington, DC: Children's Defense Fund.

Council of Chief State School Officers. (1998). *State policies to support middle school reform: A guide for policymakers.* Washington, DC: Council of Chief State School Officers.

Council of Chief State School Officers. (2002). *Ready for success: Tools for expanding effective early childhood education.* Washington, DC: Council of Chief State School Officers.

Davies, D. (March 1989). Poor parents, teachers, and the schools: Comments about practice, policy, and research. Paper presented at the annual meeting of the American Educational Research Association. San Francisco.

Elkind, D. (1991). *Perspectives on early childhood education.* Washington, DC: National Education Association.

Funkhouser, J., Gonzales, M., & Policy Studies Associates. (2005). *Family involvement in children's education: Successful local approaches, an idea book.* Washington, DC: U.S. Department of Education.

Henderson, A., Mapp, K., Johnson, V., & Davies, D. (2007). *Beyond the bake sale: The essential guide to family/school partnerships.* New York: New Press.

Henniger, M. (1987). Parental rights and responsibilities in the educational process. *The Clearinghouse, 60,* 226–229.

Kugler, E. (2002). *Debunking the middle-class myth: Why diverse schools are good for all kids.* Lanham, MD: Scarecrow Education.

Long, C. (2007). Parents in the Picture. *NEA Today, 26*(1), 26–31.

Lyons, P., Robbins, A., & Smith, A. (1982). *Involving parents: A handbook for participation in schools.* Ypsilanti, MI: High/Scope Press.

Moles, O. (1987). Who wants parent involvement? Interest, skills, and opportunities among parents and educators. *Education and Urban Society, 19*(2), 137–145.

Rasinski, T., & Fredericks, A. (November 1989). Dimensions of parent involvement. *The Reading Teacher,* 180–182.

Turnbull, R. (1992). Family empowerment. *Families and Disability Newsletter, 4.* Lawrence, KS: Beach Center on Families and Disability, 2–3.

Zipper, I., Hinton, C., Weil, M., & Rounds, K. (1993). *Service coordination for early intervention: Parents and professionals.* Cambridge, MA: Brookline Books.

KEY TERMS

Nursery School—An early childhood program, usually for children aged 3–5 years, that encourages educational play experiences rather than custodial child care.

War on Poverty—Legislation introduced by President Lyndon Johnson in his 1964 State of the Union Address. It described the federal government's response to national poverty. Head Start and the Job Corps are remaining initiatives.

Parent Adviser—A parent participating in a formal or informal capacity to represent parent perspectives in developing policy on an advisory committee, on a board, or in a focus group.

Task Force—A community coalition, frequently developed by educational programs, organizations, or government and business interests, which focuses on a particular issue or concern.

CHAPTER 12

Utilizing Community Networks and Collaborations: Linking Education and Human Services for Family Support

STUDENT LEARNING OUTCOMES

After reading this chapter, you should be able to

- Recognize challenges within existing family service delivery systems.

- Develop a rationale for education and human service collaboration in support of young children and families.

- Identify common resources and components of a community infrastructure for family support.

- Explain ways to enhance the collaborative process of service delivery through educational linkages.

- Indicate ways teachers can empower families and assist them in seeking family supports.

- Describe opportunities educators have to advocate for families and services and to provide leadership for collaborative networking.

Parents are key members in school and community partnerships. Via their children, they provide a direct link to the school and its mission of educating the future generations. The bar for educational success has been raised by national, state, and local expectations. With the complex issues facing students and their families, schools are looking beyond the school walls and reaching out to build community bridges to help assure success in preparing the next generation of citizens, leaders, and workers.

As discussed in previous chapters, the rapid and complex changes in American social structure have created undesirable stresses for families. The stressors arising from the economic and social revolution of the past 50 years threaten family systems and create a high risk for dysfunction, evidenced by increases in child abuse, violence, young parents, alcohol and other drug abuse, and family dissolution. These symptoms are more than typical family responses to the normal change process, as they reflect major structural changes in society. Families increasingly face not one but several difficult issues.

Undeniably, economics plays a central role in family stress. Demand for highly educated workers, employment uncertainty, wage instability, the impact of technology upon the work force, and the increased cost of living (particularly the increased cost of child rearing) all have combined to create a powder keg. For example, within the family system, the initial difficulty for a parent may be the loss of his or her job when an employer lays off workers or downsizes. For the parent, the impact of joblessness and the accompanying frustrations may result in depression and maladaptive coping, such as depression, alcohol abuse, or negative behaviors toward family members. There may be discomfort in the need to temporarily access unfamiliar family supports, such as food stamps, medical clinics, or thrift shops. It may be necessary to refine skills, such as job hunting, preparing inexpensive but healthful meals, or coping with the changes thrust upon the family. These family stressors and responses may become part of a child's or family's eligibility for particular programs or services. They also become risk factors in the child's development. Even without extraordinary issues, the ordinary challenges of child rearing can be stressful for families. Parenting isn't easy, and good parents may have to work at acquiring skills to help developing children meet their potential.

Amid this evolution of change, schools are under scrutiny. They are criticized for failing in their responsibility of adequately educating children in the United States. The media frequently reports statistics that compare the ranking of U.S. students with those in other countries. Government has attempted to legislate educational improvements and control educational outcomes. Yet the real solutions may be found in the neighborhoods, communities, and the programs and schools that are the **stakeholders.**

NEW COMMUNITY PARTNERSHIPS

There is a need for educators who recognize the interconnectedness of family involvement and school success to become proactive in the emerging movement toward community collaborations. As funding for social service programs decreases, and family needs for intervention escalate, it is not only logical but also essential for those with a vested concern for children and families to work together in a new kind of partnership. Parents, educators, social service workers, and health-care providers are among those creating a unique, interagency paradigm in an effort to provide multidimensional interventions for the complex problems that challenge parents or place families in jeopardy.

This approach to an **integrated service system** for children and families is built upon the individual community supports provided by programs, schools, hospitals, agency services, government, organizations, volunteers, and businesses. The call to develop community networks and coordinate services for children and families is being heard in all corners of the country. Schools and educational programs frequently are the hubs for these initiatives. Therefore, it is crucial for educators to recognize these opportunities, develop skills that contribute to successful collaborations, and network resources for enhanced educational, social-emotional, economic, and medical outcomes for families.

Community–school partnerships often provide comprehensive services, including medical care for children and families. *Courtesy of ECE Photo Library.*

Educators traditionally have sought out resources and services to support "their" children and families. Working with families to utilize and broaden their networks of support is a primary strategy for empowering parents. The new age of collaboration also offers leadership opportunities for educators and families to develop community networks that broaden the service base of individual programs and brighten the future for children. Although these initiatives may not currently operate in all areas, the new trend toward collaborations offers new promise for parent involvement.

A SERVICE SYSTEM PARADOX POSES PROBLEMS FOR FAMILIES

Responses to Family Needs

The increasing number of economic and social stressors has contributed to changes in family dynamics. Adequate supports for coping with these changes, however, have not been universally available for families. Although governmental and community agencies exist to address family needs, these programs may have internal obstacles that make it difficult to deliver services effectively. Families as clients seldom have input into program development, and professionals often are frustrated by rigid rules and restrictions. Programs may make it difficult to access their services due to variations in eligibility requirements (for individuals, families, or households) and inaccessible hours or locations. This creates enormous difficulties for families with multiple problems and limited means. A mother with no dependable transportation who must walk with her young children through violent neighborhoods may choose not to keep an appointment for special services, even if it is conveniently located. Just as the problems that families experience are interrelated, logical solutions should be integrated, multidimensional, and coordinated in order to address more than one problem at a time.

Educators must realize that many community social service systems are not as holistic or responsive as they could be to the situational needs of the family. Teachers may find it easy to fault parents for not providing all the basic needs for their children, or for not securing all the services available to help families in need. Those educators may not fully comprehend the difficulties posed by the social service system.

Challenges of Providing Services

The current assortment of education, health, and human services for children and their families is essentially a collection owned by a variety of programs, not a unified system. By dividing the problems of children and their families into rigid and distinct categories, irrespective of interrelated causes and solutions, agencies and programs may fail to serve their target clients. Historically, the educational system has been one of the major sources of assistance in dealing with the dynamics of social change. Schools, the "bastions of society," traditionally have been expected to preserve the essence of a collective culture and transmit it to the children, in addition to educating them. Educational programs and schools, whose goal is to teach children and bring them all to a level of academic excellence, are challenged by the realities of what is required for a child to be ready to learn. Children who do not receive adequate nutrition during their growing years, who are affected by environmental toxins, or who are stressed by home and societal conflicts cannot easily reach their potentials. Yet the educational system is disabled in its ability to respond to the structural changes in society and to the family systems and communities it is supposed to serve. Frequently outmoded school designs for space, time, curriculum content, and family policy prohibit responsiveness to the educational support needs of today (Swick & Graves, 1993).

Children under 6 and their families are paying the greatest price for the social revolution. Teachers of young children working with both children and their families on the "front lines" are acutely aware of this. Educators of children at all levels are frustrated by the number of children coming to their programs with recognizable problems related to housing, nutrition, medical care, and other environmental concerns that interfere with their ability to learn and succeed in school. Educators are often challenged by difficulties in accessing the systems that were designed to assist families.

In times of financial stress, reduced governmental funding for social services may affect an agency's ability to respond to increased community needs. These challenges to funding, personnel, and service options can threaten a program's effectiveness, stability, and very existence. This results in a greater need to collaborate and network within a community to maximize available resources for families and children.

A CALL FOR COMMUNITY ACTION

The first national education goal of the 1989 report *America 2000* stated, "By the Year 2000, all children in America will start school ready to learn." The U.S. Department of Education challenged states and communities to clarify what contributions for readiness were already in place and to determine what could be done to enhance readiness and support to families to achieve this goal (U.S. Department of Education, 1989). Many state agencies and community task forces responded, assessed resources, and defined action plans to increase collaborative efforts toward achieving this goal.

The National School Readiness Task Force, chaired by then-Governor Bill Clinton, asserted that the system of family services must support the development of caring communities. These communities provide comprehensive support for young children from birth through 4 years and their families by filling in gaps in health care, family support, and child care. Service linkages to bring more continuous and convenient help to families were encouraged. This often required a reorganization of state funding services or operations. Community-based family support programs grew, but the momentum slowed behind Goals 2000 as the magnitude of the task became apparent and political winds shifted. Local collaborative programs, however, have been able to reach families and deliver the services needed to route them on a path of self-sufficiency when systems have failed.

Linkages are vital to increasing students' educational success. Progressive schools have piloted programs to bring together community supports for basic needs and educational enrichment. These schools not only implement developmentally appropriate teaching and assessment practices, increase parent involvement, and provide professional development for staff, but they also work in greater numbers with community agencies to provide appropriate and effective services to children and families (Epstein, 2004; Kunish, 1993).

Communities Look to Schools

Society is again looking to schools, the central structures in each community, to provide more than education. Programs for young children throughout the nation are forging new projects that offer support services for education, health care, and family and child care. The addition of both the parent involvement and family empowerment components make these education service coalitions unique. Getting parents involved in their children's program is a beginning step, followed by active involvement in goal setting and other decision making about their children. These programs are sometimes described as being "pro-family." According to Melaville, Blank, and Asayesh (1993), pro-family systems are:

- **Comprehensive:** A variety of opportunities and services are available, from prevention to crisis intervention.
- **Preventive:** Prevention initiatives receive the most emphasis.
- **Family-centered and family-driven:** Families are seen and served holistically, with sensitivity to their needs and respect for their abilities.
- **Integrated:** Separate services share information so that families face less repetition and confusion.
- **Developmental:** Family plans are revised as needs change.
- **Flexible:** Policies that govern responsivity to family needs are adaptable.
- **Sensitive to cultural, gender, and racial concerns:** The system is sensitive to diversity in policy and practice.
- **Outcomes oriented:** Performance is measured by improved outcomes for children and families, not just the number of families served.

Some at-risk families receive a patchwork of services from a variety of sources: for example, a state-funded preschool for a younger child, violence **prevention services** for an adolescent, and job assistance for parents. This trend is clearly a call to collaborate. By reducing the number of separate interventions and individuals working with the family, resources can be better utilized.

Not all families and children with **risk indicators,** however, are receiving a variety of services. For example, parents of preschoolers may benefit from parenting guidance, joint problem solving, or encouragement, but may not need other social services. These families simply need collaboration with a caring adult, such as a teacher or community service worker. Even if the child is doing well in the neighborhood or school, the community itself may pose a health and safety threat to the well-being of *all* children and families. Violence and societal health issues like HIV/AIDS are examples of this rationale for collaboration. Interventions to these and other complex societal problems can be community-wide, and all groups can have ownership in the solution.

The Price of Ownership

The notion of ownership, when it comes to the troubles in our country's social service system, is an interesting one. There appears to be a great deal of "finger pointing" whenever difficulties affecting child welfare surface. Education has been a source of much attention in this regard. The variable consequence of ownership is the issue of financing the solution. Society has been hesitant to commit financial or personnel resources to assist families, programs, or schools until children are seriously harmed or the situation has become a crisis.

It is widely accepted that prevention is usually cheaper and more effective than crisis intervention and remediation. Increasingly, prevention is becoming a focus of comprehensive program planning. By sharing the ownership of societal problems, collaborative funding mechanisms enhance the responsiveness of the system to communities. Collaborative models frequently interest policy makers because the mission (and funding) is diffused throughout the collaboration. Much of the awareness of collaboration and its benefits comes from the business arena. As economic conditions fluctuated and became more complex in the 1970s and early 1980s, businesses (such as the automotive and computer technology industries) studied the potential courses of action, joined together, and documented their collaborative management strategies. In the 1990s and into the next century, as financial resources became more scarce, collaborations such as partnerships with designated vendors became accepted as cost-effective in the restructuring of service strategies.

Funding program and school community initiatives can be challenging, even collaborative ones where partners may be able to contribute funds, personnel, or **in-kind contributions** (such as meeting space, computer paper, or furniture). Programs and schools may look outside the community for funding assistance. Various federal and state programs permit family programming. Small state and organization grants can be sought to provide funds to pay staff or parents for planning time, for trips to visit other school involvement programs, or for start-up needs once the location of a parent center is identified.

Challenges to Collaboration

Family–school–community collaborations are wonderful initiatives that have remarkable benefits. They do, however, have identifiable potential problems:

- Teachers and staff often need training to be family-friendly, effective liaisons to partnership, and potential barriers in those relationships need to be addressed.

- Collaborations are very time consuming to prepare for, establish, and maintain. Individuals who are identified as key players must have the capability, time, and resources to fulfill their responsibilities. The responsibility of establishing and overseeing a family–community program is too large to be an addition to a full-time staff member's workload. Strong programs have a parent liaison or coordinator who networks with families and community partners, plans programs, develops communication, and assists teachers in helping the project succeed.

- Efforts made in collaboration need to be recognized and appreciated. Volunteers are typically not paid, so by acknowledging, supporting, and helping them develop new skills, programs can compensate key people in the process.

- Collaborations need funding to operate smoothly. Family or community members may be able to assist with grant writing to apply for monies to hire a coordinator or initiate collaborative planning.

- As school facilities are utilized more and as new partners from the community share the school's space, new issues can arise. Planning must include how to respect physical and programmatic "turf," security, use of space, additional maintenance needs, storage, and use of materials and equipment (Caplan, 1998).

In recognizing these potential challenges, collaboration leadership and participants may be able to avoid difficulties and ensure success.

COMMUNITY SCHOOLS

The public response to these community needs has prompted a new vision for partnership. Schools and other community organizations and agencies are working together to create community schools that offer supports and opportunities to allow all children to learn and be successful and to help families and communities prosper. Several national organizations are at the forefront to provide leadership, training, and technical assistance in developing these new paradigms for schools. The National Network of Partnership Schools and the Coalition for Community Schools both aim to strengthen community–school partnerships. Through coalitions with community partners, the school is a hub for supports and opportunities for children and families. Their focus is to achieve the goals of having children ready to learn and able to achieve high standards for academic and societal success; to produce young citizens who are well prepared for their adult roles in the workplace and as future parents; to support families and neighborhoods to develop environments that are safe and nurturing; and to help families and community members to become involved with the school and interested in their own lifelong learning (Blank, 2000; Epstein, 2004; Heifets & Blank, 2004).

Community schools invite youth, families, and community residents to be equal partners with schools and other community resource providers to develop programs in five areas: quality education, youth development, family support, family and community engagement, and community development. Although there are many models of community school design, they all share central operating principles. These include the goals of fostering strong partnerships, sharing accountability for results, setting high expectations for all, building on the community's strengths, and embracing diversity and avoiding "cookie-cutter" solutions. Community schools involve the community at deeper levels and support community members' participation. Rarely do schools have the funds, staff, or space for all the family involvement activities they want or need to offer. In an effort to resolve this dilemma, schools have forged partnerships with a wide variety of community partners (Blank, 2000). These are illustrated in Table 12.1.

Table 12.1 Community School Partners

Community school partners can include the following:	
Civic groups	Chambers of commerce
Churches	Charitable organizations
Public agencies	Local businesses
Media	Local colleges and universities
Libraries	Youth development organizations
Senior citizen groups	Neighborhood associations
Military groups	Local government
Health and human services agencies	

Community schools frequently offer extended hours, including before- and after-school care. *Courtesy of ECE Photo Library.*

Communities, families, and children become involved in activities that are meaningful and valuable to them. In an effort to best meet family needs, some community schools have extended school hours (such as early morning, evenings, and weekends) to enable families to access adult education, parenting classes, and recreational and learning activities. Through collaborations with community medical service providers, they offer services such as medical exams for school physicals, dental exams, and vision and hearing screenings. They are effective in facilitating linkages between agencies that provide services and families that need them as well as in providing parenting and learning resources for all families (Boal, 2004). They have become true centers of the community. The community-schools approach provides a wide variety of programs and services through partnerships within the community. Examples of these are found in Table 12.2. In addition, community partners can help schools with academic and basic survival needs of the students. Hairstylists can come to a program or school to offer free student haircuts. Uninsured students can receive free dental check-ups from students at a local dental college. Business partners can provide volunteers for mentoring and tutoring, reading rewards for books read at home, or pizza parties for classrooms with the most parent volunteers or attendees at an event (Funkhouser, Gonzales, & Policy Studies Associates, 2005).

Table 12.2 Community Collaborations

Community collaborations can offer supports such as the following:	
Before- and after-school care	Health services
Adult education and enrichment	Citizenship classes
ESL classes	Computer classes
Drug and alcohol prevention	GED classes
Parenting workshops	Educational enrichments
Violence/abuse prevention	Social activities (scouts, 4-H, yoga, dance, etc.)
Transportation	
Refreshments for events	Technology services (for school websites or homework hotlines)
Improvements to facilities	
Furniture, equipment, and materials	Internet/cable services

Business partners can provide volunteers for mentoring and tutoring. *Courtesy of ECE Photo Library.*

FAMILY RESOURCE CENTERS

School–community coalitions frequently sponsor Family Resource Centers that provide assistance to families in their many roles. They may provide parenting classes and information and ideas to help parents better understand school curriculum and help their children with homework. Child care and assistance with referrals for housing, health services, or employment services may also be provided. Connecticut supports school-linked **family resource centers** throughout the state. The West Hartford School District's parent center has space for a parent library and for meeting teachers during lunch. It helps families connect to child care resources, counseling services, and adult education classes. Children can check out a toy for the weekend or register for an enrichment mini-course. Greensville County Public Schools in Virginia have a mobile parent resource center that makes services more accessible for rural families. Housed in a 34-foot customized bus, the resource center travels to four sites a day and serves 12 to 18 parents of children receiving Title I services per stop. The bus has two fully equipped classrooms as well as instructional materials for parents to check out. Parents are trained to be tutors for their children. Many area businesses allow the mobile center to visit their work sites so eligible employees can visit before or after work (Funkhouser, Gonzales, & Policy Studies Associates, 2005).

INCENTIVES FOR EDUCATIONAL SYSTEM INVOLVEMENT

The educational reform movement, through state and local school improvement efforts, also has provided some incentive for schools to more seriously view relationships with parents and to seek out community resource networks. Schools are useful for facilitating collaborations for many reasons. They offer a common access to the majority of children and families whose diverse needs may cross multiple service systems, thus ensuring a more equitable distribution of services. The community or neighborhood school provides a central location where some services may be provided, thus minimizing expenses and service duplications and maximizing staff time. School linkages increase opportunities to reach families and children with information and services, thus enhancing services and building public support and advocacy for care and education. Schools also open the doors to creative, integrated service options. Most families are familiar with the elementary or secondary schools in their community and many have a network of families they know through school. Successful initiatives also involve school staff in planning, operating, and governing the program or system. By the nature of their business, educational systems are concerned with the quality of services for children and families. A common collaborative initiative that demonstrates these concepts is a community literacy initiative. Adult education agencies, community colleges, community libraries, government agencies, private industry, local volunteers, and preschool programs join forces to provide classes in adult literacy, English as a Second Language, or GED preparation.

District and State Support for School–Family Partnerships

Nationwide, there is evidence of state and district supports for family involvement. This includes supports in policies, funding, training, and family services that contribute to success. With this degree of backing, schools can draw upon a broad system of experience and expertise. District-run or state-run parent centers are one example of how schools can benefit.

In 2005, the U.S. Department of Education highlighted successful local approaches in family–school involvement that utilized a variety of funding strategies. The Texas Alliance Schools Initiative, for example, is a partnership among the Texas Education Agency, the Texas Interfaith Education Fund, and the Texas Industrial Areas Foundation. The goal of the initiative is to develop a strong decision-making, community-based constituency of parents, teachers, and community leaders in an effort to improve student achievement in low-income communities throughout the state. Schools that are willing to redesign and implement reform strategies can receive competitive grants for staff development, parent and community training, curriculum improvement, and enrichment programming. Jefferson County Public Schools, near Louisville, Kentucky, contracted with the Right Question Project to improve parent involvement in supporting education at home. In Wisconsin, the DeForest School District joined forces with the local public library (also an Even Start site) to sponsor a family involvement literacy program that included adult basic education, ESL, and parenting activities. Other schools have utilized Title I funds to conduct workshops and increase parent understanding of testing, as well as to provide parents with suggestions for enriching their children's vocabularies. In California, family centers celebrate and reach out to diverse groups of families with ESL, citizenship, and adult enrichment classes in subjects such as computer skills (Funkhouser, Gonzales, & Policy Studies Associates, 2005).

Local Support for School–Family Partnerships

At the local level, teachers are often frustrated by the limitations of their role. There may not be enough time to attempt to meet families' needs for information or to make personal contacts with them. The school and community have often created unique solutions to these issues. In one school, when a home visit was necessary, the principal and teacher worked out the logistics so the principal could cover the classroom while the teacher met with parents. In other communities, volunteers staff lunchrooms or provide playground supervision so teachers can call or meet with families.

A GUIDE TO SOCIAL SERVICES

Teachers are increasingly aware of or involved in parent education and prevention activities designed to strengthen family functioning and parenting skills. Communication flows both to and from families in the continued sharing of information. The flyer sent home concerning an upcoming public health vaccination clinic or the availability of school physicals is a small step toward programmatic collaboration. Community program and resource information often is shared by social workers within the schools and incorporated within parent involvement strategies like program newsletters, home visits, or parent meetings. Educators learn firsthand from the families of the children they teach about the social, economic, physical, and educational issues that are of greatest concern. Teachers may recognize a need for prevention services or be the first persons outside the family to be aware of a potential crisis situation. Trusting partnerships with educators allows families to confide troubling circumstances affecting them that require specialized services.

It is crucial that teachers recognize the need for and assist the family in locating services; however, these situations require an awareness of available community resources. Although preservice education for some educators includes information on social service networking, many teachers scramble for information to share with families when the need arises. This is sometimes complicated by a lack of familiarity with available services, especially if the teachers live outside of the community in which they teach or have not previously had a need for service referrals. Some educators are hesitant to offer assistance, as they may be apprehensive that the family's situation may require assistance outside of their realm of expertise.

Family Support Program Models

Families that have developed trust with an educator may hesitate to go outside their "comfort zone" of professionals for assistance with personal difficulties. Many early childhood programs, such as Head Start, have a small team of professionals who work closely with families. This team may include teachers, social workers, or parent/family coordinators whose role is to assist families in accessing parent involvement activities sponsored by the program or in locating resources in the community. When it is not possible to delegate the family concerns to another team member, the teacher may assume a family liaison role to facilitate service access and to empower the family to seek assistance. Head Start has been successful in using federal funds to assist with community initiatives to provide early childhood programming, health services, job training, GED and parenting classes, and child care for younger children at one site.

Government grants, charitable foundations, and organization initiatives are funding sources for family support programs. Programs frequently target a particular client group for services, such as urban or rural families, migrant families, a particular cultural or ethnic group, teenage parents, young military families, parents of children with disabilities, or families with children at risk for abuse or neglect. Epstein (1994) documented involvement with two parent-support models, the Parent-to-Parent Dissemination Project and the Child Survival/Fair Start project. In *A Guide to Developing Community-Based Family Support Programs* (1994), Epstein, Larner, and Halpern offer a design for program development that includes these steps:

1. **Identify a client population.** Decide how narrow or broad the definition for eligibility will be. How many families, with what types of needs, can be helped?

2. **Set program goals.** Identify realistic objectives based on the resources of the program and the needs of the families. Family support program goals address concerns for parents, for children, and for communities.

3. **Select a program format.** Typically, programs offer one or more of these types of service delivery: home-based programs, stand-alone programs, group-based programs, and family support centers.

4. **Determine how services will be scheduled.** The onset, frequency, and duration of services must be considered and weighed against the desired outcomes of the program.

5. **Select a curriculum.** Programs may adopt a packaged curriculum, modify an existing curriculum, or design a curriculum individualized to their own needs.

6. **Establish a staffing structure.** Staff roles and responsibilities must be defined. Programs typically have a supervisor and family workers. Issues regarding staff recruitment, staff development, and the establishment of a working relationship with families must be resolved.

7. **Determine the evaluation design and conduct the evaluation.** Both formative (what was done, how was it done, numbers served, frequency and content, etc.) and summative (outcomes related to gains, improvements, etc.) evaluations should be included.

Informal Models

Social service assistance may present a confusing web of eligibility requirements, paperwork, access issues, waiting lists, and information from within the same agency. Educators have the best opportunity to assist families. Depending on the ability of the family to help itself and the educator's relationship with the family, teachers may assist families with initial telephone contacts to find out requirements, locations, office hours, and understanding questions on applications. When the family members have no one to assist them, educators may help with application paperwork or cryptic scholarship applications. Some visionary social service providers and neighborhood schools have developed strategies through collaborations to minimize the bureaucratic paperwork a family must initiate in order to receive or access supports.

LOCATING SERVICES FOR FAMILIES

Throughout the United States, there is great diversity in the services available to families and children. Federal, state, business, foundation, local, and private sponsorships make a wide variety of programs available. These variations make it difficult to develop a comprehensive list of programs for the nation. Some federal programs are unilateral and can be located in every state; some federal initiatives may be model, pilot, or grant-sponsored and available only to a selected geographical area or community population, and perhaps only until funding ceases. These variations in support services are evidence that local communities and regions benefit from uniquely designed program responses. They also reflect the inequality of funding that provides concentrated services in selected areas of a state. This can be confusing for families who relocate and search unsuccessfully for particular supports, and for educators who learn that colleagues in another area have resource programs they cannot locally access.

Each state, region, or community must therefore develop a directory of services available to families within the designated boundaries. With the heightened awareness of the benefits of community networking, many initiatives have developed a **social service directory** or list as one of their initial activities. Some communities have produced collaborative directories; others have lists focused on specific needs. These resources provide information on existing programs or social services that are readily available. School district social workers, Head Start programs, and local interagency councils are highly recommended sources of information on community services. Hospitals and clinics, along with mental health, public health, and child and family service programs, also have access to resource information that can be shared. If a program wants to develop its own directory, a format similar to the one in Table 12.3 may be used.

Federally Funded Programs

Head Start programs have provided comprehensive models for community and parental involvement. In addition to the traditional part-day, center-based program, options include year-round, full-day services; a Transition Project of demonstration grants for Head Start agencies collaborating with local schools;

Table 12.3 Community Resource Information

Name of organization/agency:	
Sponsoring organization/agency:	
Address:	
Telephone:	Fax:
Director:	Contact person:
Months of operation:	Days of operation:
Hours of operation:	Service area boundaries:
Description of organization/agency:	
Population served:	Ages:
	Definition:
	Income:
	Geographic area:
	Other:
Description of eligibility criteria/referral criteria:	
Length of service availability:	
Fee description:	
How do consumers gain access to services?	
Coordination/collaborative linkages with:	

and Parent and Child Centers, which provide prenatal and postnatal services to Head Start–eligible parents and children up to age 3.

Even Start is a federal family literacy program that combines early childhood education for children ages 1 to 7 with adult education for parents with poor literacy skills. These programs are typically found in communities with a concentration of low-income families. Opportunities exist to renew or reform social service policies in Congress and state legislatures. Citizens and the political system at large have crucial decisions to make that will affect services to children and families.

State-Funded Programs

All states commit some general revenues to programs that serve or benefit children. There is great variation in the size, scope, and focus of these initiatives. These efforts include dependent care tax credits, child care, preschool education, expansion or enhancement of Head Start, and elementary and parent education. States also have preschool education initiatives (many of which target at-risk preschoolers) in addition to Head Start.

Many states now support preschool education initiatives through grants to school districts. *Courtesy of ECE Photo Library.*

Despite such diversity of programs and initiatives, some detective work may be necessary to locate specific services. The state lead agency for early intervention services may publish a state services directory. The state department of public health or education also may have a comprehensive guide to services for children and their families. A computerized information service on resources and family supports is typically available on the Internet at the state, regional, or local level. Community libraries, hospitals, agencies, local police, and the telephone book are sources of assistance. Regionally developed and state-developed resource linkages found in the Useful Websites section of this chapter illustrate technological access to information.

REVIEWING EDUCATIONAL SYSTEMS: A VITAL LINK

The systems-wide trend toward collaboration challenges the traditional education system to broaden its policies and programming to meet the needs of families and communities. Early childhood educators are in a unique position to model this process for the entire educational system. Pro-family practices in quality early childhood programs also can become the starting point for developing family-sensitive practices in the entire school and community. All of the previously detailed elements of parent involvement—early partnerships with families, educator skills in communicating sensitively with families, and meaningful parent involvement in order to encourage positive parenting skills—come together to prepare for successful collaborations. Schools and programs can identify and put into practice educational experiences that communicate a commitment to parent partnerships, support families in developing healthy ways of living and interacting, and integrate parents into the instructional process at all levels.

This integration involves looking at the roles of programs, schools, and education in new ways. In order for this work to expand beyond a token, trial initiative, schools must examine their philosophical understanding of pro-family parent involvement and view their role as an extended family support. In order for educators and schools to achieve their goals for children, partnerships with families must be developed and maintained. Through community partnerships and collaborative resourcing, families can receive assistance in meeting needs and successfully nurturing upcoming generations.

Reciprocal Benefits

The African proverb "It takes a whole village to raise a child" has become a slogan of community collaborations. The interconnectedness of resources, the ability to respond, and the corresponding need become evident in many community linkages, especially in education. United Way is a useful source of agency contacts. Table 12.4 outlines possible lines of collaboration between schools or programs and agencies and organizations that provide services.

By providing opportunities for families and the community to visit schools via the collaborative programs, schools make the community know they are welcome partners. Activities discussed in previous chapters, such as parent information nights, open houses, and parent–child activities that focus on curriculum, homework, and child development, communicate the invitation to help all children in the "community village" succeed. A school's philosophy of parent and community involvement is reflected in what it does and how it communicates to the community. In Westerly, Rhode Island, for example, Tower Street School has a lawn sign that reads, "Tower Street School—Where Everybody is Somebody" (Patton, 2006).

Educators and educational systems can provide the following:

- **Awareness** to communities of the value of parent involvement
- **Information, resources, support, and training** to communities and businesses to promote family-centered practices
- **A model for communities of respectful practices** and valuing families
- **Guidance** to communities on the changing roles of parents, families, and communities

Table 12.4 Sample Analysis of One Area's Local Services

Services	Agency/Organization
Family assessment	Head Start
Developmental screening	Special education
Hearing/vision screening	School district, Arc, Easter Seals
Psychological evaluation	Head Start
Audiological evaluation	Dept. of Human Services or local school district
Medical evaluation	Community/county hospital
Service coordination	WIC
Special education class	School district
Home-based program	Early Intervention program
Speech/language therapy	Special education
Transportation services	Local clubs and organizations
Parent education/training	Local/community hospital
Parent counseling/therapy	Mental Health Dept.
Parent support group	Churches
Parent library loan	Family Resource Center
Parent-to-Parent	Parent Resource Center
Medical services	Visiting Nurses
Dental services	Dental school
Child care	Child Care Resource and Referral
Respite care	Churches/Early Intervention links
Nursing services	Visiting Nurses/hospice
Prevention services	Public Health Dept.
Food bank/thrift shop	Good Will, Church Alliance
Infant program	Early Intervention, Parents As Teachers
Financial counseling	Local credit counseling
Substance counseling	Mental Health Dept.
Housing	Public Assistance
Nutrition counseling	Hospital/clinic/WIC
Crisis services	Local shelter
Supplemental Security Income	Public Assistance
WIC	Public Assistance
Legal	Legal Aid
Recreation	YMCA, 4-H, scouts, Boys and Girls Clubs, Big Brothers Big Sisters

- **Recognition programs** for parents, community organizations, and businesses that are sensitive to families
- **Partnership opportunities** for parents, organizations, businesses, and communities
- **Parent-to-parent network information** for parents, organizations, and communities

- **Special education and educational support services** for children and parents
- **Locations** for community meetings, health-care services, counseling, employment training for parents, and community organizations
- **On-site parent education programs** at the workplace for businesses and organizations.
- **Educational programs** like English as a Second Language, GED studies, and literacy for all in the community
- **Sites and services** for before- and after-school child care, latchkey child programs, and summer programs for children and parents

Educators and educational systems can receive:

- **Information, resources, support, and training** from organizations for family-centered involvement
- **Support** from everyone for early education and family programs
- **Transportation services** from businesses for family events
- **Volunteer support** from everyone for school and family programs
- **Technical assistance** from businesses for marketing school events, public awareness campaigns, grant writing, and so on
- **Job training** from businesses for families
- **Support for the dissemination of information** and a location for parenting resources from the community

Individual and Professional Contributions to Collaborations

Educators can develop skills in their expanded role as collaborator, liaison, or family resource person. Frequently the teacher will be called upon to introduce the program and types of parent involvement to parents, agencies, other teachers, administrators, and the community, much as a public relations specialist does. As a collaborator, the teacher's style of communication and interpersonal interactions should promote openness and respect for the expertise of others as new relationships are formed or expanded outside the education system. Projecting a positive attitude and a willingness to share will help in communicating, planning, and problem solving with others in the networks built with each agency and organization. Patience with people and with the process of collaboration will be vital. Collaboration pushes all parties into the unfamiliar when a first contact is made. Time and a commitment to making meaningful linkages are valuable assets.

As school–community activities focus on student learning and success, students benefit; however, schools, families, and communities also gain. Some businesses have a "Take your child to work day," which gives children a better idea of what happens when a parent goes "to work." Such programs also enable students to see the connection between academic skills and school curriculum and the skills needed in the workplace. Businesses might support a field trip to a museum by sponsoring the transportation. The focus, however, isn't always on what the community can do for the school. Students can reach out to seniors or individuals in the military by writing letters to them, which also provides real-world practice in communication and writing skills. Students can provide artwork to a community organization not only to brighten and beautify its facility but also to remind the community that the students can be productive and positive young contributors. Older students can be encouraged to be community service volunteers at library reading programs, at centers or residences for senior citizens, or for other community events.

INTERPERSONAL DYNAMICS OF COLLABORATION WITH FAMILIES

Parent–teacher collaborations, like all parent involvement contacts, are based on mutual respect; an understanding of each other's perspective and role; and the sharing of knowledge, information, and skills. As in any partnership, each individual brings unique values, ideas, perspectives, and skills to the relationship; therefore, each parent partnership will be different. Family-centered practice emphasizes the family's central role in planning and making decisions about services for their child and other family members. The teacher can assist parents in assessing their child's strengths and needs, family resources, priorities, and concerns and can help identify goals and services with the family. As a family resource provider as well as an educator, the teacher can assist by helping to locate the services the family desires and by facilitating parent involvement with other professionals and agencies.

Empowering parents and families to actualize a plan to meet their needs or to problem-solve requires positive attitudes and expectations toward them. Enabling parents to make their own decisions and empowering them to become resourceful in their own lives require teachers to respect family autonomy and assist families in responding to their perceived needs.

Families do not want the educator to view their needs and risk attributes as personal or family deficits. They often may experience rejection and treatment as a "problem" family by the community. Throughout their lives, other forces may have shaped their perception of themselves as somewhat powerless and unable to make better choices for their lives. These perceptions are critical to the parents' ability to guide themselves and their children in proactive directions. Through childhood experiences, education, interpersonal dynamics, and cultural and subcultural parameters, parents will have developed belief systems about themselves and their abilities. If this system has negative messages that are not confronted by positive, proactive ones, the parent's ability to function as a self-empowered individual may be diminished. These feelings of powerlessness and low self-esteem affect the parent's relations with others and the perspective from which events and life circumstances are viewed. Parental behavior patterns and interpersonal relationships are indicators of their locus of control. They may ask the question, "Do I control my life (internal locus) or do life events or other people control me (external locus)?"

The role of the educator may be to assist parents in viewing the possibility of choices in their environment and in their lives. As the concept of potential develops, parents will increase their participation in life decisions. Feelings of frustration along with a lack of self-determination create a potential for destructiveness and dysfunctional responses. Problems, both real and imagined, appear unsolvable and promote pessimistic responses to life. Stress and anxiety arise from these interpretations of reality.

These parents may feel overwhelmed that they do not have the resources or ideas to cope with their problems; however, the parents often do not realize the risk factors confronting the family. Poverty, intergenerational abuse, and poor family and school experiences may reinforce a negative, limiting perception of life. A parent with such a perception may think, "I wasn't good in school, and neither is my child. He'll have to find another way." Parents also can become dependent upon their problems for structure or social identity. Even if it may improve their life, change is threatening to them and to their social status. Some at-risk families are isolated from other views of society, and some of their rigid attitudes may come from inexperience or a lack of exposure to other ways of thinking (Swick & Graves, 1993).

Professionals can best assist these disempowered parents by being empathetic, warm, and responsive to the family's needs and concerns without being judgmental. Educators should model a positive and proactive attitude to help the family acquire a realistic understanding of the strengths and needs of their children and family system. Attention should be focused on developing autonomy and healthy self-concepts within the family relationships. Educators should emphasize collaborative strategies to facilitate the development of plans the family feels will be beneficial.

Collaboration itself builds a sense of power for the family within the helping relationship. Here are proven strategies that teachers can use to become effective collaborators with families (Children's Defense Fund, 1992; Steele, 1989; Swick & Graves, 1993).

- Recognize your motivation in assuming the helping role. This is critical.
- Emphasize the family system whenever possible, instead of focusing on an individual child or other family member.
- Treat families with respect, and honor cultural differences.
- Offer flexible, responsive services instead of single-purpose, "quick-fix" provider solutions.
- Focus on the people, not the problem. Build on family strengths instead of emphasizing deficits.
- Offer preventive services to avert crises.
- Balance your efforts as helper with opportunities for other members of the family's system to help.
- Recognize your strengths and limitations. You can't be all things in the relationship.
- Rely on your network of resources and your supports and mentors. The family itself should be encouraged to take responsibility for its progress.
- Provide the family with resource contacts through printed information, telephone links, resource fairs, and so on.
- Assist the family, if necessary, to access the resources.

COLLABORATIONS: A PART OF THE SCHOOL'S IMPROVEMENT PLAN

Teachers are often familiar with the concept of professional learning communities within schools, where professional teamwork is used to improve instruction, provide mentoring, and give moral support. A school learning community includes not only the teachers and students but also partners from the community who share a vested interest in educating students and enhancing their learning opportunities.

Collaborations and Goals for Improvement

In best practice, these community collaborations are focused upon goals in the school improvement plan and designed to increase student achievement and success. As a teacher, parent, or community member, nearly anyone can participate in the school's action team. Annual plans are made that incorporate local improvement goals and activities that are conducted by existing groups or individual teachers into a comprehensive partnership program. The National Network of Partnership Schools is linked to the Epstein model for parent involvement. It offers training, technical assistance, and examples of effective practices from throughout the United States (Epstein, 2004).

Involving community partners benefits families and agencies. *Courtesy of ECE Photo Library.*

Individual Classroom–Community Collaborations

Ideally, the leadership in the school system (district administrators and principals) takes initiative in pursuing school–community linkages and, with the ongoing support of all educators, develops them into full-fledged partnerships.

If this is not yet the case, an individual teacher can pursue classroom–community partnerships with the approval of the program administration. Collaboration is not an all-or-nothing proposition. Good things can happen for students, families, and community members on a smaller scale as well.

At the classroom level, teachers can execute the following:

- Hold a mini-workshop for families of students in the class to share specific strategies to help their children strengthen skills in various subject areas, especially reading and math. This can also be accomplished by distributing handouts with tips on how to help at home. Tip sheets and more in-depth resources are available online from a variety of organizations that support learning in various curricular areas.

- Reading partners can provide needed oral reading practice for students and give them opportunities to discuss stories for enhanced practice with comprehension. Enlist volunteers from parents, families, senior citizens, and business people.

- An individual classroom open house can highlight classroom activities with an art show or "open mike" night for students to read their works of creative writing.

- Have a hands-on "math exploriganza" to illustrate ways to help students with math at home. Idea sheets or low- or no-cost materials can be used to illustrate state math standards.

- Teachers can develop a focus on careers and educational goals by having students research careers that interest them, possibly interviewing individuals from the community or via technology. Students can develop a career path portfolio that can be shared with students, parents, and community members.

- Many teachers already have families and community members as part of the classroom curriculum when they are invited to come to class and share their interests, skills, and experiences with students. In this way, visitors can bring a field trip–like experience into the classroom.

- A student or family may have community contacts that enable an instructor of martial arts, yoga, dance, music, or sports to share their special interest with the class.

ADVOCACY FOR SERVICE SYSTEMS: WHAT TEACHERS CAN DO

Advocacy is defined as speaking or writing in support of something. In early childhood education, we advocate for children and families when we share our profession with families, colleagues, administration, community leadership, politicians, and policy makers. Although many issues are important in the field of educating children, this chapter has centered on service availability and collaborations to meet the needs of children and their families. The current system has weaknesses that allow children to fall through the cracks in society.

True system collaborations that are effective and sensitive to the needs in today's world will evolve when the "turf issues" of service delivery are addressed. Fiscal accountability will no longer ignore duplication of services and programs. Wise decisions for creating systems changes cannot be made solely from behind a desk in Washington. Policy makers must hear the stories from the field: your stories, your families' stories.

Advocacy takes many forms and has many voices. Educators should feel empowered in the role of advocate for the types of program and services they believe are best practices for children and families. Table 12.5 outlines actions that educators can take in the role of advocate.

Advocacy can also put a "human face" on community change. Developing community understanding of local needs regarding families at risk, such as the homeless or poor, happens one person at a time. Teachers (and their children)

Table 12.5 Educators As Advocates

Educators as advocates can:
- Educate themselves about state community–school coalitions and promote initiatives in their own communities.
- Support family-focused programs in their communities and states.
- Participate in family system support organizations and in professional organizations such as NAEYC.
- Encourage businesses in their communities to adopt family-friendly policies for parent employees.
- Remind school administrations about pro-family policies and school–service linkages.
- Communicate knowledgeably, sincerely, and effectively.
- Practice what they believe to be the highest quality of service for families as a model to others.
- Add a voice of commitment to the cause for quality education for all children.
- Be an active learner about their schools, their children, and the programs that serve their families.
- Expect best practices in early childhood programming and work to achieve levels of excellence.
- Participate in the democratic process of communicating their beliefs to government and support genuine leaders in education. Support candidates who support their values, and VOTE!
- Attend town meetings, talk with candidates, and educate them about the issues they see as professionals and what they believe to be acceptable courses of action for change.

Adapted from Children's Defense Fund, 1992; Nall, 1992; National PTA, 1992; and Swick & Graves, 1993.

can volunteer to support local efforts such as food drives or to work a local food pantry or thrift shop. Crisis hotlines at women's shelters can use the educator's effective listening skills, especially because many callers may be parents with children. Teachers can also be expert members of an advisory board that serves community needs.

The saying "each one, teach one" is a grassroots motto to influence the community at large. In addition to the activities listed in Table 12.5, teachers can do the following:

- Share information about local needs (of children, families, etc.) with friends, church members, and others and suggest how they could help.
- Encourage and support initiatives that address the underlying causes of family problems such as employment, housing, and health care. Advocate for funding for programs that target root socioeconomic and education issues.
- Become or train a tutor to work with children or families.
- Volunteer to renovate areas at a local family shelter, or join a Habitat for Humanity project.
- Work within organizations to collaborate on special projects and provide materials such as food, clothing, and supplies as well as financial donations.

Advocacy is a job we all share. Professional organizations have advocacy initiatives that will provide "talking points," or facts and tips to promote knowledgeable communication. The National Education Association, American Federation of Teachers, National PTA, National Association for the Education of Young Children, and special interest organizations support advocacy among their members and interested individuals. Search the Internet on topics of

Table 12.6 Tips for Writing Legislators and Public Officials

- **Avoid impersonal form letters.** Share your own personal experiences or stories. Handwritten letters are effective; they do not need to be typed or on fancy paper. Your meaningful illustrations may just end up in a speech to illustrate why others should vote for the measure!
- **Keep your letter short and to the point.** Focus on only one issue, simply told, per letter. Avoid professional jargon because the legislator may be unfamiliar with such terms.
- **Learn the facts.** Contact the League of Women Voters or other group to learn the details of the legislation. Be sure your information is correct and that it supports your position. You can also obtain updated postal and electronic addresses from the League of Women Voters, the telephone book, or the legislative website for your state or district.
- **Contact the legislator more than once to support your ideas.** Input is critical when you want to gain support for a new bill or want the legislator to sponsor a new measure; when you want the legislator to use influence to pass the proposed measure out of committee; and, finally, before the bill you support comes to a vote. Legislators at the state and federal levels have e-mail and computer access. Check online for this information.
- **Request that your legislator respond to your letter.** Include your name and address on the letter (envelopes are usually thrown away).
- **Thank your legislator if his or her vote matches your recommendations.** Be sure to add that you will share the information with others.

Adapted from Goffin & Lombardi, 1988.

concern to find specific sources of information. Information that may be helpful in communicating with public officials is found in Tables 12.6 and 12.7. Educators have a civic responsibility to "walk the talk" and become advocates for valued programs and the children who cannot speak for themselves.

Table 12.7 Salutations for Writing Public Officials

Federal Officials:	
The President	The President of the United States The White House Washington, DC 20500 *Dear Mr. President,*
U.S. Senator	The Honorable (full name) U.S. Senate Washington, DC 20510 *Dear Senator (last name),*
U.S. Representative	The Honorable (full name) U.S. House of Representatives Washington, DC 20515 *Dear Congressman/Congresswoman (last name),*
State Officials:	
Governor	The Honorable (full name) Governor, State of State Capitol City, State ZIP Code *Dear Governor (last name),*

Table 12.7 Continued

State Senator	Senator (full name) State Capitol City, State ZIP Code *Dear Senator (last name),*
State Representative	Representative (full name) State Capitol City, State ZIP Code *Dear Representative (last name),*
Local Officials:	
Mayor	The Honorable (full name) City or Town Hall City, State ZIP Code *Dear Mayor (last name),*
Members of local councils and boards	Councilman or Supervisor (full name) City, Town, or County Seat City, State ZIP Code *Dear Councilman or Supervisor (last name),*

Adapted from Goffin & Lombardi, 1988.

SUMMARY

Providing services to children and their families can become an overwhelming task until teachers begin to identify and link with a comprehensive network of colleagues in community human services. Challenges to deliver family services exist on many levels. The "community village" needs to summon all its nurturing resources to ensure the well-being of families and children. Linkages and collaborations can be made on any partnership scale imaginable: person to person, corporation to community, or national to neighborhood. Present service delivery systems are typically not keeping pace with the families needing assistance. The difficulties of systems policies, with their layers of administration and politics, have a human cost in children's success.

There is a call to communities to become their own problem solvers, and all players are asked to help. For many programs and schools, this presents a break from the traditional mold of education; for others, it is a natural outreach into the community. Teachers working with those most at risk must be open to learning and utilizing service network systems at many levels and be aware of national, state, and local programs that can help meet needs. Skills are needed to successfully communicate, motivate, and empower families to utilize these systems; consequently, the role of the educator is broadening. By helping families seek out and access needed supports, teachers can assist in empowering them. As leaders in the community, educators have opportunities to advocate as caring professionals for services that will best serve the needs of the community, its families, and especially the children.

ACTIVITIES FOR DISCUSSION, EXPANSION, AND APPLICATION

1. The existing family service delivery system has come under fire. Outline the concerns from the following perspectives: the family, the social service worker, the educator, the citizen, and the community.

2. As an educator, you would like to request a meeting for school staff with community agency program personnel. How would you justify this activity to your reluctant administrator?

3. Using suggestions from this chapter, design a chart of support services available to families in your community. For each service, indicate the type of service or program, source of the service, eligibility requirements, length of service eligibility, and additional benefits available to the family through participation in the program. You may also locate a current family resource directory available for your community and note the information above. If classmates locate a variety of directories, compare them and discuss their effectiveness for families and educators.

4. Identify typical brokers of social service network information at the national, state, and community levels. Who are the "keepers" of the information? Who accesses information about the services? How is this done? Is it user-friendly?

5. Within a center or school, identify and detail at least five strategies to empower parents to connect with community resources.

6. As an educator, discuss family support services that are not currently available in your area and for which you would advocate. How would you suggest meeting the needs?

7. Insight challenge: Elect one member of your discussion group to assume the role of a parent in search of social service assistance within your community. Have that person make telephone contact to learn what needs to be done in order to receive services. How was he or she treated? Did he or she receive the necessary information? What was positive about the contact? What difficulties, if any, were there? Would a parent without a telephone, child care, or transportation be able to access the service? How great a challenge would a lack of good communication skills be for the parent? How easy to access is the service agent (office hours, location, etc.)? Would this create any problems for working parents, non-English-speaking families, or other culturally diverse families?

CASE STUDY

Your school district has a new superintendent who would like to see each school (all buildings and educational levels) participate at a significant level in family and community involvement initiatives. Her ultimate goal is to create a pilot community coalition school. You are the committee representative from your school, which already has a positive approach toward family involvement. Considering what you have learned about community collaborations from this chapter and related resources, discuss the following:

1. What can parents and families contribute to the effort in increasing community involvement?

2. How might the teachers and director or principal bring families into a meaningful conversation about increasing the community involvement?

3. What resources could your program or school team use to meet the goal of community collaborations?

4. Who would your collaboration team target as potential collaboration members?

5. What could your program or school do to solicit their support?

6. Identify the first four tasks that would move the community collaboration toward its goal.

USEFUL WEBSITES

ccbirthto5.org

Champaign County Birth to 5 Council. This Champaign County, Illinois, program works to identify young children with special needs and to ensure that they and their families receive a coordinated, comprehensive, family-centered system of support. The website provides educational guidance for special needs services and early childhood programs, in addition to information about family resources, support groups, playgroups, and other web links.

ecap.crc.uiuc.edu

Early Childhood and Parenting Collaborative. This organization is based at the University of Illinois and hosts information on research, technical assistance, and service projects that target educating and raising young children. It provides links to various university, state, and community centers, projects, and clearinghouses.

www.brookings.edu/ccf.aspx

The Center on Children and Families. The Brookings Institution studies policies that affect the well-being of children and their parents. It provides resource information on successful collaborations between schools and communities.

www.cfpciowa.org

The Child and Family Policy Center. The CFPC heads the Technical Assistance Clearinghouse of the National Center for Service Integration, a resource center on community-based strategies to develop more comprehensive and effective services for children and families.

www.cga.ct.gov/coc

Connecticut Commission on Children. The COC has developed a Parent Leadership Training Institute designed to help parents become advocates for children and supports parent interest statewide.

www.communityschools.org

Coalition for Community Schools. The Coalition is an alliance of national, state, and local organizations that advocates for community schools in order to strengthen schools, families, and communities. It shares information on successful school–community programs, practices, and research.

www.corpschoolpartners.org

The Council for Corporate and School Partnerships. The Council researched and developed a report on Guiding Principals for Business and School Partnerships, based on successful collaborations. Their "How-To" Guide is designed to help both partners work together effectively.

www.csos.jhu.edu

Center for Social Organization of Schools. The CSOS sponsors the National Network of Partnership Schools (in menu under Programs tab). The NNPS offers training and recognizes exemplary practice with awards.

www.ctkidssuccess.org

CT Kids Succeed. The Connecticut Conference of Municipalities and the Connecticut Commission on Children have joined the National League of Cities campaign for Early Childhood Successes to provide resources to assist Connecticut municipalities and their families and children. The program focuses on early childhood success by providing resources to ensure health, learning, and safety, all provided by a municipal government project called CT Towns.

www.kidscount.org

Kids Count. Funded by the Annie E. Casey Foundation, this organization tracks national and state data to provide policy makers and citizens with benchmarks of child well-being. This is a valuable "talking points" data source. Online state-by-state data is available.

www.nea.org

National Education Association. In addition to information on parents and community, the NEA has a Legislative Action Center that highlights current issues and explains how to get involved. It also keeps data on the congressional voting records for selected issues.

www.parents4publicschools.com

Parents for Public Schools. This national organization of community-based chapters works with public school parents and other supporters to promote civic action and public advocacy. The Parent Resources tab provides a wide variety of resource links for a variety of topics, including advocacy, civic engagement, and parent/family allies. The Publications tab provides downloadable print resources: articles, newsletters, and speeches.

www.projectappleseed.org

Project Appleseed. The website for the National Campaign for Public School Improvement offers support for organizing parent involvement in public schools. It has been the national sponsoring organization for School Volunteer Week and National Parent Involvement Day.

www.ptotoday.com

PTO Today. PTO Today is a media and resource organization that serves K–8 parent–teacher group leaders with a magazine and web resources.

www.togetherwecan.org

Together We Can. This is a support organization for groups working toward collaborations for a pro-family system of education and human services. It promotes partnerships, encourages community-based awareness, and produces resources including a collaborative tool kit. The website has a listing of resource organizations that support community collaboration, a database of community collaboratives in the United States, and a bibliography of media sources that address collaboration.

www.voicesforamericaschildren.org

Voices for America's Children. This is a national organization that provides data, tools, and training for citizens wishing to support initiatives that benefit children and families. The site map provides information on organizations in each state that are part of the Voices network.

REFERENCES

Blank, M. (2000). Coalition for community schools: A call to all. *The Education Digest, 65*(6), 16–18.

Boal, C. (2004). A three-way partnership with families. *Principal, 83*(3), 26–29.

Caplan, J. (1998). *Critical issue: Constructing school partnerships with families and community groups.* Oakbrook, IL: North Central Regional Educational Laboratory.

Children's Defense Fund. (1992). *The state of America's children.* Washington, DC: Children's Defense Fund.

Epstein, A. (Fall 1994). Supporting today's families. *High/Scope Resource.* Ypsilanti, MI: High/Scope Press.

Epstein, A. (2004). Partnering with families and communities. *Educational Leadership, 61*(8), 12–18.

Epstein, A., Larner, M., & Halpern, R. (1994). *A guide to developing community-based family support programs.* Ypsilanti, MI: High/Scope Press.

Funkhouser, J., Gonzales, M., & Policy Studies Associates. (2005). *Family involvement in children's education: Successful local approaches, an idea book.* Washington, DC: U.S. Department of Education.

Goffin, S. G., & Lombardi, J. (1988). *Speaking out: Early childhood advocacy.* Washington, DC: NAEYC.

Heifets, O., & Blank, M. (January/February 2004). Community schools: Engaging parents and families. *Our Children,* 4–6.

Kunish, L. (1993). Integrating community services for young children and their families. *North Central Regional Educational Laboratory Policy Briefs, Report 3,* 1–7.

Melaville, A., Blank, M., & Asayesh, G. (1993). *Together we can: A guide for crafting a profamily system of education and human services.* Washington, DC: U.S. Department of Education and U.S. Department of Human Services.

Nall, S. (1992). A fresh look at advocacy. *National All-Day Kindergarten Network, 2*(1), 1, 3, 6.

National PTA Parent/Family Involvement Committee. (1992). *For our children: Parents and families in education.* National PTA Parent/Family Involvement Summit Report. Chicago: National PTA.

Patton, J. (2006). Family, extended. *Teaching Pre-K–8, 37*(3), 42–45.

Steele, B. (1989). *Developing community networks: A guide to resources and strategies.* Washington, DC: Association for the Care of Children's Health.

Swick, K., & Graves, S. (1993). *Empowering at-risk families during the early childhood years.* Washington, DC: National Education Association.

U.S. Department of Education. (1989). *America 2000: What other communities are doing . . . National educational goal 1.* Washington, DC: U.S. Department of Education.

KEY TERMS

Stakeholders—Individuals or groups who may be affected by an action or situation.

Integrated Service System—Collaborative, coordinated community supports for children and/or their families from programs or schools, hospitals, agency services, government, organizations, volunteers, and so on.

Prevention Services—Services provided by community agencies or programs to increase proactive behaviors that typically enhance mental or physical wellness (for example, initiatives for prevention of drug use, violence, abuse, and illness).

Risk Indicators—Factors that place an individual or family at risk for educational, physical, social, or emotional delays or maladjustment, such as poverty, low educational level, limited health care, history of health issues or special education needs, transience, child's low birth weight, parental incarceration, and so on.

In-Kind Contribution—A common type of contribution in collaborative agreements that involves materials or services, such as meeting space, refreshments, clerical services, postage, advertisements, or door prizes instead of a direct monetary donation.

Family Resource Center—A location where a wide variety of material resources and personal assistance in such areas as education, health, or human services can be provided to families. Commonly the result of community collaboration.

Social Service Directory—A print or online listing of social services from governmental, foundation, agency, local, and private providers that includes such information as description of services, target population, location, hours, and contact information.

Advocacy—Speaking or writing in support of an issue, person, cause, or idea.

Illustration Credits

Figure 5.4 Reprinted with permission of Beth Jennings, kindergarten teacher, Edwardsville, IL, Community Schools.

Figure 5.10 Reprinted by permission of Linda Pokorny, kindergarten teacher, Edwardsville, IL, Community Schools.

Figure 5.11 From Arnold, M., *Effective Communication Techniques for Child Care.* © 2005 Wadsworth, part of Cengage Learning, Inc. Reproduced by permission. www.cengage.com/permissions.

Figure 6.1 Reprinted by permission of Teresa Harris.

Figure 6.2 Reprinted by permission of Teresa Harris.

Figure 6.3 Reprinted by permission of Teresa Harris.

Figure 8.1 "Family Bookworms" taken from the Gryphon House online sample meeting of Family Bookworms, which appears in *Partnering with Parents* (ISBN 9780876592311) by R. E. Rockwell and J. R. Kniepkamp in 2003. Reprinted with permission from Gryphon House, P.O. Box 207, Beltsville, MD, 20704-0207. (800) 638-0928. www.ghbooks.com.

Figure 9.1 Reprinted by permission of Rebecca and David Touchette.

Figure 10.1 Reprinted by permission of the Anoka-Hennepin School District, Coon Rapids, MN.

Figure 10.2 Reprinted by permission of the Anoka-Hennepin School District, Coon Rapids, MN.

All photos courtesy of ECE Photo Library.

Index